General David Wooster

General David Wooster

*Hero of the American Revolution,
1710–1777*

JASON EDWIN ANDERSON

McFarland & Company, Inc., Publishers
Jefferson, North Carolina

This book has undergone peer review.

ISBN (print) 978-1-4766-9575-4
ISBN (ebook) 978-1-4766-5481-2

LIBRARY OF CONGRESS AND BRITISH LIBRARY
CATALOGUING DATA ARE AVAILABLE

Library of Congress Control Number 2024032570

Front cover: Mezzotint image of David Wooster by Thomas Hart, 1745 (Yale
University Art Gallery Collection); (left) Revolutionary flag image by David Smart
and (right) British flag image by Lightspring (both from Shutterstock).

Printed in the United States of America

McFarland & Company, Inc., Publishers
Box 611, Jefferson, North Carolina 28640
www.mcfarlandpub.com

My sincere thanks to my parents who instilled in me a love of American history, and to my lovely wife Susan, without whose support this project would never have been possible.

Table of Contents

Preface

History provides countless examples of excellence in leadership. Good leaders exude qualities which inspire, motivate, and encourage others to rise above the fray, to better themselves as well as those around them, and to perform the extraordinary in the face of adversity. These qualities are heightened when united with the spirit of loyalty. For Major General David Wooster this combination became the cornerstone of his character. On April 27, 1777, these qualities were tested beyond measure.

Two days earlier his correspondences warned that British General Tryon's men had embarked on the coast and were marching towards Danbury, which jeopardized the military supplies the Americans had stored there. Great urgency propelled him and his fellow Connecticut officers to drive the invaders from Connecticut. Wooster and the men under his command arrived on the outskirts of Danbury after an exhaustive, rain-soaked night march that had churned the country roads to mud. After a rapid execution of orders and communications, along with hours on the march, Wooster had arrived on the field.

The sixty-seven-year-old veteran had been at home in New Haven when the alarm sounded that the Tory governor of New York, William Tryon, had invaded Connecticut with British troops. With great haste he dispatched a flurry of letters and orders organizing and rallying all available troops from Connecticut for the defense of their homes. His military leadership, which spanned the past thirty-eight years of his life, had brought him full circle. Starting in defense of Connecticut in 1739, the aged soldier had fought for king and country through three major conflicts, yet now he positioned himself in the defense of American liberty and freedom and once more leading Connecticut troops in the field of battle.

Wooster had been at odds with the Continental Congress since the formation of the Continental Army in June 1775. Without a champion in the Congress, and being occupied in the defense of western Connecticut and New York while at the same time the main army gathered at Cambridge, Wooster was disconnected from the newly formed officer corps. In the spring of 1776 his military service culminated in his removal from command in Canada. Despite his being acquitted of any wrongdoing, his continued request for active command had been ignored by the Congress. However, he was quickly recommissioned as Connecticut's senior ranking major general of militia by the Connecticut General Assembly.

Wooster marched his men south towards Ridgefield in the early morning to attack General Tryon's forces from the rear, while Generals Silliman and Arnold attempted to attack the flanks. As shots rang out, Wooster placed his men in battle formation and prepared to engage the enemy. Seeing his men wavering in the early engagement, he rode forward to rally his troops. As he turned in the saddle, sword in hand, Major General David Wooster was struck in the side by an enemy ball and fell from his horse mortally wounded. The ball had shattered Wooster's spine. Soldiers removed the general's scarlet sash from around his waist, unwrapped it, and bore the dying officer from the field in the make-shift stretcher. On May 2, 1777, with his wife and son present, Major General David Wooster died. At age sixty-seven, the oldest American general in the Revolution was dead.

On June 17, 1777, the Continental Congress passed a resolution creating a committee to determine the most fitting way to honor "Brigadier Wooster."

> Resolved, That a committee of three be appointed to consider what honours are due to the memory of the late Brigadier Wooster, who died on the 2d day of May, of the wounds he received on the 27th day of April, in fighting against the enemies of American liberty: The members chosen, Mr. [Thomas] Heyward, Mr. S[amuel] Adams, and Mr. [Mann] Page…. That Governor Trumbull be requested to erect at the expence of the Continent, a Monument to the memory of General Wooster, the expence, for erecting the same, not to exceed the sum of five hundred Dollars.[1]

The responsibility fell to Connecticut Governor Jonathan Trumbull, who had highly praised Wooster in a letter to General Washington on July 13, 1775, as being "held in high estimation by our Assembly, and by the officers and troops."[2] However, due to continued British threats followed by a second attack on the Connecticut coast in 1779, the memorial was never constructed.

In 1786, the Confederation Congress officially created the Western Reserve of Connecticut in northeast Ohio, the "Firelands" as they were more commonly called. This land was made available to those in Connecticut who had lost their homes due to the devastation of the war. Wayne County was located on the southern edge of the Western Reserve and became the home of many Connecticut refugees. By 1808, Wayne County had become sufficiently populated to establish an official county seat, and the veterans who resided there took the opportunity to honor the late Major General David Wooster by naming the county seat after the fallen general, who had been dead for almost thirty-two years. Yet today the question still arises: Who was David Wooster, and why should he be remembered within the annals of eighteenth-century American history? If this man was held in such high estimation by those in power in Connecticut throughout the 1700s, why has history, and the historiography of the eighteenth century, neglected him? Wooster's experience highlighted the development and growth of American ideology throughout the 1700s that revolved around Lockean republicanism, military training, and civic leadership. His story provides new evidence which highlights the importance of eighteenth-century New England as an epicenter of political revolutionary ideology.

David Wooster was a prominent leader in Connecticut throughout the 1700s and was actively engaged in the civic, political, and military life of the colony. As historians continue to write about eighteenth-century America, as well as the Revolutionary War, David Wooster continues to evade the narrative, or at best is offered a peripheral reference. Why? By 1775 Wooster already had decades of successful military experience and was appointed the first major general of Connecticut militia before the Continental Army was even created. Yet, the historiography continues to provide only a tertiary glance at Wooster's undeniable leadership.

This book will provide a unique perspective of the major events that shaped eighteenth-century colonial Connecticut by assessing Wooster's active involvement and leadership therein. Undivided loyalty and unwavering leadership are two characteristics that defined his life. When he was a British subject and commissioned officer in the army, his loyalty to England was unquestioned in his early years. However, as political abuses of royal authority and parliamentary government in London permeated into the colonies in North America, the seeds of political discontentment were sown, and Wooster eventually refocused his political loyalty upon his home colony of Connecticut. What would make a sixty-five-year-old merchant, justice of the peace, captain of the 51st Regiment of Foot, and naval custom officer for the port of New Haven yield his royal commission in 1775 and endanger his entire livelihood to take up arms in the republican cause of independence and liberty?

The historical record of David Wooster is sparse. In 1779 British General Tryon again led a raid upon New Haven and the surrounding Connecticut countryside. Wooster's home was targeted. Many of his personal papers, including much of his correspondence, were destroyed. Thus, to recreate Wooster's place within the historic narrative requires analysis of a limited number of surviving letters and intense research to locate additional sources within the correspondences of those who wrote to Wooster. Political journals of the colonies of Connecticut, Massachusetts, and New York provide important details, as well as the *Journals of the Continental Congress*. In addition, the personal papers of Connecticut Governors, Law, Fitch, Pitkin, and Trumbull illuminate the historical record where Wooster's actions become difficult to trace. Furthermore, prominent individuals who interacted with Wooster wrote about him, such as Sir William Pepperrell, Philip Schuyler, Roger Sherman, and John Adams whose letters contain invaluable material on his life.

Manuscript collections in Peter Force's voluminous *American Archives*, and the *Public Records of the Colony of Connecticut*, also are an invaluable resource for research on the military during the Revolutionary War. Also, the New Haven Museum and Historical Society has proven to be a treasure trove of original Wooster letters, and the society has been gracious in sharing these documents for analysis. Moreover, the Connecticut State Archives and State Library in Hartford and the New Haven Museum all have numerous documents that aid in redefining Wooster's place in the colonial narrative. One handwritten letter of General Wooster to General Washington is housed at the George Washington Presidential Library at Mount Vernon, Virginia, and has been made available for study. In addition, the guidance and direction of historical authors and scholars such as John Ferling, Edward Lengel, and Andrew O'Shaughnessy have been helpful in several fields of needed research for this project.[3]

Given that Wooster served in several military campaigns throughout his life, the locations of historic forts where Wooster was stationed have also proven useful in obtaining sources. For example, the archives at Fort Ticonderoga have several Wooster related documents, as well as a canteen with his initials from 1757.

Fort Louisbourg in Nova Scotia has also provided material that has been invaluable in developing a complete military assessment of David Wooster. The Beinecke Library at Yale University has made available several original documents pertaining to Wooster's mercantile business in Connecticut that had not previously been transcribed. Lastly, the Masonic Lodge that Wooster established in New Haven, Connecticut, has offered documents that uncover Wooster's social contributions. Overall, these combined primary sources allow for a more complete analysis and assessment of David Wooster's role in eighteenth-century Connecticut.

Who, then, was David Wooster?

David Wooster was born on March 2, 1710, in Stratford, Connecticut. He attended Yale College and married Mary Clapp, the daughter of the president of Yale. They had several children, though not all survived infancy. Wooster's entrepreneurial spirit reaped great rewards. He gained military leadership experience fighting in the War of the Austrian Succession, leading Connecticut troops at the siege of Louisbourg in 1745, and in the French and Indian War where he aided in the capture of Fort Ticonderoga in 1759.

After the siege of Louisbourg, Wooster was placed in charge of a cartel ship bound for France. Once the French prisoners had disembarked, he traveled to London where he met with King George II. For his action in taking Louisbourg, Wooster was commissioned the captain of the 51st Regiment of Foot commanded by Sir William Pepperrell. No record has been found indicating any other colonial being awarded a similarly commissioned military position. He also had his portrait made.

In 1773 David Wooster assisted Phillis Wheatly in distributing and selling her first work of published poetry. In 1778, several months after Wooster's death, Wheatley wrote a heartfelt letter to Mary Wooster, in which she composed a lengthy eulogy poem to the late General Wooster. The assistance provided to Wheatley, a former slave, highlighted his character and dedication to the ideals of life, liberty, freedom, equality, and independence, ideals to which he referred often in his few surviving letters.

When the battles at Lexington and Concord erupted in April 1775, Wooster was a justice of the peace in New Haven, a merchant, and a landowner, and he retained captaincy of the 51st Royal Regiment of Foot with half-pay for life. But as the war began and his military services and experience were required, he relinquished his position with the 51st Regiment of Foot to lead Connecticut soldiers. When most enjoyed the pleasures of hearth and home, Wooster volunteered for further service. At the age of sixty-five he had everything to lose by fighting in the war, yet he did not hesitate. Wooster had an aged military wisdom filled with experience. He helped to plan the successful attack on Fort Ticonderoga, which Ethan Allan, also from Connecticut, took in May 1775. Despite anti–New England sentiment in the Congress, Wooster accepted the lower rank of brigadier general in June 1775 to lead Connecticut troops in the Continental Army.

Wooster constantly focused on the defense of Connecticut. On April 27, 1777, British troops led by New York Tory Governor Tryon invaded Connecticut. Wooster, who was again in command of Connecticut troops along with Generals Silliman and Arnold, marched to repel them. While driving against the British invaders, Wooster suffered a mortal wound and died on May 2, 1777. His death fueled a New England firestorm and became a major turning point in the Revolution.

There is a dire necessity to incorporate Wooster into the historiography of the eighteenth century and the Revolutionary War. Living in Wooster, Ohio, the very city named in his honor, I have a vested interest and responsibility to see that the void in the historical record is filled. For years I have been accumulating letters of David Wooster as well as volumes of official papers in which Wooster is mentioned. This is a project long in the making, and one for which great preparations have been made. To produce the most comprehensive biography of David Wooster, research is never-ending. Some modern historians have denigrated Wooster in their publications, and these sources will be analyzed to evaluate their claims. The purpose of this book is not to elevate Wooster, but rather to study his many varied leadership roles to provide a deeper understanding of the events that shaped eighteenth-century Connecticut. Thus, an analysis of this important eighteenth-century colonial figure will improve and elevate the current historiography of the era and provide a historically accurate leadership assessment of Wooster.

No book has yet been written on David Wooster's legacy of leadership in Connecticut. There are four themes that shaped the development of his leadership and his character: eighteenth-century republicanism; political loyalty; colonial economics; and his military involvement which culminated in the Revolutionary War.[4] Current trends in the historiography of the Revolution and colonial America focus on regional history and the impact that the common citizen made during the eighteenth century. This study aligns with these current trends to provide a biography of an extraordinary citizen of Connecticut who involved himself in many facets of civilian and military life.

This life of David Wooster will be presented chronologically as well as thematically. Chapter 1 explores his youth, his upbringing, and his education while placing him in the contexts of the early 1700s in Connecticut. The development of colonial economics, higher education, and political activity of the colony are interwoven in the experiences of Wooster. His rise in leadership in the colony, especially in the military during the 1740s and leading up to the siege of Louisbourg in 1745, will be the focus of chapter 2. Here Wooster began his disciplined training in military affairs, not only in terms of field command, but also the rigor of providing structure to an army on the march and bivouacked in camp. He developed and fine-tuned these skills throughout his life.

No empire maintains its integrity, nor its dominion, without the loyalty of its subjects. Great Britain was no exception. The third chapter will examine Wooster as a devout loyalist to the British crown and will compare him to other notable loyalists from Connecticut who, like Wooster, were forced to change their allegiance by the 1770s. The causes of these changes were rooted in the altering economic conditions of colonial Connecticut, as well as the growing republican ideology that swept through the American colonies in 1763. Chapter 4 will examine his additional military experience gained during the French and Indian War. Coupled with an acute awareness of what colonial leaders saw as an aggressive and corrupt British political system, American patriot leaders saw themselves as the champions of *Magna*

Carta in upholding republican values. It was their duty to hold the line against this ever-encroaching political corruption of the crown and Parliament. Wooster agreed. Chapter 5 will also explore the economic and political changes that impacted Wooster's mercantile business and his political allegiance in the years leading up to the Revolutionary War.

The culmination of Wooster's life experience, leadership, and disciplined training are seen in his actions during the Revolutionary War. His military experience and leadership from 1775 to his death on the battlefield in 1777 will be examined in chapters 6, 7, and 8. The impact of his death and as a brief assessment of his legacy will be discussed in chapter 9.

There is a void in the historical record of a concise narrative on David Wooster. Others have written the historical record according to their perspective and agenda. This book aims to provide an additional layer to the record and thus may prove to alter preconceived notions and misinterpretations that have dominated the field for more than two hundred years enhancing the current understanding of eighteenth-century colonial life while highlighting the successes, and failures, of one leader of colonial Connecticut, David Wooster.

1

David Wooster's
Early Years (1710–1738)

By 1710 Connecticut was a well-established colony. Maritime trade anchored by numerous port cities such as New Haven along its southern coast made Connecticut a rival of early eighteenth-century cities such as Boston and New York. As mercantilism flourished, Connecticut also became a leader in the production of ships and shipping equipment. Many of the vessels that connected England to her North American colonies were built in Connecticut, and a variety of materials required for their continual up-keep were also produced there.

The colony of Connecticut received a royal charter from King Charles II in 1662. It is noteworthy that Connecticut was legally chartered by same king who himself would be forced from the throne by citizens who opposed his divine right to lead them, which led to the "Glorious Revolution," temporarily replacing the monarchy with civilian rule until the crown's restoration under James II. James II disavowed the royal charters and sought to reorganize what he referred to as the "Dominion of New England." In defiance, the colonists of Connecticut refused to relinquish their charter and, according to historian Erin Strogoff, hid the charter in the trunk of a large oak tree to prevent the king's envoy from seizing it. The hidden charter was reinstated after James II was overthrown in 1689 and remained the governing document for Connecticut until 1818.[1]

The English Civil Wars of the 1640s, followed by the Cromwellian protectorate, the Restoration, and finally, the Glorious Revolution that brought William and Mary to the throne were all political, economic, religious, and military events that shaped the lives of the Woosters who emigrated to Connecticut in the mid–1600s. Their European experience would greatly influence their American settlement. They found Connecticut a land of opportunity, and free from the monarchical taint that they left abroad following decades of political turmoil and uncertainty. By 1710, the colony of Connecticut was quickly becoming a leader in economic activity, education, Protestant religious fervor, and the teaching of republican ideology. This was the world into which David Wooster was born.

The historical genealogy of David Wooster's family contains errors and other challenges for historians. Many original documents pertaining to Wooster's lineage were destroyed along with his own personal papers in 1780. It appears that other Wooster descendants did not maintain accurate genealogical records. In the 1880s, as popular local histories were being published, genealogies were also printed. The earliest genealogy of the Wooster family was written by Samuel Orcutt and Ambrose Beardsley.[2] *The History of the old town of Derby, Connecticut, 1642–1880* (1880) was followed by several other historical narratives which perpetuated the same lineage, however inaccurate it actually was.[3] One of these authors was a Wooster, named after Major General David Wooster himself, with the hopes that one day a descendant would write a biography of the late general for posterity's sake. In 1921, historian Donald Lines Jacobus analyzed five different historical genealogical accounts of the Wooster family and traced their inaccuracies to the 1880 Samuel Orcutt's *Genealogy of Woosters in America*.[4] Jacobus found that Orcutt, despite all good intentions, omitted family members and provided some misleading and incorrectly interpreted information. These errors were repeated throughout the additional accounts of the Wooster family until 1921 when Jacobus attempted to correct the historical record.[5] Jacobus noted that

> the errors made by Orcutt have been followed by his successors. No one of these publications presents the material that is to be found in the church and land records of Derby, and their accounts of the branches of the family which did not reside at Derby are confused and conflicting. It is the purpose of the compiler of the following account [Jacobus] to correct the inaccuracies of these publications and to set forth the lines omitted therein.[6]

The most important item that was incorrectly stated, and subsequently repeated, was the listing of the progeny of David and Mary Wooster. The number of children was inaccurately reported in the earlier genealogical record. They had four children, of which only two survived the first two years of life. Mary, their youngest daughter, lived into the 1800s, and married John Ogden who sought financial relief for Mary Wooster after the Revolution. David and Mary's only son, Thomas, was the focus of genealogical confusion. Some accounts stated that Thomas was killed with his father at the Battle of Ridgefield in 1777. Research proves this account to be incorrect. The lineage provided by Jacobus presents an accurate account of the genealogical record of Thomas Wooster. However, without clear historical records due to the destruction of Wooster's personal papers during the Revolution, recreating the family lineage is an arduous and difficult task for any historian.

Born in Stratford, Connecticut, on March 2, 1710, David Wooster was among the third generation of Woosters living in the colony of Connecticut.[7] His grandfather, Edward, was the first to emigrate from England. Based on the genealogical records, the Woosters established themselves in Derby, Connecticut. According to Jacobus, Edward Wooster died in Derby in 1689, just after the beginning of the reign of King William and Queen Mary.[8] Abraham Wooster, David's father, was baptized on March 16, 1672, or 1673. Early family information is not available, therefore the exact year of his birth, like that of his son David, is not accurately recorded. Abraham married Mary Walker on November 22, 1699. From their marriage they had seven children. David was the sixth child, having five sisters and one older brother.[9] Abraham Wooster was a prosperous landowner, owning a large farm and sawmill in Quaker's Farm near the town of Oxford. He also inherited additional lands from his father. According to Orcutt, Abraham Wooster was a stone mason by trade.[10] David was ten or eleven when the family moved to Quaker's Farm.[11]

He grew up in a military household. In 1717 his father served as ensign in the "trainband in the parish of Ripton in Stratford."[12] A "trainband" was the seventeenth-century version of the local militia, organized around one's parish church. Being an ensign meant that Abraham Wooster was responsible for carrying the militia's standard when in the field. He was promoted to captain of the trainband in May 1728. David Wooster was eighteen when his father became captain. No doubt this made an impression on the young man.

Wooster was born into the same generation as Benjamin Franklin. Franklin is well known for his personal hard work, innovation, fortitude, and social commentary as a printer, as well as his famous *Poor Richard's Almanac*. Franklin's wit and wisdom have become standards for the study of the eighteenth century by students across the country. Although contemporaries, there is a vast difference between the historical notoriety of Franklin and Wooster's obscurity. These men were a full generation older than the majority of those who would lead in the Revolutionary War. Wooster's generation was involved in far greater military and domestic issues, the defense of the frontier against Indian attacks and French incursions, as well as the campaign against Louisbourg in 1745. While Franklin wrote of the death of Blackbeard the pirate in 1719, Wooster actively defended Connecticut against the real threat of Spanish pirates in the 1740s. He gained wisdom of colonial affairs regarding mercantilism and its reliance upon British shipping and commerce, as well as military training and discipline provided by British officers and soldiers. This came with age and practical experience.

New England was a beehive of religious activity in the 1700s, and Connecticut became the epicenter for the First Great Awakening. One of the premier intentions of the original founders of Connecticut was to create a settlement where the Puritan religion would be supported and flourish. Beginning in 1662 with the granting of the original charter for the colony of Connecticut from King Charles II, the Puritan religion became the foundation for the colonists. However, by the early 1700s the earlier religious fervor had begun to subside. As with most historical cycles, and this is evident in the colonies in New England established for religious purposes, the enthusiasm of the original founders oftentimes waxes and wanes among subsequent generations. According to historian Edward E. Atwater, "Spiritual religion had much declined in New England while the second and third generations were passing over the stage."[13] By the 1710s, Wooster's generation, it had become clear that the original religious purity and interest of the colony was lacking. A new spiritual revitalization was needed to ignite the religious character of the earlier settlers, and in the 1730s, such spiritual re-awakening in Connecticut was growing and spreading.

The Great Awakening enlivened Puritans throughout New England starting in 1735, while David Wooster, then twenty-five years old, was enrolled at Yale College. New Haven became the epicenter of this early religious movement. Connecticut played a crucial role in this religious movement, and few ministers or preachers of the day had as great an impact on the growth and revitalization of American New England Puritanism as Jonathan Edwards of Connecticut. Edwards fueled the fire of this new religious revival, which was not only spread from the pulpit, but also from the classroom of the newly established Yale College.

As New England mirrored the western traditions of England, the foundation of higher education became a priority. Connecticut chartered the third oldest college in North America, Yale College, in 1701.[14] One of the founding ideas of the colony of Connecticut was to create a classical school for the betterment of all. By the 1730s, the best avenue to achieve the success that Wooster sought in colonial Connecticut was through an advanced classical education. In the eighteenth century, education was seen as a means to personal advancement and a building block to a lucrative and social career. Although the citizens of Connecticut were eager for the opening of Yale College, European wars continually postponed the successful creation of the school. Wars with Spain and France dominated discussion and decimated the colonial treasury, either for coastal defense or internal Indian aggression.[15] The vision of a college, however, soon became a reality. Yale College in New Haven was the oldest college in Connecticut and was slightly over thirty miles from Quaker's Farms, near Oxford, where the Woosters resided. The school was originally established in Saybrook, Connecticut, but was voted to relocate to New Haven in 1716, and the first buildings in New Haven were constructed in 1717. The school was named to honor Elihu Yale, who contributed books to the library and other material goods.[16] Yale College produced some of the most influential men of eighteenth-century America, including four signers of the Declaration of Independence, Philip Livingston, class of 1737, Lewis Morris, class of 1746, and Lyman Hall and Oliver Wolcott, both graduates of the class of 1747. Many members of the Continental Congress were also Yale men.[17] The school was founded to educate young men in Christianity, the sciences, and enlightened thought.[18]

By the 1730s Yale was well established with its benefactor's donation of books and resources. Yale produced many notable graduates, as mentioned, including Jonathan Edwards, class of 1720, and of course, David Wooster, class of 1738. In 1740 there was an apparent issue with students not paying for the cost of tuition. The college addressed the problem stating that "no undergraduate shall hereafter be admitted to College, until father or guardian or some person has given a sufficient bond that his quarterly dues shall be paid." There were scholarships, however, provided to some students. The cost of administration and the running of the school in 1738 was £ 701..9..6.. (701 pounds, 9 shillings, 6 pence).[19] The class of 1738, Wooster's class, saw the passing of the last of the original trustees while the academic year was in session. Significantly, the new president, Thomas Clap, would be instrumental in Wooster's adult life.

The 1738 Yale graduating class included Chauncaus Whittelsey, the minster who wrote the funeral oration for Yale President Clap, which was delivered by his own daughter Mary Clap, and Phineas Lyman, under whom Wooster serve in military during the siege of Louisbourg.[20] The records of Yale noted that David Wooster was twenty-three and a half years of age when he entered college. There is no indication of specific courses he studied, or grades received. Wooster left Yale upon graduation and became a lawyer in New Haven shortly thereafter. His son, Thomas, also attended Yale and graduated in 1768. Numerous Yale graduates served with David Wooster during the Revolutionary War.[21]

The courses of study for the early 1700s at Yale exemplified the influence of enlightenment thought coupled to religious conviction. Thomas Clap, president of Yale College from 1739 to 1766, and subsequently the father-in-law to David Wooster, wrote several tracts and pamphlets about the courses of study undertaken by a student at Yale. In 1766, he wrote:

> Each Class is under the immediate Instruction of a particular Tutor; who carries them thro' a Course of Studies, for three Years; and the President completes their Instruction in the fourth. At their Admission they are able well to construe and parse *Tully's Orations, Virgil* and the *Greek* Testament; and understand the Rules of common Arithmetick. In the first Year, they learn *Hebrew*; and principally pursue the Study of the Languages, and make a Beginning in Logick, and some Parts of the Mathematicks. In the second Year, they study the Languages; but principally recite Logick, Rhetorick, Oratory, Geography and natural Philosophy: And some of them make good Proficiency in Trigonometry and Algebra. In the third Year, they still pursue the Study of natural Philosophy; and most Branches of the Mathematicks: Many of them well understand Surveying, Navigation, and the Calculation of the Eclipses; and some of them are considerable Proficients in Conic Sections and Fluxions. In the fourth Year they principally study and recite Metaphysicks,[22] Ethicks and Divinity.[23]

During the years that Wooster attended Yale, the tutors he would have received instruction from included John Sergeant, William Adams, Samuel Whittelsey, William Woscott, Abel Stiles, and James Lockwood.[24] In addition to the course of study outlined by President Clap, students were also engaged in debate and rhetoric.

> The two upper Classes exercise their Powers in disputing every Monday in the Syllogistick Form,[25] and every Tuesday in the Forensick; which gives a greater Scope to their Genius, and is better adapted to the common Use and Practice of Mankind, in the Conduct of Publick Affairs.
>
> When they have alternately gone through all their Arguments, the Moderator recapitulates those which seem to be the most plausible on each Side, shews their real Force or Weakness, and gives his Opinion upon the Whole. The Questions are taken from every Subject, which occurs in the whole Circle of Literature, and upon almost all the doubtful Points, which have been publickly disputed among Mankind.
>
> Twice a Week five or six deliver a Declamation memoriter[26] from the oratorical Rostrum; the President makes some Observations upon the Manner of Delivery and sometimes upon the Subject; and sometimes gives some small Laurel to him who best acts the Part of an Orator.[27]

Religious instruction was the core of academic life at Yale College in the 1700s, as well as the central reason for the school's charter.[28] The First Great Awakening had taken root in Connecticut, and the school was entrusted with the religious education of the young men sent there for their academic success.[29] In the fervor of the First Great Awakening, a divide arose between the Old Lights and the New Lights who favored the preaching of George Whitefield. Thomas Clap was initially a solid Old Light and instituted a new expulsion policy at Yale College in the 1740s that prohibited any student from criticizing or commenting on the religious beliefs of the faculty. From 1742 to 1745, three students were expelled from Yale for criticizing the religious devotion of their tutors. By the 1750s, the fanaticism of the New Lights had subsided, however the antagonism of the Old Lights had intensified. Clap began to alter his view and eventually sided with the New Lights, as he saw their religious ideology more aligned with his own.[30] Religious instruction of the youth was first and foremost on his mind. He wrote:

Special Care is taken to form the Morals of the Youth; to keep them (as much as may be) from all Excesses and Extravagancies; from all vain Affectations of Show, which occasion unnecessary Expences and divert their Minds from the Pursuit of those Things which are of greater Importance; to instil into their Minds true Notions of Honor, Politeness, and a Love of Virtue: And to impress upon them a Sense, that the End of their Creation, and of all their special Advantages, is not ultimately for themselves, or their own Sakes; but to qualify them for the special Service of God; and to render them most useful to their Fellow-Men.

Above all, Care is taken to instil into their Minds, the Principles of true Religion, in Doctrine and Pratice, by publick and private Discourses and personal Conversations. To this End they are obliged to attend the publick Worship of God in the Chapel every Lord's-Day, and Morning and Evening Prayers; at which, Occasion is frequently taken, from the Portion of Scripture read, to excite them to some particular Duty, and to Caution them against some particular Sin.[31]

The religious fervor of the Great Awakening, combined with the teaching of Lockean enlightened thought at Yale, began to challenge the status quo of loyalism in Connecticut. Wooster's religious-based Yale education created a solid foundation for both the intellectual and practical development of eighteenth-century republicanism, which was rooted in the English tradition of Magna Carta. Throughout his youth, he was surrounded with leaders who instilled a Puritan religious philosophy linked to natural rights and law into his education and daily life. Adding military tradition and service of the Wooster family in the colony of Connecticut to his early years, David Wooster was well situated to take an active leadership role. International conflicts in the British North American colonies in the late 1730s and early 1740s, first with Spain and then with France, provided an excellent classroom for the future major general. The skills thus far learned at Yale propelled Wooster to military leadership success in the war with Spain as well as in the siege of the French port city of Louisbourg.

2

First Military Action (1739–1746)

The War of the Austrian Succession and the Siege of Louisbourg

Preparations for military defense were an ever-constant necessity in the British colonies in North America. Throughout the eighteenth century the colonies in New England raised militia units for both internal and external protection. Military discipline and customs had become a foundation of David Wooster's youth. This military tradition was directed towards native Indian tribes, the French who had established outpost settlements in Nova Scotia and Upper and Lower Canada, and the Spanish in Florida and the Caribbean sugar islands. The economic activity of the New England fishing industry, coupled with maritime trade, required a constant defensive position. Great Britain did not provide a standing army in the North American colonies. Therefore, this necessity fell to the colonists themselves. Wooster's father had been an ensign and captain in a local militia company. The twenty-eight-year-old Wooster was molded and shaped by the tradition of military discipline, rigor, and service.

In 1739, just one year after graduating from Yale, Wooster enlisted in the military defense of Connecticut. External threats from Spain necessitated protection of the coast. Britain and Spain were engaged in the ongoing War of the Austrian Succession, which lasted from October 22, 1739, to October 18, 1748. This European conflict spilled into the American colonies. Tensions rose in 1731 when the British ship *Rebecca* was attacked and boarded off the coast of Florida by the crew of the Spanish ship *La Isabela*. British captain Robert Jenkins was forced to surrender his vessel. From this engagement, the war in North America was more commonly referred to as the War of Jenkins' Ear and became a struggle for domination of the Caribbean sugar islands.[1] As members of the British Empire, the American colonists found themselves engaged in a global war. Many of the colonies were asked to provide manpower to aid the empire in this fight.[2] Since Connecticut depended heavily upon trade with England for its economic survival, the General Assembly ordered a ship to be built for the protection of the Connecticut coastline. In May 1740, the sloop *Defense* was ordered built for that purpose.[3]

David Wooster graduated from Yale College at the age of twenty-eight, and his knowledge of navigation and mathematics equipped him with the necessary tools to sail, and lead, the newly constructed sloop. When the *Defense* was completed and put into action in early 1741, Wooster was commissioned by the lower house of the Connecticut General Assembly as the 1st Lieutenant of the ship under the command of Captain George Phillips of Middletown, the town where the *Defense* was built.[4] A year later Wooster was commissioned captain of the sloop. In 1742, Wooster wrote to Governor Jonathan Law concerning the military action onboard the *Defense*.

> May it Please your Honour,
>
> I Have Rec'd the Coloney Sloop Defense and Inlisted Twenty men Officers included I have also got her Grav'd and her Decks and Upper works Cork'd which were very Open & I hope to Git her Ready for a Caruze by the middle of next week if need Require. Cap't Burnham being Ingaged on a Voyage to y'e West Indies Cant be Released As I am Inform'd to go in the Coloney Sloop therefore I have Shipt another man to Master at Present I Cant Send your Honour a Coppy of my Commission Because it is not Yet Come but Expect it Daily Two Capt'ns of Vessels Arriv'd here a few Days Ago who have been taken by a Spanish Privateer and they Suppose that She is now on Our Coast for they were Set att Liberty att the Western Islands and the Commander told them that when he had Clean'd his Vessel he would Come on y'e Coast of New England they Say also that while they were on Board Sd Privateer they Came on Our Coast to y'e Latt: of 39'd 30'm wherefore if your Honour Sees fit to send me out on a Caruze In a short time I should be Glad to have Orders to Inlist men from your Hon'r By the Next Post. wherefore having nothing further to add I Subscribe my Self Your Honr's Most Humb'le and Most Obed't Serv't To Command
>
> David Wooster[5]

The sloop had a crew of twenty-seven men. An account for pay from Captain Phillips dated September 5, 1741, provided information not only on the number of crewmen, but also their respective tasks. Of the twenty-seven, there were two officers (Phillips, and Wooster), one sailing master, one gunner, one boatswain, one carpenter, one cook, and twenty sailing mates. This made up the ship's full company. Their pay scale varied based upon individual skill and was paid by the treasury upon return. One submitted account indicated that the *Defense* had been at sea for forty-five days. For their service £ 114..9..00 (114 pounds, 9 shillings) in new bills were paid to the crew. Of that amount Lieutenant Wooster received £ 10..2..6.. (10 pounds, 2 shillings, 6 pence).[6]

Wooster served on the *Defense* from 1741 to 1743. As noted in his letter to Governor Law in 1742, the threat from a Spanish attack was very real. Protecting their shipping industry from pirate attacks was of the utmost importance for the economic vitality of Connecticut, as was defending their fishing vessels in the Grand Banks. While onboard the *Defense,* his duty was to patrol and protect the Connecticut coastline from any potential Spanish or pirate attacks. He traveled as far south as the Virginia coast to prevent such attacks. In May 1743, Wooster, now as the captain of the sloop as well as the purser, petitioned the Connecticut General Assembly for reimbursement of funds that he himself had paid to the crew. He noted that "he had expended a considerable time in attending on settlement of his accounts, paying off the men, etc., for all which he hath had no allowance." Wooster requested £ 20..16..6.. which the treasurer of the colony was ordered to pay.[7] This would not be the last time that Wooster provided payment out of his own personal finances for military costs. Despite being onboard the sloop for two years, the *Defense* never saw any naval action while Wooster was onboard.

Following the conclusion of the war with Spain, the *Defense* was engaged in transporting Connecticut troops to Louisbourg. On March 7, 1744, Governor Jonathan Law, as commander-in-chief of the armed forces in Connecticut, wrote the following to Captain John Prentis of the *Defense*:

> By and with the Advice of the Council of Warr assigned me I do hereby Order and Direct you forthwith to enlist one hundred able bodyed, effective men including Officers to serve on board the Colony Sloop Defense in the intended Expedition against Cape Britton.[8]

In 1745, Roger Wolcott, Deputy Governor of Connecticut, and a member of the Louisbourg expedition, noted in his journal that "Connecticut sent 500 land forces in transports, with Capt. Prentis in the *Defense* Sloop with 100 men for the sea service."[9] As a sloop of war, the *Defense* was active in the months following the successful assault upon Louisbourg.[10] Safeguarding the foremost economic endeavors of the colony of Connecticut, shipping and mercantile trade, had propelled David Wooster onto the vanguard of the colonial scene in the early 1740s. The larger world conflict which loomed on the horizon in 1744 would catapult the young naval captain even further into an engaging life-long military career.

Upon his return in the mid–1740s from this first experience in the military naval service, David Wooster was betrothed to Mary Clap, "an educated and exemplary lady, not likely to make a statement without ample authority."[11] She was born in Windham, Connecticut, on April 25, 1729. Her father, Thomas Clap, was a graduate of Harvard, class of 1722, before becoming the president of Yale College from 1740 to 1766. Her mother was Mary Whiting. David and Mary were married on March 6, 1745. Together they had four children. Mary, their first daughter, was born on January 21, 1746, yet died on October 20, 1748, just two years old. Thomas, born on July 30, 1751, named after his grandfather, graduated from Yale in 1768, and died in 1792. Their second daughter, Mary, was born on June 2, 1753, but unfortunately did not live past January 16, 1754. Their last child, also named Mary, was born on October 21, 1755, and lived into the early 1800s with her husband the Rev. John Cosins Ogden.[12] Mary's fortitude is exemplified in the years following the death of her husband, Major General David Wooster. From 1777 to her death on June 6, 1807, Mary Wooster fought to preserve and protect her husband's legacy in an ever-changing post–Revolution America.

The threat of French and Spanish attack was very real to the colonists in Connecticut. The most ominous of these was the fortress of Louisbourg. Located along the southeastern shore of Cape Breton Island and northeast along the Atlantic coast from the British colonies of Massachusetts Bay, Rhode Island, and Connecticut, Louisbourg posed a serious threat to the colonial fishing industry. It controlled access to the Gulf of Saint Lawrence as well as the Saint Lawrence River and the great French settlements of Quebec and Montreal. Most alarming, however, was Louisbourg's access to the Grand Banks and the numerous fishing vessels from the New England colonies that relied upon these waters for their livelihood.

Prior to the expedition against Louisbourg, the military structure in the British colonies was well established. Internal conflicts between the French and their Indian allies along the frontier precipitated a military design employed through the colonial militia system. Even in Connecticut the use of the militia served as a defense against raiding parties that had impacted the New England colonies for decades. The military tradition of Protestant New England guarded against French Catholics and their Indian allies, and the backcountry warfare perpetuated European and Indian antagonism and atrocities. All were equally involved in violent actions. King Philip's War escalated Indian–Anglo tensions in 1675. Hundreds of Connecticut men joined with men from Massachusetts and other New England colonies in the fight against the consolidated forces of King Phillip.[13] The destruction of life and property which resulted in the cultural war prevented peaceful co-existence between many of the Indian tribe and the British colonists in New England for decades. Such was the New England culture in which David Wooster matured.

The French began a series of fort construction projects in the New World in the late seventeenth and early eighteenth centuries. Louisbourg was one of a series of fortifications. Its construction added to the drain of the royal treasury of King Louis XIV. Forts at Quebec and Montreal were constructed in a similar manner.[14] Examining maps drawn of the French fortress of Louisbourg provides an image of an imposing structure, one that would not be easily captured.[15]

Although the sloop *Defense* had been decommissioned, Wooster remained involved with military matters in Connecticut. In the spring of 1744, war had once again broken out between England and France. Unfortunately for the inhabitants of the British colonies in New England, word of the official declaration of war did not reach them until after the French army and navy had attacked and successfully captured the English settlement at Canso, southwest of Cape Breton. When word of the attack reached Massachusetts and Connecticut, the colonial militia sprang into action. Despite this initial success, the French were not prepared for the military advance of New England troops and the Royal Navy upon their stronghold of Louisbourg.

According to an anonymous Frenchman who was witness to the action at Louisbourg, and the subsequent deportation of its inhabitants to France, the French military was poorly trained, low in morale, and inadequately led. Historian George Wrong translated the French account in 1897. The author of the letter noted that "on May 13–24, 1744, the French seized the English fishing station off Canso, opposite to Cape Breton on the Nova Scotia coast, and this was the first intimation which the English colonies received that war had broken out."[16]

This particular account is anonymous. In that regard it must be analyzed more critically, despite the collaborative nature to other sources cited. It is one of the few accounts of the siege of Louisbourg that presents the French perspective of events. The author claimed to be at Louisbourg before the siege and witnessed the actions of the summer of 1745. He was then transported to France on one of the cartel ships. In his writing, the author attacked the inadequacies of the French navy and their commanders in the colonies. To the author, French captains were more concerned with adding to their own personal wealth and materials gained through trade, despite the practice being against the desire of the French crown. Their attention to personal accommodations prevented them from providing needed naval security to those in Louisbourg in 1745.[17] Although not specific to Louisbourg, modern historian James

Pritchard has analyzed the inefficient nature of the French navy in the North American colonies and corroborates the complaints of the anonymous French inhabitant of Louisbourg. Pritchard argued that by the early 1700s, despite being fully invested in the economic structure of the African slave trade, there was a great deal of illegal French trade and fraud in the West Indies. This involved numerous naval officers who would ship freight home for profit, as well as ship freight to the Caribbean, which limited the navy's effectiveness as a fighting force. Several officers were arrested, and one was court martialed.[18] This led to problems with the French navy in Canada by the 1740s.

With the influx of money from the royal treasury in Paris in 1715, Pritchard stated that the French settlements in upper and lower Canada quickly developed. The beaver trade was revived, and newly designed forts were being built to protect the Hudson Valley in New York, north of Albany, as well as the Ohio territory. This increased French trade with Indians.[19] He concluded with an assessment that supports the anonymous account. The French Bourbons did not apply as good a governance as they could have in the Americas, especially in the use of their navy.[20]

To add to his critique upon the inadequacies of the French navy, the author of *Anonymous Lettre d'un Habitant De Louisbourg* noted that two French men-of-war came to Louisbourg but did nothing to aid in the defense of the city. "Negligence and fatuity conspired to make us lose our unhappy island." It is important to analyze the economic impact of the settlements in Nova Scotia regarding access to the Grand Banks. Fishing was the most important economic factor in the 1700s, and the author noted such, stating "They [English] wished to have a monopoly of the cod fishery, which is a most important trade, as experience should have convinced us."[21]

According to the author, the English would not have attacked the French settlement at Louisbourg if the French had not attacked them first at Canso. The dereliction of the French governor at Louisbourg led to the loss of the city. "Some of her subjects [English] had built a wretched town [Canso], which we burned."[22] If taken alone, the anonymous French letter could be understood as the writings of a disgruntled subject bemoaning the loss of their city, home, and way of life. The author could clearly be read as seeking a scapegoat for the inadequacies of military preparation within Louisbourg. However, the French narrative was continually verified through English accounts, both colonial and British naval records. The amount of continuity from primary source material, as well as modern historical analysis and interpretation, add a level of credibility to the anonymous author's letter.

Not only was the attack upon Canso and the threat to the fishing industry of great concern to the colonists in Connecticut and all of New England, but there was also an additional layer to the animosity of the colonists towards the French settlements to the north: religion. The Old-World religious antagonism between Catholics and Protestants had taken root in the New-World. Religious baggage came with the settlers, be they English or French. In 1711 there was a failed British attack on Quebec. French Catholics in Quebec hailed the victory as divine intervention, held several Masses in thanksgiving, and rededicated their church to Our Lady of Victory.[23] In Connecticut and Massachusetts, militia units had been raised to prevent attack from the French Catholics and their Indian allies along the frontier. Raids had taken place for generations. It was the threat of such raiding parties that caused David Wooster's father to join the militia while his son was a youth. As military planning began for the colonial attack upon Louisbourg, Protestant ministers in New England, fueled with the fire of the Great Awakening, rekindled religious animosity. "Religious antipathies were inflamed to the point of fanaticism. One clergyman armed himself with a large hatchet, with which he said he proposed chopping up into kindling wood all the Popish images he should find adorning the altars of Louisbourg."[24] As a Puritan these animosities were a part of Wooster's upbringings and would affect his interaction with French Catholics in Canada in 1775 and 1776.

Once the colonial forces reached Louisbourg the destruction of property was not only directed towards private dwellings, but included Catholic chapels and churches, or "Mass houses" as they were referred to. James Gibson, a veteran of the campaign, wrote that that the "Mass-house" within the Grand Battery was used on May 3 to have a Protestant service, not Catholic. Gibson noted in his journal and letters of the occasions where Catholic "Mass-houses" were either taken over and used for Protestant purposes or burned. He was the only writer to include such details.[25]

Samuel Niles, a Protestant preacher who lived most of his life in Rhode Island, also wrote on the religious situation in Louisbourg as a sign of divine providence, that the New England Protestant force was destined to defeat the evils of popery. French privateers had attacked his family when he was a small child, and young Niles was severely beaten by one Frenchman. Although it does not appear that Niles himself accompanied the troops to Louisbourg, he composed a lengthy thirty-four-page poem which highlighted the defeat of the French at the hands of the New England troops in 1745. As a Protestant preacher he appeared to take great delight in the fall of the Roman Catholics at Louisbourg. Unlike James Gibson, who simply recorded in his letters and journal accounts of the destruction of the various "Mass-houses" in Louisbourg, Samuel Niles composed two full pages on the evils of "Popery" and the Catholic faith which had been practiced by the French in Louisbourg. He concluded this section of the poem with the following lines:

> These Popish Rites, and Ceremonial Cants,
> Give no Relief to the poor Gallic' ants,
> In sable Darkness, they do still remain,
> From the Gygantick Force of English Men.[26]

This was the religious, economic, and military environment that David Wooster, now thirty-four years old, became part of. His initial military leadership experience onboard the *Defense* precipitated further action. Driven by his Protestant faith, his Yale education in the classics, mathematics, and rhetoric, the siege of Louisbourg became the catalyst for Wooster's military star rising on the horizon.

With the War of the Austrian Succession now a global war, and after the French attack on the English settlement at Canso, a retaliatory action was planned against the French at Louisbourg, not by the crown but rather by the colonial leaders in New England. Massachusetts Governor William Shirley led the movement for a military strike against the "Gibraltar of North America," as Louisbourg was called. For military support Shirley called upon William Pepperrell, also of Massachusetts, to lead the ground assault. As Governor Shirley planned the attack, initially envisioned as a surprise assault, King George II and Parliament were kept informed, and the support of the Royal Navy was pledged to Shirley. Louisbourg was vital to controlling the French fur trade in Canada, as it dominated the entrance of the St. Lawrence River. It was also a key location for French privateers who were operating against New England commercial shipping. The attack upon Louisbourg was thus seen as a retaliatory action only. The French settlement had presented a real threat to the livelihood of New Englanders since the early 1720s and with the completion of the fort and the attack upon Canso, the threat had become a reality. If action was not taken, British settlers in New England feared that French aggression would fall upon them next. Their course of action was to take the offensive.

Troops needed to be enlisted, along with procuring the necessities and equipage of war. Money had to be raised for the purchase of the many needed goods. Governor Shirley, James Gibson, and William Pepperrell all contributed large sums of their personal wealth to finance the expedition.[27] A joint inner-colonial military command had to be created. William Pepperrell became the commander-in-chief of the ground forces, and each colony provided military leadership. The Connecticut General Assembly, under order of the governor, met on Tuesday, February 26, 1745, at New Haven, with the express duty to appoint military leaders of the colony and to provide funding for the men from Connecticut who would undertake the action against Louisbourg.[28] Roger Wolcott, lieutenant governor of Connecticut, served as Pepperrell's second in command and was the commander-in-chief of Connecticut troops. Wolcott also oversaw the men from Connecticut, including Captain David Wooster. The assembly called for five-hundred volunteers from the colony and made provisions for those who brought their own military equipment, firelocks, swords, belt and cartridge box, and blanket. Volunteers who provided these were allotted an additional £ 3 pounds pay on top of the £ 10 pounds promised for the expedition.[29] The General Assembly also appointed "Capt. David Worster [Wooster] of a company in the regiment of foot to be raised and sent from this government on the expedition against Cape Breton, &c., and order that he be commissioned accordingly."[30]

The assembly also commissioned officers who then raised the necessary troops for their own companies for the expedition against Louisbourg. During the General Assembly meeting of March 14–19, 1745, Captain Wooster was commissioned to lead a company of foot soldiers along with Lieutenant Nathaniel Beedle and Ensign Nathan Whiting.[31] This was the first experience for Wooster at leading infantry. There was much to be learned. Although his military leadership onboard the *Defense* provided an ample beginning, preparations for Louisbourg required a different type of leadership. Not only did Wooster have to recruit men to fill the ranks of his newly formed company, but he also needed to study military manuals, learn and instruct military drill, and organize, albeit at a smaller scale, the necessary items required of soldiers: food, water, bedding, tentage, ammunition, and hygiene. No officer could afford to have illness decimate their ranks. For Wooster this was a new and exciting opportunity, and one that sharpened his Yale education and naval experience and developed life-long leadership and organizational skills.

On April 2, 1745, just four weeks after receiving his commission, Wooster wrote to Connecticut Governor Jonathan Law concerning the raising of troops for his company. This is the earliest surviving handwritten letter written by Wooster. In it he expressed his concern over the lack of weapons required to fully outfit the men of his company.

New Haven, April yᵉ 2ᵈ 1745

May it please your Honour, I have completed my company and am ready to proceed as soon as I have orders but I want a great many guns and having no press warrant[32] I cannot get 'em, therefore I desire your Honour to favor me with a press warrant for whatsoever I shall want for the expedition this from your Honours very humblᵈ Servᵗ to Command,

David Wooster[33]

The New England forces joined William Pepperrell near the coast of Cape Breton on April 24, 1745. The French quickly abandoned the Royal Battery, also referred to as the Grand Battery, which was positioned on the opposite side of the harbor from the fort and commanded the harbor. The anonymous French account lambasted the French commander, Pierre Morpain, for this move and wrote that the defense of Louisbourg was futile once the military abandoned the battery.[34] Major General Roger Wolcott related the preparations made for the English encampments around Louisbourg, and also detailed the process of repairing of the French guns taken at the Grand Battery, which had been poorly spiked by their crews as they abandoned the fortification.

We now spent several days in landing our tents and stores, fixing our camp, setting up our store-houses and hospitals, sending out advanced parties to meet any of the enemy that might be patrolling about and reduce the adjacent settlements. Workmen were employed to drill the cannon at the grand battery, which the enemy had plugged up, others were employed to view the ground where we might erect our batteries to the best advantage. As soon as the cannon were freed, they began a very brisk fire upon the town to the great annoyance of the enemy.[35]

William Pepperrell described the arrival and deployment of the Connecticut troops in his journal[36]:

March, 25th, 1745,

…and were join'd the 25th of the same Month [March] by the Connecticut Forces, being Five Hundred and Sixteen Men, including Commission-Officers.[37]

April 18th, 1745,

From thence Two Armed Sloops were sent to Bay Verte, to take and destroy some Vessels that, according to Information, were to carry Provisions from thence to Louisbourg. And the 18th of April the *Renomee*, a French Ship of War, of Thirty Guns Nine-Pounders, with Three Hundred Seamen, and Fifty Marines, being charged with Publick Dispatches, fell in with the Armed Vessels in the Service of the Massachusetts Government, before Louisbourg Harbour: Where she maintained a running Fight with them; but got clear by out-sailing them. This Ship afterwards fell in with the Connecticut Troops, under the Convoy of their own Colony Sloop and the Rhode-Island Colony Sloop; the latter of which she attacked and damaged considerably.[38]

For many of the Connecticut soldiers at Louisbourg, including David Wooster, this was their first experience in the infantry. Along with the thrill of battle came the boredom and tedious activity of camp life. The equipment provided to the soldiers was of poor quality at best. Camp life included a variety of work details. Constructing new placements for artillery batteries was physically exhausting to the New England volunteers. William Shirley recalled the work done by the English troops in erecting two additional batteries that were used to fire into the city. He presented a grueling account of the difficulty in moving the heavy cannon through the mud:

> in which the Cannon were upon Wheels, they several Times sink so deep as not only to bury the Carriages, but the whole Body of the Cannon likewise: Horses and Oxen could not be employed in this Service, but all must be drawn by Men themselves, up to the knees in Mud at the same Time; the Nights in which the Work was to be done, cold and Foggy, their Tents bad, there being no proper Materials for Tents to be had in New-England, at the Outset of the Expedition.[39]

Once the new battery had been erected, the men were exhausted and there were up to "1500 Men incapable of Duty" with the flux.[40] Accounts of the siege of Louisbourg mention the difficulty of erecting new batteries to reduce the fortress. Despite the challenging conditions of terrain, the New England troops prevailed.[41] Camp discipline was lax, and Wooster learned from this experience. Applying discipline to volunteers who were on the expedition on their own accord was a grave military concern. British Commodore Warren was able to enforce strict naval discipline among his crew in the Royal Navy, but similar discipline would not be tolerated within the ranks of the New England volunteers. Yet, adherence to military disciple was a necessity.

The colonial action at Louisbourg was not entirely a glorious achievement. Captain Joseph Goldthwaite, adjutant to Sir William Pepperrell, presented the stark reality of the condition of the troops laying siege at Louisbourg, and provided a more somber perspective on the campaign.

> The utter lack of experience of the New England men at the outset; the long discouraging delay at Canseau; the dangers and difficulties to be overcome at Flat Point and Fresh Water Cove; the dreadful strain of hauling the guns across the marshes in the depressing gloom of darkness and dense fogs; the want of tents, shoes and proper clothing; the prevalence of disease, at one time over 2,000 men being unfit for duty; the incessant cannonading, night and day, to which they were subjected; the heroic assaults and repulses at the Island Battery; the long and wearisome duty in the garrison; the rare patience, courage, good temper and poor pay (25s per month, or less the 6d per day, the soldier furnishing his own clothes and gun); all these tried the souls of men unused to war.[42]

Major General Roger Wolcott led the 1st Connecticut Regiment. Colonel Andrew Burr commanded the eight companies of the regiment, and Captain David Wooster commanded the first of these eight companies. All ground forces were under the command of William Pepperrell, while naval forces were led by Commodore Warren whose squadron had sailed north from the Caribbean to assist in the siege. On June 11, the anniversary of the coronation of King George II, the British forces began a massive artillery bombardment of the fortress at noon which caused tremendous destruction both to the French defenses and the morale of the garrison. The great French fortress of Louisbourg fell to the combined British land and naval forces on June 17, 1745. Sir William Pepperrell wrote of the event in his journal:

> Hostages were exchanged; and on the 17th of June the City and Fortresses were surrender'd, and the Garrison, and all the Inhabitants, to the Number of Two Thousand capable of bearing Arms, made Prisoners, to be transported to France with all their Personal Effects.[43]

As the surrender was underway, troops from New England were prohibited from ransacking and plundering the inhabitants of the town, much to their disappointment. The pay that they received was lower in relation to their length of service and time away from home. They had hoped to supplement their pay with the spoils of war. In comparison, the British ships under Commodore Warren continued to lure French ships into the harbor at Louisbourg and take them as prizes, from which the monetary gain was divided among the crew. None of this was shared with the New England troops who became angered at the unequal distribution of bounty.[44] Despite attempts to prohibit looting and plunder, both inevitably occurred.[45]

There is an interesting anecdote articulated at the dedication of the memorial monument to General Wooster in 1854, delivered by Henry C. Deming at Danbury. It recounts an action during the attack at Louisbourg between Wooster and another British officer:

> A British captain had ventured to apply his ratan quite freely to the shoulders of one of Captain Wooster's men, a respectable freeholder and church-member from Connecticut. Wooster remonstrated with the regular for so grossly abusing official superiority. The Briton resented this advice in unmeasured terms, and finally drew his sword to chastise the adviser upon the spot. Wooster successfully parried his thrusts and speedily disarmed him. Applying his own sword to his adversary's breast, he told him that the life he had just forfeited could only be redeemed by asking pardon, and promising that he would never again disgrace with a blow, any soldier in the service. The terms were accepted without a parley. The jeers of his companions soon drove the officer from the army, while Wooster won the title of the soldier's protector and friend.[46]

Although it is difficult to verify this anecdote, it does fit into and solidify the narrative of Wooster's dedication to duty, loyalty, and leadership as perceived by his contemporaries.

On July 4, 1745, following the surrender of the French forces at Louisbourg, Wooster was placed in charge of a cartel ship filled with French soldiers and civilians who were being removed from Louisbourg. He was given the responsibility of taking a portion of these prisoners back to France due to his bravery and leadership in aiding the reduction of the fort. In a letter to Connecticut Governor Jonathan Law, Colonel Andrew Burr reported:

> three of our Transports were taken into the Kings pay ye 24th of June Last and are Gone to France to Carry Prisoners—Capt Wooster is since Gone in a snow belonging to ye Army for ye same purpose. the french are most of them transported to France & Boston, as to ye Number of Troops that are to keep Garrison here ye General and Council of warr here will not as yet determine, but wait for the Coming of Govr Shirley or advice from him.[47]

When the ship arrived at the port of Rochefort on the western coast of France, there was a prisoner exchange of the French prisoners from Louisbourg for three-hundred and fifty English prisoners being held in France. Captain Wooster was not allowed to leave the ship or set foot on French soil. James Gibson traveled with Wooster to France along with the French prisoners and civilians. At the conclusion of Gibson's journal, which included his hand-drawn map of the attack against Louisbourg and the placement of colonial troops, is an attached letter which described the ill treatment of all the British forces upon their arrival at Rochefort.

Wooster and Gibson were both onboard the *Launceston*. Gibson's letter provided details that were corroborated by Wooster's testimony to the Lord High Admiralty Court in London in October 1745. He complained that as soon as the British cartel ship entered the roads at Rochefort, the French commander, Mac Lemarrough, onboard a French seventy-four-gun man-of-war, ordered all incoming vessels to anchor. Private letters, journals, maps, and other papers were seized from the British and no Englishman was permitted to go on shore or to any of the other cartel ships. Gibson further wrote that the captain of the *Launceston* become violently ill with fever, yet the French garrison commander refused any aid. The English were not even allowed to take on fresh water or provision. In his journal Gibson wrote of the French "Commodore Mac Lemarrough, who, like an inhuman Savage, turn'd a deaf Ear to our Complaints, and rather added to our Miseries, than any ways reliev'd us."[48] The cartel ships were permitted to leave Rochefort on September 19, much the worse for wear.

Following his forced detainment, Wooster left France and headed to London. Upon arriving in England, Wooster and John Marston, captain of the ship *St. Dominique* and the HMS *Eagle*, reported to the Lord High Admiralty Court on October 8, 1745, concerning the events that had taken place at Rochefort and the condition of the French fleet there. Wooster and Marston gave detailed accounts of the enemy that they encountered as well as the number and condition of the French seamen at Rochefort. After the interview Wooster was sent to be introduced to His Grace, the Duke of Newcastle, and from there was afforded the opportunity to be received by His Royal Britannic Majesty, King George II, at His Majesty's request.[49]

While in London, Wooster's accolades accumulated. For his involvement at the siege of Louisbourg, King George II awarded him the position of Captain of the Regulars in the 51st Regiment of Foot. This regiment was under the command of Sir William Pepperrell, the officer that led the colonial troops at Louisbourg.[50] Pepperrell wrote to Governor Law on August 19, 1746, informing him that "Capt Wooster has a Commission for Capt in my Regiment" and would receive half-pay for life with this position, a tremendous honor to be bestowed upon a colonial.[51] When the regiment was engaged in active duty, Wooster received full pay as a captain of regulars. However, whenever the regiment was not called into action, he received half of his commission until he died.[52] On January 15, 1746, Governor Law wrote to Roger Wolcott that he had just received word that Captain Wooster had just returned home from England, and that the governor was eager to receive word on the particulars of his trip to Europe.[53]

Wooster had his official portrait made in London. This is the only known image of Wooster ever produced in his lifetime. In the image, he wears his Connecticut Regimental British uniform and carries an officer's spontoon, which is a large pike. He is depicted leaning on the barrel of a large cannon while the ramparts of Louisbourg loom behind him. Many other images of Wooster have subsequently been made from this original print. The original is thought to be at Yale University.[54] The title of the print refers to "David Wooster, Esqr." This is the first occasion in which Wooster is addressed with the honorary title "esquire."[55]

Upon arriving back home in Connecticut, following his transporting of

French prisoners and his subsequent meeting with King George II, Wooster began to organize his company of colonial infantry in the 51st Regiment of Foot. This included providing all the necessary armament required of a regiment in the British army. Clothing was an additional expense, as it was a necessity, and easily became threadbare, especially if the regiment was on active duty. A clothing allotment for eighty men of Captain Wooster, Starr, and Burr amounted to £ 58..0..50.. (58 pounds, 50 shillings) in July 1746.[56] Such organizational skills as clothing allotments for his men served as one of the many foundational tools of Wooster's success as a military leader.

Troops who had sailed to France and England in 1745 after the reduction of Louisbourg found the extended detainment in Rochefort had greatly prolonged their return to Connecticut. Many were without funds and were forced to petition the Connecticut General Assembly for reimbursement for their stay, since they were without pay for the duration of the expedition. Others who had taken ill at Louisbourg never returned home. Additional petitions from the families of men under Wooster's command requested assistance from

DAVID WOOSTER, Esq.ʳ
Commander in Chief of the Provincial Army *against* QUEBEC.
Published as the Act directs 26. *March* 1776, *by* Thoˢ Hart London.

Mezzotint image of David Wooster. This image was made during Wooster's 1745 visit to England following the return of the French prisoners to the port of Rochefort after the capture of Louisbourg. The inscription of the print reads: "Commander in Chief of the Provincial Army against Quebec, Published as the Act directs 26. March 1776, by Thos Hart London" (Yale University Art Gallery Collection).

the General Assembly in paying the cost of shipping the bodies of their lost family member's home.[57] Administering to these types of needs added to the leadership experiences of Captain David Wooster.

Wooster's military leadership continued. In September 1746 he, along with Captains Starr and Hall, received orders from Connecticut Governor Law to procure an ample supply of military equipment and food for their expedition, including "half a pound of powder & two pounds of bullets.... Such a Quantity of Lead as will be sufficient to make two pounds of bullets fit for each man Gunn and half a Dozen flints for each man, and … such Quantity of bread and other Provisions as you shall Judge Necessary on your March."[58] All of these items were to be kept secure until the men were underway—especially the powder and lead which was extremely valuable.

American colonial troops, including Connecticut forces, helped to occupy Louisbourg well into 1746. Meanwhile, Sir William Pepperrell sought to either be granted command of the garrison there, or to be relieved of command by replacements from England. Louisbourg had heightened Wooster's awareness of military life. In the following years he attempted to balance a civilian and military career to the best of his ability.

Historian Samuel Adams Drake has analyzed the impact of Louisbourg upon the New England republican spirit. According to Drake:

> In the trenches of Louisbourg was the training-school for the future captains of the republic. Louisbourg became a watchword and a tradition to a people intensely proud of their traditions. Not only had they made themselves felt across the ocean, but they now first awoke to a better knowledge of their own resources, their own capacities, their own place in the empire. And here began the growth of that independent spirit which, but for the prompt seizure of a golden opportunity, might have laid dormant for years.[59]

The siege of Louisbourg was a pivotal moment in the intellectual and military development of David Wooster. On the field at Louisbourg, Wooster experienced for the first time the complexities of a military campaign and, after his return from France and England in 1746, he reflected on the importance of Connecticut's role within the British Empire.

In 1748, the Treaty of Aix-la-Chapelle officially ended the War of the Austrian Succession. As part of the treaty negotiations, Louisbourg was returned to the French. Wooster, with his new familial responsibilities, sought to reapply his entrepreneurial spirit at home. From 1748 to 1754, David Wooster refocused his military leadership towards civic responsibility and the establishment of a thriving mercantile business. Throughout his life, Wooster was focused upon establishing and maintaining a successful business in Connecticut, which drove him to become a leader in New Haven, and to develop a flourishing mercantile industry. These years at home with his growing family would be short lived, however, as the drums of war sounded once again.

3

Civilian Life (1747–1753)

The colonial military success at Louisbourg in 1745 had temporarily eliminated the French threat against New England's commercial shipping and the extremely lucrative fishing industry. Although frontier conflict between colonists and the native Indians continued, the years following the surrender of Louisbourg brought relative peace and prosperity to Connecticut and to David Wooster's domestic situation. Newly commissioned as a captain in the 51st Regiment of Foot under Sir William Pepperrell, the regiment saw little military action aside from drill and marching maneuvers. Although the regiment was outfitted for the Canadian campaign against Quebec and Montreal, a continuation of the aggression in the American colonies during the War of the Austrian Succession, it was never called upon for active service.[1] Wooster's experience at Cape Breton instilled in him a desire for military leadership which was bound to a deep sense of duty. It also provided a practical application for his Yale education, religious devotion, and personal discipline. Meanwhile, domestic tranquility would broaden new and exciting economic and civic venues within his developing colonial leadership.

After transporting the French prisoners taken at Louisbourg back to France, Wooster arrived home in early January 1746. He had been married for less than a year, and his wife was expecting their first child.[2] On January 21, 1746, she gave birth to a daughter, Mary, the first of their four children. Despite the excitement of new parenthood, however, their joy was not to last long. Mary died on October 20, 1748, just twenty-one months old. This would not be the last death of a child the Woosters would have to endure.[3]

A fissure developed in 1748 between Great Britain and the New England colonies. In order to protect their economic interests, the colonies of New England had planned and financed the successful military expedition against the French stronghold of Louisbourg three years earlier. Despite receiving praise from the crown, and eventual monetary reimbursement, a critical blow came against the colonies as news of the Treaty of Aix-la-Chapelle reached New England. Great Britain claimed victory in the conflict, and France was forced to sign the treaty on October 18, 1748. One of the terms of the conclusion of the War of the Austrian Succession, however, was the return of Louisbourg to the French, in exchange for the city of Madras in India, as well as the return of the Austrian Netherlands to Habsburg rule. To the colonists who participated in the siege of Louisbourg, and most especially to those who lost family and friends in the expedition, this was seen as a tremendous betrayal of their loyalty to the British Empire. The seeds of rebellion were sown in New England in the winter of 1748–49.

Despite the loss of their daughter, and the news of Louisbourg, the Wooster's began their new life in earnest in New Haven, which, in the 1740s, was rapidly developing. New Haven had been a town slow to develop. After the Louisbourg expedition and the alleviation of the French and Spanish threats, the development of New Haven became a priority to her citizens. An examination of the 1748 "Plan of the Town of New Haven" displayed the dwellings of the inhabitants of the town, as well as their occupation. New Haven was the home to mariners, farmers, sextons (one who takes care of the local protestant churches), shoemakers, coopers, tailors, ship's carpenters, joiners, blacksmiths, innkeepers, tanners (one who cures and prepares hides for leather use), schoolmasters, lawyers, hatters, physicians, priests, clothiers, merchants, along with one miller, silversmith, barber, wheelwright, clockmaker, laborer, and saddler (one who makes and repairs saddles for horses). Aside from the twenty farmers listed on the map, New Haven's second most common profession was represented by its eleven merchants.[4] David Wooster was one of these, along with his partner and former Yale classmate, Aaron Day.

Aaron Day was born on August 11, 1715, and after graduating from Yale in 1738 with Wooster, he gained employment at the college. During the years following the New England attack upon Louisbourg, Day was authorized by the General Assembly of Connecticut to procure and store all weapons and powder that had been authorized for the expedition against Montreal and Quebec. In October 1747, Day was authorized to secure the arms issued to Colonel Samuel Talcott's troops raised for the intended expedition against Canada, as it was too far to the arms to Hartford.[5] In that month, he was authorized to do the same for Captain Elihu Hall.[6] In 1748, he was listed as a merchant in the town of New Haven and joined with Wooster in this business endeavor. He continued his colonial military service and secured approval of the storage and distribution of gunpowder by the New Haven Assembly in October 1750, upon the death of Joseph Whitney, Esq., who had previously held that responsibility.[7]

The Woosters moved into their new home on George Street overlooking the intersection of College Street. Behind the house ran the West Creek, or West River. This was broad and deep enough to allow ocean going ships to sail up to a small dock behind the Wooster's property from which mercantile goods could be easily unloaded and brought into his warehouse. In *History of the City of New Haven to the Present Time* (1887), historian Edward Atwater mentioned the use of the West Creek by Wooster. "The West Creek was used in early times for the navigation nearly up to the corner of York and George streets, and vessels of considerable size unloaded their cargo at College Street, as has been shown by the discovery of a ship's skeleton in the rear of the old Wooster House."[8] One block to the northeast of their home was the residence of Thomas Clap, president of Yale College and father of Mary Wooster. Across the street from his home was Yale College itself. The public green was the center of town, geographically, socially, economically, and educationally. It was comprised of the New Haven Meeting House, the public "gaol" (jail), a grammar school, and the first courthouse, which was erected in 1747. The public green was also the training ground for the community militia, which Wooster would lead in the years to come.

The early town of New Haven was comprised of a nine-block quadrant running parallel to West Creek, which opened to New Haven Harbor. It was ideally situated for incoming trade and commerce and afforded ample opportunity for growth in the shipping industry. On a 1748 map of New Haven can be seen a wharf which extended into the harbor and allowed ocean going vessels ease of access to the Connecticut town. With Wooster's leadership the town became a leading commercial center in Connecticut and in New England. The shipping industry was the economic corner-stone of New Haven, and, in the 1740s, it was transformed into a commercial port to rival New York and Boston. The economic prosperity of New Haven depended upon the shipping-based mercantile businesses created in the 1740s and 1750s. Wooster and Day greatly contributed to the success of the booming town.

Shipping was the lifeline of many in Connecticut in the 1700s. The entire south-ern coast was lined with important towns and a variety of inlets, points, and bays. Four major harbors, Ship Harbour, Sachem's Harbour, Stronington Harbour, and New Haven Harbour, were central hubs of import-export business, bringing goods into Connecticut from across the British Empire as well as transporting the goods of the colony overseas. Of the four harbors, New Haven was the largest in the 1700s. A ship's captain, sailing due west along the southern coast of Massachusetts and Rhode Island, could easily navigate the waters of the Long Island Sound. Upon entering the sound, any merchant vessel could sail along the 55.2° north latitude into New Haven Harbor. From New Haven imported goods could easily be transported to coastal towns as well as to the capital, Hartford, by several roads that were constructed by the 1770s. These same roads allowed for farmers to bring their crops to New Haven to be shipped to other colonies or to Europe.[9]

Connecticut also became instrumental in the ship building trade. Many of the merchant vessels involved in the Atlantic trade were either built in Connecti-cut or repaired there after extensive use. By the 1760s and 1770s, New Haven Har-bor had become an epicenter for nautical trade. An eighteenth-century wooden ship, even if kept in good working order, could expect twenty years of good service before the wear and tear of the high seas took its toll. There are several accounts of the *Defense*, the sloop that Wooster commanded in the 1740s, needing to be overhauled and repaired. The caulking lines wore thin. Oakum, which was flax or hemp fibers, coated in tar, was required to be driven into gaps in the planking to alleviate leaking. Connecticut was a major exporter of flax, the by-product of which was used in the shipping trade to make rope, which was as vital to the ship building trade as wood. By the end of the 1700s, several ropewalks could be seen on the maps of New Hav-en.[10] Ships' carpenters, joiners, and blacksmiths were all employed in New Haven to provide for the busy maritime trade of the New England colonies.

To advance the development of New Haven, the existing wharf needed to be extended. The building of the "Long Wharf" was thus the focus of Wooster and other merchants. Without the extension New Haven could not possibly compete with the great wharves of Boston and New York. In 1745, the Long Wharf only extended three hundred and thirty feet into the harbor.[11] In order to extend the wharf and allow

New Haven to become more economically competitive, funds needed to be raised to pay for the construction project. Wooster led an effort to raise the necessary funds required to extend Long Wharf through the sale of lottery tickets which would hopefully provide the required amount requested, not to exceed £ 660. The Connecticut General Assembly met in New Haven from October 10 through October 31, 1754, and approved the petition of Wooster to orchestrate the lottery.

> Resolved by this Assembly That there be a public lottery in said New Haven for the raising six hundred- and sixty-pounds lawful money, concerted and drawn in the usual and proper form of public lotteries, for the carrying on and finishing said wharf and for the charge of said lottery.[12]

Lotteries were advertised in the local paper, both for the selling of lottery tickets as well as the posting of the winning numbers once the lottery had taken place. This particular proposal was designed to create a larger wharf at Ferry Point, and therefore increase the economic productivity through trade in New Haven and allow more ships of the Atlantic trade to dock and unload cargo in the safety of New Haven Harbor. The larger the wharf, the more incentive for broader foreign markets to trade for colonial goods. Additionally, New Haven businesses, warehouses, storerooms, inns, and taverns all benefited due to the increased nautical traffic. The entrepreneurial spirit of Wooster and other merchants in New Haven made this project a reality through the sale of lottery tickets which raised the required funding for the construction of the wharf.

By the middle of the eighteenth-century New Haven had become a major economic and social epicenter along the southern coast of Connecticut. Yale College was firmly established and added to its campus with the building of "Connecticut Hall" in 1750. Construction of a new chapel on the campus began in 1761.[13] A milestone to encourage involvement in the news of the day came in 1755 with the establishment of the first newspaper printed in New Haven, *The Connecticut Gazette*.[14] The *Gazette* connected New Haven with the news of the British Empire, but more importantly, with all the major cities throughout the American colonies. The colonial press was vitally important in disseminating the news, and *The Connecticut Gazette* kept New Haven well informed of the events of the day, both foreign and domestic. Wooster made his newspaper debut in 1755. It was customary to advertise when anyone had received a letter, and a notice was placed in the June 14, 1755, edition that he had a letter "now remaining in the Post-Office at New-Haven, Capt. Wooster, New-Haven."[15]

The development and growth of New Haven was reflected in the new additions to the Wooster family. On July 30, 1751, Thomas Wooster was born. He was named in honor of his grandfather, Thomas Clap, president of Yale College. Like his father David, Thomas also attended Yale and graduated with the class of 1768. After attempts in the mercantile trade, he joined the army during the Revolution and served with his father. Thomas was their only son. The joy brought by the birth of their first son was overshadowed by the loss of their second child, a girl, also named Mary. She was born on June 2, 1753, but only lived for seven months, passing on January 16, 1754. Their last child, a girl whom they named Mary, was born on October

21, 1755. Mary and Thomas were the only children to survive infancy in the Wooster household.

New Haven's continued economic and social growth was visibly evident in the number of homes built and businesses added. Tax records from the 1700s indicated a substantial growth in the number of estates owned in New Haven. The increase in the number of ships entering the port of New Haven by 1750 also reflected this development. From the 1760s to the 1770s, trade and commerce propelled New Haven to actively compete with other ports-of-call in New England.[16] However, there was still one major hurdle for the merchants of New Haven to overcome: the lack of hard currency within the colony of Connecticut.

In 1751, the British Parliament passed a law that forbade the issuing of bills of credit in the colonies because too many merchants were paying for goods with either lines of credit that they could never pay, or with useless colonial currency which held little-to-no value in England. In 1709, Connecticut had started to print its own paper currency. As a developing economic center, New Haven felt the burden of extending lines of credit, not to English merchants, but to neighboring colonies. On May 6, 1751, thirty-one merchants of the county of New Haven wrote a petition, referred to as a memorial, to the Connecticut General Assembly in Hartford concerning the issue of bills of credit. Wooster was the second to sign the petition followed by his business partner Aaron Day. In the memorial the merchants' stated that they "think themselves in danger of being great Loosers & Sufferes by the Depreciation of this Medium of trade I fear Least the trade of this Colony be totally ruined." There are several economic points that Wooster and his companions brought to the attention of the assembly. First was the rising amount of credit offered, and accepted, by neighboring colonies, especially Rhode Island. The businessmen of New Haven feared economic enslavement to outside "governments" to which they would be financially bound. Farmers in New Haven were being forced to pay exorbitant amounts to ship their goods elsewhere, when in fact their goods could earn fair prices within the colony itself. It also appeared that Rhode Island was issuing new bills of credit which would devastate the financial stability of Connecticut and its merchants if they were accepted by the government in Hartford.[17] According to historian Charles Levermore, between 1756 and 1758, "Connecticut called in all her bills of credit, paying one-nineth of their value and repudiating all the rest."[18] This aided in the stability of Connecticut currency as well as staving off the continuous drain of hard currency which was already at extremely low levels. It also provided a glimpse into the negotiations and cooperation, or lack thereof, in dealing with inter-colonial economics. These actions of the Connecticut assembly proved the idea that each of the British colonies in North America perceived themselves as separate economic entities despite their geographic proximity to one another. This perception continued well into the early 1800s.

Much was changing in the colony of Connecticut in the 1750s. The town of New Haven exemplified Yankee ingenuity, entrepreneurship, and military discipline, and David Wooster was actively involved in it all. One major change occurred that affected all subjects of the British Empire. In 1752, the yearly calendar was altered dramatically by an act of Parliament to realign the British calendar to the one used by most European countries. Prior to the Act, the calendar year began on March 25, the date set to the Annunciation, or the incarnation, of Christ. Due to a necessary adjustment to realign the British calendar to the procession of the equinox it was decided to remove eleven days from the month of September in 1752. September 3 then became September 14, and one day was to be added to the month of February every fourth year, leap year, to realign the yearly calendar to match the rest of Western Christendom. The beginning of the new year would now be on January 1, rather than the previously noted March 25.[19] Although there are no written records from Wooster concerning the change in the yearly calendar, as a businessman this had to have caused a great deal of confusion, let alone delay, in shipping schedules, arrivals, departures, and payments of debt.

Although Connecticut's economy was developing and growing, one element of society was beginning to fracture. Since the Rev. George Whitefield's visit to New Haven on October 23, 1740, differing religious views and interpretations began to divide the town. The First Great Awakening sparked a great religious revival in the 1730s and, by the late 1740s and 1750s, the split between the Old Lights and the New Lights was seen as a very serious social and religious division. Although both groups were Puritan in nature, their beliefs and ideology started to polarize. The New Light faction in New Haven broke from the Old Lights and petitioned the General Assembly for permission to form their own separate congregation, or "society." Permission was granted, and the new congregation was formed in 1742. By 1748, the new "White Haven Society" had constructed a meeting house located on the corner of Church and Elm Street directly across from the public square and meeting house. David Wooster was one of the founding members of the White Haven Society. Taxes were levied to support the public ministers of the congregations. The formation of new congregations divided the community both spiritually and financially.

As membership within the White Haven Society fluctuated, so did the interest in additional religious factions. For example, division arose in the late 1760s over a new minister for the White Haven congregation. Some sought to obtain Jonathan Edwards, Jr.; others were adamantly opposed. Edwards, recently ordained a minister in 1769, was known for his lengthy, intellectual sermons. The son of the well-known minister of the Great Awakening, Jonathan Edwards the younger procured the position at New Haven and eventually performed the marriage ceremony for David Wooster's daughter Mary and Mr. John Ogden in 1774.

Connecticut was deeply rooted in the spirit of eighteenth-century republicanism. From the original charter of 1662 to the Glorious Revolution of 1688 that overthrew the Stuart line in England, English patriotism flourished in the colony. The founders of Connecticut drew a connection between their political situation in the New World and the foundational ideology of Magna Carta. Many American colonial newspaper articles from the 1750s through the 1770s cited Magna Carta as the anchor of their rights as Englishmen. The ideas of republicanism were visible in the structure of the various Puritan congregations and how they voted to appoint their ministers or remove them from the pulpit. Allowing the creation of new "societies" by the General Assembly, which was an elected body, demonstrated these ideas. Students attending Yale College received instruction on the ideas of John Locke, which were reinforced from the pulpit. The growth of New Haven brought an increase in foreign trade, and with that, a wider scope of news from throughout the empire, along with books and pamphlets printed overseas and in other colonies. In sum, Connecticut, along with Massachusetts, led the way in promoting a form of republicanism which transformed New England and eventually all the British colonies in North America. The idea of a growing political conspiracy within the British government to remove all liberty and freedom in the American Colonies was, in fact, more than just a theory. An analysis of pamphlets written in the 1760s and 1770s indicated an ideological change in the judiciary, the legislature, and the monarchy itself. Historian Bernard Bailyn, in his work *The Ideological Origins of the American Revolution*, analyzed numerous political pamphlets written in the American colonies which referenced key enlightened thinkers such as Locke, Gordon, and Trenchard, the influence of their republican ideology upon colonial politics, and validated the proposed conspiracy that was afoot in the American colonies in the eighteenth century.[20]

No one was as influential in the development and understanding of political philosophy as John Locke. Born in England in 1632, just twenty-five years after the founding of Jamestown, Virginia, Locke solidified political theory and advanced the ideas of the old world into the new. Nowhere did John Locke's influence on political philosophy, the state of nature, and the role of the monarch, the right of revolution, and the emergence of representative government take hold and flourish as well as in the British colonies in North America.

John Locke's most influential work, the *Second Treatise of Government*, written in 1689, revolutionized political philosophy. It became the pillar of political thought and republicanism in the 1700s. This monumental work influenced the writings of French Enlightenment thinkers such as Voltaire, Jean Jacques Rousseau, David Hume, and Immanuel Kant, as well as notable American thinkers George Mason, Thomas Jefferson, John Adams, and Thomas Paine. The foundations of American political thought can be traced to the theories and writings of John Locke. This ideology became useful in the establishment and perpetuation of a brotherhood that had taken root in Europe and which would quickly spread to the North American colonies—Freemasonry.

In 1696, five years after the writing of the *Second Treatise of Government*, Locke wrote a letter that was later published in *The Gentleman's Magazine* in London. Locke analyzes an "ancient" text on Freemasonry for the benefit of the Earl of Pembroke, who himself was intrigued by the organization, yet requested the advice of Locke. In the letter Locke commented that "I know not what effect the sight of this old paper may have upon your LORDSHIP; but for my own part I cannot deny, that it has so much raised my curiosity; as to induce me to enter myself into the fraternity; which I am determined to do (if I may be admitted) the next time I go to LONDON (and that will be shortly)."[21]

By the early 1700s social clubs were becoming popular in London, and the structure of medieval guild organizations laid the foundation for the masonic movement. This new fraternal organization centered around the study of history, mathematics, philosophy, and science, rather than a specific trade or occupation. The first Grand Lodge of Freemasons was established in London in 1717. With increased travel abroad, the fraternity rapidly spread to other countries. By 1750 Freemasonry was established with lodges in seventeen foreign countries and eight American locations, including Philadelphia (1730), Boston (1730), Savannah (1733 and 1734), New York (1738 and 1739), Virginia (1741), Maryland (1749), and New Haven, Connecticut (1750).[22]

Freemasonry in the British American colonies took on a new approach to membership by the 1750s and began to include artisans as well as those in the upper echelon of urban colonial society. The masons had long been established in Boston but had little growth in the early 1700s. After Wooster's return from England, however, the fraternal organization rapidly spread throughout New England. According to historian Steven C. Bullock, the masonic movement in Colonial America was perpetuated by the excitement of its seriousness and academic interests, despite being shrouded in secrecy. The mystique of Freemasonry also attracted much criticism and anti-masonic attacks through the various colonial newspapers of the day. Yet the movement served as a vehicle to transform colonial society "from a hierarchical society of superiors and inferiors to a republican society of independent citizens."[23]

Not only did Wooster develop as a leader through his military experience, his mercantile business endeavors, and his prominence within the growing religious fervor in Connecticut, he also established an organizational branch of Freemasonry in New Haven that bound the changing political atmosphere in the colonies to the ideology of Locke. Freemasonry, the European fraternal organization, encompassed the philosophical, political, and educational awakening taking shape in the colonies at that time. Connecting both the Lockean ideas of eighteenth-century republicanism with Freemasonry solidified this new organization's standing among the urban elites in the American colonies.

It is believed that Wooster became a Freemason in England during his visit in 1745–46.[24] To charter a new Freemason lodge in Connecticut, Wooster was required to seek permission from the oldest lodge in New England, the St. John's Lodge in Boston. Thomas Oxnard, Provincial Grand Master of the St. John's Lodge in Boston, granted the charter, which is referred to as the "Oxnard Charter."[25] The name "Hiram" granted to the lodge in New Haven took its origin from the foundation of Freemasonry itself. According to ancient legend, Hiram Abiff was the master workman in the construction of King Solomon's temple. He guarded a "secret word" which provided key information concerning those involved with the construction, but was also thought to have a deeper, secret meaning. Abiff was accosted by workers at the temple construction and murdered when he refused to reveal the secret word. This legend became one of the foundational elements to the secret fraternity, along with its emphasis upon the knowledge of the ancient world in mathematics, history, and philosophy, all of which the masons believed had been lost to modernity.[26] After the founding of Hiram Lodge, Freemasonry spread throughout the colony of Connecticut.[27] Wooster received the first charter for Hiram Lodge No. 1 on November 12 and the members held their first meeting on December 27, 1750. The original minute book from the Hiram Lodge recorded twelve members of the lodge in attendance, including Wooster. Each member paid thirty shillings for dues for the years. Brother

Jehiel Tuttle's hosted the first meeting at his home in New Haven on Saint John the
Evangelist Day.[28]

The ideals of Freemasonry were thus connected to eighteenth-century republicanism, and as tensions arose between the American colonies and England, Freemasonry provided an avenue to support and develop the republican principles of
self-government, representation, and independence. Although politics and religion
were topics forbidden in discussion at Freemason meetings, those who became leaders in the revolutionary movement were also leaders in their respective masonic
lodges. As the 1770s approached, membership changed to include the non-elite of
the colonies and to create a broader base for the fraternal organization.

By 1753, Wooster began to reap the rewards of a successful career. Now forty-three years old, his leadership in the siege of Louisbourg had propelled him onto
the colonial stage. Meanwhile, his mercantile enterprise that he had started with
his Yale College partner was an established and prosperous business. The development of the Long Wharf in New Haven brought more overall trade and commerce
into the town that would only continue to increase. The religious fervor of the Great
Awakening elevated Wooster to leadership within the White Haven Society, the
newly established religious society in his hometown, and among the many accolades and emoluments which he brought from his trip to England five years earlier was his enrollment into the fraternal society of the Freemasons. These successes
combined to encapsulate Wooster within a leadership niche in Connecticut from
which he would grow in political savvy and in intellectual prowess. Meanwhile, as
France increased their aspiration of empire in North America, his focus was redirected towards military preparation in the colonies as the drums of war sounded
again, and the age-old nemesis, France, once more became the target of British military aggression.

4

The French and Indian War
(1753–1764)

In 1754, a young and inexperienced Colonel George Washington led a detachment of Virginia militia and Native American allies into the backwoods of Pennsylvania. His assignment was to verify an account of a French fort being built at the forks of the Ohio River, where the Ohio, Allegheny and Monongahela Rivers all converge. The result of this expedition was the assassination of a French official, Joseph Coulon de Villiers de Joumonville, and the start of a world war. American history often presents a rather Virginia-centric view of the first years of the French and Indian War, and this perspective is certainly widespread as taught in classrooms and reprinted in textbooks. Although the actions of Washington and the assassination ignited the powder keg of the British and French conflict in western Pennsylvania in 1754, military buildup, training, and preparation had been underway in New England since the conclusion of the War of the Austrian Succession. David Wooster took a preeminent role in Connecticut for this preparation, both as a civic leader and a military commander, even though the role that New England, and Connecticut in particular, played in this world conflict has been long overshadowed and largely forgotten.

Connecticut played a crucial role in the execution and outcome of this world conflict in North America. Up to now, Wooster's involvement in the war, both on the home front and on campaign, has been ignored. In the context of his life this era certainly presented a large void in the historical scholarship, with only the slightest bit of information available to pinpoint his location and activity from 1755 to the conclusion of the war in 1763. His active role, and that of numerous others in Connecticut, received little attention because of the tumultuous years that followed. This argument is well articulated by historian Frank D. Andrews who noted that the military actions of Connecticut soldiers in the French and Indian War were destined to be overshadowed due to the upheaval within the British North American Colonies from 1763 to 1775. Despite the lack of attention, however, "during the campaign of 1755 and following years, the raw undisciplined farmers who responded to the call to arms became, through their military training, efficient soldiers."[1] These colonial troops would soon test their military experience against the King's own regulars.

Military readiness was a necessity in eighteenth-century Connecticut, and Wooster was raised in a military household. Having family members in the militia was a necessity of life, not simply a career choice. By the outbreak of the war in

1755, Wooster was in the prime of his life. At forty-five years old he had developed a solid character centered around a thriving mercantile business as well as his captaincy of a company of the 51st Regiment of Foot. The military experience he gained during the war propelled him into new leadership roles which continued to develop throughout the rest of his life.

The call to arms in Connecticut came in 1755 as war was officially declared. This new war-for-empire became the first truly world war, with battles in North America, the Caribbean Islands, the west coast of Africa, India, and in Europe. To Great Britain, the colonies in North America served as pawns in this global chess game. Yet Englishmen in the American Colonies viewed it quite differently. The Connecticut General Assembly, which met twice each year, once in March and again in October, quickly called for volunteers to serve in a campaign against the French in Canada. New England was concerned about a potential reprisal of French attacks against New England shipping and its important fishing industry off the Grand Banks.[2] These early enlistments served for six months in the first year of the war and fought under the command of Wooster's Yale classmate, Phineas Lyman, who became the commander-in-chief of Connecticut troops for the duration of the war.[3]

Eighteenth-century American provincial units were seasonal fighting forces. Made up primarily of farmers, who constituted much of the population, the recruitment and deployment of colonial regiments revolved around the growing seasons. When called into military service, men enlisted in the late spring after crops were planted. Colonial military service in the French and Indian in North America reflected this practicality. Troops raised in Connecticut in 1755 served from early April through early November. Despite their possible military experience at Louisbourg ten years prior, these were not professional soldiers. Although similar to the regular army, the provincial units lacked discipline, endurance, supplies, and the financial resources required by a long-term campaign. The military operations near Lake George in 1755 would test the resolve of many a Connecticut Yankee. During the siege of Louisbourg, small short-term volunteer units saw limited action in the field combined with an introduction to military discipline, albeit under local officers, many of whom were friends or neighbors. In the current conflict these colonial units saw more intense action, along with the hardships and difficulties of the march, tedium of camp life, and harsh discipline under British officers.

For soldiers in the Connecticut regiments, the 1755 campaign centered on Lake George, north of Albany in New York. General Lyman ordered a fort to be constructed south of Lake George, originally called Fort Lyman in his honor. To sustain an army in the field, a well-defended supply route was necessary. This meant that a chain of forts would need to be built that could house soldiers and defend against a possible enemy advance and that could also serve as staging areas for military attacks against the French. The Connecticut officers who had served during the siege of Louisbourg, and those who had studied French military manuals, which were as readily available in the colonies as the British versions, constructed these new forts in the new French star-shape pattern. Lyman's Fort, located on the western bend of the Hudson River directly north of Albany, was the first to be constructed by the Connecticut troops under British supervision. Following the Battle of Lake

George in 1755, Lyman's Fort was renamed Fort Edward.[4] The campaign north was totally under English authority, and the British commanders saw to it that the chain of forts were constructed in a timely manner and would defend the frontier from any possible French attack. Fort William Henry, built on the southern shore of Lake George, however, would challenge this assumption. Although not in the field in 1755, Wooster was extremely familiar with Fort Edward, Fort William Henry, and Fort Carillon, far to the north near Lake Champlain and Crown Point.

The Battle of Lake George was the fiercest that regiments from Connecticut had yet engaged in. All colonial troops were placed under the command of General William Johnson, who was wounded during the battle. Johnson's account of the battle was printed in newspapers throughout the colonies. One such account appeared in the October 9 edition of the *Maryland Gazette*.[5] The lengthy report provided a detailed account of the military action in which the British and colonial forces were victorious over the French at Lake George. After General Johnson was wounded General Lyman took command in the field and secured the victory, although he received no accolades from the commanding general for his success. With such a large military expedition underway, any news from the front was sought after, be it an official report by the officer in charge or letters from soldiers to family and friends at home. A detailed after-action report on the battle at Lake George was written by Samuel Blodget, who noted that he was "Occasionally at the Camp, when the Battle was fought." Blodget included a point-by-point map that coincided with his report of the battle. The map and printed account provided the reader with a visual image of the terrain and the order of events by which the battle was fought. For the eighteenth century, this was the best way to provide details from the front for those at home. The map also provided the location of General Johnson's headquarters, General Lyman's headquarters and regiment, as well as the six colonels' regiments. General Lyman's regiment was positioned closest to the front and bore the brunt of the day's action.[6]

Connecticut's General Assembly appointed civilians to supply the soldiers with food, especially flour and bread. Without these food items it would have been impossible to maintain an army in the field. In October 1755, weeks after the success at Lake George, the assembly directed Wooster's business partner and Yale classmate, Aaron Day, to collaborate with General Lyman on "the best and most speedy measures to be used for the supply of our troops with bread and flour."[7] These items were requisitioned and delivered to the troops stationed at Lake George. Day was also provided "warrants to impress (if need be) such numbers as shall be wanted, not exceeding one hundred men and five hundred horses, with proper furniture, provender and sacks, to proceed forthwith on said business."[8] Manpower, food, and materials of war were gathered and sent north by civilians, most at their own expense. The economic impact of this first world war weighed heavily upon the colony of Connecticut.

Not only was obtaining material items a necessity for a military campaign, but the training of officers and enlisted men alike was imperative. The 1750s and 1760s saw an influx of available military drill manuals. The printed French army manuals outnumbered the British, but overall, a variety of training books found their way into colonial Connecticut before the war started. One of the most popular was Sir Humphrey Bland's *A Treatise of Military Discipline*, first printed in 1727.[9] Bland was one of several British generals who attempted to create uniformity and consistency within the various military units, based upon actual field experience, not just military theory. At over four-hundred pages, including several fold-out sections that provided detailed diagrams for military maneuvers, Bland's manual could be found in all the British colonies in North American. These manuals not only taught the rudiments of handling a musket, loading, firing, and marching maneuvers, they also instructed the best way to erect and fortify an encampment, the posting of guards, and establishing discipline within the camp. Several military manuals even began to emphasize the importance of camp hygiene to prevent the outbreak of disease among the soldiers. As a colonel during the French and Indian War, Wooster sharpened his military knowledge of the regimentation of the British Army by studying such military books. Field manuals were required reading for officers of the army.[10] Sandra Powers, Library Director Emerita of the Society of the Cincinnati in Washington, D.C., has cataloged the eighteenth-century military manuals in their collection. There are at least forty-four different manuals dating from the time of the French and Indian War which are owned by the Society of the Cincinnati. Many books and pamphlets were sent from England, and by the 1750s several editions were being re-printed in colonial cities such as Boston and New York.[11] A compilation of military manuals owned by George Washington exemplifies the colonial interest in modern tactics and historical commentary on military matters. Not only did eighteenth-century officers carry drill manuals, they also read Polybius and Caesar and analyzed military tactics of antiquity to learn from both their successes and failures. Virginia Steele Wood, at the Library of Congress, has documented the manuals owned by Washington throughout his military career. The list of fifty manuals included many used by New Englanders during the French and Indian War, as well as several sources written in French.[12]

As the campaign season of 1755 came to a successful conclusion, it was evident that the conflict was far from over. The Connecticut General Assembly and Governor Thomas Fitch, governor of Connecticut from 1754 to 1766, directed the raising of more troops for the 1756 campaign. At the March session of the assembly, Wooster was among the new field officers and was appointed colonel of the second regiment and captain of the first company of that regiment. Major General William Johnson was replaced by John Winslow due to Johnson's wounds the previous year at Lake George, and General Phineas Lyman remained at his post. By March 1756, Wooster was more than prepared to lead Connecticut troops in the field. He took command of the 2nd Connecticut Regiment and left New Haven for Albany. Crown Point was their destination.[13]

The prospect of a second year of campaigning meant a continued financial burden to Connecticut. The colony was required to provide the necessary provisions for their own troops. Above and beyond the obvious sundry items such as clothing, firearms, powder, shot, and accoutrements, soldiers also required adequate tentage. Learning from the experience at Louisbourg, the troops under Wooster's command would not be left to find refuge from the elements among the gullies, ravines, and scrub brush as they had in 1745. However, providing adequate tentage also included supplies of wooden poles, tent stakes, or nails, as they referred to them, as well as twine and rope. Not all recruits took to military service with the same zeal as Wooster, in fact some deserted the ranks. Wooster ran an advertisement in the *Connecticut Gazette* for three consecutive weeks starting on May 29, 1756, which stated:

> Deserted from Col. David Wooster's Regiment and Company John Broadstreet, an Irishman about five Feet nine Inches high, wears his own Hair, of a pale Complextion, something Pocketbroken, called himself a Barber; and likewise an Indian Fellow names Isaac James, of a short Stature, and well sett, said he was born at Dartmouth: Whoever will apprehend and confine them in any of the common Gaols in this Government, and make Report thereof to any of the Commissaries in this Colony shall be well rewarded for their Trouble.
> Norwalk, May 20, 1756.
>
> David Wooster, Colonel[14]

While in camp soldiers were required to cook their rations, making kettles and various pots necessary items. Military food rations were needed to provide adequate nutrition to the men, while also lasting as long as possible before rotting or spoiling. Items such as flour, bread, vinegar, sugar, raisins, dried apples, ginger, bushels of beans, cheese, pork, cornmeal, and oats were provided to Wooster and his men, all from Connecticut. In addition, no military campaign could be successful without the rations of rum, and Wooster's men were supplied with that as well.[15]

Marching north from Albany, Wooster's regiment bivouacked near Fort Edward, which was located southeast of Fort William Henry along the Hudson River. Maps of the area indicated trails that connected Fort Edward and Fort William Henry, as well as northeast routes to Fort Ticonderoga. Cartography was an art in the 1750s. Map-making required great skill and attention to detail. At Yale, one of the required courses of study was mathematics and the skills of navigation. These included the same skills necessary for surveying. Wooster had practical experience in all of these. Since printing was a great expense, and printed bound books were considered the most expensive of personal property, printed maps were equally expensive. Since the printing plates on any given press were limited in size, often large maps required numerous engraved plates to print an entire map. For example, the 1755 Mitchell map was printed on eight separate sheets of paper, and Henry Popple's map, finished in 1733, was made up of twenty printed sheets. If the maps were printed for field use, and not simply to ornament a wall, the sheets were glued to a large piece of material, usually a coarse muslin, with a slight gap in between the sheets to allow for the map to be folded and carried. Maps of more localized regions were also drawn and engraved. Valuable tools during military campaigns, they provided those at home with an image of terrain that often coincided with tales of battle.

Following the Battle at Lake George in 1755, Samuel Blodget wrote a step-by-step account of the first and second engagement. The written account provided numbers of events and specifically numbered locations of troops and officers that coincided with an engraved map of the camp with the corresponding numbers. Similarly, Thomas Johnston created an engraved map of the Battle of Lake George which was printed in 1756 and provided detailed locations and designs of Fort William Henry and Fort Edward. Both depictions of the battle included a side map which detailed the routes that New England troops took to Albany, as well as the newly constructed forts towards Lake Champlain.[16]

Now entering its third year, the campaign season of 1757 proved to be the most economically taxing and militarily challenging of the war. Connecticut continued to provide for another season, not only sending troops but supplies as well. The military goals of 1757 continued to focus upon the capture of Crown Point and to drive the encroaching French back into Canada. The advance of the French into northern territory claimed by Great Britain, specifically New York and western Pennsylvania continued to alarm Americans along the frontier and especially in New England. The British goal of capturing Fort Duquesne had not been met, and the death of British General Edward Braddock on July 13, 1755, added to the military frustration.

In May, Wooster was elected to represent New Haven in the Connecticut General Assembly.[17] Maintaining his rank of colonel, Wooster remained in New Haven during the 1757 campaign season to pursue a different military route. The general assembly, in their March session, ordered one regiment of fourteen companies, totaling 1,400 men, to be raised. These troops were to march to Fort Edward. As a newly elected official and with his past naval experience, Wooster, along with two other officers, were directed by the legislature to form a committee to outfit a vessel of war.[18] The purpose being to protect the valuable shipping lanes along the coast of Connecticut. With their experience of French naval incursion which had led to the military expedition against Louisbourg, the New England colonies sought to do all that they could to ensure the safety of their most valuable commodity—the shipping trade. The Connecticut Assembly allotted one thousand pounds for the vessel which would be equipped for war and made ready with all haste.[19]

Word reached Connecticut in September of the horrific massacre of British troops and civilians who were returning to Albany after the surrender of Fort William Henry, which had taken place weeks earlier. The story of the slaughter spread throughout the colonies. Newspapers printed and reprinted stories which fanned the flame of outrage against the French and their Indian allies. Connecticut soldiers stationed at Fort Edward wrote home that they could hear the siege guns at Fort William Henry, and eagerly awaited marching orders for them to turn out and come to the relief of their comrades at William Henry, but no such orders ever came. The lack of military response to aid those at Fort William Henry, some of whom were from Connecticut, sparked early disgruntled discussion of military competency among colonial volunteers regarding their British officers. Despite the loss of Fort William Henry, the general assembly, in October, called for additional troops to be raised and sent north to Fort Edward for the duration of the winter.[20] There was a renewed fear of Indian attacks along the frontier, and Connecticut, being well acquainted with Indian aggression, reenforced the outposts with needed soldiers.

In mid–December, news reached New Haven that British troops stationed in New England would likely need quartering over the winter months. Wooster was chosen as one of five men to head a committee to "provide Suitable houses to Quarter Such Soldiers and Consider the Extraordinary Charge Such houses will be at for Entertaining Such Soldiers and report the Same to the Town which Extraordinary Charge this Town will pay."[21] This was a cost that New Haven would be forced to endure in the short term, and that would, hopefully, be paid by the general treasury after the war was concluded. The issue of quartering troops was more an economic burden for whomever played the role of host. There is no record of the actual cost incurred for quartering His Majesty's troops, nor any account of reimbursement.

Drastic military, political, and economic changes were underway for the British army following the surrender of Fort William Henry and the massacre of its garrison. All of which impacted the colonies. First, General James Abercrombie was appointed military commander in the campaign against the French at Lake George. General Abercrombie lead New England troops to take Fort Carillon, renamed Fort Ticonderoga by the British. On the political front, England had a new prime minister, William Pitt. Pitt directed a new strategy in the global war effort and saw that those in the colonies who had funded that effort on their own accord would be reimbursed, although no specific timetable was ever established for payment.

In this new approach, Wooster was commissioned in March as colonel of the 4th Regiment, and captain for the first company within that regiment. As economic pressure to fund the war continued, new financial burdens arose. It became evident to the Connecticut officers that their commissions provided substantially less pay for their service than other officers of equal rank in adjacent colonies. To alleviate this discrepancy, twenty-two officers signed a memorial petition sent to the Connecticut General Assembly in May 1758, requesting an increase in their pay as officers in the service of the colony of Connecticut. Colonel Wooster's signature was next to General Lyman's. The pay for officers was determined by each colony. Wooster, and the other officers, noted that New York, Massachusetts, and other New England governments paid their officers more than Connecticut. Despite the petitioner's request, the secretary placed a notation upon the letter stating that the issue was "Resolved in the Negative." Connecticut officers remained the lowest paid during the French and Indian War.[22]

Wooster and his men were stationed at Fort Edward during the summer of 1758. An examination of the few records that remain shed light on the voluminous daily paperwork required to be completed of officers in the British army. Many items required documentation: the loss of arms or equipment; hospital accounts listing men wounded or too ill for active service; bills for blankets; bills for medical treatment; and sundry items, mostly clothing, shirts, stockings, etc., delivered to the men in the field, and all of these required some type of official documentation. Several of these items listed are available and provide a glimpse of additional responsibilities placed upon officers, as Colonel Wooster's returns indicated.

General Abercrombie ordered the army north on July 5, 1758, to take the French at Fort Carillon, which had been abandoned. The British army of 15,000 men marched from Fort Edward to Lake George and then proceeded down the lake, north, in a massive flotilla. Over three hundred whaleboats and one-thousand bateaux were employed in moving the army through Lake George in an organized fashion, which took up the width of the lake. Wooster's regiments were in bateaux on the right flank along with Colonels Babcock, Fitch, and Johnson. Others were on the left and the center. The armada resembled "two floating castles on the lake." The flotilla reached its destination, disembarked, and, in high spirits, made ready for the march to Fort Carillon.[23]

The French commander, General Louis-Joseph de Montcalm, was greatly out-numbered, but Abercrombie's plan of attacking the French position was greatly flawed. On July 8, 1758, wave after wave of men advanced against the strong French position. During the actual engagement, Wooster's regiment was part of the rear guard comprised of Connecticut and New Jersey troops.[24] Abercrombie ordered a retreat following the battle which further added to the sting of defeat.

Wooster lost two men killed in the attack on Fort Carillon in July 1758, and an additional soldier was wounded when his gun exploded. While engaged at Fort Carillon, a soldier under Wooster's command was wounded and sent home on July 27. Soldiers wounded in battle were often deprived of their pay for the time that they were not in the field, or in active service. Joseph Hoit, the wounded soldier in Colonel Wooster's regiment, remained at home and was tended to by his father until November the same year. Payment for military service came from individual colonial treasuries, and Hoit had to petition the Connecticut Assembly for payment lost while recuperating. He was provided eight pounds from the Connecticut treasury for the loss of his income.[25]

Despite the changes in strategy, 1758 did not end in total military failure. Fort Duquesne, built at the confluence of the Ohio, Allegheny, and Monongahela Rivers in western Pennsylvania was captured by the troops under British General Forbes. By the close of 1758, the war began to turn in favor of the British.

As the war moved into its fifth year, Colonel Wooster commanded the 3rd Connecticut Regiment, and, just as in years prior, was also captain of the first company of that regiment. The war was weighing heavily upon the men under arms as well as the civilians in New Haven. The nature of war in the eighteenth century did not preclude daily life: farms continued to require the attention of the farmer, shipments of goods required the merchant to unload and sell, laws continued to be passed, classrooms required instructors, and the pulpits demanded preachers. Despite a war to the north, nothing stopped at home. Life continued.

War can develop a deeper spiritual awakening and, coupled with the religious fervor of the Great Awakening, religious devotion appeared to grow in New Haven. A petition was submitted at the October general assembly's meeting to request permission to divide the current ecclesiastical society in New Haven into two. For several months the congregation had been meeting in two different places, one location not being large enough to house everyone. The general assembly approved the division, and Wooster joined the new society. This act of the legislature officially established the White Haven Society. Members of the new ecclesiastical society chose the Rev. Mr. Samuel Bird as their minister. It is interesting to note that Wooster's business partner and Yale College classmate, Aaron Day, remained with the older society.[26] This division is the last recorded note of any collaboration between Wooster and Day.

Prior to leaving New Haven in 1759 and heading for the front with his men, Wooster called upon the Rev. Mr. Samuel Bird to give a blessing to his troops. Wooster's Puritan devotion was the core of his strong character and disciplined leadership. Bird spoke to Wooster and his men on Wednesday, April 27, 1759. The sermon encompassed all the ideals that Wooster had grown up with, the very notions that encapsulated the religious fervor of the Great Awakening, political ideology, and the rhetoric of eighteenth-century republicanism, as well as service and duty, both to God and to country.

The sermon was divided into several sections. First, Bird provided an overview and Biblical reference to the very nature and necessity of war. "War is in its self very undesirable; but nevertheless, it is some Times an indispensable Duty, of absolute Necessity, and of great Importance to undertake it. A just War is rather to be chosen, than an unjust Peace."[27] The focus of aggression was placed upon France, and Bird justified the actions of the British colonies as both a religious Puritanical endeavor against the French Catholics, as well as a defense of the dominion of New England against "Ambitious France, who to increase her Dominion and extend her arbitrary Sway, has had nothing less in View, than to root us out of the Inheritance which God gave to our Fathers, and had hitherto continued to us."[28] The fiery pulpit convinced those in attendance that "nothing remains to us, but to dispute at the Point of the Sword, at the Mouth of thundering Cannon, Fire Arms, and other Instruments of Slaughter, the Claim and Possession of North America, and all that is dear to us, of a civil and sacred Nature."[29]

Bird provided an excellent example of the skill in which Puritan ministers intertwined republicanism with religion in their sermons. To the soldiers, as well as the civilians who were to remain in New Haven, he stated that he was concerned that there were those "who have no just Sense of the Liberties and Privileges of their Country, no great Concern for its Wellfare, nor are desirous to do its Business; who instead of serving their Country, mean nothing but to serve themselves."[30] As the first portion of the sermon came to a close, the spirt of the Great Awakening arose from the pulpit. To Bird nothing good could be accomplished without the repentance of sin by all those in the community:

> the putting away the Evil of our Doings, by a sincere Repentance, and returning to him; is the only likely Way to engage his Preference with our Armies. A thorough Reformation in Persons of every Rank, would do more towards recovering our invaded Rights, the securing of our Possessions, the expelling our Enemies, the bringing on an honourable Peace, and the Lengthening out of our Tranquility; than all our military Strength, warlike Preparations, formidable Fleets, and numerous Armies.[31]

The second portion of the sermon was directed to Colonel Wooster who was sitting in the assembly. He had become a prominent member of New Haven society, and great responsibility rested upon him. The sermon continued:

> Honour'd and worthy Sir,
>
> I presume not to instruct you in the Art of War, in which you have considerable Experience; but, permit me to assume the Preacher, and address you out of sincere Regard to the Honour of God, your Honour, and the Honour of our Country; all which, I humbly hope, lie, with some just Weight, upon your Mind, and are wisely connected and properly balanced; and were the prevailing Motives of your Entering into the Country's Service. I presume it is needless to tell you, that your Trust is great, and that the Eyes of Multitudes will be upon you, to observe you in the Character of a Man, a Leading Officer, and a Christian. Permit me to tell you, that to you, with others, as Instruments, doth the Country look, and on you, under God, depend, as Guardians to defend, and, if possible, to secure the natural, civil, and religious Life, the Liberties and Properties of a free-born People.[32]

The invocation of God, and the utmost duty to fight for "KING GEORGE, the best of Kings, against proud LEWIS" inspired many of those listening attentively to the preacher's words. The age-old animosity between the French Catholics in Canada and the Puritans in New England once more reared its ugly head. Several times throughout the sermon Bird challenged those who were to go on the expedition to destroy the "Popish Enemies" and to "secure to us our religious Privileges, which are dearer to us than our Lives."[33]

The sermon was then directed to the officers who were to serve under Wooster. To them Bird stated "I wish you Health, Protection, and every needed Blessing; that you, with others, through the Aids of divine Providence may give the decisive Blow to our Enemies, finish the Dispute in North-America, return victorious, and be crowned with deserved Laurels of Honour."[34] The sermon concluded by addressing the soldiers preparing to march off to war, and to the civilians who remained behind. The craft of sermonizing was well-polished in the final section, and the reader envisions a Whitefield/Edwards style approach as Bird declared that

> our Sins persisted in and unrepented of, may bring a Blast upon our Arms, and a Curse upon our dear Countrymen, who for our Lives and Safety expose their own. Let us not only abstain from Acts of Sin, but labour to mortify the inward Love of Sin; and betake ourselves to the Practice of every Duty. Let us awake to Righteousness, and not against GOD. Let Tavern-Haunter abandon their Cups. Let Liars learn to the Neighbours. Let the foul-mouth'd Swearer no longer defile the Air with his contagious Breath, and disgrace his glorious Maker. Let carnal Frolickers down with the Riots; surely this is no Time to be merry and vain, when our Country is bleeding in almost every Vein.[35]

This twenty-four-page sermon embodied all the elements of eighteenth-century life in colonial Connecticut. As the French and Indian War continued into its fourth year, with no clear end in sight, the burdens of military conflict and economic depression began to take its toll on the home front. If historical foreshadowing could be noted, Bird's sermon of 1759 was the alarm bell in the night.

> One of these we have to choose; either to gird on the Sword, rush into Battle, jeopard our Lives in the high Places of the Field, and conquer, or die like Men; or be enslaved with a happy Country, to the lawless Ambition and arbitrary Rule of the proudest of Princes: The former of which is infinitely rather to be chosen, by every considerable noble Mind, capable of relishing the Sweets of Liberty and Property, *Englishmen's* Darlings: Surely an honourable Death, in the Defense of our Country, is much rather to be chosen, than a Life of most wretched Slavery.[36]

Although the sermon delivered to Wooster and his men focused on the threat from France, the republican sentiments would soon be used against, not the King of France, but rather the King of England. By the mid–1700s the ideology of John Locke had become deeply rooted in the Connecticut experience, and the *Englishmen's* Darlings," Liberty and Property, would never be relinquished voluntarily.

During the 1759 campaign, Colonel Wooster and the 3rd Connecticut Regiment were under the command of British General Jeffery Amherst. The 3rd Regiment spent the campaign season in New York at Fort Edward, Lake George, Fort Ticonderoga, and Crown Point.[37] Fort Carillon commanded the approach to Lake Champlain from the south. It would be impossible to take Crown Point without first reducing and capturing Fort Carillon. Water routes were essential for supplying troops and the numerous fortifications erected to defend the northern frontier. Whoever controlled Lake George and Lake Champlain would control upper New York and the approach to Canada. The French Fort Carillon sat on a tall bluff and commanded the lake below. General Abercrombie had underestimated the French troops stationed there, resulting in the British and colonial troops' unsuccessful attack against Fort Ticonderoga in 1758. They were eager for a second attempt in 1759.

Under General Jeffery Amherst the British and colonial forces placed cannon on ground that commanded Fort Carillon, and after two days of fighting, July 26–27, the fort was taken. The French commander surrendered the fort and attempted to blow it up by igniting the powder magazine. Despite some structural damage to the fort the British troops were able to quickly make necessary repairs. The fort was then officially renamed Fort Ticonderoga.

Soldiers on guard duty at Fort Ticonderoga often came under fire. Although positioning men on the periphery of camp to keep watch against the advance of the French and Indians ensured the safety and security of the soldiers within the fort, guard duty could be tiring and monotonous. Fear of being caught asleep while on guard duty, and the subsequent court martial and punishment which ensued, was often motivation enough to remain alert while on guard. There were accounts of British and colonial soldiers engaging fire with the enemy while on post. One of Wooster's men, Abraham Dan, was wounded while on guard duty. Like Joseph Hoit, who had been wounded at Fort Carillon, Dan petitioned the Connecticut Assembly for compensation for his injury. He stated that "he was so unfortunate as to receive a shot in his right arm from an enemy Indian lurking in the bushes adjacent to his post, by means of which shot the bones of his said arm were very much broken and shattered to pieces, and since have been taken out, and his arm is rendered thereby so useless that he cannot so much as lift it to any service or office for which it was made." The Assembly granted him fifty pounds in compensation.[38]

With Fort Ticonderoga in British hands, the army set to the task of making the necessary repairs to strengthen the fort against any impending French advance. Wooster and his men remained at Fort Ticonderoga throughout the fall. With the British and colonial army encamped on the northern point of Lake George the greatest test of military skill and leadership was about to fall upon Wooster. Leading an army on the march or in the heat of battle was one task. Maintaining order, discipline, and morale while in a sedentary camp far from home was quite another.

While stationed at Fort Ticonderoga, Wooster often served as the "officer of the day." As such, one of his responsibilities was to write out field orders for the commanders of the various regiments. Colonel Wooster's sixty-nine-page *Orderly Book* provided a detailed account of the military activities in the fall of 1759, especially for the army in camp at Fort Ticonderoga. Wooster continued to develop his military skill and knowledge through his experiences at Ticonderoga. While stationed there, he served with Colonel Phillip Schuyler. Schuyler was from New York and was twenty-two years Wooster's junior. Although both men served together under Amherst, there is no record of them interacting during the 1759 campaign. Their interaction would have unprecedented results in 1775–76, and ironically in the same theater of war. Colonel Wooster's regiment was stationed at Fort Ticonderoga from July 23, 1759, through October 8, 1759, a total of seventy-eight days of continual military leadership which solidified his foundational military instruction and provide him invaluable experience that he would call upon in 1775.

The campaign of 1759 was critically important for Wooster's future military career. In the early years of the war, British and provincial forces were dealt one defeat after another. The early British campaigns produced nothing noteworthy in land gained or victories won. However, the fall of Fort Duquesne in 1758 marked a pivotal change in war strategy and planning. By the campaign of 1759, the tide of war had changed in North America. Wooster gained practical leadership knowledge from some of the greatest British generals in North America. He also learned from the mistakes of men such as Abercrombie. Serving under Amherst allowed for the colonial officer to apply his newly gained military knowledge in a successful campaign. He not only learned the intricacies of managing a battalion of infantry, but he also perfected his leadership style and skills that would serve him well in the years to come. Issuing food rations in a timely manner, structuring a soldier's daily routine while not engaged in battle, the timely paying of soldiers, providing them goods to purchase from camp sutlers, and oversight of camp hygiene were all critically important skills required to successfully run the army. Wooster mastered all of these.

Field maneuvers, marching the army, or your regiment, from one encampment to another in an orderly and timely manner was yet another set of skills that Wooster fine-tuned. He noted the length of travel and time necessary to move troops from Connecticut to Crown Point, New York. At the bequest of the Connecticut General Assembly, Wooster used his knowledge of the topography of the area around Lake George, Fort Edward, William Henry, and Carillion that he gained in the campaigns of 1758 and 1759 to plan the successful American attack on Fort Ticonderoga sixteen years later.[39]

Wooster's *Orderly Book* is filled with detailed orders of march, camp activities, work details, passwords, paroles, and countersigns for each day. Analysis of his book provided a view of the practical military education that a colonel under British command would have gained in 1758–59. It revealed the specifics of daily military structure and life that Wooster applied as he continued to develop and refine his leadership skills. Generals Amherst and Forbes served as military tutors for Wooster on these campaigns. Wooster already had military experience while on campaign against Louisbourg in 1745, and service under these officers continued to refine his own military leadership.[40]

Colonel Wooster developed his practical military knowledge while on the British expedition of 1759. Topographical skills were essential in determining exact movements of the army, and accurate maps were highly valued by commanders.[41] The expedition began at Fort Edward, June 19 and 20, and continued to Lake George from June 21 through July 21; the sawmills near Lake George on June 22; and Fort Ticonderoga from July 23 to October 8. It concluded at Crown Point on October 10. He worked alongside grenadiers, light infantry, rangers, provincials, of which his Connecticut force made up several regiments, British regulars, engineers, and

Inniskilling fusiliers (Irish soldiers). Great organizational skill was required to keep the army fed, clothed, and disciplined. Field music played a key role in the daily activity and delivery of field orders to the army. Colonel Wooster was responsible for organizing regimental movements, the issuing of rations, making sure that bread was baked, assigning work details and preventing camp sutlers from selling strong liquor to soldiers, waggoners, and Indians without permission.[42] Those under Wooster's direct authority were his officers of the line: regimental commanders (captains, lieutenants, non-commissioned officers, sergeants, and corporals), chaplains, surgeons and surgeons' assistants, adjutants (those helping to complete the mountains of military paperwork required daily), armorers (responsible for repairing weapons), and the quartermaster.

The physical well-being of his soldiers was a constant concern, and to that end a field hospital was built at Lake George. Wooster posted daily orders to instruct officers and men alike on the issue of soldierly hygiene, without which disease would run rampant. Lice and vermin were constant problems in camp and required the employment of barbers to not only shave the men, but also to cut hair.[43] To commanders in the army, however, the greatest threat to the army was the outbreak of smallpox. This deadly disease killed more men than enemy bullets. The outbreak of smallpox was as devastating to entire communities as to the army in the 1700s.

Leading regular troops was far different than commanding volunteers from one's community. Wooster relied heavily upon the information he plied from the numerous military manuals available to him. British naval officers had used force to maintain discipline at Louisbourg in 1745, yet the New England troops had received little corporal punishment for infractions. Fighting in the French and Indian War, one theater of a global British conflict waged by the British Empire, and one that by 1759 was well into its fifth year, required strict discipline of both men and officers. Without discipline, military command would disintegrate. Court martials were the tools in which discipline could be maintained while justice was amply served, albeit cruel and harsh justice in many instances. Cuthbertson's 1759 manual entitled *A System for the Complete Interior Management and Economy of a Battalion of Infantry* dedicated an entire section to the necessity of Court-Martial trials and punishments in the army:

> As Subordination, and strict Discipline, can not (from the general depravity of the Soldiery) be properly supported without having recourse to the severest punishments, it often becomes necessary for Officers, to require the authority of a Court-martial, to enable them to take such rigorous methods; in doing which however, the greatest caution must be used, that the nature of the offence may be equal to an application of such consequences, nothing making the importance of a Court-martial, sink so low in the opinion of Soldiers, as seeing them ordered on the most trivial occasions.[44]

Discipline was essential to maintaining order in the army. The first court martial was held on June 28 with the punishment immediately enforced. While on the 1759 campaign, Wooster recorded forty-two separate court martial cases. These ranged from stealing and striking an officer, to desertion. The punishments were very specific: from 100 lashes with a cat-of-nine-tails to up to 1,500 lashes. Three of the cases resulted in execution. In one case of desertion the soldier was caught in a French uniform. His punishment was to be immediately hanged in his French coat, to be displayed throughout the day for all to see, followed by being buried "in a deep hole" still in his French coat. The regimentation of army life, and the rapid movement of the army necessitated that the dispensation of military justice had to be placed on hold at times. The orders were given on August 2 that the army was "marching for the reduction of all Canada," and therefore, with no time for punishment, a general pardon was granted to several soldiers who had been convicted in their court martial cases.[45]

Soldier's pay was insufficient at best. Still, as Wooster wrote on several occasions regarding the unequal distribution of pay for Connecticut troops, common soldiers did have a means to make a few extra pence while at Lake George. If they retrieved shot and shell left behind by the French, they were compensated based on the size and condition of the spent ammunition. This was also the case while the army was encamped at Fort Ticonderoga after the French surrender.

On July 24, as the army reached Fort Ticonderoga, Wooster placed an "Advertisement" in the *Orderly Book*, the only such item in this volume. The advertisement read:

> Col. Wooster, having left a small bed, 4 Blankets a small bedquilt + bolster and white pillows marked D.W. all were in a canvas sack + through mistake were sent in a wrong Batteau at the camp of Lake George. Therefore whoever can + do inform of the same shall be well rewarded by David Wooster—Col.[46]

From June to October 1759, Wooster served as the "Colonel of the Day" a total of seventy-three times, including the last sixty-five days of the campaign. As the army drew closer to engaging the French at Fort Ticonderoga, the commanding general of the British forces began calling for a colonel of the day for the regulars, and a colonel of the day for the provincials. Wooster served as both.

By 1759, the financial burden placed upon the Connecticut officers had become an economic strain on them and their families. The officers wrote to the Connecticut General Assembly requesting, once again, an adjustment to their pay. This second attempt was more direct, yet non-threatening. These men, including Wooster, stated clearly that the additional requirements of time and resources to perform their tasks was far greater and lasted longer than the term of their enlistments. Asking for equal compensation to those serving from neighboring colonies was, to them, a just request. Once more their request was denied.

A letter was then sent to General Amherst, North American commander-in-chief, from the Connecticut officers who proposed an extraordinary idea. To alleviate their financial situation, the officers stated that "from a Consideration of the small Allowance made us as Pay from the Governments to which We belong, it is Easy to Conclude We were Induced by Other Motives to Engage in said Service: We do Assure your Excellency, that it was by None stronger than a Zeal for His Majesty's Honor and Interest, and the Welfare of Our Country."[47]

The officers sought to procure a sizeable tract of land recently gained from the French near Crown Point to establish a British settlement there. The land would be given to the Connecticut officers, and they would be responsible for improving the land with settlement and badly needed roads. Since this land was newly acquired, the Connecticut officer's proposal would benefit the king as well as themselves. In the eighteenth-century land ownership equaled wealth. Owning land in the west was a financial investment. The officers humbly asked Amherst if he would present their petition to the king at his earliest convenience. It was also proposed that such a settlement, made up of soldiers from the Connecticut regiments, would be well prepared to defend the frontier of New England against any future Indian incursions.

General Amherst replied that because of "Your readiness and Alacrity, for Promoting the good of the Service, upon all Occasions, during the Course of this Campaign, are Sufficient Testimonies that you were Induced to Engage into it, thro' no other Motives, than that of Zeal for His Majesty's Honor and Interest, and the Welfare of Your Country," he would readily "transmit Your Memorial" to the king himself.[48] The settlement of newly claimed land from Crown Point south along a newly cut army road would have created a buffer between the French in Canada and the rest of New England. Having this settlement inhabited by soldiers would have guaranteed a strong military settlement, yet, despite their specific offer, the plan was never put into action.[49] Wooster was not finished with his vision of land settlement in the area near Lake George, however, and would revisit his plan after the war.

By 1760, fighting in North America had all but ended. Wooster retained the position of colonel of the 3rd Regiment of Connecticut troops, and the captaincy of its first company. Wooster's men traveled west of Crown Point into Iroquois Country. Hospital returns for Wooster's men in 1760 indicate the army had marched west from Fort Edward and Oswegatchie.[50] Oswegatchie is located on the Saint Lawrence River almost due west from Crown Point. Originally a French settlement called La Gallette, the British renamed it Oswegatchie after the French and Indian War. An examination of maps made during the 1750s and 1760s do not show the British name, but the French name La Gallette is marked on each one. This is the farthest Wooster and his men traveled during the war.

Men wounded during a military campaign found little financial relief upon their return home. Wounds often chained the individual to a life of increased difficulty and financial ruin. In some cases, as previously mentioned, wounded soldiers petitioned the General Assembly for compensation for wounds received while under military service. Records of the Connecticut Assembly contain numerous petitions from soldiers who had fought under Colonel Wooster throughout the French and Indian War. Some received significant compensation, while others, like Joshua Mudge, benefited far less while surviving with more debilitating wounds. Upon receiving a facial wound from a cannon ball while on the campaign against Oswagatchy, which resulted in the loss of his right eye, Mudge received fifteen pounds from the Connecticut Assembly.[51] These petitions not only highlight the dangers of colonial military service, but also demonstrate the very real financial burden placed upon wounded soldiers and their families after serving in the army in the eighteenth century.

Wooster's experience in the British army during the French and Indian War was monumental towards his development as a military leader. The art of military management, organizing and leading large numbers of troops, and maintaining discipline in the most difficult of situations were lessons not gained through text-book study, but rather through experience in the field. He learned the importance of training troops in the latest military maneuvers, as well as the value of working with qualified quartermasters to provide adequate and timely rations to his men, and the value placed on proper hygiene within an army encampment. These skills became vitally important during the Revolutionary War when leaders such as Wooster were difficult to find.

Fearful of continued French or Indian aggression, the Connecticut General Assembly once more called for the raising of troops to prepare for yet another possible military campaign. By the spring of 1761, Colonel Wooster closed his military accounts, records, and returns, and began to look to what the future might bring. Despite having commanded in the field for much of the war, his mercantile business continued, and shipping coming into New Haven would once more begin to flourish. The economy of New Haven was strong enough to support the construction of a new chapel at Yale College which would be completed in 1763.

Just as normalcy returned, devastating news reached New England. On January 22, 1761, the *Connecticut Gazette* printed the official account of the death of His Royal Britannic Majesty, King George II. To show due respect for the loss of the monarch, despite the inclement January weather, the militia was called out, comprised of two troops of Horse, and four companies of Foot, as the Governor, select men of honor in the colony, read the official proclamation of the death of the king. The proclamation concluded with ceremonial praise to the new monarch, King George III.

> We therefore the Governor and Company, assisted with numbers of the principal Inhabitants of this Colony, do now, hereby with one full voice and consent of tongue and heart, publish and proclaim, that the high and mighty Prince George, Prince of Wales, is now by the death of our late sovereign, of happy and glorious memory, become our only lawful and rightful Liege, Lord George the Third, by the Grace of God, King of Great Britain, France and Ireland, Defender of the faith, Supreme Lord of the said Colony of Connecticut in New England, and all other his late Majesty's dominions and Territories in America, to whom we do acknowledge all Faith and constant obedience, with all hearty and humble affection; beseeching God, by whom Kings and Queens do reign, to bless the Royal King George the Third, with long and happy years to reign over us. Given at the Council Chamber at New Haven, the Twenty-second day of January, in the first year of the reign of our Sovereign Lord George the Third King of Great Britain, France and Ireland, Defender of the Faith, &c. Annoque Domini 1761.
> GOD SAVE THE KING.[52]

Wooster had met King George II following the siege of Louisbourg in the fall of 1745. The late monarch had bestowed accolades upon him, including the captaincy of the 51st Regiment of Foot. Despite victory over the French, the future within the empire was uncertain, and the conclusion of the current war left much to be determined and settled.

Following the printed proclamation announcing the death of King George II, and upon receiving the news of the coronation of the new King of England, George III, the governor of Connecticut, Thomas Fitch, and fifty-two "principal Inhabitants of this Colony" signed a proclamation on January 22, 1761. Wooster was one of those fifty-two. The proclamation repeated the ceremonial praise that had been printed in the newspaper earlier that month. As the French and Indian war drew to a close, Wooster declared his loyalty to King George III just as had to the previous monarch. As financial crisis loomed on the horizon, the next fourteen years would test his allegiance to the crown. In historic hindsight, there is great irony in the concluding line of the pledge which Wooster signed in 1761. The proclamation stated that "we do acknowledge all Faith and Constant Obedience, I with all Hearty and humble Affection; beseeching God, by whom Kings and Queens do reign, to bless the Royal King George the Third with long and happy Years to Reign over Us."[53]

Writing a petition to the Connecticut General Assembly, this time on his own, but on behalf of all Connecticut officers who served in the French and Indian War, Wooster humbly requested compensation equal to that provided to all other colonial officers during the war. His letter referenced the proclamation of the king regarding the payment of soldiers, as well as the required equal distribution of rations. The third and final petition of October 13, 1761, was noted as were the two previous requests, by both the lower and the upper house of the general assembly and "Resolved in the Negative."[54] From the perspective of the members of the assembly, the economic pressures placed upon the colony to provide for their own men in the field during the course of the six years of war, as well as their pay and that of the officers, were too great and they were unable to provide the increase that Wooster and other officers requested. The looming economic situation would only worsen in the years following the Treaty of Paris in 1763.

Perhaps the most important benefit Wooster gleaned from his military experience in the French and Indian War were the skills required to maintain supplies to troops in the field. Without food, clothing, and the needed military and medical supplies, an army could not last through a campaign season. For almost five years he had led a colonial regiment in the field and met the challenges of supplying the army. As an elected official and leading merchant in New Haven, Wooster also experienced the economic impact of a war-weary colony whose treasury was strained. He felt this firsthand with the several rejections to his petitions for equal pay and rations. The colony of Connecticut simply could not increase pay and continue to supply her men.

Geography provided an additional challenge to supplying troops during the campaigns near Fort Edward, William Henry, and Ticonderoga. Road travel to Albany from Connecticut was not terribly difficult, and there were several roads that led north from Albany to Fort Edward which was the southernmost British fort near Lake George. The Hudson River also provided a navigable route to Fort Edward before the river turned westward. Military roads had been built from Fort Edward northwest to Fort William Henry. From William Henry roads allowed for travel along the western edge of Lake George to Fort Ticonderoga. As seen in the 1758 Abercrombie expedition, as well as the 1759 Amherst campaign against Fort Carillon (Ticonderoga), Lake George provided an all-water route to Fort Ticonderoga located on the northern most point of Lake George. Barges and bateaux, flat-bottom boats, were used to transport supplies north to Ticonderoga or to Crown Point. Transporting military supplies during the spring, summer, and fall campaign season was possible, yet taxing. However, once winter set in, supply routes became treacherous and oftentimes impassable. Winter campaigns in areas north of Crown Point became a supply nightmare, as rivers and lakes froze, preventing barge and bateaux transportation.

The French and Indian War was officially concluded with the signing of the Treaty of Paris on February 10, 1763. In North America, Great Britain gained all land east of the Mississippi River as well as rights to the fishing of the Grand Banks near Nova Scotia. To New England, the protection of the fishing industry was essential. For merchants in New Haven such as Wooster, the freedom of navigation and commerce once more allowed for uninterrupted trade with Europe. In addition, although little monetary compensation was provided to Connecticut or the other American colonies to alleviate their debt incurred during the war, the new monarch, King George III, issued a royal decree on October 7, 1763, which allowed the several governors of the colonies in American to grant land to all men who served in the late war with France. Field officers received 5,000 acres; captains, 3,000; subalterns and staff, 2,000; non-commissioned officers, 200; and privates received 50 acres.[55] This Royal Proclamation also established what was commonly referred to as the Proclamation Line of 1763, forbidding British colonists in North America to settle west of the Appalachian Mountains without proper government consent or license. For Wooster and other Connecticut veterans of the late war, the prospect of new land was a welcomed incentive, yet with the same stroke of the pen, the king had placed these new lands beyond their reach. Not only would the 1759 proposal for settlements near Lake George no longer be considered, all settlement and land acquisitions westward were now in question. Wooster wrote to New York Governor Cadwallader Colden in December 1763, petitioning for his allotted 3,000 acres "on the East side of Lake Champlain opposite to the Fort at Crown Point, to be bounded Westerly by the said Lake, on the Terms expressed in the Royal Proclamation."[56] Records indicate that Wooster did receive 3,000 acres of land in New York.[57] These lands would be tremendously valuable to him in the coming years.

Wooster had thus reached a high position within Connecticut society. He was one of the fifty-two men to sign the proclamation of congratulations to their new Britannic Majesty King George III. Now fifty-one years old, married with children, a successful merchant, and officer with half-pay for life as the captain of the 51st Regiment of Foot, Wooster remained a devoted subject of the crown, so long as the crown and Parliament, in his view, continued to protect the rights and privileges of Englishmen in the North American colonies. The war, however, had changed colonial attitudes towards England. Louisbourg had proven that Connecticut was more than prepared for military defense, both with domestic insurrection, and foreign threats to shipping and trade. The active involvement of Connecticut troops and officers in the French and Indian War demonstrated their drive and fortitude in becoming a true disciplined fighting force. This was especially true for David Wooster.

Given that military discipline was necessary to maintain order in the British army, applying these learned principles become crucial to controlling soldiers in the American militia army of 1775. Throughout the Revolutionary War, Wooster would be pressed to execute British style discipline among volunteer troops that enlisted for short terms of service. He was often challenged by fellow officers in the

Continental Army when court martials were necessary and punishments had to be enforced. The leadership skills gained in the French and Indian War became invaluable to Wooster.

The lessons learned from both military actions, entwined with the republican lessons of Locke and the fervor of the Great Awakening were invaluable. The continual development of republican ideology, along with the economic turmoil, both during the war and those that were to come, soon tested ideological loyalty which became the core of David Wooster. No one would have expected that the closing lines from the Reverend Bird's 1759 sermon would foreshadow the numerous impending challenges soon to face Wooster and others in Connecticut. The pressures to maintain economic independence, freedom, and liberty, all in the context of the ever-encroaching political and economic might of Great Britain, began to weigh heavily. Bird's concluding lines rang true:

> One of these we have to choose; either to gird on the Sword, rush into Battle, jeopard our Lives in the high Places of the Field, and conquer, or die like Men; or be enslaved with a happy Country, to the lawless Ambition and arbitrary Rule of the proudest of Princes: *The former of which is infinitely rather to be chosen, by every considerable noble Mind, capable of relishing the Sweets of Liberty and Property, Englishmen's Darlings: Surely an honourable Death, in the Defense of our Country, is much rather to be chosen, than a Life of most wretched Slavery.*[58]

5

The Brewing Storm
(1763–1774)

The Royal Proclamation of 1763 provided land to veterans of the French and Indian War, yet it also set the stage for unprecedented actions within the British colonies in North America. David Wooster's entire life had been structured around the ideas of Locke that protected and defended the natural rights of life, liberty, and property. However, the ensuing actions of the British Parliament in the years following the conclusion of the war appeared to challenge these core principles. Wooster became actively engaged in the civic life of New Haven while closely watching the growing division and animosity perpetuated by the very representative body that, in theory, spoke for all members of the British Empire.[1] He had developed a sense of dedication and honor which had been instilled in his from his family, his education at Yale, his years of military training, and from the pulpit. This devotion and loyalty hinged upon the rights of Englishmen to own property, to engage in open business, and to enjoy the liberties granted through Magna Carta of political involvement without oppression and free from tyranny. After the French and Indian war everything changed.

Historians have estimated that Great Britain was approximately £ 145 million pounds sterling in debt in 1763. War is the most expensive thing that mankind can engage in, and after decades of war, England was reeling under the tremendous burden of the price of military success and conquest. In order to alleviate this debt, Parliament instituted a series of taxes upon all British subjects, including those across the Atlantic.

Parliament had attempted to control the commerce of Britain's North American colonies for over one hundred years, mostly through duties on shipping. By the end of the French and Indian War, however, there had been a perpetuated sense of abandonment on the part of the American colonies, referred to as salutary neglect. The colonies had felt that their active economic participation within the empire had been satisfied through the mercantile system, and certainly had been diligently adhered to during the last war. British shipping and vessels of war were the backbone of their military success, and the New England colonies provided the resources and tools for the continuation of that success. Naval stores, wharves, and nautical craftsmen provided Great Britain necessary supplies of oakum and pitch for repairing and caulking ship's hulls, rope and hemp for rigging, and the best quality of masts in the empire.[2] New England was one of the best areas for ship building, and Connecticut rivaled the other New England colonies for naval production. The ports of Boston, New Haven, and New York provided the Royal Navy a location to repair and refit their ships during the French and Indian War. *Rule, Britannia! Britannia Rule the Waves!* A chorus refrain from the popular 1763 version of the song by the same title by James Thompson highlighted the importance of British naval superiority. As a leading merchant and importer of goods, Wooster was keenly aware of the growing tension over British naval strength, parliamentary pressures to alleviate the surmounted debt, and restraint on colonial commercial shipping.

Parliament, the representative body within the British government, had levied navigation acts since 1651. These were designed to control commerce between Great Britain and her colonies throughout the world. They also sought to force the colonists to only use British vessels when shipping goods to and from England. Furthermore, they required a bond to be placed on all cargo shipped. These bonds amounted to a type of insurance policy upon the goods. In the event of storm, piracy, or ship lost at sea, these bonds provided some protection for both the shipper and the London merchants. With each new navigation act passed the restrictions placed upon Connecticut merchants, for example, become more and more cumbersome. By the mid–1700s Connecticut had become a major center of ship building, which challenged the notion that all goods shipped must be on British vessels from England. Many in the American colonies simply ignored the acts and continued using their own ships or engaged in the business of smuggling.

Tensions were on the rise. The interaction of British regulars and their officers alongside colonial provincial officers and soldiers during the French and Indian War had accentuated the growing divide in the way in which Englishmen and colonists viewed one another. Changes in attitude created uneasiness and a growing "second class citizen status" emerged. Coupled with the concern of new tax policy, Wooster and other merchants in New Haven aligned themselves with merchants in Boston, as the two major commercial centers in New England tried to anticipate the inevitable actions of Parliament.

On February 22, 1763, at a town meeting in New Haven, a committee addressed a letter from the "Selectmen of the Town of Boston to the Selectmen of this Town to consider of some measure to be agreed upon for promoting Economy, Manufacturing, etc." The New Haven committee responded to the Boston letter by creating a list of non-importation items which would ensure the stability and growth of colonial business. The report of the committee stated that to support their brethren in Massachusetts, Connecticut, merchants would no longer import the following items after March 31:

> Carriages of all sorts, Horse Furniture, Men's and Women's Hats, Men's and Women's Apparel ready-made, Household Furniture, Men's and Women's Shoes, Sole-Leather, Gold, Silver, and Thread-Lace, Gold and Silver Buttons, wrought Plate, Diamond, Stone and Paste-Ware, Clocks, Silversmith's and Jeweller's Ware, Broad-cloths that cost above ten Shillings Sterling per yard, Muffs, Furs, and Tippets, Starch, Women's and Children's Toys, Silk and Cotton Velvets, Gauze, Linseed Oil, Malt Liquors, and Cheese.[3]

Self-sufficient actions became the rallying cry. The select committee in New Haven went so far as to "promote the saving of Linen Rags and other materials proper for making paper in this colony."[4]

The New Haven report was approved. This is one of the earliest examples of non-importation agreements within the colonies and predates those of the southern colony of Virginia which are synonymous with the lead up to the Revolution. The actions of Parliament strengthened the bond connecting Boston and New Haven, and the merchants of those cities set their resolve against British imports. The non-importation acts certainly placed an added financial burden upon those whose livelihood centered on shipping and trade. However, the looming actions of the administration of prime minister George Greenville in London, with new forms of taxation, dominated the economic situation.

Parliament continued to search for ways to raise revenue to eliminate the ever-growing national debt. Coupled with the prohibition to settle the western lands mandated by the Royal Proclamation of 1763, Parliament tightened the reigns upon colonial currency, only adding to the developing sense of animosity in the American colonies. On April 10, after much consternation from London merchants and creditors who bitterly objected to receiving payment in worthless colonial script, Parliament issued the Currency Act. This act required payment to merchants in London and other major English cities to be made in pounds sterling.

With great concern for perpetual "enslavement" to British merchants and their inability to pay bills of credit, Wooster, and other merchants throughout New Haven began to devise a plan that would maintain their entrepreneurial integrity and independence within the Empire. In the meantime, the Molasses Act of 1733 was set to expire at the end of the 1763 session. This previous act had raised the cost of importing foreign molasses into the British American colonies, thus promoting the purchase of British molasses while inflating the price of French product with an added tax. Colonists in New England relied upon imported molasses to produce rum. There was a concern that, with soldiers returning from the French and Indian War, there would be a large demand for rum, thus increasing the necessity for imported molasses from the Caribbean sugar islands.

On September 29, 1764, the new Sugar Act took the place of the expired Molasses Act. The law attempted to raise revenue for "defraying the expences of defending, protecting, and securing the said colonies and plantations." This act of Parliament contained forty-seven sections, each a specific punitive addition.[5] However, Article VII stated that, along with a renewed tax on imported foreign molasses, the Sugar Act included a tax on "foreign white or clayed sugars, foreign indigo, foreign coffee, wines, wrought silks, bengals, and stuffs, mixed with silk or herbs, callico, cambricks, French lawns, and foreign molasses or syrups."[6] For Wooster, as a merchant, whose sole endeavor was importing goods from across the British Empire, these restrictions became a tremendous hinderance to the success and freedom of his business.

In addition to the levies implemented by the Sugar Act, there were several articles that increased the authority of Royal Customs' Officials. These officials were leading men in their respective colonies who were offered positions as royal tax collectors. At any other time, this might have been seen as a great honor. To prevent smuggling, customs officials were required to assess a ship's cargo manifest upon entering port. If the manifest was not in order, or if there were goods being smuggled into port, the customs official was authorized to bring the captain of the ship up on charges in Vice Admiralty Court. This was not a jury trial and thus further inhibited the rights and liberties of the colonists.

Rumors circulated that Parliament was set to issue a new external tax in 1765. The new "Stamp Act" would levy additional taxes to numerous items. It is important to note that these taxes which Parliament issued were well known in the British American colonies before they were enacted into law. Discussion about the new tax was met with great animosity in New Haven and in the fall session of the general assembly a state paper was issued from the legislature which decried the potential passage of the new act.[7] The resolve of Wooster and his countrymen of Connecticut to uphold, secure, and defend the rights of Englishmen against tyranny, both foreign and domestic, would be tested the following year.

Despite the actions of Parliament, the city of New Haven thrived and flourished in the years following the French and Indian War. Wooster played a key role in the continual development of the shipping industry as well as the continuation of the Long Wharf project. By 1765, the Long Wharf had extended a significant distance into New Haven harbor, allowing for additional merchant vessels, and increasing New Haven's prominence as a competitive New England center of commerce.

Yet the concern over the passage of the Stamp Act weighed heavily upon businessmen such as Wooster. If this act passed, what would it do to import businesses in New Haven? Would it destroy the entrepreneurial spirit that had been flourishing in the American colonies? Parliament had passed an amended version of the Iron Act in 1765, which allowed for some transportation of bar and pig iron manufactured in America along the coastal regions. However, it continued to restrict any manufacturing of finished iron goods in the colonies. Pots, pans, cooking irons, all such finished goods were required to be purchased from England and shipped to America.[8]

Since no individual, or individuals, specifically represented the colonies in Parliament, the American colonists had no actual vote on the passage of any type of legislation. The Selectmen of New Haven chose to send Mr. Jared Ingersoll to speak on their behalf regarding the upcoming Stamp Act debate. Ingersoll met with Benjamin Franklin in London to discuss presenting the resolution passed in October 1765 by the Connecticut General Assembly, which stated, in their opinion, why the Stamp Act should not be passed. While in London Mr. Ingersoll was present in Parliament when Colonel Isaac Barré, an Irish British officer who had served in America during the French and Indian War and subsequently elected as a member of the House of Commons in Parliament, spoke against the passage of the act.[9] His reply was recorded by Ingersoll and reprinted in the Connecticut newspapers. Barré, a champion of the American colonies, argued against the ability to tax "the children planted by our care, nourished by our indulgence, and protected by our arms" as noted by one Parliamentarian:

> They planted by *your* care! No! Your oppressions planted them in America. They fled from your tyranny to a then uncultivated and inhospitable country, where they exposed themselves to almost all the hardships to which human nature is liable; and among others, to the cruelties of a savage foe, the most subtle, and, I take it upon me to say the most formidable of all people upon the face of God's earth; and yet actuated by principles of true English liberty, they met these hardships.

They nourished by *your* indulgence! They grew by your neglect of them. As soon as you began to care about them that care was exercised in sending persons to rule over them ... sent to spy out their liberties, to misrepresent their actions, and to prey upon them.

They protected by *your* arms! They have nobly taken up arms in your defense; have exerted a valor amidst their constant and laborious industry for the defense of a country whose frontier was drenched in blood, while its interior was yielding all its little savings to your enrichment.[10]

The members of Parliament passed the Stamp Act on March 22, 1765. While in England, and as the official representative of the British colony of Connecticut, Jared Ingersoll, Sr., was offered the position of Royal Stamp Collector for the colony, an offer he accepted. When news of the passage of the Stamp Act reached Connecticut, Governor Thomas Fitch alluded that he would support the act. There was a great deal of growing resentment and animosity in Massachusetts which, by the very proximity of the colony, began to make its way into Connecticut. Riotous mobs met in Boston, yet the Connecticut governor wished to prevent destructive action in his colony. However, when time came to enforce the Stamp Act, Connecticut Lieutenant Governor Timothy Pitkin and Jonathan Trumbull, a councilman at the time and future governor of Connecticut, left the chamber rather than pledge themselves to the act's enforcement.[11]

The Stamp Act taxed paper products, playing cards, and legal documents. In fact, the sixty-three separate articles delineated not only the type of paper or vellum to be taxed but went further into the specified use for the paper. For printing a declaration of the court of law the tax levied was three pence. A university degree; two pounds. A printed warrant for a court; one shilling. And an appointment of a lawyer; ten pounds. There are forty-two total distinctions for the tax on printed vellum, parchment, or sheets of paper, and all taxed differently. Playing cards were taxed one shilling, and a pair of dice ten shillings.[12] The act went further to prescribe detailed penalties for infringing upon the act or the collection of the tax.

In addition, Parliament issued the Quartering Act in May which established the permanent garrisoning of large numbers of British troops in the American colonies in peacetime, including housing them in public houses.[13] With the implementation of this measure so soon after the Stamp Act, many in America began to question the motives behind such a militarized action during a time of peace. This would lead to one of the major issues of contention in the years to follow, the maintenance of standing armies in times of peace could only be used for tyrannical purposes.

Ingersoll returned to Connecticut as the official collector of the new stamp tax. By the time he had arrived colonial opposition was clear. Effigies of the stamp collector in Boston were displayed and burned, and Ingersoll received similar treatment in Connecticut. He placed a notice in the *Connecticut Gazette* on August 24, 1765, to quell the growing anti-stamp fervor in the colony. Much of this agitation was being fueled by discontented groups in Massachusetts, and being so close, this same was funneled into Connecticut. No one was being forced to purchase the stamped paper, Ingersoll stated. Furthermore, he assured the readers that his intention was never to cause confusion or animosity throughout Connecticut, but rather to simply do his duty as a collector of the said tax. If anyone found themselves in need of paper for whatever reason, he hoped that they would come to him to purchase the necessary item, which, in turn, contained the stamp tax. Ingersoll expressed his own concern over the rising violence aimed at the collectors of the tax. Such expressions, however, did little to alleviate the growing violence aimed at the distributor, and collector, of the tax:

> I cannot but wish you would think more how to get rid of the stamp act than of the Officers who are to supply you with the Paper, and that you had learnt more of the nature of my Office, before you had undertaken to be very angry at it.[14]

There was a growing uneasiness in New Haven over the act and the collection of the tax. No report was made of Ingersoll being tarred and feathered as took place in Boston. However, in early September, while enroute to Hartford for the meeting of the general assembly, Ingersoll was "accompanied" by an accumulation of citizens, all on horseback, who forced him into a roadside tavern and released him only after he signed an affidavit that he would resign as the stamp collector. Ingersoll stated that he would be glad to do so at the request of the general assembly; however, this statement did not appease the growing crowd. Eventually he did sign the note which was delivered to the assembly and printed in newspapers throughout Connecticut. He resignation dated September 19, 1765, read:

> I do hereby promise, that I will never receive any Stampt-Papers, which may arrive from Europe, in consequence of any act lately passed in the Parliament of Great Britain, nor officiate in any manner as Stamp Master, or Distributor of Stamps within the Colony of Connecticut, either directly or indirectly, and I do hereby request all the Inhabitants of this his majesty's Colony of Connecticut (notwithstanding the said Office or Trust has been committed to me) not to apply to me, ever hereafter, for any such stamped Papers, hereby declaring, that I do resign said Office, and execute these Presents of my own free will and accord, without any Equivocation or mental Reservation.[15]

Although Ingersoll was forced to resign, the anger over the Stamp Act continued to spread throughout New England until May 1766. He and his family moved to Philadelphia in 1771 yet returned to New Haven in 1777. Despite being a noted Tory during the Revolution, Jared Ingersoll, Sr., remained in New Haven until his death in 1781.[16]

Animosity grew against the Stamp Act throughout 1765 and into 1766. Opposition to the act appeared to make little to no impression upon the members of Parliament. Those like Barré were in the minority in England. Meanwhile the continuation of external taxation abroad fueled increasing unrest in America. The Sugar Act and the Stamp Act had enlivened the spirit of republicanism in New England. Boston became the center of violence and aggression towards the tax collectors, while New Haven attempted to keep the peace and prohibit riotous action. A renewed interest in the non-importation of British goods, refusal to pay for the "Stampt Papers," and growing animosity towards the tax collectors placed added pressure on Parliament to repeal the Stamp Act.

In March 1766, under mounting pressure from the London mercantile establishment that forced the new prime minister, the Marquess of Rockingham, to push for repeal, as well as continued agitation from its American colonies, Parliament repealed the Stamp Act. This was proceeded by a reprimand to the American colonists entitled the Declaratory Act. The main point of this most recent action was not for immediate financial gain, but rather "for the better securing the dependency of his majesty's dominions in America upon the crown and parliament of Great Britain." The Act mentioned that the legislative bodies in the British North American Colonies had "claimed to themselves" the authority to tax the citizens residing in their respective British colonies, while at the same time denouncing the authority of Parliament to levy taxation upon them. Subordination to the authority in Great Britain was paramount and was slipping like grains of sand held in one's clenched fingers. To reclaim lost authority, and to re-clarify the political, economic, and social boundaries that their North American colonists had crossed, it was noted that the aforementioned "have been, are, and of right ought to be, subordinate unto, and dependent upon the imperial crown and parliament of Great Britain." To conclude this act any laws, resolutions, or additional proceedings within the North American colonies which denied Parliament this authority was hereby declared null and void.[17]

From the perspective of those in Great Britain, the Declaratory Act made it extremely clear who maintained political and economic authority over the American colonies. This prohibited any political action or protest which opposed Parliament's authority, and in doing so, inadvertently established therein a solid foundation of republican ideology.

In the meantime, colonial actions began to shift towards more coordinated protest. The taxes of Parliament levied since the conclusion of the last war had created a movement within the American colonies which led to the calling of the Stamp Act Congress in 1766. Aside from the Albany Plan of Union in 1754, this was the first successful political gathering of colonies to discuss the economic and political issues affecting North America. Not all of the colonies sent representatives; several royal governors refused to acknowledge the assembly. Connecticut sent as representatives to the Stamp Act Congress Eliphalet Dyer, who served with Wooster in the French and Indian War, David Rowland, and William Samuel Johnson. The congress adopted a series of fourteen grievances which would later serve as underlying principles for the calling of the First Continental Congress in 1774.

On May 19, news of the repeal of the Stamp Act reached New Haven. The *Connecticut Gazette* printed the following article on Friday, May 23, detailing the city's response:

> Last Monday morning early, an Express arrived here with the charming news; soon after which many of the Inhabitants were awakened with the noise of small-arms from different quarters of the town; all the Bells were rung; and cannon roared the glad tidings. In the afternoon the Clergy publickly returned thanks for the blessing, and a company of Militia were collected under the principal direction of Colonel Wooster. In the evening was Illumination, Bonfire and Dances—all without any remarkable indecency or disorder. The arrival of the regular Post from Boston last night, had completed our joy for the wise and interesting repeal of the stamp act.—Business will soon be transacted as usual in this loyal Colony.—In short, every thing in nature seems to wear a more cheerful aspect than usual—to a great majority.[18]

Wooster, who remained a colonel of the New Haven militia, was prominent at the celebration, leading the local troops in the community's celebration. As a civic leader the news of the repeal of the tax had to have been a welcome message to him. The article hinted that, with the passage and application of the tax, commerce, trade, and local business had suffered. The *Gazette* noted on May 23, 1766, that "business will soon be transacted as usual in this loyal Colony."[19]

While the colonies were entangled with internal and external taxation, Wooster devoted a portion of his time and attention to the requirements of religious devotion. As New Haven expanded both in population and in business activity due to the expansion of the Long Wharf following the French and Indian War, so, too, did the congregation of the White Haven Society. In 1766, the meeting house for the White Haven Ecclesiastical Society was in need of repair and expansion. Wooster oversaw the additions to the building, which, according to the historical maps of New Haven, was located adjacent to the public green and was given a fine coat of blue paint.[20] He also worked to sell a portion of land in Canada, which was owned by his wife prior to their marriage, to a business associate in New Haven.[21] Mary Wooster was "highly esteemed in her day for her dignity, hospitality, and benevolence," and referred to as "an educated and exemplary lady, not likely to have made a statement without ample authority."[22]

The news of 1766 contained an interesting side story worth mentioning. Benedict Arnold, also from Connecticut, appeared in the *Connecticut Gazette* in January. The story is becoming of the young revolutionary. Born on January 14, 1741, thirty-one years younger than Wooster, Arnold retained a youthful "zeal" according to accounts of his actions. Whereas Wooster had developed an aged wisdom refined over years of experience, both is business and in military matters, Arnold was seen as a "hot-headed youth."[23] In the reported account, Arnold, a merchant, and ship-owner, had been accused of smuggling goods into New Haven by a member of his crew, Peter Boole. Upon hearing the accusation, Arnold and several of his associates called upon Boole and required the following confession from him which was printed in the local paper. The intensity of the statement is certainly worth noting:

> I, Peter Boole, not having the fear of God before my Eyes, but being instigated by the Devil, did, on the 24th instant, make information, or endeavor to do the same, to one of the Custom House Officers for the Port of New Haven, against Benedict Arnold for importing contraband goods, do hereby acknowledge I justly deserve a Haiter for my malicious, wicked and cruel intentions.
>
> I do now solemnly swear I will never hereafter make information, directly or indirectly, or cause the same to be done against any person or persons, whatever, for importing Contraband or any other goods into this Colony, or any Port of America; and that I will immediately leave New Haven and never enter the same again. *So help me God.*[24]

According to Arnold's account, Boole did not leave New Haven immediately and he waited "nearly four hours after," since Boole had still not yet left town, Arnold and his associates confronted him and whipped him upon the public pillory. In an attempt to defend himself, and his character, Arnold made a public statement upon the matter which was printed in the *Connecticut Gazette*. His report stated that

> I then made one of the party and took him to the Whipping-Post, where he received near forty lashes with a small cord, and was conducted out of town; since which on his return, the affair was submitted to Col. David Wooster and Mr. Enos Allen, (Gentlemen of reputed good judgement and understanding) who were of opinion that the fellow was not whipped too much, and gave him 50s, [shillings] damages only.[25]

This was the first recorded encounter between David Wooster and the "hot-headed youth" Benedict Arnold. Over the next ten years the two encountered each other again in rather unpleasant circumstances. If truth is to be found in this incident of 1766, it would certainly be consistent with Arnold's brazen action towards Wooster nine years later.

Despite a temporary lull in the political scene in London regarding their colonies in North America, political activity continued in Connecticut. Wooster had become a prominent member of the community and was often asked to serve the Connecticut General Assembly in a variety of ways in which his expertise dictated. At the October session of the general assembly, he was requested to examine the petition of several sutlers who were still owed money from goods sold on campaign during the French and Indian War.[26] As the Assembly met only twice each year, once in the spring and again in the fall, obtaining financial or legal relief could be a lengthy process. It became more cumbersome in attempting to recuperate post-war debt. Wooster, along with Jabez Hamlin and Thomas Darling, were appointed by the Assembly to judge the case involving the repayment of sutler fees for the amount of £78..5s..5., which was no small debt. The case had previously gone before the superior court in Windham.[27]

The record does not indicate when these soldiers incurred their debt, or if their inability to pay for the goods received were in any way connected to the continual taxes administered by Parliament. However, this narrative of 1767, four years following the end of the war, does coincide with the struggling citizens, and merchants, who attempted to keep their own financial situation above board amid mounting economic uncertainty. Wooster advanced his civic leadership by applying his military and mercantile experience to the political climate of the post-war years in New Haven. He gained a reputation as a trusted and reliable leader in Connecticut, which was exemplified by growing public confidence in his actions and abilities.

Parliament renewed its attempt at reducing the national debt by instituting a new series of taxes upon the American colonies on November 20, 1767. The Townshend Acts not only levied new taxes on imported goods, but it also renewed older taxes enacted under previous monarchs that had expired. Items such a plate glass, lead, painter's colors, tea, paste or mill boards, coffee, cocoa nuts, foreign lace, silk, ribbon, rice, and over sixty-three different types and colors of paper were all taxed under the new act of Parliament. Additional penalties were added for non-collection or for smuggling of goods into the colonies.[28] The Townshend Acts were met with stiff resistance. Protests were common and New Haven continued to keep an even-keel approach to the burgeoning economic crisis.

By 1768, just five years after the end of the French and Indian War, the Parliament issued numerous taxes and reissued older ones that had expired, all of which did more than simply raise revenue to pay down the national debt. They punished any infringement of the laws with heavy fines while stemming well established commerce between the American colonies and foreign nations. They were oppressive to colonial business ventures which had been thriving on their own. Wooster was not opposed to paying taxes, so long as they were duly passed by elected officials who represented him in the general assembly. No one in the British North American colonies had a say regarding the acts passed by Parliament. Those, like Wooster, in all the thirteen colonies, had representation within their colonial legislatures, the very essence of Lockean republicanism. Yet these additional taxes were levied without any colonial consent given, the very essence of abusive government and absolutism. Here began the breach between liberty, freedom, and republicanism, versus the yoke of tyranny.

As often as tyranny was the subject of conversation, so, too, did the idea of loyalty spread in the taverns, shops, pulpits, and classrooms in New Haven, and other New England towns. The question of loyalty was very complex. What exactly did loyalty mean? To whom must you remain loyal? Or rather, to what did you owe loyalty? The answers to these questions drove public debate throughout the 1760s and the 1770s. Loyalists in the colonies noted that Britain was a parliamentary monarchy, not an absolute monarchy like many nations on the European continent. Under that system more liberties were granted to Englishmen. Men like William Samuel Johnson, one of the three representatives sent from Connecticut to the Stamp Act Congress in 1766, were undecided upon the question. As he saw it, the actions of England were, in fact, abusive and perhaps bordered on tyranny; however, he did not support the militant actions of the Sons of Liberty. Johnson, and many like him, saw their violent actions as a form of tyranny in and of itself. Wooster often wrote in the 1770s of liberty and freedom, and of the rights of Englishmen, yet his surviving correspondence through the 1760s does not specifically articulate his position.

Wooster was a republican and remained loyal to those ideas. To him the government that protected citizens' rights to life, liberty, and property was the very institution to which his loyalty was given. He never wavered from that ideology. Locke was part of his intellectual upbringing. To him the defense of property was an absolute necessity and a right. As a student of history, he read stories of tyrants, but the larger challenge was to act against tyranny in one's own lifetime. Wooster was prepared to do just that. He was not a radical, or a member of the Sons of Liberty, but he was duly concerned about the economic oppression that the levied acts of Parliament were inflicting upon his business and his home.

In 1768, Wooster was in correspondence with Governor William Pitkin concerning the creation of the position of a naval customs officer in New Haven. This royal post was performed in the service of the Governor, similar to the customs officer in Boston. Governor Pitkin, the father of Wooster's brother-in-law, asked him to review the official royal proclamation that allowed for the creation of the custom's official. Wooster's knowledge of British Common-Law and political history of Great Britain—especially when concerned with colonial charters and connections—were invaluable to the governor. After a careful study he clarified and summarized the listed requirements for the Commissioner of his Majesties Customs at Boston, which would be applied in Connecticut.

Concern plagued him. Under the position of the custom's officer, it was uncertain where the authority of the post would originate—the governor or the king? To Wooster it also placed colonial loyalty to the test. If challenged, where would the loyalty of the Custom's Officer lie, again to the king or to the governor? Defending the charter of Connecticut, Wooster commented that

I look upon it that that Naval Officers under your Honour are oblig^d to make all necessary
Returns to his Majesty of to the Person or Persons whom his Majesty appoint to receive the
same as required by act of Parliament, by virtue of their Commission Received from and
securities given to your Honour for that purpose, therefore the requisition of the Commissioners not only supersedes our Charter Privileges but also the very act of Parliament it self,
for it is manifest by the act of the 22^d of Charles ye 2^d, Ch: 26th the Governours are answerable to his Majesty for the execution of the Duty Containt^d in that act, and as I observed
before the Naval Officer appointed by the Govr becomes answerable to the Govr to perform
that Duty—therefore it appears to be very inconsistent for an officer after he has given sufficient account to the authority from whom he receives his Commission (for the due execution
of the Trust reposed in him) to be also oblig^d to give security to the authority to whom he is to
report.[29]

At a town meeting on April 10, 1769, the Selectmen of the town of New Haven "voted
that Col: Wooster be Collector on the Goods Imported into this Town, according
to the act of this Colony made in may Last."[30] His duties included the collection of
import taxes which were paid to the crown and were defined in an act of the Connecticut General Assembly in May 1768.[31]

Wooster accepted the position as a naval officer, and no record of public discontent is documented towards his execution of the office. Many such officials were
threatened or forced from their posts in cities such as Boston, Philadelphia, and New
York.

The acts of Parliament instituted in the 1760s caused great economic upheaval
in New Haven, and Wooster's mercantile business began to feel the brunt of these
external taxes. There was renewed interest in a non-importation agreement amongst
the colonies. In 1770, New York refused to follow the non-importation agreements
established by Massachusetts, Connecticut, and Pennsylvania. In light of that stance,
New Haven merchants pressed to cease all trade with New York and reroute their
imports to Philadelphia and Boston instead. On September 13, 1770, a committee
was formed to establish a revised non-importation list from Great Britain. Wooster
was among the thirty-eight merchants who signed the petition. Among the items on
the list were "Powder and Shot, German Steel, Hemp and Duck, Wool-Cards, Card-
Wire and Tacks, Implitnents for Cloathiere' Trades, Fishhooks and lines, Tin-plates,
Hatters' Trimmings, Salt-peter, Sickles, Bar Lead, Pins and Needles, Copperas and
Allum. Brimstone and Sea-Coal, Sheep-Shears, Shoemakers' Awls and Tacks, Sheet
Copper, Apothecaries' Drugs, Paper Moulds, Books, Chalk, and Salt."[32]

During the tumultuous period following the French and Indian War, Wooster
found himself financially secure upon his return to civilian life. With his degree
from Yale, his military experience, and his mercantile business, his return to the private sector was no less hectic nor less busy than his military career had been. Three
major themes concerned Wooster from 1763 to 1775: Land, both in New York and
his investments in the Susquehanna Company; the success of his mercantile business, David Wooster and Co.; and his political involvement which included continued correspondence with the governors of Connecticut as well as serving as
customs naval officer and justice of the peace for New Haven. In addition, he continued his post with the 51st Regiment under the late Sir William Pepperrell of Massachusetts, being placed on the half-pay list.[33] The bond between Massachusetts and

Connecticut was strengthened through the 1770s as both collaborated in non-importation of British imports. Political and military tension were heightened after word reached New Haven of the Boston Massacre in March 1770.

Wooster received a new position in 1771, in which he capitalized on applying his legal knowledge. During the May session of the general assembly, he was appointed as a justice of the peace for New Haven County. This first appointment lasted until the spring assembly session in 1772.[34] The responsibilities of a justice of the peace in the 1770s centered upon the maintenance of order, specifically regarding criminal proceedings. They also were empowered to perform marriages and various additional "administrative duties" as seen fit by the legislature. Prior to the Revolution the position of justice of the peace was significant in establishing and keeping law and order as the legal system matured in the colonies.[35] Several petitions were forwarded to him by the legislature, in which he now had the legal authority to resolve the matter.[36]

As a landholder, merchant, colonel of militia, and now a civil officer, Wooster had a profound interest in seeing Connecticut prosper. He defended Connecticut's land claims in a dispute over western territory in the Wyoming Valley throughout the 1760s and 70s. Pennsylvania also claimed the rights to the same land, as did the Iroquois Six Nations. Known as the "Susquehanna Affair," this incident demonstrated the devout loyalty of Wooster, and foreshadowed divisions among the thirteen American Colonies that would reappear during the upcoming Revolutionary War.

A group of individuals from Connecticut sought to gain western lands in an area north of the Susquehanna River, west of the New York chartered lands. These lands were traditional hunting grounds for the Six Nations. In the 1740s, Puritan missionaries from Connecticut had traveled to this area of the frontier and preached among the Indians. During the early 1750s, the Susquehanna Company attempted to purchase these lands from the various tribes of the Six Nations. The petition of the Susquehanna Company to purchase and settle the western lands in the Wyoming Valley was granted by the Connecticut General Assembly in May 1751:

> Resolved by this Assembly, that they are of opinion that the peaceably and orderly erecting and carrying on some new and well regulated colony or plantation on the lands abovesaid would greatly tend to fix and secure said Indian nations in allegiance to his Majesty and friendship with his subjects, and accordingly hereby manifest their ready acquiescence therein, if it should be his Majesty's royal pleasure to grant said lands to said petitioners and thereon erect and settle a new colony in such form and under such regulations as might be consistent with his royal wisdom, and also take leave humbly to recommend the said petitioners to his royal favour in the premises.[37]

In May the following year Wooster invested in the Susquehanna Company and paid nine dollars for one whole share in the company.[38]

By 1754, their attempts had proved successful. A close examination of the original charter for Connecticut indicated that the lands in question did, in fact, belong to Connecticut, and the Susquehanna Company, now officially recognized by the general assembly, gained the necessary signatures of Iroquois chiefs to acquire the land. This was accomplished during the Albany conference in 1754. This gathering brought together several colonial representatives; however, more Indian leaders were present which allowed for the successful transaction of the sale of the land.[39]

From 1750–1755, conflict arose over the ownership of the Wyoming Valley and proved a hot bed of contention. To those in Pennsylvania the forceful claim to this land by Connecticut was seen as tantamount to a civil war. By 1754, both those in Pennsylvania, the Proprietaries, and those in Connecticut laid claim to the land. According to Wooster the issue was a private matter and did not involve the governments of either Connecticut or Pennsylvania, as the Indians of the Six Nations had sold their rights to the land.[40] Only the onset of the French and Indian War in 1754 temporarily tempered the impending crisis.

Years of military experience, together with his business endeavors, college education at Yale, and political involvement all provided Wooster with an insight into the land dispute with the colony of Pennsylvania. As the colony of Connecticut was chartered, the land patent went from the Atlantic Ocean to the "South Sea," meaning the Pacific. Pennsylvania, however, was chartered years after Connecticut. Connecticut Governor Pitkin approved western settlement in the Susquehanna Valley, in what is now northern Pennsylvania, in 1769, and his successor, Governor Trumbull, voted to establish the western Connecticut settlements in 1774.

In May 1770, a committee was formed to research all recorded colonial land charters, grants, and patents for the colony of Connecticut. Unfortunately, their research was incomplete by the October session of the general assembly yet was finished for the spring session. In May 1771, the committee provided their completed work on colonial land charters of the colony of Connecticut to the assembly. In their report it was noted that the lands "west of Delaware River and in the latitude of that part of this Colony eastward of the Province of New York are well contained within the boundaries and descriptions of the Charter granted by King Charles 2d."[41]

Following the case in law of 1771, the Connecticut General Assembly stated that "this Assembly at this time will assert their claim and in some proper way support such claim to those lands contained within the limits and boundaries of the charter of this Colony, which are westward of the Province of New York," and passed "An Act concerning the Western Lands, so called, lying west-ward of Delaware River within the Boundaries of this Colony."[42]

By 1773, the Susquehanna Company, with the consent of the Connecticut General Assembly, began settlement in the Wyoming Valley, the newly claimed western lands of Connecticut. The land dispute no longer centered around ownership regarding the Six Nations of the Iroquois, it now became a heated dispute between Pennsylvania and Connecticut. At the January 1774 meeting of the general assembly, Connecticut approved a resolution to prepare all necessary papers, land claims and patents, and colonial charters to be sent along with a delegation to London for His Majesty to decide the final proper ownership of these chartered lands. Meanwhile, the Connecticut General Assembly also passed a resolution supporting those who had traveled and settled in the Wyoming Valley and guaranteed them the rights and privileges of citizens of Connecticut so long as they remained upon the chartered land grants and did not incorporate additional lands.[43]

Once the report of the case presented to the lawyers in London was completed, a thirty-seven-page pamphlet was printed in Connecticut which outlined the details of the decision. The pamphlet stated:

> Their Opinion Was given in Favor of the Right and title of the Governor and Company to said Lands—and they directed the Course of Proceedings legal and expedient for the Governor and—Company of Connecticut to pursue to be either amicably and in Concurrence with the Proprietaries of Pennsylvania, or in Cafe of the Refusal of those Proprietaries without them to apply to the King and Council praying his Majesty to appoint Commissioners in America to decide the Question with the usual Power of Appeal.[44]

Wooster displayed a sound grasp of the chartered history of Connecticut, as well as a profound understanding of the land rights of the citizens therein. He wrote an extensive four-page historical defense of the claim of the colony of Connecticut to the lands in dispute with the Penn family. Written on the reverse of a 1773 broadside advertisement from the David Wooster and Co., he constructed a historical time-line listing each of the charters and land patents issued to Connecticut, starting with King James I in 1620. It continued through the land charters of 1631 and 1644, as well as the letter patent incorporating the colony of Connecticut by King Charles II in 1662.[45] Throughout the entire second page of his treatise, Wooster described the boundaries as set forth through the land patent, establishing the colony with reference to lines of latitude and longitude. The remaining two pages described Connecticut's legal claim to this land in the west. Wooster's defense supported Connecticut's land claims, and his understanding of legal matters went unquestioned as he eloquently demonstrated, through the historical record, that the charter and land patents granted to Connecticut did, in fact, grant the land in the Wyoming Valley to the colony. Unfortunately, these claims ultimately resulted in violence between settlers in the Wyoming Valley in the months leading up to the Revolution. It was the alarm bell which sounded from Lexington and Concord in April 1775 that stymied violence in the western lands and refocused colonial armed efforts towards the east coast against Great Britain.

The confusion over the land grants and patents first arose in the years prior to the French and Indian War; lands granted from the king of France overlapped those granted by the king of England. However, there were many potentially violent inter-colonial disputes that centered on charters and land patent irregularities. Many of the original colonies received land patents which claimed lands far beyond their reach. The Susquehanna incident illustrated the division between one American British colony and another, as well as the fiercely independent nature of defending legal chartered claims against an encroaching power, even if that dispute was with a neighboring colony.

Earlier Wooster and seven others undertook a building project to construct the Long Wharf in New Haven. The construction of this massive project helped to grow commerce. The initial expansion did increase the economic activity in New Haven. In 1773 another expansion to the Long Wharf was made. As before, the project was funded by the sale of lottery tickets, and Wooster again led the effort. The lottery was advertised in the *Connecticut Gazette* as was the official lottery drawing done later in the year.[46]

Wooster's mercantile business became his primary concern during this period.

In 1763, his shipping and trade business with London began to import vast goods into Connecticut from all parts of the British Empire, as demonstrated by the January 1, 1773, broadside which advertised:

Just Imported from London, in the Ship Albany,
via New-York, By
David Wooster and Co.
And to be sold Wholesale, As cheap as can be bought in New-York, or Boston,
At the STORE in NEW HAVEN;
A large Assortment of English and India GOODS,
Suitable for all Seasons of the Year; but more particularly for the present.

Wooster's mercantile company imported a variety of items into New Haven, including thirty-four different types of cloth ranging from Irish linens to velvets, cottons, taffaties, and gauzes, to handkerchiefs, ribbons, fur trim, gloves, hose (men and women's stockings), sewing threads and lace, felt hats, shoes and sewing tapes, textile wares such as brass kettles, warming pans, looking glass (mirrors), window glass, German steel, nails, pins and needles, pewter items such as dishes, plates, basons, porringers (small bowls used for oatmeal and cornmeal), quart and pint cups, hard metal teapots, [gun]powder and shot, English sailcloth, Ticklenburgh (a type of coarse material sold in the West Indies), "the best purple Indigo," and a whole host of spices including nutmeg and pepper.[47]

By 1773, the various goods that Wooster's company imported had been subject to a variety of taxes for over ten years. These had been levied through numerous acts of Parliament which attempted to pay down the astronomical national debt, and Wooster did his fair share in providing that taxable revenue. The colonies of Connecticut and Massachusetts, being geographically connected, continued to support one another, especially with the growth of the anti-taxation movement in Boston.

The most harmful act of Parliament in the years following the French and Indian War to the David Wooster and Co. mercantile was the Townshend Duties of 1767. This placed an external tax upon many of the items that he imported for his company. As any businessman knows, if there is an increase in the cost of goods, the owner has two primary choices: first, pay the cost of the increase himself and potentially lose revenue, or second, pass along the cost to the customer by raising the prices of the goods sold, thus absorbing the tax in the new elevated price of the goods being sold, and still run the risk of lost revenue due to decreased sales.

Despite colonial reaction to these acts of Parliament; calling for the Stamp Act Congress in 1766; violence directed towards royal tax collectors by methods such as tarring and feathering, or intimidation as seen with Jared Ingersoll of New Haven; or rioting, Parliament took little action to further incite the heated situation in the American colonies. There appeared to be a lull in Parliamentary actions regarding additional taxes over the next three years. The Boston Massacre in March 1770 increased revolutionary rhetoric in the colonies and reminded everyone of the mounting political and military situation in America. That, too, began to decline from 1770 to 1773. The calm and tranquility, however, were short lived.

In 1773, Parliament passed the controversial Tea Act, which granted a monopoly of the sale of tea in the American colonies to the East India Company, a large,

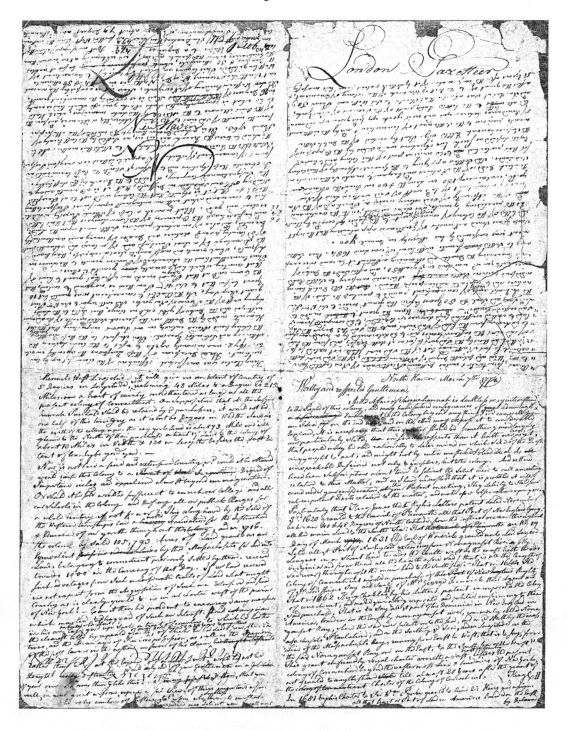

Reverse of the Wooster & Co. broadside which reveals a four-page letter written by David Wooster defending Connecticut's land claims to the Wyoming Valley, known as the Susquehanna Affair (Beinecke Rare Book and Manuscript Library, Yale University Library Collection).

powerful, and extremely influential mercantile company in London. This, in turn, led to the Boston Tea Party in December 1773. As a result of the destruction of the tea shipment in the port of Boston on the night of December 16, Parliament levied a series of acts designed to regain political, economic, and military control over the colonies in New England, especially Boston. Known as the Intolerable Acts, or Coercive Acts, these acts were a clear signal to the New England colonies that the powers in London no longer viewed their American colonies as a co-equal participant in the empire, but rather as rebels to be subjugated. According to some in the colonies, King George III and Parliament had become authoritarian and tyrannical by their actions. By 1774, the Lockean ideals of life, liberty, and property no longer appeared to be protected by the government in London. Members of the Sons of Liberty, as well as colonists writing in the *Connecticut Journal* spoke of attempts to reduce the colonies to the absolute control of Parliament and the king.[48] Relations between England and her American colonies continued to worsen.

In a series of four separate actions the Intolerable Acts did what many eighteenth-century colonial republicans feared. First, the Boston Port Bill official closed the port of Boston until repayment was made to the East India Company for the tea destroyed in December. For any city that relied upon their sea trade and commerce for its livelihood this was devastating. Parliament also sent troops to control the port city of Boston. Second, with the Massachusetts Government Act the legislature in the colony was prohibited to meet. Thirdly, the Administration of Justice Act gave Massachusetts a royal governor and provided British soldiers who were charged with a crime in the colonies the opportunity to be sent to England for a "fair" trial. Lastly, the Quartering Act forced civilians to house and feed the British Regulars now stationed in Massachusetts.

The implementation of the Intolerable Acts, the financial hardships inflicted by the Townsend and Stamp Acts, and the limitations placed upon western settlement forced Wooster to reexamine the political bond which connected the British government and its American subjects. Throughout his life he had remained loyal to the government that protected the inalienable rights of life, liberty, and property. By the 1770s Wooster had become a true republican and his actions demonstrated his ardent zeal for the defense of these principles. He placed the needs of his country above personal self-interest through his continual military service and leadership. Not to overstate his convictions, Wooster realized the necessary connection between the success of both. His involvement in a variety of elected positions which ranged from a member of the Connecticut General Assembly, justice of the peace, and surveyor of highways, exemplified eighteenth-century colonial republicanism in action. Things were dramatically changing, militarily, politically, and economically. The moment soon arrived in which drastic action was required, and Wooster, with all his experience, was prepared for such an event.

Wooster corresponded often with various governors of Connecticut. As a prominent citizen concerned with the betterment of the colony, he found it important to stay connected with those leading the colony on behalf of the crown. He had written to Governor Law in the 1740s, and Governor Pitkin in the 1760s. By the 1770s, Wooster was a well-known figure in New Haven and well connected to leading

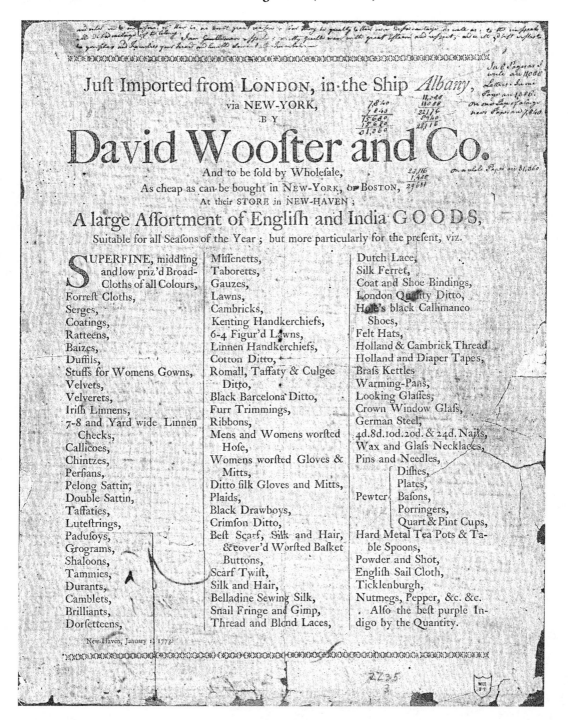

Broadside image of the Wooster & Co. Mercantile, New Haven, Connecticut. This 1773 broadside was also published in the *Connecticut Journal*, announcing the items newly arrived from London (Beinecke Rare Book and Manuscript Library, Yale University Library Collection).

political figures of his day, some through marriage. He remained in close correspondence with the next three colonial governors. His appointment as a justice of peace, first in 1771 and subsequently each year after through 1776, demonstrated his reliability, good judgment, and wisdom that came from years of service and experience.

His judicial responsibilities continued into 1773 as justice of the peace for New Haven County. That year he received petitions for two separate cases. The first submission in May involved Thomas Dowd, a jointer by trade who could not pay his debt. Wooster was on the committee for this case and ordered that, instead of debtors' prison, the majority of Dowd's tools would be seized until his debts were paid.[49] The second case came in October and involved Nathaniel Shaw the New London lighthouse keeper. Shaw had petitioned the general assembly for a stipend from the treasury to assist in the financial burden placed upon him for the maintenance of the lighthouse. His petition was approved.[50]

Wooster was a devoutly religious man, and as mentioned previously, was acquainted with the Rev. Jonathan Edwards, whom he asked to address his unit prior to departing for action in the French and Indian War. His education at Yale furthered his Puritan devotion. He owned several religious books, some voluminous tomes, including one large Bible, one volume of Watt's *Sermons* and one *Journal of Revelation*.[51] In the eighteenth-century books were extremely expensive and owning one, or several, was a sign of one's personal wealth. These books alone would be a symbol of pride for one's family in colonial Connecticut.

The White Haven Society in New Haven experienced a decline in membership in the 1770s. Their first building was constructed in 1744, and in 1764 they had built a much larger meeting hall. As with most religious denominations that begin by breaking away from a more established structure, the White Haven Society was not exempt from decline. In 1773, Wooster signed off on a ledger account for the White Haven Society for items to be paid for by the society. Oak planking was one item listed, which was used for repairs of the meeting hall, and other enumerated items included payments to members of the society for services rendered. The ledger accounts were approved for the 1772–1773 fiscal year and signed by David Wooster.[52] He remained a member of the White Haven Society for the rest of his life.

Wooster was a man of diverse interests grounded in republican principles, including the rights to life and equality. He received a noteworthy letter of correspondence in the fall of 1773 from Phillis Wheatley. Wheatley, a former enslaved woman, was a famous poet in colonial America, whose first volume of poetry was published in England in 1773. Her letter to Wooster indicated a level of familiarity between the two. Wheatley wrote to Wooster from Boston on October 18, 1773, and recounted her recent travels to England, noted the many prominent citizens she met there, recounted her freedom gained from her master upon her return, and pressed Wooster with an important request regarding her soon-to-be published first work of poetry. The letter demonstrated a sense a familiarity which was solidified upon his death in 1777.[53]

Wheatley described in her letter to Wooster the challenges she faced as a newly freed black woman in Boston, as well as the difficulties of publishing a work of poetry while preventing other printers from illegally making their own copies. This was a time when copyright laws did not apply and without them the author was not guaranteed any type of income from their work. There is no record of a reply to Wheatley from Wooster; however, it is a fair assessment to state that their association was well founded. Wheatley wrote a lengthy letter to Mary Wooster in July 1778, expressing her sincere condolences for the loss of Wooster following his death at the Battle of Ridgefield in 1777. Included in this letter to Mary Wooster was a three-stanza eulogy poem entitled "On the Death of General Wooster." The closing remarks of the letter addressed the books he had in his possession that remained unsold, and Wheatly mentioned that she would like to retrieve them at the earliest convenience and sell them herself.

Additional legal and familial duties required his attention in 1773. His son Thomas had gotten into financial straits in England in 1773 and had been arrested. An account of his situation was presented by Roger Lamb, a former sergeant in the Royal Welsch Fusiliers and stationed in America during the Revolution. Lamb recalled that Thomas Wooster was completing his education in England and:

> When the American troubles broke out, he came over to Ireland, and the rupture between the two countries preventing the regularity of his remittances from America, his circumstances became, from youthful extravagances, much involved, until at last he was arrested, and thrown into the Four Courts Marshalsea. All the letters and remittances from his father being of course intercepted by the British government, the young man remained in confinement, until general Wooster, through another channel, sent him money to pay his debts, the remainder of which enabled him, (thought contrary to his father's commands) to leave the country. The general, fearful of the issue of the American struggle, had positively enjoined young Wooster to remain in England until the war was terminated. This injunction however he disobeyed; as soon as he gained the American shore, actually joined the part of the continental army which his father commanded.[54]

For Thomas to be released his debt had to be paid, which amounted to a bond of £814..13..7.. (814 pounds, 13 shillings, 7 pence).[55] Raising the revenue cost David Wooster a great amount of his personal wealth, which fell short of the needed amount. To provide the remainder he relied upon the colony of Connecticut to secure a loan. Wooster found it necessary to sell most of his land holdings in New York. In April 1773, he sold several plots to John Gilbert of New Haven, which helped recuperate some of the financial loss that he incurred to gain his son's release.[56] Due to his son's confinement Wooster was unable to attend the May 1773 election. The only important item that he mentioned to John Lawrance, treasurer of Connecticut, was in regards to the Naval Office post which he held, in which he provided "the true State of the Revenue at present, but I done expect it will be Collected without the assistance of the attornies, as Paying Duties Don't Seem to be a pleasant thing to the Tribe of Zebulon."[57] A meeting was arranged at Hartford with Lawrance the following week to go over the financial accounts.

Wooster's economic situation, due to years of levied taxes, had been greatly reduced. Ownership of land was paramount to his success and being forced to liquidate property to raise the necessary funds for his son's release was a hard blow. He was unable to raise the amount required for the bond, and in 1774 petitioned the Connecticut General Assembly for a loan of the said amount. In the petition he referenced the "misfortune in trade" due to the acts of Parliament as well as the "confinement of his son." Following the approval of the loan from the Connecticut treasury he orchestrated the payment of his son's debt and procured release from prison.

His debt plagued him. Although the loan from the colony of Connecticut allowed him to balance his finances, both for his family and for his mercantile business, the renewed taxes of Parliament placed new financial straits upon him. As the loan came due, Wooster requested an extension and provided security in real estate. He was granted a two-year extension for repayment. Three men were appointed by the Assembly to receive the said real estate from Wooster until the loan of £ 814..13..7 was repaid in full.[58]

Upon the eve of the passage of the Intolerable Acts in 1774, the Secretary of State to his Majesty King George III sent a list of questions to the various governors in the American colonies, and in turn the governors asked various leaders in their respective colonies to reply to the queries. The crown sought information on the economic condition of the colonies, their imports, and exports, as well as domestic manufacturing. As a leading merchant in New Haven, Wooster was asked by Governor Trumbull to reply. His response to seven of the questions remains.[59] Those that he addressed pertained directly to the development and growth of the harbor of New Haven and the economic importance of the shipping industry.

Wooster's responses to the queries posted provided an invaluable analysis of New Haven in 1774, as well as an insight to his status in Connecticut as one whose opinion was sought after and valued. They also construct a clear image of the items imported and exported from the town, and the importance of inter-colonial trade with port cities such as New York and Boston. At the same time, Wooster was appointed as justice of the peace for the county of New Haven. By 1774, he had held this position of esteem and authority for three years and would continue until his death in 1777.

The political atmosphere in New Haven was highly charged in 1774, and on June 20 the town electorate voted in favor of a general congress to be called to discuss a response to the Intolerable Acts enforced earlier that year. The town selectmen voted "That a General Congress is desired as soon as it may be, and that a general annual Congress would have a great tendency to promote the welfare and happiness of all the American Colonies."[60] Not long afterward, the First Continental Congress was called. Delegates from several of the colonies attended the congress held in Philadelphia. Chosen to represent the colony of Connecticut were Silas Deane, Eliphalet Dyer and Roger Sherman.

In the fall of 1774, Connecticut began to make the necessary provisions to prepare for war. The general assembly voted to secure powder and shot, procure necessary cannon carriages, and reinvigorated the militia, the trainband, and required appropriate drill and muster of the militia in the various towns. A fee was levied if anyone of proper age did not respond to militia drill. The lower house of the legislature drafted an eleven-point petition which stated their allegiance to the king, yet also stated "That it is an indispensible duty which we owe to our King, our country, ourselves and our posterity, by all lawful ways and means in our power, to maintain, defend and preserve these our rights and liberties, and to transmit them entire and inviolate to the latest generations; and that it is our fixed, determined and unalterable resolution faithfully to discharge this our duty."[61] The upper house unanimously approved the resolution and voted to have numerous copies printed and distributed throughout the colony.

Connecticut veterans of the French and Indian War knew of one place in which weapons could be procured for the defense of their colony: Fort Ticonderoga. Wooster had led troops in the region around Lake George throughout much of the war and in the fall of 1774, along with Silas Deane, Samuel Wyllys, and Mr. Parsons, planned a possible attack upon the British held fort. According to historian Charles H. Levermore, "These gentlemen, and others, borrowed upon their own security the necessary funds from the Colonial Treasury. They dispatched a scout to investigate the feasibility of the undertaking, and were, in short, responsible for the risk and the success of the enterprise."[62]

It is fitting to conclude this section of Wooster's life again referring to eighteenth-century republicanism. The Rev. David Brooks prepared a sermon, and "at the request of his kinsman, Gen. David Wooster" delivered it in Derby, Connecticut, in 1774. The sermon entitled "The Religion of the Revolution" encapsulated the depth to which Lockean ideology had rooted itself in the very fabric of Connecticut. Brooks prefaced the sermon by clarifying that "the very notion of oppression and injustice supposes that men have some rights which they have a title to." He then referenced the major points concerning these rights, for example "What these Rights are," "How they are infringed upon of the manner of Oppression," and finally to "Make good the assertion that Better is a letter with Righteousness, than great Revenues without Right." He went on to say that men have a right to life, as in a state of nature. Second was the right to liberty, in which he commented that "liberty gives us the right to conduct as we choose, and to dispose of our property by our own free and voluntary consent. Is it consonant with reason, that a superior force should dictate my understanding, and prescribe rules for me to walk by, enforced by the penalties of stripes, imprisonment, death, or whatever they see fit?"[63] Third, the right to property. Fourth listed the right "by nature ... to deeds of kindness and benevolence." Lastly was, according to Brooks, the right to fairness and truth. He then spoke to the core of republicanism:

Those rights that belong to mankind by compact are various as the forms of government under which they are included. To point out all the rights that belong to every form of government, would require more time, and an abler pen than my own. I shall therefore point out one or two that belong to our civil Constitution, and proceed to the other heads of this discourse. And

First: We have a right to choose our Legislative body. We have this right as well as favor that our Governors are of ourselves, and that our rulers proceed from the midst of us.

Second: We have a right to tax ourselves, and consult our own abilities in it, and the most equitable, equal, and proper method to impose and collect taxes to defray the public charges.

Third: We have a right to make our own laws.

Fourth: We have a right to be tried in cases that touch both life and property, by our own peers of the vicinage.

Fifth: We have a right to a full and fair trial with our wit- nesses and proofs, and no one can be condemned unquestioned and unheard.

Sixth: We have a right to lands, tenements, &c. In fine, we have the plighted faith of kings to secure these rights inviolable.[64]

Throughout the sermon Brooks highlighted key republican elements that Wooster and those in Connecticut, as well as the adjacent New England colonies, espoused. These ideas emerged into an American identity. To solidify that identity, the individual right to property had to be protected. Brooks addressed the right to be secure in private property:

by which we have a just claim to our estates; and for any but a superior force to impose taxes on, or take them from us without our consent, is a practical declaration that we have no title to them, and it is a flagrant violation of this right which the God of Nature has put into our hands.[65]

Consent of the governed, that establish Lockean idea, had certainly taken roots in the colony of Connecticut on the eve of the Revolution. Wooster wrote on it, as did his contemporaries. The abuse of political authority—tyranny—was a real threat to liberty. This abuse not only applied to the king and Parliament, but it also extended to the jurisdiction of the court as well. Further in the same sermon, Brooks espoused the fear of the looming encroachment of government upon the rights, liberty, and property of those in the British North American colonies, especially Connecticut:

But if that Court may impose rates and duties, and bind us in all cases whatever, without our consent, then what right have we to property, or the disposal of it? It cannot be true that we have liberty and a sole right to our property, and yet at the same time others have a right to seize it for the selfish purpose of enriching and aggrandizing themselves.

Therefore, the aforesaid acts of the British Parliament are not only unjust, but a direct infringement upon our right to property. Our native right to benevolence and kindness shares the same unhappy fate. Can you, my hearers, once imagine it to be the genuine and hearty expression of kindness and benevolence to blockade our ports, deprive us in many cases of trial by jury, indemnify those who (as the affair might happen,) should murder us, and openly violate these three sacred and native rights, Life, Liberty,—and Property?[66]

Political gatherings began to increase in the 1770s. Fiery debates ensued over what the colonies saw as flagrant violations of their rights as Englishmen. Towards the conclusion of the sermon, he queried "To what part of the world have humanity and justice fled, when it is judged in the mother country illegal for the Colonists to unite in preferring remonstrances and memorials to his Majesty on account of our violated rights?"[67]

If one document, one sermon, could combine and contain all that Wooster thought and believed it would be *The Religion of the Revolution*. This sermon, delivered by his second cousin, addressed the many layers of eighteenth-century American political thought that continued to prove to those who were devoted to republican ideology that they were the true defenders of liberty and that Parliament had truly become tyrannical and oppressive in their governance and greed.

There has been a search for a singular event that could pinpoint that one defining moment that altered the personal loyalty and allegiance of colonists in America from the French and Indian War to the start of the Revolution. There were those who aligned with the American cause for personal financial gain. Some participated for political motives. Some were pulled in by public mob frenzy and outcry after the

Stamp Act or the Intolerable Acts. Still others were for independence from the very beginning.

What about David Wooster? How did someone with such a solid, devoted connection to king and country become the ranking major general of the Connecticut militia, and the third highest ranking brigadier general in the newly formed Continental Army in the summer of 1775? To some this may appear as a dramatic shift, perhaps even as a contradiction to the very essence of loyalty. As previously stated, loyalty takes many forms. It is easier to declare loyalty when personal wellbeing and material possessions are secured and not at risk of loss. It becomes much more difficult when they are seized, and personal liberty and freedom are denied. Wooster's loyalty was to an ideal that had been instilled in him and had developed his entire life. Loyalty to him encapsulated the essential notions of the right to life, liberty, and property. To him loyalty was given to his home colony of Connecticut. Loyalty was also given to king and country provided that the political body defended these natural rights. What caused Wooster to risk everything; land given in the service of the King; his position as the captain of the 51st Regiment of Foot with half-pay for life; his mercantile business; his political involvement in Connecticut; and the economic stability of his family? Simply put, his understanding of the republican ideals of representative government, and the rights of Englishmen to enjoy life, liberty, and personal property. To these Wooster held great loyalty. To him upholding the honor of republican idealism was the "religion of the revolution." By the end of 1774 his ideology, devotion, and leadership were put to the ultimate test as the great military conflict with Great Britain appeared inevitable.

6

Wooster's Involvement
in the Revolutionary War 1775

By 1775, the economic and military foreign policy of Great Britain had created a fissure within the empire which led to armed, open rebellion within her North American colonies. David Wooster had been greatly impacted by these ever-changing policies, as the analysis of the previous chapters demonstrates. Those who favored rebellion in 1775 did not anticipate a lengthy, drawn-out war that would eventually result in the American colonies declaring political independence from Great Britain. Certainly, some colonists did seek a new independent nation, but many simply looked to reclaim their liberty as Englishmen in America, which they believed had been taken from them. Republicanism and liberty did not necessarily equate independence.

Armed conflict between Great Britain and her New England colonies was inevitable by the spring of 1775. Wooster had seen the storm of conflict building over the past ten years and, despite his advanced age of sixty-five, was prepared; economically, militarily, and politically. He was the oldest general in the American army, twenty-two years older than George Washington and thirty-one years older than Benedict Arnold. He retained an aged wisdom built upon years of experience that few brought to the Revolution.

Despite his previous military experience, however, Wooster was at the point in life when most would have retired from active military service. Also, his previous positions within the army were of lower rank and he commanded smaller forces. Wooster expressed great interest and enthusiasm to continue to serve in the upcoming rebellion and lead troops in the field. However, that did not take into account his advanced age, his physical condition, or his growing impatience towards those younger officers who served with him during the war. There is no indication of ailment, or reduction in mental capacity in the historic record. Despite the physical challenges which accompany lengthy military service, his focus on the execution of his duty and his loyalty to defend liberty never wavered regardless of who he followed, or who he led.

The beginning of his education in the art of war started at the siege of Louisburg in 1745 and was forged in the fire of the French and Indian War eleven years later. His entrepreneurship in the years preceding the Revolution further developed his ability to traverse economic uncertainty, which would help in supplying and paying his troops in desperate situations. His loyalty never wavered. To Wooster and many others, it was Parliament that had strayed from the protection of the rights to life, liberty, and property, and the securing of these rights of Englishmen became the primary goal of American patriots.

On April 26, 1775, the general assembly of the colony of Connecticut began the process of raising six regiments as well as appointing appropriate officers to lead them. This was done almost two months prior to the Continental Congress creating the military structure for the Continental Army:

> This Assembly do appoint the persons hereafter named to the respective offices, to take the command of the inhabitants to be enlisted and assembled for the special defense and safety of this Colony, to lead and conduct them as the General Assembly shall order, and his Honour the Governor is desired, and he is herby authorized and empowered, to give Commissions according to the form provided and ordered for each respective Officer, according to his office and rank, and Warrents to such as are appointed in the Staff, viz:
> This Assembly do appoint David Wooster, Esquire, to be Major General.
> Joseph Spencer, Esquire, to be Brigadier General.
> Israel Putnam, Esquire, to be Second Brigadier General.
> First Company in the First Regiment.—Major General David Wooster, Esquire, to be Colonel of the First Regiment, and Captain.[1]

In the meantime, the legislative assembly of Connecticut watched the events unfolding in Massachusetts. At their April session they appointed Wooster as the first major general of Connecticut troops, placing him in charge of six newly raised regiments for the defense of the colony. Samuel Lockwood was appointed his secretary and remained with Wooster until the general returned from the Canadian campaign in May the following year. Both William Douglas and Samuel Blagden served as aides-de-camp to Wooster.[2] Joseph Spencer and Israel Putnam were also appointed brigadier generals. These were positions within the colony of Connecticut, as the Continental Army had not yet been formed. These three men were the senior military leaders for the colony in 1775. Each of them carried similar regimental flags into battle, with the armorial seal of Connecticut on one side, and the motto of Massachusetts "An Appeal to Heaven" on the opposite. Wooster's flag for the 1st Regiment of Connecticut Militia was made of yellow material with the seal and motto painted on.[3] The placement of the motto of Massachusetts on the Connecticut battle flags indicated just how significant the connection was between the two. Massachusetts and Connecticut had forged a tight-knit bond from years of economic hardship, as well as decades of military cooperation, with Indian wars on the frontier, the siege of Louisbourg, and the challenges of the French and Indian War. This type of cooperation did not exist between Connecticut and New York, her neighbor to the west.

In the spring of 1775, final plans were made for the reduction and capture of Canada. Wooster found his prior military experience to be of great benefit as he helped to plan the capture of Fort Ticonderoga and the military stores held there.[4] The post had been in British hands since 1759, following Amherst's successful reduction of the fort during the French and Indian War. Wooster knew of its key strategic location as well as the number of arms and ammunition stored there. Taking Fort Ticonderoga would be no small feat. The growing insurrection in the Dominion of

New England led to open hostilities following the Battles of Lexington and Concord on April 19. The initial planning to capture Ticonderoga began in Connecticut in the fall of 1774, and Wooster was present.[5] With the aggression against the colonists in Massachusetts, and the closure of the port of Boston the year earlier, it was decided that seizing the fort in the New York highlands would level the military playing field in New England. Wooster's experience in the British army as a provincial officer at Ticonderoga made his presence a logical choice when planning for the assault upon the fort. Along with several other leading men of New Haven he assisted in raising funds to pay for the expedition.

Benedict Arnold had burst upon the scene in April as word reached New Haven of the battle at Lexington and Concord. The general assembly was in session when news of the actions reached the town. The Committee of Safety was meeting as well. Arnold, who was the commander of the "Governor's Guards" had also heard of the battle and formed his volunteer company to respond to the emergency:

> Mr. Benedict Arnold of New Haven, had been chosen captain of a volunteer company, by the inhabitants, when they began to prepare for whatever might happen. No sooner did the Lexington news reach him, than he called his company together, and asked them whether they would march off with him the next morning for the neighbourhood of Boston, distant 150 miles.—They agreed; and at the proper time paraded before the tavern where 'a committee was fitting. He applied to the gentlemen for powder and ball; they demurred suplying him, as he was not duly authorized. The captain, in haste to fly to the help of his suffering brethren, proposed procuring the supply by force if needful, to which the volunteers consented. He then sent to the committee, and informed them what he was determined upon. Colonel Wooster came out, and would have persuaded him to wait till he had received proper orders; to which capt. Arnold answered, "None but God Almighty shall prevent my marching." The committee perceiving his fixed resolution, supplied him; and he marched off instantly, and with his company reached the American head-quarters by the 29th of April.[6]

By 1831, this original story had been embellished, as seen in J.W. Barber's *History and Antiquities of New Haven*:

> Being in want of ammunition, Arnold requested the Town Authorities to furnish the company, which they refused to do. The next day, immediately before they started, Arnold marched his company to the house where the selectmen were sitting, and after forming them in front of the building, sent in word that if the keys of the powder house were not delivered up to him in five minutes, he would order the company to break it open and furnish themselves.[7]

Wooster was not mentioned in this narrative of New Haven history until 1855 in *The History of Connecticut from the first Settlers of the Colony to the Adoption of the Present Constitution* written by G.H. Hollister. In that work "Colonel Wooster went out and endeavored to persuade him [Arnold] to wait for proper orders, before starting for the scene of conflict."[8]

With the expedition against Ticonderoga planned, the command was given to Connecticut native, Colonel Ethan Allen. Allen was joined enroute by Benedict Arnold, who had taken the "Governor's Guards" to Boston in late April. Despite Arnold's attempt he was unable to take command of the expedition, which remained under Ethan Allen. Even though Wooster did not lead troops to take Ticonderoga his strategic plan allowed for the successful capture of the fort. Ticonderoga was taken by Allen, his "Green Mountain Boys," and Arnold's troops on May 10, 1775. The Americans now had their first clearly planned and successfully executed military victory. Without the initial success of the various militia units on April 19 which forced the British to retreat to Boston, the capture of Fort Ticonderoga would not have taken place, at least not in the spring of 1775. Wooster and those who worked with him starting in the fall of 1774 had planned and orchestrated a bold move which had been based upon solid military experience. The Continental Congress ordered that everything be cataloged at Fort Ticonderoga, so that all the equipment could be restored once the conflict had been resolved. They, too, did not anticipate a lengthy conflict. The items from Ticonderoga were never returned.

As with previous colonial wars, daily life continued in New Haven as best as could be expected throughout the Revolution. The general assembly met in May and, again, elected Wooster as a justice of the peace for New Haven County. However, an additional committee was formed that would oversee future military planning for the colony when the general assembly was not in session, called the Committee of Safety and War. Before they adjourned the assembly provided Wooster with £ 4 pounds sterling to pay for a military secretary in camp.[9]

Similar to the French and Indian War, Wooster asked that prayers be delivered for him and his men prior to their departure. Deacon Nathan Beers, a soldier in the Revolution, remarked years afterwards of seeing General Wooster march off to the service of his country. In his recollection Beers commented that

> the last time I saw General Wooster was in June 1775. He was at the head of his regiment, which was then embodied on the Green, in front of where the centre church now stands. They were ready for a march, with their arms glittering, and their knapsacks on their backs. Colonel Wooster had already dispatched a messenger for his minister, the Rev. Jonathan Edwards, with a request that he would meet the regiment and pray with them before their departure. He then conducted his men in military order into the meeting house, and seated himself in his own pew, awaiting the return of the messenger. He was speedily informed that the clergyman was absent from home. Colonel Wooster immediately stepped into the deacon's seat in front of the pulpit, and calling his men to attend to prayers, offered up a humble petition for his beloved country, for himself, the men under his immediate command, and for the success of the cause in which they were engaged. His prayers were offered with the fervent zeal of an apostle, and in such pathetic language, that it drew tears from many an eye, and affected many a heart. When he had closed, he left the house with his men in the same order they had entered it, and the regiment took up its line of march for New York. With such a prayer on his lips he entered the Revolution.[10]

A sermon was also delivered to his troops, extolling the honor and virtue of the endeavor upon which they were to embark. The anonymous sermon was reprinted as a broadside that could have been posted throughout Connecticut. The rhetoric exudes the spirit and "religion of the revolution" as delivered in 1774. This was printed in a poetic fashion and extolled Wooster and his men marching off to defend liberty against the tyrant King. "But Frederick's son now fills the British throne, Who seeks to make our property his own; Imposing taxes with tyrannie sway..." "Heroic leader! General of the field! Intrepid WOOSTER! May you never yield ... we know your military skill, Your martial courage, and heroic zeal, Your firm attachment to your country's cause, Your great abhorrence of tyrannic laws; May heaven protect you."[11] Such was the tone and enthusiasm of those who supported and encouraged their brethren into the fray in the early months of the conflict.

The military fervor that spread throughout New England in the spring of 1775 necessitated the calling of a collaborative inter-colonial assembly. The First Continental Congress had met briefly in the fall the year prior and by late spring the Second Continental Congress was to convene. However, it was not set to convene in Philadelphia until May. In the meantime, the colonies had to act independently, as they had always done, for their own defense and protection. It is important to note that each separate colony had an established military structure of its own, with appointed military commanders, specific manuals-of-arms used for the training of officers and men, a set scheduled routine for military drill, and the necessary stores of powder and shot, and in some cases the ability to produce such on their own. The colonies had also become politically self-sufficient.

The establishment of the Continental Congress in 1775 drew together representatives from all thirteen colonies. Their overall goal throughout 1775 was to create a governing body which all the colonies would adhere, be equally represented in, and work collaboratively in concert with one another. In addition to this, and for the military success of the Revolution, albeit in its infantile stage, the Continental Congress needed to create a large colonial military force. No such thing existed prior to 1775, and there were few with notable military experience or training to lead the new Continental Army. This would be a much more difficult task to complete as colonial rivalries, egos, and age, most certainly inhibited the success of this newly formed Continental Army. To accomplish the task of creating a unified front, each colony would need to relinquish some autonomy, both politically and militarily, to ensure the success of the common cause. In the same token, to maintain the delicate balance of power, the Congress could not afford to offend or reject input provided by the individual colonies. Without them the Congress could not exist, and financial support from the colonies was an absolute necessity for the Continental Congress, and the Continental Army, to survive.

The uncertainty as to who oversaw colonial military forces in America was evident in June 1775. Wooster's troops, and his initial military commission, were from Connecticut. Therefore, he only answered to the Connecticut General Assembly, the Connecticut Committee of Safety and War, and Governor Trumbull. Was he also responsible for assisting the neighboring colonies, like New York? If so, whose authority was he under? Did he answer only to the newly formed Continental Congress in Philadelphia? Only time would provide answers to these questions. Simply because the colonies had called for and convened the Second Continental Congress did not guarantee its success, nor did it precipitate immediate and well-grounded allegiance from the thirteen separate colonies, and it certainly did not alleviate the growing uncertainty within the military structure of the various militias called for service.

Military preparedness had been underway by the general assembly of Connecticut for decades. By 1775, the newly formed Committee of Safety and War began issuing orders to Wooster regarding the deployment of his troops. On June 20, he was ordered to send two companies to New London and march with his remaining seven regiments, and all of those under Colonel Waterbury, to positions within five miles of New York. Additionally, he was to serve under the direction of the General and Provincial Congress of New York until further ordered.[12] Orders such as these demonstrated the origin of colonial military confusion and animosity. Wooster was commissioned as a major general of the Connecticut Militia and thus under the direction of the Connecticut General Assembly. But, as the orders state from June 20, he was also under the direction of the Continental Congress, as well as the New York assembly. This caused tremendous confusion and frustration with its lack of clarity and direction. From June 14 to the June 20, Wooster received fourteen different orders that required him and his men to defend New York City, prevent livestock on Long Island from being stolen, send troops to support the forces stationed around Boston, and securing any Tory or spy within New York. All this while also preparing for an arrival of several British troop transports that were bringing troops from Ireland to invade New York.[13] There were even more orders throughout July and August.

On June 15, amidst the series of letters to the New York Assembly, Wooster wrote to Connecticut Governor Jonathan Trumbull to inform him of a loyalist, Angus McDonald, who was captured and sent to Wooster's camp as a prisoner. McDonald had raised forty-three troops in New York against the colonies. Wooster also informed Trumbull of the expected arrival of the four regiments from Ireland. As military stores were very valuable, the most significant portion of this letter described a store house at Turtle Bay which had "fallen into our [Wooster's] hands." In this store house Wooster reported capturing "about five hundred good horse harnesses, a very considerable number of thirteen and ten-inch carcasses, cohorns, and stinkpots, all well charged; a very great plenty of grape-shot; cannon ball, from twenty-four pounders down to three, &c."[14] Military supplies which belonged to the king during this time of open rebellion were considered spoils of war. With continued shortages, military equipment became increasingly valuable and harder to come by. Not only were weapons highly valued, but equipment and food items also became scarce commodities.

Further confusion became apparent in a letter from Wooster to Trumbull concerning the possible arrival of the troops from Ireland. He was uncertain if he should oppose their landing since the Continental Congress had not yet officially created an army, nor was there any formal declaration of war, or any proposal for independence. It was Wooster's opinion that "they ought not to be suffered to land."[15]

In another letter addressed to Trumbull, Wooster indicated that the troops under his command had been divided up; some sent to Ticonderoga, some to Boston, others were in New Haven, some to Greenwich, and still more to New York.[16] These orders arrived from the New York Assembly, Trumbull, and the Continental Congress.[17] Despite this military tug-of-war, Wooster continued to write in the affirmative regarding his devotion to his duty as well as his country. The New York Assembly wrote to him and expressed their gratitude for his "high sense of the readiness which you shew to assist our Colony. That honest zeal which inspirits the bosoms of our countrymen in Connecticut commands our admiration and praise."[18]

The day before Wooster was ordered to Greenwich, Connecticut, which is located near New York, the Continental Congress in Philadelphia appointed George Washington to command the Continental Army in the hopes that by selecting a Virginian to lead the newly formed army, other southern colonies would eagerly join in the Revolution, which up to now had been centered around Boston. Washington, a delegate to the Second Continental Congress from Virginia, retained valuable experience serving alongside British officers in the French and Indian War. He, like Wooster, valued the importance of a well-trained and disciplined army. At the age of forty-three, Washington brought a vigor and vitality to military leadership that older officers lacked. His athleticism and equestrian skills were well known and revered among his peers, and his analytical skills provided a calm thoughtfulness that was greatly needed to lead the military which was gathered from the various American colonies. Not only did the Continental Congress hope to unify the colonies in political action, but they also anticipated a collective military effort. Would a Virginian be able to lead New England troops in what was up to that point a New England fight? There was a great necessity to establish a solid officer corps for the new Continental Army and this required the appointment of officers from all the colonies. Two days later Wooster's continental commission as brigadier general was approved.

Sergeant Roger Lamb provided a unique British perspective on the organization of the Continental Army. He wrote that "the congress ... determined likewise to call forth into action the greatest military talents which American could furnish.... More than one third of the soldiers in the American ranks had formerly been in the British service; and were indefatigable in training the raw recruits to the use of arms." He further reported that upon gaining the rank of major general in Connecticut, Wooster was "immediately struck off the half-pay list" of the 51st Regiment of Foot.[19] Regarding those, like Wooster, who were employed in the active service of Great Britain in 1775 Lamb noted:

> It was an unhappy circumstance for England, that some of the bravest and most experienced officers in her pay, then residing in America, turned against her and supported the insurrection. To this, perhaps, much more than to any other cause, was America indebted for her ultimate success. This was precisely the case with regard to general Wooster.[20]

On June 22, 1775, the Congress created a military structure similar to the British army. There was one commander-in-chief of the army, George Washington. Horatio Gates became adjutant general. Four men were appointed as major generals; Artemas Ward, Charles Lee, Philip Schuyler, and Israel Putnam, and seven were made brigadier generals; Seth Pomeroy, Richard Montgomery, David Wooster, William Heath, Joseph Spencer, John Thomas, and Nathaniel Greene.[21] Within the newly created Continental Army structure three officers were from Connecticut: Wooster, Spencer, and Putnam. Wooster outranked them in the Connecticut militia, but not, however, in the new Continental Army. He was placed in charge of the 1st Regiment of Continental troops, yet his rank with the newly established Continental Army amounted to a demotion for him.[22] Wooster's new commission to the rank of brigadier-general of the Continental Army conflicted with his commission of major general of Connecticut militia. For Wooster there was a certainty, and a stability, within the colonial military structure of Connecticut. The new Continental Army was neither well supplied, fully officered, nor funded. Most significantly, in June 1775, there were no troops to command in the field.

Within the 1st Continental Regiment, Wooster's friend, the Rev. Benjamin Trumbull, served as the regimental chaplain. Wooster himself was listed as colonel of the regiment and captain of the first company in the regiment.[23] The best commanders surround themselves with excellent leaders, and Wooster's selection of military secretaries and aides-de-camps were from the best graduates of Yale College. Peter Colt, military secretary to General Wooster, graduated from Yale in 1764, Samuel Lockwood, military secretary, graduated in 1766, Mark Levenworth, adjutant general to Wooster, graduated in 1771, Stephen Row Bradley, who became his aide-de-camp in 1777, graduated in 1775, and lastly, his own son, Thomas Wooster, graduated from Yale in 1768, served his father as aide-de-camp in 1777.[24]

Tensions rose when, despite Connecticut's requests to the Continental Congress for equal placement of their colony's officer corps within the newly formed Continental Army, David Wooster, Connecticut's only major general and oldest officer, was given a commission in the new command structure below that of his Connecticut rank. As younger officers were needed for service in the field, the Continental Congress sought those men who could withstand the vigor of field command. At sixty-five, Wooster was far removed from the boundaries of youthful vitality that the Congress favored with their commissions. The Connecticut delegation wrote to Governor Trumbull that "we hope that his Appointment [Israel Putnam] will give no umbrage to General Wooster or General Spencer as they are honorably provided for."[25] To the delegation, offering Wooster the position of brigadier general considering his advanced age, should be viewed as an honor, not a criticism of his previous service. Despite this slight, Wooster remained in the service of both the colony of Connecticut and the Continental Congress.

The Continental Congress had to some extent created a fire-storm due to their military appointments. Knowing that Wooster had been commissioned as a lower ranking officer by the Continental Congress, the Connecticut legislature wrote to Trumbull on July 5 requesting that he

> write to the honorable Continental Congress, and acquaint them with the estimation in which General Wooster and General Spencer are held by this Assembly, and the Officers and troops under their command; of their concern that they have been so far overlooked in the appointment of General Officers by them, and of the probable inconveniences that may ensure; at the same time testifying their sense of the singular merit of Gen' Putnam, and requesting them, if practicable, to devise some method of obviating the difficulties apprehended.[26]

The lower house of the Connecticut legislature altered the letter to the governor by requesting that he write to the Connecticut delegation to the Continental Congress instead of the Congress itself.

Delegates of the Second Continental Congress had taken some "liberties" when they created the military structure for the newly formed Continental Army in June 1775. Wooster was the only major general from any colony to not retain his same rank in the Continental Army command structure. Although only eight years younger than Wooster, due to his successful action in the French and Indian War, serving in Roger's Rangers and leading during Pontiac's Rebellion, and his actions near Boston earlier in 1775, Connecticut's Israel Putman was given a higher rank than either Wooster or General Joseph Spencer. Spencer was outraged and left the camp to return to Connecticut. Wooster was disgusted by the sleight of hand of the Congress, complained openly, yet remained in camp and accepted his Continental rank as a brigadier general. In a letter from John Adams to James Warren, July 23, 1775, Adams commented on this uneasy situation caused by the Congress:

> But, in the Case of the Connecticut officers, We [the Congress] took a Liberty to alter the Rank established by the Colony, and by that Means made much Uneasiness: so that We were sure to do Mischief whether We conformed or deviated from Colony Arrangements. I rejoice that Thomas [John Thomas of Massachusetts], had more Wisdom than Spencer or Wooster [Wooster], and that he did not leave the Camp, nor talk imprudently, if he had We should have lost him from the Continental service: for I assure you, Spencer, by going off, and Wooster [Wooster] by unguarded Speeches have given high offence here.[27]

On June 23, after the Congress created the officer corps for the new Continental Army, Roger Sherman wrote to Wooster to inform him of the newly created positions. The selection was by ballot, as Sherman noted to Wooster. Sherman, one of the most influential politicians from Connecticut, was a good friend and supporter of Wooster. He had attempted to secure the rank of major general for Wooster in the Congress but was unsuccessful. In his letter, Sherman attempted to calm any agitation that had arisen from the diminution of Wooster's rank.[28]

Despite the necessity of express riders, news still traveled slowly during the war. An express reached Wooster on June 25 with news of the Battle at Bunker's Hill which had taken place on June 17. The report was written on the twenty-second, giving three days to reach Wooster who was stationed in Greenwich.[29]

Wooster received his official commission from General George Washington who, while enroute to Boston, visited Wooster at La Rochelle in New York on June 27. General Schuyler traveled with the new commander-in-chief from Philadelphia to New York City where Schuyler then took command of the Northern Department. Washington personally delivered the commission prior to taking command of the Continental forces, rather than having it sent by express. This was the first encounter between Wooster and the new commander-in-chief of the Continental Army. Unfortunately, there is no documentation from Wooster on this meeting aside from the receipt of his commission.

Washington had written to the Congress two days earlier expressing his concern about the condition of Wooster's troops: "How they [the troops] are provided for in General Wooster's camp I have not been able yet to learn."[30] The two generals corresponded throughout the next several months, although their letters were less than cordial. This was due in large part to Washington's opinion towards New Englanders prior to taking command of the army. New England Puritan ideas of republicanism and liberty were more openly pronounced than similar notions in the southern colonies. Although Washington had visited New Haven prior to the outbreak of the war, his experience with New England provincial regiments was somewhat limited. Upon his arrival at Cambridge to take command of the army, he witnessed a most unprofessional assortment of armed citizens attempting to pass for soldiers. Order and discipline were greatly needed if the rabble was to be turned into a fighting force. It took Washington quite some time to understand and appreciate the New England soldiers and their commanders.[31]

While Washington was meeting with Wooster in New York, Justus Bellamy, a soldier in Wooster's regiment, brought a captured British officer to headquarters. Wooster trusted Bellamy with hazardous missions and had requested Bellamy to select six of his comrades and move north of New York with all speed and capture British General Skene who was heading to Canada. Bellamy and his squad apprehended Skene, secured him in his own carriage, and escorted him to headquarters. According to Bellamy, "General Wooster and General Washington complimented us highly for our exploit in taking so important a prisoner."[32] Bellamy continued to be given dangerous assignments under Wooster's command, which he performed with great skill and success.

Following his meeting with Washington, and upon reflection of his commission and demotion in rank, Wooster replied to Sherman on July 7, 1775. He wrote from his headquarters near New York and vented his frustration:

Dear Sir,

Your favor of the 23rd ult I received, in which you inform me that you recommended me, but without effect to the Congress for the berth of Major General. Your friendship I never doubted, and this fresh instance I shall ever gratefully remember.

I enclose with this the commission delivered to me by General Washington. You will see that somehow by mistake it was never dated. You will be good enough to deliver it to Mr. Hancock with my best compliments, and desire him not to return to it me. I have already a commission from the assembly of Connecticut. No man feels more sensibly for his distressed country, not would more readily exert his utmost for its defense, than myself. My life has been ever devoted to the service of my country from my youth up; though never before in a cause like this, a cause which I could most cheerfully risk, nay lay down my life to defend.

Thirty years I have served as a soldier; my character was never impeached not called in questions before. The Congress have seen fit, for what reason I know not, to point me out as the only officer among all that have been commissioned in the different colonies, who is unfit for the post assigned him. The subject is a delicate one. For further particulars, as well as for an account of the stores taken at Turtle Bay, I must refer you to my letter of this date to Col. Dyer. I am, Sir, in haste your sincere friend and humble servant

David Wooster[33]

Wooster's letter to Sherman provided a multi-layered view into his personal conviction. He demonstrated his contentment in serving Connecticut and viewed the service to the newly formed Continental Congress and the Continental Army as less than alluring. Yet it also showed a perspective of Wooster not seen in any of his other papers. Stating that he had no idea why the Congress would "point me out as the only officer … who is unfit for the post assigned him" after thirty years of service indicated his uncertainty of political collaboration with the newly formed Continental Congress. The honorary position provided him, as noted by the Connecticut delegation to the Congress, illuminated their perspective that, despite his excellent prior service, younger men were needed within the newly formed Continental Army. Perhaps it can be viewed as arbitrary that he returned the commission unsigned to the president of the Congress, which more than likely provided insult to some in the Congress who did not know him. However, upon examining the *Letters of Members of the Continental Congress*, and the *Journals of the Continental Congress*, no negative mention of Wooster was made, nor recorded in private letters that are within the historic record.[34] Wooster held a true Yankee devotion and duty to his country. The letter to Sherman highlighted his undivided loyalty, while hinting at a growing sense of impatience and possible fatigue.

There was one notable member of Connecticut society that did not view Wooster and Sullivan's actions in a meritorious light: Silas Deane. Writing to his wife upon hearing of the actions taken by the two Connecticut generals, Deane commented to her that

> I am informed that the late arrangement of affairs is highly displeasing to Wooster and Spencer, and that high words have passed on the occasion; that Wooster talks high of his thirty years' service, and that Spencer left his force to shift for themselves, though expecting hourly to be attacked, to return home and pray an alteration.
> When Wooster was appointed, I washed my hands of the consequences, by declaring him, in my opinion, totally unequal to the service. This I did openly in the face of the Assembly. And if I thought him unfit for a Major General of Connecticut forces only, could any one think I would oppose the voice of the Continent and my own sentiments by laboring to prefer him to Putnam, on whom by every acc^t the whole army has depended ever since the Lexington battle? I wish all such men would leave our army at once.[35]

John Adams also provided his opinion regarding the appointment of Wooster in a letter to James Warren. Adams noted:

> But, in the Case of the Connecticut officers, We took a Liberty to alter the Rank established by the Colony, and by that Means made much uneasiness: so that We were sure to do Mischief whether We conformed or deviated from Colony Arrangements.
> I rejoice that Thomas had more Wisdom that Spencer or Woorster, and that he did not leave the Camp or talk imprudently, if he had We should have lost his from the Continental service: for I assure you Spencer by going off, and Woorster by unguarded Speeches have given high offense here.[36]

Concluding the analysis of Wooster's demotion within the Continental Army includes the final correspondence on the issue between John Adams and Governor Trumbull. The Connecticut delegation to the Continental Congress had been adjusted in late 1775 and, after a cordial beginning of his letter, Trumbull addressed Adams query as to why the change was made—simply because members of the Connecticut delegation, Silas Deane in particular, did not adequately represent the will of the Connecticut Assembly or the people at large.[37]

Silas Deane was replaced, and Trumbull later mentioned that "Deane is a young Man, and one who never courted Popularity by cringing to the People, or affecting an extraordinary sanctity of manners; a man whose freedom of Speech and pointedness of Sarcasm has made him as many enemies, as have been raised against him by envy."[38]

Wooster eventually accepted the Continental commission and served as a brigadier general in the Continental Army. He continued to write of his service to the republican cause of liberty. However, his apparent vocal disappointment in July required him to continually state his conviction and devotion to the American cause time and again to those less convinced by his actions.

Late in June, Wooster and his men marched to New York City. James Rivington, a Tory printer in New York, printed in his paper the *Rivington Gazetteer* that General Wooster and seven companies of his regiment, along with Colonel Waterbury and his regiment, arrived in New York on June 29. The two Connecticut regiments encamped outside of the city.[39] The following week the *New York Gazette* announced a military review of Continental troops that included General Wooster as well in their paper. The account of the "exercises and evolutions" of military drill performed for the public, concluded with the bold reflection that a "country can never be enslaved, whose rights are defended by the hands of its citizens."[40]

To top off the arrival of General Wooster and his troops, a fine dinner and entertainment was provided at Mr. Samuel Frances on July 5. "The day was spent in the utmost harmony, every thing conspiring to please, being all of one mind, and one heart" read the article. The dinner, as reported in the *Rivington Gazette*, was a huge success and included a rousing round of loyalty toasts, eighteen in all.[41]

Despite the warm welcome Wooster and his troops received upon their arrival in New York, his letters continued to reflect the sense of confusion in the command structure and organization of the army versus the authority of the various colonial governments who held on to their own political autonomy. Being appointed first as a major general in Connecticut, the militia being a long-established institution within the colony, and now a brigadier general in the new Continental Army, which was still in its infancy, exactly whose orders took precedent? Those from the governor of Connecticut, or those from the president of the Continental Congress? Where did the New York Assembly and Committee of Safety fit into this structure? Initial collaboration between Connecticut and New York was well under way as demonstrated at an emergency session of the Connecticut General Assembly called by Governor Trumbull on July 1. At this session Trumbull not only called for raising 1,4000 troops but he also proposed the motion to provide money to both Massachusetts and New York, and to extend a line of credit to General Schuyler near Lake George in the amount of £ 15,000 pounds.[42] From July through August, Wooster's dealings with the New York Assembly began to wear on him. A letter from the general to the New York Congress expressed further confusion in dealing with individuals in New York who had retained men under his command. All the while he remained sensitive to the fact that he was not under the direct authority of the New York Assembly:

Camp near New York, July 7, 1775

To Peter V.B. Livingston, esq,'
President of the Provincial Congress

Sir:

We have among the Connecticut Troops a number of apprentices, and indented servants who ran away from their masters in the city, and have enlisted themselves, and received their pay in Connecticut. Since our arrival in this place, many of them have been detained in town by their masters. As the Governor of Connecticut has subjected me and the Troops under my command to the direction of the Continental and Provincial Congress, I desire you, Sir, to take the opinion of your Congress, and advise me what plan of conduct I shall pursue with regard to such persons, and you will oblige, Sir, your humble servant,

David Wooster[43]

From the beginning of the war, it was clear to Wooster that divided loyalty, especially between various colonies and the Congress, would prove detrimental to the cause. Never did his loyalty to Connecticut or to the newly established Continental Congress diminish. Yet the fact that he had to answer to, and assist, the New York General Assembly proved taxing. This added to the enlarged geographic perspective of the war which now encompassed more than the coastal regions of Connecticut or Long Island Sound. In June, Wooster was required to return to the area near New York to help keep communications open between the city and surrounding countryside, while also helping to stop marauders from stealing food that could be used by the army. He was in constant contact with Governor Trumbull for orders throughout his actions in the war, despite being pulled from New York to Connecticut and back again. Initially there was a sense of collaboration between Connecticut and New York, but this began to wear thin as the New York General Assembly continually demanded of Wooster his time, attention, and troops, sometimes against the defense of Connecticut or elsewhere.

Wooster was pressed with two major concerns regarding the New York General Assembly in 1775. First was the issue of loyalists within the city who might cause trouble. A second was a report from "Captain Thompson, who arrived here last night from Cork, in Ireland, that four full Regiments have embarked in Ireland for this City, and may be expected here every hour...."[44] With news reports constantly changing, letters such as Thompson's caused a great deal of concern, and in some cases, panic. Between June and July, Wooster, encamped with his men five miles from New York City, needed to keep one eye on New York, and one on his home of Connecticut. Not only was he requested to march with his troops to New York, but he was also required to bring as much military equipment as necessary, as the New York General Assembly informed him that they did not have enough of their own to provide his men. Wooster had years of military training in the field under British commanders in the past; however, this new political style of military collaboration tried Wooster's patience. No one had the foresight to tell exactly when or where a British force might land. New York was the obvious target, however in 1775 it was anyone's guess for certain. Wooster was pressed to provide optimal protection regardless of the time or the place of invasion along southern New York and Connecticut.

An attempt to resolve the question of who had authority over colonial troops was addressed by the commander-in-chief himself. General Washington issued an order from his headquarters in Cambridge on July 4, which stated:

> The Continental Congress having now taken all the Troops of the several Colonies, which have been raised, or which may be hereafter raised, for the support and defence of the Liberties of America into their Pay and Service; They are now the Troops of the United Provinces of North America; and it is to be hoped that all Distinctions of Colonies will be laid aside: so that one and the same spirit may animate the whole, and the only Contest be, who shall render on this great and trying occasion, the most essential Service to the great and common cause in which we are all engaged[45]

The uncertainty of war caused excitement to those in New York as reports continued to come in concerning the stealing of livestock in and around Long Island.

Wooster and his men were routinely shuffled from one end of the island to the other in order to prevent the British from landing and removing cattle to feed their own troops stationed in Boston. In June the 64-gun third-rate ship of the line, HMS *Asia*, was stationed outside of New York to transport British troops and protect British commercial vessels. Fearing retribution from rebels in the city, New York Governor, and Lieutenant General in the British army, William Tryon, removed himself to the *Asia* in late 1775. Wooster was in command of troops stationed just outside of New York City while the *Asia* lay at anchor. Loyalists, fearful of the situation in New York, used the protection of the 64-gun ship-of-the-line to attempt to free fellow loyalists being detained in General Wooster's camp. On July 10, one such loyalist, Peter Herring, was caught taking prisoners to the *Asia*. He was detained while Wooster corresponded with the New York Committee of Safety asking directions on what exactly to do with Herring. Wooster ended up sending Herring to the Committee for questioning.[46] Two days later Wooster received another message from the Committee of Safety for the colony of New York in which the committee members accused Wooster's men of stealing a boat that belonged "to His Majesty's Ship *Asia*," arresting the crew, and then breaking into "His Majesty's store-house" and stealing items stored there.[47] This situation added to Wooster's growing agitation towards those in New York. Which side, exactly, was the New York legislature and Committee of Safety on? Three months had passed since the shots fired at Lexington and Concord. In the view of the Committee of Safety for the colony of New York, were material goods owned by the king untouchable, not to be seized as spoils of war, or were these vitally important materials of war to be taken and used by the rebels? This only added to the growing animosity of Connecticut officers and soldiers towards their New York counterparts, who appeared to carry the olive branch in one hand, the sword in the other, and, if possible, require of their Connecticut neighbors all the military protection needed for their own safety.

By the middle of July, it became apparent to Wooster that maintaining order and discipline in camp was becoming problematic with having the army so near to New York. He wrote to the New York Assembly and informed them that

> having found by experience that the Troops under my command, from the situation of their encampment, are subjected to many difficulties, which render it next to impossible to maintain that good order and discipline of an Army, my officers agree with me in sentiment, that it will be much for the benefit of the service to remove the Troops to a further distance for the Town.[48]

Not only was the Continental Army plagued with a lack of resources, food, gunpowder, clothing, and other critical supplies throughout the war, but those in command were faced with the daunting task of training a volunteer army. As short-term enlistments expired, troops returned home. Some never returned. From a command perspective this was a disastrous way to wage war. To civilians and politicians in New York who wished for the protection of Wooster's troops, moving his men outside of the city was unwarranted. Wooster saw it as a necessity for maintaining order, discipline, and training. Another issue that Wooster dealt with was the political infighting, maneuvering, and backstabbing. Even though this had gone on throughout his military career, he had not previously been forced to deal directly with it as a younger, lower-ranking officer. Dealing with a myriad of political situations was new for those within the Continental Army officer corps. All of Wooster's military colleagues had to attend to these pressing situations and adverse personalities, and his age perhaps limited his patience with such challenges.

New orders had reached Wooster in July to make all preparations to move his troops to join General Schuyler at Albany. Schuyler had sent a request to Wooster on July 17 to send 1,000 men north to support him.[49] Wooster, encamped at Harlem, made ready for the march north. He received orders from the president of the Continental Congress, and replied to him on July 22:

> Sir;
>
> I received your orders of the seventeenth instant, and immediately contracted for vessels to carry the Troops to Albany.... And indeed, Sir, you may depend upon my utmost exertion and assiduity for carrying into execution every order within my department, for the good of the common cause, notwithstanding some discouragements that I have met with, after a series of thirty-four years in the service of my King and Country. The forces under my command are in general good health and high spirits, and rejoice to have it in their power to go where they may have an opportunity to do their Country some service.[50]

In all of Wooster's correspondence in 1775, he continually reiterated his loyalty to his country. He reminded those of the slight in his demotion in rank, and that he had served his country for over three decades. Understandably, as seen in the letter to Hancock, not even one month after the time he received the disappointing news, there remained a bit of resentment as the undertone of his letter indicated. To some members of Congress, however, younger more energetic officers were required of the arduous task set before them.

By mid–July continental forces were starting to organize in the Northern Department under the command of General Philip Schuyler of New York. The Continental Congress passed a resolution that the president of Congress write to Wooster "directing him to send, in the most expeditious manner, one thousand of the Connecticut Forces under his command to Albany, there to remain encamped until they shall receive orders form General Schuyler as to their future proceedings."[51] To that end Wooster organized his troops and gathered all necessary supplies that were required to assist Schuyler. By the end of July, he was prepared to leave his camp at Harlem to proceed to Albany.

Wooster received word from General Washington's secretary, Colonel Joseph Reed, at the end of July, that three British ships had sailed from Boston and were heading east-by-southeast; their destination was thought to be New York. Wooster's preparation for the defense of New York was critically important. He boosted the patriotic spirit in the New York area in 1775.[52] Over the past two months Wooster and his men had been in New Haven, Greenwich, New York, Harlem, Long Island, and Oyster Pond. Now they were preparing to march to Albany. However, this order would prove to be fraught with contradiction, as Wooster soon discovered.

Communication became a hinderance in August. As Wooster, following orders, prepared to leave Harlem and travel north to Albany, the New York Assembly requested him to protect the livestock once again on Long Island. This was compounded with the request for two-hundred pounds of gunpowder for the defense of the colony. Most of the gunpowder seized at the capture of Fort Ticonderoga had been distributed to the army, and New York had acquired an ample supply at that time. Finding himself in a precarious position, Wooster wrote to Governor Trumbull requesting powder for his own men as they headed east toward Oyster Pond on Long Island. The late summer of 1775 found Wooster sending troops back and forth into the eastern end of Long Island, at the request of the New York Provincial Council, as he continually requested shipments of gunpowder from Trumbull in Connecticut, as New York had none.[53]

With continued economic hardships, the Connecticut General Assembly relied upon leading men of the colony to assist in financing the military preparations required. Wooster utilized his own finances as collateral to outfit his troops from the colony, as a few others did. In a letter to Governor Trumbull on August 9, 1775, Wooster addressed key issues that plagued the army throughout the war: the lack of gunpowder and lack of food. The British removed cattle from areas on Long Island, and Wooster was dispatched to help secure the rest, while asking the governor to send him gunpowder as soon as possible.[54]

On August 14, Wooster detained a Church of England Clergyman, the Rev. James Lyon, for being "the main spring of all the tories on that part of Long Island." Wooster noted that "the Committees of the several adjacent Towns; thinking him a very dangerous person to remain among them, have desired me to take care of him. I shall, therefore, by the first opportunity send him to the care of the Committee of Hartford, till they can receive your Honor's orders concerning him."[55] While in New York, Wooster's men seized the printing press type blocks from the Tory printer, James Rivington. He was known for his anti-republican sentiments and continued to print false articles against the patriot cause. The printing press was left intact; however, Wooster ordered the type to be melted down and turned into bullets. Wooster's men also disarmed many Tories on their way to and from Connecticut in 1775. Isaac Sears, a soldier in Wooster's regiment, wrote to Roger Sherman, Eliphalet Dyer, and Silas Deane, explaining the event:

New Haven, 28 November, 1775,

Gentlemen,—I have to inform you of an Expedition which I, with about 100 Volunteers from this and the other Towns Westward in this Government, set out upon for New York & in which was to disarm Tories, and to deprive that Traitor to his Country James Rivington of the means of circulating pison [poison] in print, the latter of which we happily effected by taking away his Types, and which may be a great means of puting an end to the Tory Faction there, for his press hath been as it were the very life and Soul of it—and I believe it wou'd not otherwise have been done, as there are not Spirited and Leading men enough in N. York to undertake such a Business, or it wou'd have been done long ago: and as there are many Enemies to the cause of Freedom, in that place, it is most likely I shall meet with many Censures for undertaking such an Enterprise.[56]

One key element of keeping troops in the field was the necessity of feeding them, which was a constant challenge throughout the war. Wooster and his men continually drove cattle and sheep out of the hands of the British who, in 1775, were sailing to Long Island to seize livestock to take back to Boston where most of the British army was encamped. Keeping New York safe and his own troops fed was a vitally important task. However, after working with the New York Assembly back and forth since early June, his correspondences with Governor Trumbull indicated his doubt in continuing under the authority of New York politicians:

> I expect by next Monday to sail for New York. Your Honor well knows the suspicious light in which the New-York Congress are viewed by the rest of the Continent; I must therefore beg of your Honour to alter that part of your orders to me, in which you subject me to the direction of that body of men. I have no faith in their honesty in the cause. I must, therefore, think it not only a disgrace to me, but a dishonour to my employers, that I am subject to them. You know not, Sir, half their tricks.[57]

Wooster's apprehension of the sharply divided and volatile New York political sphere intensified due to his dealings with one key man: Philip Schuyler. Schuyler was twenty-three years younger than Wooster. He had also served in the French and Indian War in the British Army as a colonel along with Wooster at Fort Ticonderoga in 1759. As a member of the New York gentry, he joined the New York Assembly where he served until the war broke out in 1775. Schuyler was politically well connected and received a commission in 1775 when the Continental army was formed. Oftentimes political positioning carries more weight than experience; this was the case with Schuyler. To Wooster, and many others, the New York Assembly was more concerned with their political well-being than the cause for which the Revolution was being fought. As was the case with various colonial legislatures, the New York Assembly, reflective of the citizenry, was divided over its loyalty to the crown or the patriot cause. In 1775 no one could have predicted how long the struggle would last. The newspapers of the day provided an insight to the day-to-day concern and confusion expressed by colonial Americans as events played out. The editorials, often anonymous or with a pen name, encouraged both the support of the patriot cause or liberty, as well as loyalty to the king.

Schuyler was under orders to plan for the invasion of Canada. He marched north to Fort Ticonderoga for that purpose. He and the New York Provincial Council had instructed Wooster to send three companies to his assistance at Ticonderoga. Wooster received information from Washington that several British ships were headed towards New York from Boston.[58] He assured the New York Assembly that their interests were aligned with his; however, he doubted that General Schuyler would have ordered three companies of his men north to Ticonderoga had he been aware of the potential threat from the British ships enroute to Long Island. With that in mind he informed the New York Assembly that he would not be returning to Harlem until the current threat to Long Island had passed.

In the meantime, Schuyler, whose forces were gathering near Fort Ticonderoga, had encountered a looming problem for the Northern Department: the lack of military supplies. His initial request for troops had been fulfilled. Wooster had sent one regiment to him as well. However, in a letter to Connecticut Governor Trumbull on August 31, Schuyler informed him that no more men should be sent north, as there were not enough supplies in that region to provide for them, especially tents. This was the first of a series of letters from officers in the Northern Department that addressed the total lack of resources and supplies.[59] By the end of the year Wooster experienced this himself.

Wooster wrote to the new commander-in-chief in late August concerning the movements of his troops and questioned the requests placed upon him by the New York Assembly and by General Schuyler. Washington replied that Schuyler's mission was of utmost importance and that Wooster should assist him in any way possible. Upon reflecting on Wooster's situation, being ordered by several separate entities to spread his troops across the area, Washington added to the New York Assembly on the urgency of retaining the military force in one location stating that "separating the Army into a number of small detachments, who would be harassed in fruitless marches and countermarches, after an enemy whose conveyance and shipping is so advantageous that they might keep the whole cost in constant alarm, without our being able perhaps, at any time, to give them vigorous opposition." Washington further noted that "no Provincial Congress can, with any propriety, interfere in the disposition of Troops on the Continental establishment, much less control the orders of any General Officer."[60] This was the first indication to Wooster that the military orders given by the Continental Congress did in fact supersede all others, including the New York Assembly.

Washington was faced with the tremendous task of establishing the legitimate authority of the Continental Congress, which had only been in existence for four months at this point, versus the authority of the general assemblies and governors of the thirteen established colonies. Connecticut, for example, had been self-governing under the authority of the crown since 1662, and New York had done the same since 1664. To officers like Wooster, the cause for which they were all fighting in 1775 was clearly defined. Yet, determining the legitimate authority in which to fulfill the goals of the American cause was another question entirely.

This struggle between Wooster and the New York Assembly for the control of military troops came to a head in September. The legislature sent an order to him demanding that his force, most of whom were Connecticut troops, return to Harlem. Wooster, having received the order from Washington that all provincial orders were secondary to the Continental Congress, cited the commander-in-chief's directive and stated that the request from New York was predicated upon a June request, one sent prior to the Continental Army being fully organized. Therefore, Wooster noted, the Provincial Assembly of New York did not have authority over the orders given to him by Washington. Wooster was thus loyal to the higher governing body and the commander-in-chief.[61] The time delay in writing, sending, receiving, and eventually replying to eighteenth-century correspondence added to the confusion of this situation. Upon examination of letters of correspondence and orders written, it is evident that the overlap between sending and receiving added to growing military frustration.

Having established the chain of command regarding the deployment of his men, Wooster wrote to the New York Committee of Safety following yet another request for his troops to construct and utilize new batteries to be placed around New York City. Despite what he viewed as mistreatment at the hands of the Continental Congress, once fully commissioned Wooster's loyalty was solidly placed with the new command structure under General Washington. Given the distrust and animosity that he felt towards the New York Committee of Safety, having the backing of

Washington certainly had its personal benefits. Since his orders came directly from His Excellency, Wooster noted the difficult position he would be placed in had he succumbed to the orders of the New York Committee of Safety rather than the Commander in Chief. As a final shot, Wooster commented that "I have authority to say that no Provincial Congress can, with any propriety, interfere in the disposition of Continental Troops, much less control the orders of any Commander-in-Chief."[62] The collaborative efforts between New England and New York continued to deteriorate throughout the remainder of 1775.

Following the prescribed orders given to Wooster and his men from June through September 1775 would be similar to viewing a Wimbledon tennis tournament. Between Governor Trumbull, the New York Assembly, the New York Committee of Safety, General Schuyler, and the Continental Congress, the continual change in orders mirrored the uncertainty of the war. It led to increased frustration and challenged military leadership. Being able to provide and receive the best available information in a timely fashion became a daily struggle. Wooster made certain that his actions were specific and well-grounded. September would witness an escalation of action, with Wooster now firmly in the right, defended by the direct orders of General Washington.

On September 20, the New York Provincial Congress wrote to Hancock requesting the Congress to order Wooster to march immediately to Albany to assist Schuyler with as many Connecticut troops as were available. Wooster, stationed at Harlem, received the orders, and sent a letter to Schuyler stating that he and his men were on their way north. Two days later, the New York Committee of Safety sent an additional letter to the Congress stating that Wooster had four-hundred men who "appear to be unemployed" and therefore to request him to send one full company back to New York to erect forts along the Hudson. Keeping in mind the delay in communication, Wooster received his orders from the Congress, signed by John Hancock, on September 23, in which he was ordered to march to Albany with his troops "there to await the orderd of General Schuyler, in case he should want your assistance; and you will please, without loss of time, to proceed."[63] Wooster immediately replied to Hancock the same day, stating that "your favour of the 20th instant I have just received, and shall with the greatest expedition proceed with the Troops under my command to Albany, and there wait General Schuyler's orders, according to direction of Congress. I am sir, in haste, your most obedient humble servant, David Wooster."[64]

An additional letter was sent to Washington from Wooster on September 28, informing His Excellency that he was embarking for Albany that very afternoon. One important item of note is length of time between a written letter, the receipt of that letter, and the return notice. In this situation the first letter was written from New York to John Hancock in Philadelphia. The letter from Hancock was sent to Wooster on September 20 and was received at his encampment at Harlem on September 23. On September 28, Wooster replied to Washington's letter of September 2 (in which Wooster was ordered from Long Island to Harlem) and informed the commander-in-chief that he would leave that day for Albany.

These correspondences highlighted two key elements that emerged in 1775.

First, they demonstrated the reality and the uncertainty that war presents to those active participants, be they military officers, politicians, or common citizens. The fear of the unknown in a time of war, where the enemy may appear, when battle will be engaged, or whose livelihood will be impacted, permeate these letters. Secondly, despite his age and growing agitation with those in New York, they show Wooster's commitment to his duty as an officer in the Continental Army, and his subordination to those in the Congress, regardless of his opinion towards members of that body. He was determined, as ever, to carry out his orders to the best of his ability.

Schuyler was placed in charge of the Northern Department as a major general by the Continental Army, one rank higher than Wooster. He had requested Wooster to bring troops north to Ticonderoga for the planning and invasion of Canada. In late September, Wooster moved his troops north from Harlem to Albany and then to Ticonderoga. His letters to both Hancock and Washington restate his service in the army, despite the incident of June, and continually reaffirm his commitment to the cause and the orders given to him by the Congress.

By the fall of 1775, the political infighting of war began to rear its ugly head. As Benedict Arnold's force struggled through the Maine wilderness towards Canada, Philip Schuyler had taken ill at Fort Ticonderoga. This illness prevented him from taking to the field but would not prevent him from writing a constant stream of correspondence, both to Congress and General Washington.

A change in the command structure of the Northern Department was underway, due to Schuyler falling ill to the "flux." He alerted Washington to his condition and that he was considering leaving the army in order to recover. After providing condolences for Schuyler's illness and, since Schuyler was unable to command, Washington informed him that

> "General Wooster, as the oldest Brigadier, will take rank and command of Mr. Montgomery. General Wooster, I am informed, is not of such activity as to press through difficulties with which that service is environed. I am, therefore, much alarmed for Arnold, whose expedition is built upon yours, and who will infallibly perish, if the invasion and entry into Canada are abandoned by your successor [Wooster].
> Should this find you at Albany, and General Wooster about taking the command, I entreat you to impress upon him strongly with the importance and necessity of preceding, or so to conduct that Arnold may have time to retreat."[65]

Washington's concern over Wooster's ability and speed was noted in several letters, all to Philip Schuyler. Perhaps included in the commander-in-chief's apprehension was the advanced age of the brigadier from Connecticut. Regardless, Schuyler was reluctant to leave the field if Wooster was to become the next commander instead of General Richard Montgomery. In a reply to Washington's letter of October 6, Schuyler informed the commander-in-chief that "Mr. Wooster is the younger [junior] Brigadier of the two, but lest any uneasiness should be occasioned, I will keep him here."[66]

Meanwhile, Wooster and the troops under his command were enroute to Lake George, arriving there on the evening on October 18. As he was making his way up the Hudson River, both the New York Provincial Congress and the Continental Congress attempted to alter his marching orders once more. The body in

Philadelphia ordered Wooster to return to the Highlands to erect forts and batteries for the defense of New York, if "he had no orders to the contrary from general Schuyler."[67] Fortunately for Wooster, these orders did not reach him in time for his return. By the middle of October, he was finally out of reach of the New York Assembly and Committee of Safety, but their influence upon him was far from over.

The working relationship between Wooster and Schuyler was agitated in October 1775 by one man: Gunning Bedford. Bedford, a New Yorker, and friend of Schuyler, had been given the position of muster master for the Northern Department. A muster master oversaw mustering or getting soldiers to either enlist or reenlist. With the creation of the Continental Army by Congress also came the publication of new official Articles of War. Schuyler required all new Continental troops, officers, and enlisted men alike, to sign the Articles, therefore pledging their support to the Continental Army and Congress. Wooster's Connecticut men had been enlisted under the Articles of War ratified by the Connecticut assembly, as they had been in the service long before the Continental Army had been in existence. This could cause a dire situation in determining the allegiance of individual colonial units. If Connecticut troops were not held to the same standards as the Continental Army, would they follow orders of Continental officers, or only those serving from Connecticut? It is possible to examine this action as the troops themselves saw it, as steps taken by colonial volunteers who could not foresee the longevity of the war before them. This was to be a short campaign into Canada, and they were to return home before the end of the year. In a letter to John Hancock, dated August 30, Bedford complained:

> I have to inform you, Sir, that after receiving my commission I made the best of my way to New-York, when I waited on General Wooster, to know whether he had any orders for me to muster his Troops. He told me he had none, neither did he think he had the authority to give me any, not thinking himself a Continental officer; however, he gave me a general return of his forces, which I brought forward to General Schuyler.
>
> On my arrival here, Gen. Schuyler gave it our in orders that the Captains should prepare their muster-rolls for a general muster, according to the forms to be given out by the Muster-Master. When I gave them the forms, I showed them the articles (in the general body of rules for the regulation of the Army) which respect my particular department. I found the Connecticut Troops had none of them signed them; on which I applied to the General, who told me it had been given out in general orders that they should sign them, and he thought it had been done. On calling the officers on the subject, they told the General they knew they had disobeyed orders in not urging the matter to the soldiery, but they found it would raise a defection in their minds which would injure the cause, as the soldiers thought their signing the articles would dissolve their present obligations, for a limited time, to their own Colony, with many disadvantages to both officers and soldiers, and involve them in a service, the end of which was uncertain, and would leave them, perhaps, on no better footing than that of Regulars.
>
> On hearing the many reasons that were urges against it, the General thought it prudent to drop the matter for the present; however, thought proper the men should be mustered. The same reasons were urged against signing the muster-rolls, as against the rules and articles for the regulation of the Army. On this I was obliged to give up the matter.[68]

Bedford went further by an additional letter written to Schuyler on October 15. The general received Bedford's missive after he and Wooster had met and was relieved to find Wooster had accepted his position within the Continental service. Two additional comments, however, fueled Schuyler's discontent. He nurtured his fragile ego as much as his ill health. Bedford informed Schuyler that while at Lake George, Wooster had called a court martial. Wooster certainly had the experience and the mastery of military etiquette and discipline to call and hold such a court and he did not see any reason to gain permission. However, Schuyler, as the overall commander of the Northern Department, had not been informed prior to Wooster's actions, which was contrary to military protocol. Schuyler was informed that

> Mr. Cobb, the commissary here, is a Connecticut man (but who despises them thoroughly in his heart) and was let into his [Wooster] counsels. He was present when General Wooster was about calling a court-martial. He had not officers enough of his own to form it, and how to get others he did not know, without signing himself brigadier-general. He mentioned the difficulty to his officers, "Why," one of them replied, you have two strings to your bow; "another," "take care you don't pull on the weakest"; and a third, "you may pull on both, on occasion." Cobb says he believes he signed brigadier-general, but would not be certain; however, it might be found out by getting the orders.[69]

He also stated that Wooster and his Connecticut troops had marched north. "They are making great preparations, as if all the execution of the army was to be done by them alone. He brings provisions of his own, they tell me, to serve his regiment for the campaign. They will not touch Continental stores, nor eat Continental provisions!"[70] To this end, Bedford informed Schuyler that Wooster had even brought his own sutlers to provide supplies to his men. The outrage displayed by the New Yorker, who only continued to add fuel to the growing fire between Connecticut and New York, demonstrated a total disconnect and lack of military knowledge that Wooster had obtained through years of service north of Albany. He was aware of the difficulties and challenges of marching north, and, as Schuyler had already noted, the lack of supplies. With years of experience Wooster knew that the only way to lead a successful campaign north was to equip the force with all the necessary supplies first and take them on the campaign. His dealing with the Continental Congress, not to mention the inexperience and, in some instances, ineptness of the New York Assembly and Committee of Safety, most certainly did not place any amount of trust that they would provide the necessary materials to supply the army of the Northern Department. How could any newly formed organization such as the Continental Army, having only been in existence for less than four months, possibly provide the required military support? Wooster knew what was needed and made sure that his men marched north with the necessities of war for a successful campaign in Canada. What Bedford reported as an abandonment of the Continental Army, Schuyler interpreted as usurping his own authority and military command, and put simply, Wooster viewed as nothing more than applicable wisdom and military leadership.

After reading Bedford's letter of October 15, Schuyler, who at this time was incapacitated with the "flux," wrote to Washington complaining about the actions of Wooster. Wooster had ordered a court martial at Fort George over the issuing of the 1775 Articles of War newly passed and printed by the Continental Congress. These were harsher and stricter than what Wooster's men had agreed to while in Connecticut, and many officers refused to sign these newly issued directives. Wooster, ever the disciplinarian, ordered the trials, since these men had joined the army under Connecticut regulations, and would not now pledge to the new Articles of War.

This was a potentially devastating problem for unity within the Continental Army. Schuyler was offended that a junior officer should supersede his command and that of General Montgomery. Schuyler complained openly to the president of the Congress, John Hancock:

> General Wooster having ordered a Court-Martial at Fort George, of which I was informed only this morning, which he be no means had the right to do, and apprehensive, from the extraordinary conduct, that he might create difficulties if he should join the Army under General Montgomery (from which I cannot dissuade him, nor dare I order him to stay lest the Regiment should refuse to go, which he says they will do), I thought it my indispensable duty to write him a letter, of which the enclosed is a copy, and to which I received an answer, copy of which you have also enclosed. I have since received letters advising me that he has presumed to discharge men of Hinman's and Waterbury's Regiments. I assure you, Sir, that I feel these insults from a General Officer with all that keen sensibility that a man of honour ought; and I should be ashamed to mention them to Congress, but that the critical situation of our publick affairs at this period require that I should sacrifice a just resentment to them, and I would wish to have it remembered that to that cause only must be imputed that I have suffered a personal indignity.[71]

Lake George is located south of Fort Ticonderoga where Schuyler was stationed. The situation which caused such "personal indignity" to Schuyler was twofold. First, General Wooster ordered a court martial for troops who refused to sign the newly issued Articles of War, which were approved by the Continental Congress. Second that Wooster "discharged men" under two separate regiments. Schuyler's letter to Congress stressed that he "should be ashamed to mention them to Congress," referring to the insults he received from Wooster, yet he openly expressed his views and opinions regarding the general to the Congress throughout 1775 and well into 1776.

The correspondence between Wooster, Schuyler, Washington, and the Continental Congress over this issue is truly remarkable. Wooster saw his responsibility to keep the troops under his command well-disciplined, supplied, and healthy. This situation demonstrated several points of military confusion. First, the notion of a short war in 1775 was seen by the men themselves who grew restless under the pretense that they were sent into Canada for a short campaign season and sought to return home by December. Second, it highlighted the conflict, and confusion, of maintaining two simultaneous, separate military commissions, as Wooster did, as well as whose authority the Connecticut troops were placed under. Solutions were provided as the war dragged on, however for the infantile congress and Continental Army in 1775 these were serious challenges. Schuyler, feeling that his authority had been usurped, complained bitterly, and felt that Wooster and his troops would not really be needed in the Northern Department, as he feared that Wooster and Montgomery would clash over the court martial issue. There is no evidence that Wooster and Montgomery ever had words on this issue. Wooster noted that he and Montgomery were good friends and treated one another as gentlemen; treatment that Wooster felt he did not receive from Schuyler.[72] In fact, Wooster and Montgomery collaborated on the successful reduction of Fort St. John in November, whereupon John Hancock wrote a praiseworthy congratulations to Wooster upon his success.

On October 18, General Schuyler wrote to the president of the Congress from Fort Ticonderoga and gave an update on the army's situation and its advance into Canada. Several requests from Montgomery were stated in the letter, including the great need for men, money, and discipline among his troops. These were some of the very same issues which Wooster wrote about yet would be criticized for during the winter of 1776 while he was in command at Montreal and Quebec. Schuyler was fully aware of the lack of supplies in the Northern Department. The antagonism with Wooster was further noted as Schuyler reported:

> Two hundred and fifty-three of General Wooster's Regiment came across Lake George on Sunday, the General is not yet arrived, and they do not choose to move until he does. Do not choose to move! Strange language in an Army; but the irresistible force of necessity obliges me to put up with it. This morning I gave orders to Lieutenant-Colonel Ward to send a subaltern, a sergeant, corporal, and twenty privates, in two bateaus, to carry powder, artillery stores, and rum. The Colonel (who is a good man) called upon me to know if he would not be blamed by General Wooster for obeying my orders. I begged him to send the men, and urged the necessity. The men, I believe, will condescended to go. I could give many instances of a similar nature.[73]

Before Schuyler sent the letter, Wooster arrived in camp. The tenor of Schuyler's note changed once Wooster visited him and pledged to support his commander. Schuyler noted this exchange further in his correspondence:

> General Wooster is just arrived here. As he was appointed a Major-General by the Colony of Connecticut, and as I did not know his sentiments with respect to the rank he considered himself in, in the Continental Army, my intentions were to have him remain at this post; but assuring me that his Regiment would not move without him, and that although he thought hard of being superseded, yet he would most readily put himself under the command of General Montgomery; that his only views were the publick service, and that no obstructions, of any kind, would be given by him; this spirited and sensible declaration I received with inexpressible satisfaction, and he moves tomorrow with the first division of his Regiment.[74]

Unfortunately, the heated rhetoric from General Schuyler continued the following day, as both were now at Ticonderoga the usual time-lapse in communication was not applicable. On October 19, Schuyler wrote to Wooster the following:

> Sir;
>
> The Continental Congress having taken the six first Regiments, raised this year in the Colony of Connecticut, (of which your is one,) into the pay and service of the associated Colonies, at the earnest request of the honourable Delegates representing the Colony of Connecticut, and you having in a variety of instances obeyed the orders of Congress, who have conferred on you the rank of Brigadier-General in the Army of the associated Colonies, I was taught to believe you considered yourself as such, both from what I have observed, and from your declarations to me yesterday; but I am now informed, that you have called a General Court-Martial, at Fort George, in your way up here—a conduct which I cannot account for, unless you consider yourself my superior; and that cannot be in virtue of your appointment by Congress, by which you are a younger Brigadier-General than Mr. Montgomery; and unless you consider yourself a s such, I cannot, consistent with the duty I owe to the publick, permit you to join that part of the Army now under Brigadier-General Montgomery's command, lest a confusion and disagreement should arise that might prove fatal to our operations in Canada. You will therefore, Sir, please to give me your explicit answer to this question: whether you consider yourself and your Regiment in the service of the associated Colonies, and yourself a younger Brigadier-General in that service than Mr. Montgomery or not, that no misapprehensions or misrepresentations may hereafter arise.
>
> I am, Sir, with much respect, your
most obedient humble servant,
>
> Philip Schuyler[75]

After four months of aggravation at the hands of the New York Assembly and Committee of Safety, followed by the growing animosity of General Schuyler, one could only imagine the way this letter was received, and read. No military manual ever written taught an officer how to deal with internal tensions, yet Wooster's reply provided not only a clear explanation to all the ambiguous charges raised against him but went further to publicly state his dedication to the cause once more. His reply was sent shortly after receiving Schuyler's letter. First Wooster explained the necessity of the court martial being called at Lake George. Taking into consideration his experience during the French and Indian War, he was extremely well versed in the application of discipline and use of a general court martial:

> Sir:
>
> In answer to your favour of this day, give me leave to acquaint you, that immediately upon my receiving the Continental articles of war, I gave them out to the different Captains and commanders of Companies in my Regiment, but they universally declined signing them; of consequence, in the discipline of the troops under my command, I was obliged to continue in the use of the law martial of Connecticut, under which they were raised, which I certainly had a right to do, by virtue of my commission from the Colony. Upon the same principle, I ordered a General Court-Martial at Fort George, which, whether right or not, was never designed in the least to contradict or counteract your authority as Commander-in-Chief of the troops under this department.

He redirected the question of his allegiance in a powerful statement that can only be read in light of months of questioning and political antagonism amidst the uncertainty of war and rebellion:

> With regard to the other question, my appointment in the Continental Army, you are sensible could not be very agreeable to me, notwithstanding which, I never should have continued in the service, had I not determined to observe the rules of the Army. No, Sir, I have the cause of my Country too much at heart to attempt to make any difficulty or uneasiness in the Army, upon whom the success of an enterprise of almost infinite importance to the Country is now depending. I shall consider my rank in the Army what my commission from the Continental Congress makes it, and shall not attempt to dispute the command with General Montgomery at St. John's. As to my Regiment, I consider them as what they really are, according to the tenor of their enlistments, and compact with the Colony of Connecticut, by whom they were raised, and now acting in conjunction with the troops of the other Colonies in the service, and for the defense of the associated Colonies in general. You may depend, Sir, that I shall exert myself as much as possible to promote the strictest union and harmony among both officers and soldiers in the Army, and use every means in my power to give success to the expedition.
>
> > I am, Sir, with much respect, your
> > most obedient servant,
>
> > David Wooster[76]

The entanglement of communication regarding the issuing of orders and counter orders became apparent in the fall of 1775. On the same day that Wooster and Schuyler took pen in hand towards one another, the Continental Congress had written the order that recalled Wooster to New York to fortify the Highlands and the batteries being erected along the Hudson River. Schuyler had issued an order prior to the receipt of the letter from Congress that indicated his need of Wooster and his troops. Schuyler yielded to his initial proposal of removing Wooster and sending him back to New York and had ordered him north to assist Montgomery on his move towards Canada. His decision was supported by General Washington.[77]

A resolution was passed by the Connecticut General Assembly that stated all troops raised in the colony of Connecticut "then employed against the ministerial troops in Canada, shall be subject to the rules, orders, regulations, and discipline of the Congress of the twelve United Colonies during the time of their enlistment." Unfortunately, their enlistments were set to expire on December 10.[78] This was in accord with Washington's directive.

It appeared that the tensions between Schuyler and Wooster had subsided, for on October 23, as Wooster marched to St. John's, Schuyler wrote to him giving him leave to attempt to take the fort there if he thought he could do so, granted the loss of life would be minimal.[79] Although he permitted Wooster to take part in the reduction of Chambly and St. John's, three days later he wrote to Washington stating that "I wrote your Excellency that I should not send Gen Wooster, but, as his Regiment refused to go without him, I was obliged to suffer him to go."[80] Schuyler continued the personal attack against Wooster in a letter to Governor Trumbull on October 27, telling the governor that the reduction of St. John's was imminent, and that "General Wooster, with his Regiment of three hundred and thirty-five effectives, officers included, left this on the 22d—most of the men, and many of the officers, with great reluctance."[81]

Prior to the attack against St. John, with the knowledge that the enlistments for his Connecticut troops were soon to expire, Wooster successfully convinced his men to stay with him in the field until December. Again, Justus Bellamy provided an eye-wittiness account of what transpired:

> General Wooster informed us that our term of enlistment was about out and that he should not go any further without we engaged to go ahead and stand by him until the end of the Canada campaign. He said he wished all those who were sick or lame, or had rheumatism, to step out, and they might go home. Six or seven stepped out forward of the line as being unable or unwilling to go. General Wooster then commenced limping like a lame man and asked if there were no more lame or had the rheumatism in his whole army, and after doing so a minute of two, all returned to the ranks save two who were discharged on the spot. General Wooster then praised his men and remarked that with such hope he could go to hell and back with them safe, and from thence we marched to St. Johns in Canada.[82]

Analyzing the impact that Wooster had upon the Northern Department by simply reading the letters from Schuyler presents a rather negative image. Even though he had taken ill at Ticonderoga while the troops under the command of Generals Montgomery and Wooster were sent north to secure St. John, Schuyler's letters provide only one side of the story. While very few of Wooster's correspondence survived the destruction of his home and personal papers in 1780, his voice was further stymied by the record of men such as Schuyler, who survived the war. Official copies of letters sent to the Congress provide one insight into the man, yet current historical research provides additional letters and journals from soldiers who fought under his command in Canada in 1775. One such account came from the Rev. Benjamin Trumbull.[83]

Trumbull, a Connecticut soldier and chaplain, kept a journal of movements of his regiment in 1775 in Canada. Several entries in his journal specifically mentioned General Wooster's arrival as he and General Montgomery held a council of war.[84] It is worth noting the account of this "interview" between Wooster and Montgomery. According to Justus Bellamy, one of Wooster's soldiers who overheard the conversation held between Montgomery and Wooster, Montgomery said "I welcome you to this place. I am heartily glad to see you. My commission is older than yours, and I must command, and I think it a goddamned shame. I am but a young man, and you are and old man, experienced in war. I shall always take your advice as a son would that of a father."[85]

Likely this conversation was meant to appease the older general who continued to harbor resentment towards his appointed rank in the Continental Army. No doubt this greeting made a significant impact, as the two collaborated well in the reduction of St. John and the capture of Montreal.

Although born in Ireland, General Richard Montgomery had married into a wealthy New York family, and to some degree was considered a New Yorker. He was challenged by the republican spirit of the New England troops under Wooster's command. Montgomery summed up his opinion in a letter to Schuyler earlier in October. "Troops who carry the spirit of freedom into the field, and think for themselves' will not bear either subordination or discipline."[86] Wooster and his men took their ideals of republican virtue with them to the front, even though this very independent spirit prohibited unified military subordination to the Continental Congress, and possibly even to the commander of the Northern Department.

Trumbull provided an image of the hardships of war through the eyes of a common soldier as Wooster's men marched north to Montreal. Extreme conditions, grueling weather, and the constant exposure to the November elements quickly took their toll on the men. Throughout November rains deluged the army, churning the roads into impassable mud and mire.[87] The enemy, in the meantime, was well defended and prepared for the advance of Wooster.

Not only were the conditions in Canada in October and November bad for the soldiers, but it was equally miserable for the women and children. When the British surrendered the fort at St. John's the garrison was permitted to leave under the honors of war. Trumbull witnessed the conditions of the civilians as they left the fort. However, the same conditions befell the civilians who accompanied the Connecticut troops northward. By mid–November as the army moved north the rains changed to snow and ice. "Some of the Regulars Wives and Children this morning came up from Montreal in a miserable Plight, Women badly clothed, Children bare foot and almost naked & covered almost with Mud and Water, and have in these Circumstances to go on 400 miles to New England. My Heart pitied them, and I wished to be able to help them."[88] The weather, coupled with disease and lack of hygiene, plagued the Continental Army in Canada in 1775. Smallpox ravaged the camps as winter bore down upon them.

Throughout the Canadian campaign, with all its challenges and hardships, Justus Bellamy continued to serve Wooster by preforming special military actions at the request of the general. One such incident occurred prior to the capture of St. John. Bellamy was placed on a secret guard detail and ordered to capture anyone who came in his direction from the fort, not to shoot them, but to bring them to headquarters. During the night, Bellamy took a British prisoner and stated in his pension record the following account:

> [Bellamy] saw him put something to his mouth, but he could not tell what it was because it was so dark. [Bellamy] took him to General Wooster and informed the general of all the particulars. The general searched him but could find nothing, and he affirmed that he had nothing about him. He would not talk much. The general compelled him to take a physic and kept a guard over him. [Bellamy] stayed by him all night, though he had not slept at all in three nights. In about two hours after taking the physic, the prisoner discharged the ball, which on being examined was found to be of silver and went together with a screw, and on taking it apart it contained a small bit of paper on which was written these words: "Hold out and you shall be relieved."[89]

It is important to see how Connecticut soldiers viewed their general. Examined through the perspective given in the orders and letters from delegates to the Continental Congress from New York, Wooster received a dismal mark. Even Washington, only meeting Wooster once thus far, viewed him as lacking enthusiasm and drive. These images were perpetuated through the letters of General Schuyler both to the Congress and the commander-in-chief. Connecticut solders, however, had a drastically different view as recorded by Trumbull in 1775:

> The Arrival of General Wooster and his troops, his great activity and Engagedness in the Service, as well as that of his men, animated and gave a Spring to the whole Army, and served to intimidate the Enemy. The taking of Chamblee with so many Prisoners and such large Stores, on the 16th of October contributed its Influence, to this happy Event, and especially the Defeat of Governor Carlton at Longale on the 30th of October, by Colonel Warner.
>
> General Wooster though he is not insensible that he is abused by not having his Rank in the Continental Army pursues the general good of the country with great Steadfastness and vigour. There appears to be great Harmony between him and other Generals. General Montgomery does nothing of importance without General Woosters advice; and though there has not been that harmony by any means in the Army which is absolutely necessary in Order to having measures prosecuted with vigour and Success, yet all those uneasinesses seem to have subsided on General Woosters arrival, and great Harmony now prevails in the Army.[90]
>
> Our Men have had such a Taste of the Officers in the New York department, that I am persuaded they would never proceed any further were not General Wooster with them, and I believe it will be impossible ever to enlist them to Serve this Way again under any Officers but their own; and perhaps it is well worthy of Consideration, whether the Common Cause will not Suffer should not General Wooster, before another Season, have his Rank in the Army.

The enthusiasm of Wooster's arrival in Canada was expressed in letters home and were reprinted in the local newspapers. As was the custom, letters printed in the papers oftentimes were left anonymous, as is the case with one dated November 22, titled "Extract of a Letter from a Gentleman at St. John's." In this letter the "gentleman" stated that "we expect to march immediately for Montreal, which we think must of course fall into our hands. Gen. Wooster is very hearty and has pushed matters with the greatest possible expedition—since his arrival, the whole camp has been almost continually on duty. There is the greatest harmony between him and Gen. Montgomery."[91]

Even though Silas Deane did not value Wooster's leadership, that did not prevent those who did write highly of the general. Samuel Lockwood, General Wooster's military secretary, expressed to Deane from Fort George in October, praising Wooster while stating the obvious reality of the disdain Connecticut soldiers and officers held towards their New York counterparts:

> I have already informed you that the New England Troops are universally disaffected with General Schuyler. I find, since, that the disaffection is by no means confined to the New England Troops, there being none who return from across the Lake, a few of his particular friends excepted, that speak well of him. But they all agree that the whole of the Army (even the New York Forces, the best of whom were originally New England people, being raised upon the Skirts of the Province,) were fervently praying for the arrival of General Wooster, who will push on as fast as possible.
>
> I am sure he [Wooster] will exert himself to prevent every mischief & to give success to the enterprise; but their being two Gen^rls above him, I know not what he can do to quiet the minds of the Troops. The most of the Officers upon this Station, who are all of this province, have already waited upon General Wooster with Complaints, in hopes it would be in his power to relieve them. In short, Sir, there never was an Army in such confusion & such a general uneasiness through all Ranks, Officers as well as Soldiers.
>
> I understand that the Congress have ordered a large supply of cloathing for this department. I could wish they had also ordered the Troops that are to wear them, for those who now compose the Army declare in the most positive manner they will not stay one minute after their time is up under the present commanding Officer. As they are so anxious to see Gen^rl Wooster, I hope he can persuade them to make a push & do something which, from the representations I can collect, is almost the only rational hope I have left.[92]

It is impressive to see such a viewpoint provided from a fellow soldier like Lockwood, yet a different perspective by a politician like Deane. Trumbull captured an almost exact opposite view of Wooster than those from New York; a view which would be repeated by others who served directly under him in battle and on campaign. The Continental Congress itself praised Wooster for his actions in taking St. John. It would be the last time that the Congress would offer their open praise and congratulations. Over the next six months they would do everything in their power to place the blame of the failure in the Canadian Campaign—their failure—squarely upon the shoulders of David Wooster.[93]

The campaign of 1775 ended on a very tenuous note for Brigadier General Wooster. After the reduction of St. John, the army under Montgomery's command captured Montreal. Wooster remained with his force at Montreal to secure that place from enemy activity. In the meantime, Montgomery marched with a small force to seize Quebec. By early December, Wooster had secured Montreal and much of the surrounding area, while Montgomery's forces were outside of Quebec. During the early weeks of December, Montgomery was occupied with planning for the attack against the great city. While there, reports arrived of a Canadian plan to cut off Montgomery's communications with the rest of the American army. Wooster dispatched Colonel Ritzema and a select group of men to capture Louis St. Luke de la Corne, known for inciting the Indians against the Americans during the French and Indian War, and who was behind this latest aggressive act against the Americans in Canada.[94] An officer in the American army wrote home that "General Wooster is taking the most prudent and spirited measures to put in the best order of defense possible."[95] Wooster provided the leadership that was needed. His years of military training were put to great use while stationed in Montreal in 1775.

Letters between Wooster, Montgomery, and Schuyler demonstrated the need for supplies, the constant concern with expiring enlistments of the men, the lack of hard currency, and the ever-increasing hostilities against the American troops by Canadians. British General Carleton had arrived to defend Quebec, bringing with him reinforcements and supplies. There was continued miscommunication between Schuyler and Wooster as to troops that had been discharged enroute between Albany and Ft. Ticonderoga. Schuyler demanded an account of these men, to which Wooster replied on December 18, informing him that he had discharged no one, but had granted several Connecticut officers, who were responsible for the pay of their soldiers, a furlough to return to New England where they might secure the necessary pay for their men, after which they were to return to Canada.[96]

Montgomery's plans for the reduction of Quebec were provided in detail in several letters both to Wooster and to Schuyler in the weeks prior to the ill-fated attack on the city. On December 26, Montgomery wrote to Schuyler of the situation near Quebec. There were some in the ranks who were uneasy with the current situation, being far from home for such an extended amount of time, as is seen with Montgomery himself, although he was determined to reduce the town if possible before returning home. One pressing complaint was the lack of funds, for the Canadians were not willing to accept Continental scrip. Wishing to return home, Montgomery pressed the Congress for permission to do just that, while leaving the "management of affairs in General Wooster's hands.."[97] He was not granted his request.

On December 31, Montgomery led his troops in an attack against Quebec. While at Montreal, Wooster received the disheartening news of the defeat of the American attack against the city, and more importantly, of the death of General Montgomery. Two separate letters informed Wooster of this, the first from Colonel Benedict Arnold, the second from Colonel Donald Campbell.[98] Arnold had led troops in the attack on Quebec and was seriously wounded in the leg. He informed Wooster that Montgomery had been killed. With one military action, and Schuyler convalescing, Wooster became the overall commander of the forces in Canada, and thus inherited all the problems that had been brewing for months.

7

1776

The new year did not bring much celebration to the Northern Department nor to the Continental Army in Canada. A continual litany of wants and dire needs wound their way throughout the winter months of 1775 and well into the spring of 1776 in Canada: men, money, medicine, ammunition, powder, food, and cannon. The failed attack upon Quebec, the death of General Richard Montgomery, and the wounded Benedict Arnold, all made the situation in Canada critical for the Continental forces. Fully aware of the expired enlistments of many Connecticut troops in December 1775, David Wooster had done everything in his power to encourage continual service or reenlistment, knowing the fragile nature of the army in Canada. He organized a provincial regiment to serve from December 1775 through the spring of 1776.[1] Early in January, Wooster faced the daunting task of reorganizing and restructuring the armies both at Quebec and at Montreal. The first order was to determine the number of men killed in action or taken prisoner at Quebec, and to ascertain the exact situation of the Continental Army there. His correspondence with Benedict Arnold, who was recovering in a field hospital near Quebec, was extremely helpful.

His priority was to maintain a strong presence in Montreal. Upon examination of the troop strength, informed Arnold that, at least in January, he ascertained that there were not enough men at Montreal to send reinforcements to the army outside of Quebec. Despite their military defeat he hoped that Arnold would be able to keep up the siege as best he could until reinforcements could arrive from Albany or some other quarter. Wooster wrote to General Philip Schuyler often, who, although ill and totally absent from the Canadian frontier, was still the ranking commander in the Northern Department. His letters pressed Schuyler for men, food, powder, lead, and hard currency. In a letter from Quebec on January 2, Colonel David Campbell informed Wooster of yet another urgent issue. "Some good men are gone, (and some, even without discharge,) and carried off their arms, which I wish could be recovered, as being in much demand here."[2] With the enlistments expiring, some were leaving for home of their own accord. Some disappeared in the night. One officer took his entire regiment home. How could they keep the men in Canada for the winter months after the disaster at Quebec? A lack of medicine was another key problem facing the American army. Benedict Arnold wrote that he eagerly looked forward to General Wooster arriving at Quebec to take charge of the situation there.[3] Unfortunately, with the lack of resources, and the tenuous hold that Wooster held on Montreal, the general would not be in Quebec until the first of April. It was extremely difficult to wage war in the winter months, especially a distance from home for an unknown length of time, and with a volunteer army.

All these issues were brought to Schuyler's attention.[4] Wooster wrote informing him that, with the large number of troops lost at Quebec, either killed in battle, missing, or taken prisoner, as well as those ill, he was unable to send an adequate force to support Arnold at Quebec and at the same time maintain control of Montreal. "I little expect, that with the troops who remain, to be able to continue the siege; in short our situation in this country is, at present, and will be, till we can have relief from the Colonies, very critical and dangerous."[5] Not only was Arnold in desperate need of reinforcement if Quebec was to be taken, but he was also desperate for money. The lack of hard currency for the Canadian expedition continually haunted the army in the Northern Department throughout 1775 and 1776.

To alleviate the lack of troops Wooster ordered that no one was permitted to leave the army regardless of the termination of their enlistment, at least until reinforcements were sent north.[6] This did not resolve the pressing issue, and Wooster needed new troops to prevent his dwindling force in Canada from disappearing. He wrote to Colonel Warner of his solution, albeit a short-term one. Wooster encouraged the Green Mountain corps under Warner's command to be brought to the Canadian front. Apparently, an earlier disagreement between Warner and Montgomery had prevented Warner's Green Mountain Boys from joining the army in Canada. Now, under Wooster's command, Warner eagerly brought his corps forward to the assistance of the army.[7]

All the while, Wooster was faced with the daunting task of encouraging the Canadians to join the American cause. Washington expressed a great desire to bring Canada into the American fold. In November 1775, Washington had written a field order for the army in Canada to not offend the French Catholic Canadians by burning effigies of Guy Fawkes or the pope on Guy Fawkes Day.[8] General Wooster found that the Catholic clergy in Montreal and Quebec "almost universally refuse absolution to those who are our friends, and preach to the people that it is not now too late to take arms against us."[9] Wooster detained a number of Catholic priests after an incident where a group of forty Canadians, led by their priest, attempted to ambush Wooster's men. The plot failed, but not without loss of life on both sides. Wooster felt that these religious leaders compromised the safety of his army in Canada. He was criticized for arresting Catholic priests and limiting the celebration of the Mass in Montreal.

On January 16, 1776, Washington wrote to Schuyler from his headquarters in Cambridge regarding the situations in Canada. At the conclusion of this letter, Washington commented on a recent letter received from Wooster and declared that he was surprised to see that Wooster had granted furloughs to his Connecticut troops. In Washington's opinion it would have been better had Wooster discharged his men rather than allowing them to return home on furlough, which would have saved a great deal of money—discharged men were not paid, whereas men on furlough were.[10] Wooster saw the situation from a different perspective.

As a veteran military commander, and now responsible for keeping the army intact and equipped in Canada in the winter, Wooster saw it best to send these troops home on a temporary furlough, still employed in the service of the army, rather than discharge them altogether. Some were colonial paymasters who returned with much needed pay for the army. Others went to enlist new troops who were as badly needed as specie. As noted earlier, two soldiers were sent home due to rheumatism.[11] Washington's letter articulated the challenge he faced as commander-in-chief with the mounting problems that befell his army in Canada as well as accepting varied solutions to these problems offered by his officers in the field.

Wooster wrote to inform the commander-in-chief of the actions taken at Montreal and Quebec on January 21. He explained why he had not yet moved with the army to Quebec, as Washington had received word from Schuyler and Arnold, both of whom were in no position to direct the forces in the field, whereas Wooster was. To Washington, he stated:

> I should have gone down, immediately, upon hearing of the defeat, to the camp before Quebec, but the necessity of securing this place [Montreal], and the country round, in our interest, induced all the officers and our friends here, to request me not to leave this place, till we should have a reinforcement from the Colonies; when they arrive, I expect to proceed on with them. We have many enemies in this Province, particularly among the Clergy, who are using every artifice to excite the Canadians to take up arms against us; but I hope to be able to prevent any thing of the kind.
>
> The taking of Quebec must be a matter of the greatest consequence to the Colonies, but at present we are very ill provided for it. The place is strong.[12]

Conflict quickly arose once more between Wooster and Schuyler over the return of prisoners to the front, those who had been sent to Ticonderoga or Albany for safe keeping. Wooster had detained several key Canadians who were seen to be causing trouble for the Continental Army near Montreal and Quebec. In accordance with the Articles of War, these prisoners were sent away from the front to Schuyler at Fort Ticonderoga. One of Wooster's challenges was dealing with prisoners and spies. Many individuals were sent to Schuyler who, in turn, sent many of these men and women back north to Wooster. This caused no end of frustration for the success of the army in Canada. Wooster wrote to Schuyler expressing that

> some of the persons you have sent back have really behaved very illy, indeed. One Sears, whom I have now in confinement, immediately upon coming into the country circulated a report, that the Colonies had given over the thoughts of keeping this Province; that there were no soldiers at Ticonderoga or Fort George, nor any expected, &c., &c.; a story very illy calculated for us at this time. Some others, I hear, have made themselves very busy with the people. I expect, therefore, to be obliged to return to you some of them, with the other prisoners who are in this country, in a few days.[13]

He replied to Schuyler's letter of January 14 and reiterated the need to keep political and military agitators out of Canada. He complained to Schuyler about one in particular, stating that "Major Campbell has behaved in a very extraordinary manner, and has thrown out most ungenerous and illiberal invectives against my character. He told Captain Benedict at Chambly, that I was a damned old scoundrel, and had broke my faith with him."[14] Major Campbell was the son-in-law to the infamous and dangerous French Indian Agent in Canada, Mr. St. Luke La Carne, who had been promised the opportunity to return north for business. Wooster, who had much to contend with, refused the promise that General Montgomery had given months earlier to Campbell, and prohibited him from venturing into Canada, preventing further problems among the population there. Wooster closed his letter to Schuyler, as he had stated in every one of his letters to the commander of the Northern Department, by stressing once more the need of men and cannon if Quebec was to be taken. He had, however, found a local Canadian who was able to cast shot and shell for any cannon that Schuyler could send to him from Ticonderoga; all Wooster needed to know was the size of cannon hopefully to be supplied to him.

Wooster was also extremely conscious of the impact that the weather had upon any army stationed in Canada, American and British. He was well aware that the Saint Lawrence River would freeze mid-winter and prevent any British supplies from reaching Quebec, foods items or troop reinforcements. At the same time, this allowed a window of opportunity to the American troops to take the city, if more troops were rushed north. However, he had been informed that this window of opportunity was rather small and by March, all hope of taking Quebec would be lost. The river would begin to thaw, and large ice chunks would make it impassable. At the same time all roads in the area became muddy quagmires.[15] If too much time elapsed, British General Guy Carleton would have the city heavily reenforced.

Tensions continued to rise between Wooster and Schuyler throughout January and February 1775. Schuyler continually sent information to the Continental Congress, and to Washington, relating to the tensions in the army, as well as what he viewed as increased insubordination of Wooster. Meanwhile, Wooster was left to deal with the situation at hand in Canada. He faced an insurmountable task considering the way the commander of the Northern Army treated him. Schuyler fumed over Wooster returning detainees to him that he had sent north, informing the general that their personal request to return peacefully home to their families seemed reasonable enough and, therefore, he returned them north. Schuyler escalated the situation by sending the following missive to Wooster:

> Resolved, sir, to be treated with the respect due to me as a gentleman, and as an officer intrusted with a command by the honourable the Representatives of Thirteen Colonies, it is my positive order that you cause all persons as have had my permit to return to Canada be called before you, and there confronted with their accusers, that they may have an opportunity to exculpate themselves, if they can, from the charges which are made against them, and, if you find them guilty, then send them here in close confinement, together with the affidavits ascertaining their guilt.[16]

At the same time, he wrote to Washington and included copies of Wooster's letters, all the while complaining that Wooster "has before wrote to me on the occasion, with an unbecoming subacity."[17] Schuyler's pen made an impact on Washington's opinion of New England officers and of Wooster in particular. To Schuyler Washington wrote on January that there was "little hope of Arnold's continuing the blockade without assistance from Wooster, which he is determined not to give, whether with propriety or not, I shall not, at this distance, undertake to decide."[18] Unbeknownst to Washington, Wooster had sent Arnold one-hundred-and-fifty men, a small amount to be sure, but an abundance when considering that he had very few to send him. While Schuyler wrote scathing letters complaining of Wooster's ill-treatment towards him, the Continental Congress ordered one ton of powder shipped to Wooster in Canada, as did Governor Trumbull. Wooster wrote to the governor thanking him for the shipment which he received in late January.[19]

From January through March 1776, a flurry of correspondence took place between Wooster, Schuyler, Washington, and the Continental Congress concerning the situation in Canada. A majority dealt with the necessity of hard currency being brought up to pay the soldiers and to compensate the Canadians for military purchases, such as food for the soldiers, and fodder for the horses and cattle. By mid–January Canadians refused to accept anything but hard currency from the Continental Army for goods purchased. To them the Continental script was worthless, and the army's credit was running dangerously low. Wooster had a solution to this crisis. In a letter to Schuyler, dated January 14, 1776, he proposed the following:

> Will it not be well, in order in some measure to remedy the great difficulty of procuring hard money, to encourage a number of sutlers to bring across the Lakes all kinds of West-India and other liquors, sugar, and other articles, which can be procured in the Colonies, and wanted by the Army, for which they can be paid in paper money? I am confident that rum, wine, sugar, &c., can be well transported from Albany here and sold as a great profit, and yet be much cheaper than what we now give for it.

In a second letter to Schuyler the same day he further stated his point:

> All kinds of liquors and West-India goods, are so extravagantly dear here, that I am confident they may be brought over the Lakes to great advantage. In order, therefore, in some measure, to remedy the great difficulty in procuring hard cash, suppose rum and sugar should be forwarded for the soldiers, and a number of Sutlers should be encouraged to come over with every kind of article wanted in the Army, for which we are obliged to pay hard money here at the most extravagant rates. The Sutlers would be able to sell them to us full as low, and many things much lower, and take in pay Continental money. The people in the country seeing the money pass freely among us, perhaps will be induced to give it a currency.[20]

Bringing sutlers into Canada to sell goods to the soldiers was a solution to the lack of supplies. Wooster foresaw this earlier as he had his army bring supplies with them the previous fall. The sutlers would be under contract by the Continental Congress, and as such, would accept the Continental script as payment from the soldiers in the field. Once they returned, they would be reimbursed by the Congress in Philadelphia. If Canadians saw them accepting this payment, then the Continental script would be seen as sound currency, and they would be encouraged to accept it as legal tender in the absence of hard cash. Wooster pressed this idea several times. Procuring specie was too long in coming. As a successful merchant from New Haven, he knew the potential of this type of supply and demand economics. He also sent the proposal to the president of the Continental Congress on January 27, 1775, upon receipt of their notice of congratulation for the success at St. John two months earlier.[21] The idea was never adopted, adding yet another impossible hurdle to the success of the Canadian expedition.

His leadership never waned. Throughout the winter months of early 1776 Wooster planned for ways to integrate Canadians into the Continental system, although most saw the Americans as invaders. First, he challenged those who had received military commissions from British General Guy Carleton to transfer them into commissions provided by the Congress. Those who refused would be considered traitors and seized. In the orders of January 27, 1775, it was posted that

> the General [Wooster] must consider all those gentlemen who insist upon retaining their commissions under Governor Carleton, as enemies to the United Colonies, and not a private citizen, and as such include in the treaty with this town. He cannot see the propriety or consistency of their holding out friendship in one hand, and the sword in the other.
>
> By Order of GENERAL WOOSTER
>
> James Van Rensselaer, Aid-de-Camp [signed][22]

Second, he proposed a brilliant, and radical plan to create an extension of the Continental Congress in Canada, something that no one else had attempted. If an invading army with similar western traditions and history sought to include new territory and peoples into their dominion, what better way to do so than to allow them some element of self-government and a voice within the newly formed governing body in America? He wrote of his proposal to General Schuyler:

> I am also about establishing a Committee of Safety in this town [Montreal], which will be, also, a Committee of Correspondence. They will, by settling a thousand trifling disputes, ease me of a very great burden. But I have something further in view: when it is once established in this town, perhaps other places in this country will be inclined to follow the example, and by degrees they may possibly be led to choose a Provincial Congress, and, of course, Delegates for the Continental Congress. I confess, to me there appears at least a plausibility in the scheme, What we wish, we easily believe.[23]

Neither of Wooster's proposals, the use of sutlers in Canada who received Continental script for payment, or the ideal of an extension of the Continental Congress in Canada were ever adopted. The struggle for supplies, money, and troops continued into February.

From his headquarters in Cambridge, Washington, himself overburdened by the sheer scale and scope of managing to entire army now active in numerous military departments, and under pressure from the Continental Congress, wrote to Wooster about the utmost urgency of taking Canada:

> I need not mention to you the importance of Canada in the scale of our affair—to whomever it belongs, in their favour, probably, will the balance turn. If it is ours, success will crown our virtuous struggles; if our enemy's, the contest, at best, will be doubtful, hazardous, and bloody.[24]

Faced with similar predicaments, Washington certainly could have appreciated the dire straits in which Wooster had been placed. As the war dragged on, Washington experienced first-hand the same types of political wrangling and military divisiveness from his own generals that Wooster faced in Canada in 1776.

Early in February there appeared a glimmer of hope from the correspondences within the Northern Department. Collaboration and cooperation between Wooster and Schuyler appeared to be on the mend, or at least several letters had hinted. Schuyler had sent copies of letters to John Hancock that praised Wooster. In one Schuyler wrote:

May Heaven graciously be pleased to extricate you out of the perilous situation you [Wooster] are in. At this distance it would be presumption in me to direct what measures should be taken; these can only be determined by events as they turn up. May God guide your councils and bless your operations.

Further, in replying to Wooster's request to aid Arnold's retreat from Quebec, Schuyler encouraged him to assist in securing the retreat of Colonel Arnold, and to be prepared to secure the town in the event that General Carleton should follow and attack. He hoped that Wooster would do his duty and defend the town to his utmost. Schuyler praised Wooster for his idea in bringing sutlers into Canada:

The hint General Wooster has given, in sending Sutlers to Canada, is a very good one. If I can get any good men to go, I will venture to assist them, on proper security, with money out of the military chest here, to purchase the necessary articles, and let them repay it in Canada.[25]

Unfortunately, as the military situation in Canada worsened for the Americans, so to would the cooperation between the two men. The number of soldiers remaining in Canada following the defeat at Quebec, along with number of desertions and end-of-enlistment departures, had yielded a staggeringly low number of soldiers who remained on active duty. Those who did remain were also subject to the ravages of smallpox that continued to plague the northern army. Schuyler wrote to the Congress of the poor condition and decreased number of men in the Northern Department who were able to take the field after the Battle of Quebec. He wrote:

General Wooster, in a letter of the 20th untimo says:
I have just received intelligence from our army before Quebeck; they still continue the blockade with spirit, yet are greatly distressed for want of men, being alarmed almost every night, and having so few men, if not assisted in a little time, good as they are (and men never behaved better) they must be worn out.[26]
    Yesterday Colonel Ritzema arrived from Canada, and brought me a letter from General Wooster, copy whereof enclose. Colonel Ritzema does not think it possible to complete two regiments out of the last campaign's troops, now in Canada. I shall be agreeably disappointed if one can be raised there.[27]

To continue the successful campaign in Canada, Wooster needed men by the thousands; ammunition, which needed to be specially made for their cannon; food (pork would be sent by the barrel from Fort Ticonderoga, however the price to ship them to Wooster was at a tremendous cost); medicine (smallpox was beginning to ravage both the camp at Montreal and Quebec); and hard currency. As the winter months rolled on, Wooster faced a more dangerous enemy, the Canadian winter. As February dragged into March, and few of the required supplies arrived, his letters stressed the timeliness of action as the window of opportunity for reducing Canada was getting smaller by the day. The garrison at Quebec had enough provisions inside the fort to last them until spring, the same time the British would sail up the St. Lawrence and resupply the city. In the meantime, the roads approaching Quebec would become impassable due to mud. The best way to supply Wooster and his men was by sled over the rivers and frozen lakes. Faced with mounting impossibilities, including pressure to take Canada, Wooster wrote to the Continental Congress on February 11, 1776, that "besides the operations of war, there are so many civil and political affairs that require the greatest care and most delicate management, that I could wish a Committee of Congress might be sent into this Province."[28] In the same letter he noted that Arnold had been sufficiently resupplied to avert any immediate crisis and allowed him to keep up the siege of Quebec. Wooster noted that "Quebec must be taken before May."[29]

Yet, while Wooster did his utmost to provide for his men in Canada, his feud with Schuyler escalated. Schuyler continued to send letters to members of Congress and leading generals degrading and complaining about Wooster's leadership of the army in Canada. Not one to sit idly by when his own honor and character was under attack and showing his growing impatience with the situation in Canada, coupled with his advanced age, Wooster took to the pen. Congress was alerted of the improbability of holding Canada without sufficient supplies and troops. He defended his position against the abuses, as he saw them, from his commander and informed Congress of the dispute:

He [Schuyler] writes to me that he had observed to Congress that I had wrote him with unbecoming subacity. I think he might have pointed out to me the exceptionable parts of my letters, before he made his observations to Congress. It gives me pain that I am obliged, in my own defense, to trouble you with examining and determining which of us has the greatest reason to complain of ill treatment.

I am conscious that my conduct will bear the strictest scrutiny. I have ever studiously avoided entering into any altercation with him, fearing that the publick interest might suffer by it. He began to insult me immediately on my joining the Army, as you will see by his letter of the 23rd of October last, though I know of no reason under Heaven why he should treat me thus cavalierly, but merely to indulge his capricious humour, which in the course of the last year, he has dealt out very liberally upon many of the officers who have served in this Department, complaints of which have frequently been made to me. Happy would it be for him, and for our cause, if he could learn to bridle his passions. The letters between him and me will speak for themselves. I shall send him a copy of this letter, and also enclose with this a copy of my letter to him, of this date. No personal ill treatment will ever prevent my steadily and invariably continuing to pursue those measures which shall appear most conducive to the publick good, and shall think myself happy, if, by doing every thing in my power, I can be in the least instrumental in maintaining and preserving the rights and liberties of my country.[30]

True to his word, he wrote to Schuyler that same day relaying his perspective of their dispute. After months of frustration under Schuyler's command, Wooster sent the following letter to his commander, which he had copied to the Congress:

Sir:

Your letter of the 26th ultimo, I have received; in answer to which, give me leave to observe to you, that I, also, claim a right to be treated with respect due to me as a gentleman and an officer intrusted with a command from the honourable the Representatives of thirteen Colonies. Why, sir, are these positive mandates? Have I ever disputed your orders? Since I have been in the Army, I have exerted every faculty to promote a union among the officers, and have carefully avoided every thing that might have the least tendency to cause jealousies; in short, sir, I have steadily and invariably pursued those measures that appeared to me conducive to the true interest of our county. How ungenerous therefore, is it, that an advantage should be taken of my conciliating disposition; yet you will pardon me if I misjudge, I cannot account for your imperious conduct towards me upon any other principle. You will remember your letter to me while I was at St. John's, founded in falsehood, and which you could have no other motive for writing but to insult me. I thought it, at that time, not worth answering, and shall, at present, take no further notice of it. I shall, however, send a copy of it to Congress, and of your last letter, together with copies of my own, except for the one you observed was wrote with unbecoming subacity. As you have already complained to the honourable Congress, I have thought it my duty to show them what passed between us, and they will judge which of us has the greatest reason to complain of ill treatment. For the present, let the matter rest. They will doubtless do justice. This is no time to altercate, the whole of our time is little enough to attend to the operations absolutely necessary for the defense of our country.

You will give me leave to inform you, that the commanding officer who is with this Army is to give out orders, and is the only competent judge of what is proper, and what is not, for the internal regulations of the Army, and for the immediate safety of the country. Since the death of the worthy and brave General Montgomery (with whom I had the happiness to serve in the strictest harmony and friendship, and who ever treated me like a gentleman) the command devolves upon me, and I shall give out such orders as appears to me necessary for the publick good, and shall send out of the country all prisoners and such persons as may be thought dangerous to our cause. As soon as it can be done with convenience, the returns of the Army shall be made out and transmitted to you. I shall, also, take care that your orders to General Montgomery are executed as far as possible. I shall do every thing in my power to carry into execution every resolve of Congress

P.S. I will just observe, further, that I think it would have been much more generous in you to have pointed out to me the exceptionable parts of my letters, before you complained to Congress.[31]

This postscript exemplified the relationship between these two men. The disrespect and pettiness that Schuyler exhibited towards Wooster never changed while the two men worked together in the Northern Department. Despite the growing animosity, Wooster was conscious to follow the strictest military protocol, even if his immediate superior had been absent from the field due to illness. In late January, Wooster sought Schuyler's permission to hold a general court martial for several prisoners and made sure to follow military protocol as he awaited a response. He did not wish to repeat the situation that had earlier caused such consternation.

Just three weeks from his sixty-sixth birthday, Wooster's frustration with the Continental Congress, their lack of apparent interest in supplying the very army in Canada that they continued to press for action in taking Quebec, his dealings with Schuyler, and his old age prompted him to write to his friend, Roger Sherman. This letter of February 11 was filled with every pent-up emotion the aged commander had restrained himself in expressing earlier. He began by thanking his friend for his letter of January 20, added a few niceties, stressed the need for more, and then confided his utmost agitation:

Dear Sir,

I am much obliged to you for your favor of the 20th ult. I was happy to hear that the Congress had made provision for our speedy reinforcement in this Province. Yet I fear it will not be sufficient if, as many conjecture, the ministry should send a large army here early in the Spring. Mr. Walker and Mr. Price, two gentlemen zealously attached to our cause, I have requested to go to Congress. They are the best acquainted with this province and with the tempers and dispositions of the Canadians, of perhaps any men in it. They will inform you much better that I can, of everything concerning them.

I have sent to Congress copies of several letters which have passed between General Schuyler and me. By which, and my letter upon the subject you will see that we are not upon the most friendly terms. Which of us has occasioned the coolness the Congress will judge upon examining the letters. I think it a great unhappiness that we cannot agree among ourselves. I am conscious however of no fault or neglect of mine to occasion it. I can write freely to you. As you have lately been in Connecticut you must have heard the general dissatisfaction (among the troops of that Colony who were employed in this department) at the treatment they met with from General Schuyler. It was much as I could do to keep them easy and in the service, and had it not been for their expectations of my arrival among them the consequences might have been fatal to our operations in this country. You will not think that this proceeds from vanity or private pique, be assured, Sir, it is from a real concern for our country. The uneasiness in the army was and is now by no means confined to the Connecticut troops, but is universal among all who have served under him. And should he come into this country to take the command many of the best officers in the army would immediately throw up their commissions provided it can be done without risking every thing. I wish I had as much consideration.

It is not from ambitious views of keeping the command myself that I make these observations, though my services and experience might possibly entitle me to it. I should have been happy to have served under General Montgomery. He once, from some trouble he met with from some of his officers determined to leave the service and actually resigned the command to me, but apprehending unhappy consequences might follow from it, I persuaded him, though with great difficulty to reassume it. You will readily perceive the terrible consequences that may follow from a want of confidence in the commanding officer. I greatly fear in the first place that it will be difficult to raise the men, and when they are raised they will soon catch the opinions of those now in the army. I hope the evils apprehended will prove less than our fears.

Col. Hazen and Col. Antill both inform me that the Congress have appointed me Maj. General. As General Schulyer has not informed me of it and there is nothing of it in the extracts of the Resolves of Congress sent to me by him, I shall be obliged to you for information. You will be pleased to remember me respectfully to Messrs Huntington and Woolcot and believe me with the greatest truth and sincerity your real friend and most obedient

Very humble servant,

David Wooster[32]

The feud between Schuyler and Wooster continued. Upon receipt of Wooster's letter of February 11, stating that he had sent copies of their correspondence to the Congress, Schuyler penned a note of feigned outrage to the Congress:

Congress will perceive by General Wooster's letter of the 11th instant, to them, and that of the same date to me, that matters are got to such a height between us, that either he or I must immediately quit this department, for I cannot, consistent with my honour or my feelings, serve with an officer, who, very early in the campaign, witnessed a contempt for my orders, and proceeded so far as to offer insults of the grossest kinds, which, as I have not the least doubt but my informants will support, I must, therefore, request that Congress will order an inquiry to be immediately made.... A respect for my country, sir, obliges me to suppress that just resentment which I felt rising in me at his conduct at Fort-George, &c.; but wounded in my honour, although willing to be spent in the glorious cause my country is engaged in, and to continue to serve her under all the disagreeable incidents attendant on a ruined constitution, yet, she cannot expect, in addition, a sacrifice of my reputation, by calmly bearing indignities. Indeed, this would render me unable to serve her.[33]

Enraged that Wooster would have the audacity to write to the Congress alerting them of his perception of the situation in Canada, which was by this point causing division between the Connecticut and New York troops, Schuyler reached his point of contention. He mentioned that Wooster did not ask permission prior to holding a court martial at Lake George the previous fall. The fact that Wooster had done this on his own initiative without following the new directives within the military structure of the new Continental Army remained a divisive point between the two. Unfortunately for Wooster, who was stationed in active command either in Montreal or Quebec, he had limited access to members of Congress and did not retain the luxury of having many supporters within the Continental Congress or the New York Assembly quite like Philip Schuyler. By the end of February 1776, Schuyler began to call upon those friends to remove Wooster from the Canadian theater once and for all.

With the army in Canada reduced in number, although some reinforcements arrived from the neighboring colonies, the army under Schuyler needed to be reorganized. Schuyler attempted to regain control of military matters and sent a lengthy order to his commanders in Montreal and Quebec informing them of the restructuring of the army, not only of the enlisted men, but of officers as well. One can only imagine the exasperation felt by Wooster upon receiving Schuyler's orders. Although they did not alter his position or command, the realigning of the regiments caused unending and unnecessary confusion. In a reply to Schuyler, Wooster commented on his plan to restructure remaining regiments in Canada. The proposed plan would place men of one colony under the command of an officer of another, thus harming the existing military cohesion. Months of antagonism between New York and Connecticut alone would prove that such a plan was dangerous to morale and to keeping men in the field. Wooster saw that such a plan would make it "very difficult, if not impossible, to persuade but very few of them to engage for a longer time than their present inlistments; yet I should be sorry that those officers who are willing to continue on the service should not have an opportunity." He also saw that it would advance younger officers in command of older ones, possibly a petty notion, but one that Wooster had personally experienced. "Suppose, sir, that the troops from Hampshire, Massachusetts, and Connecticut, should form one regiment, and the different New-York battalions another, and the officers be ranked according to seniority? From some conversation I have had with several of the officers, I am persuaded the other plan cannot be effectuated."[34] Wooster's challenge to Schuyler's plan only deepened the antagonism between the two officers.

The situation in Canada became worse by the end of February. In order to press Congress into action, any action, to alleviate the horrid condition that the army had been barely surviving under, Wooster once more alerted Congress of their dire situation, informing them that "provisions and wood cannot be obtained, nor can we pay for the transporting of any thing, but with hard cash, which, if we are not immediately supplied with, we must either starve, quit the country, or disgrace our army and the American cause, by laying the country under contribution; there is no other alternative."[35]

Wooster was limited in what he could accomplish, given the condition of his men and the lack of supplies. He requested the Congress to send supplies, for "our flour is already in a manner gone, and every other kind of provision soon will be. I understand there is a quantity of pork at Fort George, which I have desired General Schuyler to forward across the Lakes; whether he will do it or not, I cannot say; I hope he will."[36] He continued to wait for information on the type of cannon that might be sent to him and Arnold for the reduction of Quebec. Nothing of the sort arrived.

During the Canadian expedition, Wooster employed the services of French Catholics Jean Baptiste Degas and Prudent La Jeuness. Degas helped to lead prisoners to Ft. Ticonderoga. La Jeuness received a pass from General Wooster to travel, unmolested, to Philadelphia to report to Congress on the situation in Canada. It was the visit from La Jeuness that prompted the Continental Congress to finally send a delegation to Montreal and Quebec to investigate the condition of the army in Canada.

Military activity in the Northern Department necessitated the involvement of the Continental Congress. The Congress organized the Committee of Secret Correspondence, which reported on the Canadian Campaign of 1775–1776. It was clear from the volume of letters that dire help was needed, which had been repeated numerous times from all commanders in Canada, Schuyler, Montgomery, and Wooster. These requests met little action from Congress. The Committee of Secret Correspondence met and interviewed the delegation Wooster sent from Canada in late February. In their report the committee wrote that the late General Montgomery had twice asked General Schuyler to request a Congressional committee to act as a general assembly in Canada. The situation in Canada was such that the presence of a delegation from the Continental Congress who could assist in alleviating the poor condition of the army, was the only way that necessary supplies could adequately reach the army in good time. The Congress sent one delegation, which went no further than Fort Ticonderoga, where General Schuyler was stationed. Promises for future delegations were made, yet none arrived in Canada while Montgomery was still alive.[37]

As Montgomery had mentioned in 1775, and Wooster reiterated time and again, supplying the army in Canada would be challenging as the spring approach. Not only were the roads impassable, but there was also a lack of forage for horses that were required to haul the needed supplies. By the time that the paymaster arrived at Montreal on February 19, he did not bring any hard currency with him with which the army could use to buy supplies from Canadians. To highlight the severity of the situation, which now included the real lack of gunpowder, Wooster wrote to Schuyler, the Congress, and leading men in Connecticut as well. To preserve much needed powder for the troops in Canada, on February 22 the town of New Haven passed the following local law:

> a misuse of powder may prove very prejudicial, not only to the public in general, but to the Town, therefore, Resolved, that no person or persons whatsoever, shall, by sporting or fowling, fire away any of that necessary article, within the limits of the town, upon the penalty of 1d. [shilling] lawful money for each offence.[38]

The need for gunpowder was so great that a powder mill was built near New Haven in the summer of 1776 and an advertisement ran in the *Connecticut Journal* which requested a supply of "Salt Petre" and "Sulphur" to produce gunpowder.[39]

By the end of February, the Committee of Secret Correspondence had informed the Congress about the situation of the army in Canada. Prior commissions did not venture further north than Fort Ticonderoga. Following the communications from Schuyler and Wooster, and upon hearing about the reduced condition of the army, a new congressional commission was formed. The Congress finally appeared to act, and an official investigative committee was dispatched to Canada to inquire on the state of the army and resources needed to secure Montreal and Quebec, and hopefully, to encourage Canada to become an ally. This committee consisted of Benjamin Franklin of Pennsylvania, Samuel Chase, Charles Carroll of Carrollton, and the Rev. John Carroll, all from Maryland. The Revered John Carroll, a Jesuit priest, was selected to persuade the French clergy to align with the American cause. Charles Carroll of Carrollton was not a member of Congress, but was a wealthy and influential Catholic, educated in France. His journal of the trip contained minute details of who the commission met with, both civilian and military, where they stayed, and the condition of the army from their perspective. The committee left in for Canada on April 2.

Meanwhile, Wooster continued to maintain control of the situation in Canada as best he could amidst dwindling supplies, the lack of hard currency, an increasingly hostile native population, both French and Indian, and the spread of smallpox amongst his troops. These required of the aging Wooster, who on March 2 had just turned sixty-six and was the oldest general in the army, the combined skills of a military strategist, peace negotiator, and to some extent, a magician. He continued to write to Schuyler for cannon and currency, neither of which he received. Schuyler informed the Congress on March 6 that, of the required sleds needed to haul cannon to Quebec, 120, only seventy-six could be gathered, and these had not yet been sent north with the required artillery for the reduction of Quebec.[40] Schuyler attempted to remedy the situation by requesting that Connecticut supply the much needed specie rather than the Congress.[41] While this continued, Wooster sought some remedy to the number of prisoners that Schuyler continued to release and send north, all of which further exacerbated the tremendous burden placed upon him. Exhausted, he wrote to Schuyler on March 16, "I have made a calculation of what powder we have in the country, and find there is not more than sixty rounds for six thousand men, supposing we had no use for cannon." He continued, relaying that he was "very sorry that the whole of the provisions, cannon, artillery, stores, &c., which were designed for this country, could not be sent forward. I hardly know what we shall do. Our money is already gone. Hope there is some upon the road."[42] Despite his frustration, he remained optimistic about taking Quebec, saying "that he should scale the walls of that place, if there was space sufficient between them and the heavens."[43]

Unbeknownst to Wooster, who had left Montreal on March 27 and traveled to Quebec to relieve Arnold, who returned to Montreal, the congressional commission finally reached Albany, and was entertained by Schuyler on April 7. Those who journaled of their experiences wrote about his exquisite residence and commented on the comfort and hospitality shown to them. Schuyler traveled with them as far north as Fort Ticonderoga. They then proceeded north to St. John. While at St. John, Dr. Franklin, who had taken ill, returned to Congress in Philadelphia. The commissioners who would determine the fate of the army in Canada, and of Wooster, consisted of Charles Carroll of Carrollton, the Rev. Father John Carroll, and Samuel Chase, all from Maryland and all Catholic. There was not one New Englander on the commission from the Congress, and not one supporter of Wooster. Samuel Chase was the only congressman and was also a close friend and supporter of Schuyler. The deck had most certainly been stacked against Wooster.

On April 29, the commissioners were received by Benedict Arnold, who was recovering in Montreal. Arnold had fallen from his horse a second time near Quebec and re-injured his severely wounded leg. He received the original wound storming Quebec on December 31 with Montgomery. Reluctantly he requested to convalesce at Montreal, thus explaining the change of locations for Wooster and Arnold. Arnold disliked the older general, who had refused to implement the younger subordinate's suggestions for the army's actions against Quebec. While meeting with Arnold the commissioners commented on the comfort of their surroundings. However, upon examination of the army, and their conditions in Chambly, the members of the committee reported on April 23 that

> we found all things in much confusion, extreme disorder and negligence, our credit sunk, and no money to retrieve it with. We were obliged to pay three silver dollars for the carriage of three barrels of gunpowder from Little Chamblay river to Longueil, the officer who commanded the guard not having a single shilling.[44]

Wooster had repeatedly requested the presence of a congressional committee in Montreal to assist him in expediting his military and civic duties. They never arrived. At the request of Schuyler, months later, one finally arrived to examine the condition of the army and the stalled offensive against Quebec.[45] The committee was appalled at what they saw in Canada. Their report to the president of the congress stated that

> we found all things in Canada in confusion; there is little or no discipline among your troops. Your Army is badly paid; and so exhausted is your credit that even a cart cannot be procured without ready money or force. The Army is in a distressed condition, and is in want of the most necessary articles—meat, bread, tents, shoes, stockings, shirts, &c.[46]

The committee further noted that they had ordered fifteen barrels of flour to be seized from the inhabitants to bake bread and feed the army. "Men with arms in their hands will not starve when provisions can be obtained by force," the commission reported.[47] The conditions of the army in Canada, as witnessed by the commissioners, were exactly as Wooster had written about since taking command of the army in January. He had petitioned Schuyler and the Congress repeatedly over the lack of all supplies to no avail. The commissioners placed the blame of the deteriorated condition of the army on Wooster, a political move, stating in their report that "General Wooster is, in our opinion, unfit, totally unfit, to command your Army, and conduct the war; we have hitherto prevailed on him to remain in Montreal. His stay in this Colony is unnecessary, and even prejudicial to our affairs; we would therefore humbly advise his recall."[48]

The Congressional Commission left Canada on June 1, 1776. The furthest north this group traveled was to the camp at Sorel, which was one-hundred and twenty-five miles southwest of Quebec. For most of their expedition to Canada they stayed in Montreal, which itself is one-hundred and fifty miles southwest of Quebec. The commissioners only met once with Wooster, which was just prior to their departure home. All their information came from Schuyler, Arnold, and their own observations of the men and the army. The journal of Charles Carroll of Carrollton mentioned the friendship between the commissioners and Schuyler, and of the very cordial hospitality they received from Arnold; all the while Wooster, serving as the commanding general of the army in Canada, had no equal opportunity to defend himself to the commissioners. Ironically, absolutely everything that the committee had stated as dereliction of duty on Wooster's part were the exact same things found in his letters to the Congress, which had been addressed by Schuyler in the fall of 1775.

Throughout March and April, there was an additional dilemma to the American situation in Canada. News reached Wooster and Schuyler that hostile Indians in Canada were angered with the continued American presence. This was aggravated by the lack of hard currency offered by the Congress for payment of good needed by the army, as well as the congressional committee's insistence that the army "seize by force" any items that would be needed by the army, if Continental script was not accepted. Wooster was torn between removing himself to Quebec and maintaining a strong military leadership position in Montreal. His absence made possible an Indian attack on Montreal. Wooster wrote to Washington that another attempt on Quebec would be made upon the arrival of more troops and artillery for the bombardment city.[49]

Wooster knew that without any large cannon any attempt to take Quebec was pointless. He had been writing to Schuyler since January about the necessity of large artillery, which Schuyler never sent. Wooster had pressed the commander of the Northern Department for timely action. Now, in April, every letter-filled prediction Wooster had made came true; the roads were impassable, the rivers were choked with ice flows which had started to thaw, and the necessary manpower had not arrived. Wooster attempted to launch fire ships against Quebec in the hopes that these would set fire to the British ships in the harbor. Alerted by an informant, the garrison of Quebec kept a constant watch and the ill-fated attempt produced nothing of significance.[50]

Writing to John Hancock on March 6, 1776, Schuyler informed the Congress that "on the 28th ultimo I sent General Wooster something about twenty-one hundred pounds in specie, which I have collected on my notes, payable in like money, on demand. We are greatly distressed for money for the current expenses of the day."[51] Despite this temporary influx of specie, the army in Canada continued to struggle to pay for all the supplies it so greatly needed with currency that held dubious value at best to the civilians in Canada.

To add one final nail to the coffin of the Canadian expedition of the spring of 1776, a smallpox epidemic ravaged the camps and military hospitals, against which the little medicine that the army did have was inadequate to provide for the numbers of soldiers wracked with the disease. Wooster was in the process of having his men inoculated, but by the spring only half had received it.

In the meantime, the Congress, meeting in Philadelphia, reevaluated their officer corps and voted to offer promotions and new field commands to several men. On March 7, John Adams wrote to Brigadier General Thomas informing him that he had been promoted to major general in the Continental Army and was being sent to take over the forces under the command of Brigadier General David Wooster in Canada.[52] Despite having been in Canada since November 1775, Wooster was passed over for a promotion. Of the original eight brigadier generals appointed in June 1775, Thomas was sixth in seniority while Wooster was third, and remained so.

By early May 1776, word reached the American forces in Canada that British ships had entered the St. Lawrence River with reinforcements for Quebec, exactly what Wooster had warned would happen if the Congress did not reinforce and resupply the American troops there first. Depleted by smallpox, which many believed had been inflicted purposely upon the American troops by order of British General Guy Carleton, Wooster's men were in no condition to repulse an arrival of fresh British troops in Canada.[53] Short on ammunition, food, medical supplies, and cash to purchase anything from the Canadians, Wooster's hopes for success diminished. Thomas arrived in Quebec on May 1 and took command four days later. The next day, as Wooster had forewarned, British reinforcements arrived at the city. On June 8, the Americans engaged the British at the Battle of Trois-Rivieres. This resulted in a defeat of the American troops. By the end of May, British and Indian attacks unsettled the tenacious hold the Americans had on the region around Quebec and Montreal. The Battle of the Cedars undermined the thinly veiled authority that the army maintained.[54] With renewed vigor and courage the Canadian forces, British regulars, French civilians, religious leaders, and their Indian allies began to dissolve American control. With no support from the other colonies, there was little that the army could do, and a withdrawal was eminent.

The continual attacks against Wooster, both personally by Schuyler, and politically by the members of the commission, were wearing heavily upon him, as was Arnold's impatience and youthful vigor and zeal. The final blow came with the announcement that he had been replaced by a younger, subordinate general, one who had never been in the Northern Department. In a letter to Washington dated May 7, Benedict Arnold wrote that "General Thomas arrived here about seven days since and has joined the Army before Quebec. General Wooster is disgusted, and expected here daily."[55] Considering that within the previous twelve months, Wooster had gone from the highest ranking senior major general in Connecticut to being the only general officer to receive a demotion in rank within the newly formed Continental Army in the summer of 1775, disgust and frustration came as no surprise. Now, in the spring of 1776, he found himself thus further abused by the political wrangling in the Congress and replaced by another subordinate simply to end up the scapegoat for the inadequacies of the Congress and their failures in the Northern Department.

A growing contingent of hostile Indians and British soldiers were reported to be gathering for an offensive in May. Thomas, who had taken ill with smallpox, had ordered Wooster to remove any supplies at Quebec to Chambly to the south to prevent their capture, which Wooster did.[56] As Thomas succumbed to his illness, he requested that Wooster take command of the army in his absence. The commissioners from Congress, however, who were still lingering in Canada, protested that Wooster should not take command, that he should retire to Montreal, and command should fall to General Thompson. On May 30, Wooster held a Council of War at Chambly, in which the commissioners from congress were present. This was one of their final acts prior to traveling to Philadelphia to discuss the army's situation and the possible retreat of the army out of Canada. Despite the intense political maneuvering Wooster continued to serve and provide military leadership to the best of his ability.

The politics of the Revolution were extremely regionalized. While fighting the King's troops, New England was pitted against the Middle and Southern Colonies. As a New Englander, John Adams saw this firsthand in the Congress. In the fall of 1776 Adams wrote in his diary, "There were three Persons at this time, who were a standing Subject of Altercation in Congress. General Wooster, Commodore Hopkins, and a Mr. Wrixon. I never could discover any reason for the Bitterness against Wooster, but his being a New England man."[57]

Thomas Jefferson also noted the actions of Wooster in a letter to Thomas Nelson on May 16. Unlike his fellow New Englander, Wooster received no praise from Jefferson, the delegate from Virginia. Jefferson wrote: "General Wooster has the credit of this misadventure, and if he cannot give a better account of it than has yet been heard I hope he will be made an example of."[58] Wooster had every intention of providing a "better account of it."

He was faced with a difficult and extremely frustrating position concerning the report of the commission, yet his undivided loyalty and his military leadership guided him in his continued devotion to the cause for which the country was fighting, liberty and freedom. It is difficult to read through the military and political correspondence from 1775 through 1776 and not become overwhelmed at the sheer scale and scope of responsibility placed upon him. His continued attempts to alleviate the situation using sutlers for supplies, the creation of a satellite congress for Canadian representation, and the numerous letters requesting supplies for his men, all to provide success to their endeavor in Canada, demonstrated his constant dedication to, and focus on, securing republican liberty.

Early in June, Washington, received a notice from the Continental Congress informing him that the Congress had recalled Wooster from Canada. "The Congress in this situation of our affairs have resolved that General Wooster be recalled from Canada. I am therefore to request you will immediately order his to repair to Head-Quarters, at New York."[59] Washington wrote to Wooster asking him to appear at his headquarters now stationed in New York. He received the official notice on June 9, 1776, from Washington, which stated:

> The Congress have been pleased to direct your recall, as you will perceive by the enclosed copy of their resolution. I am, therefore, in compliance with their request, to make it my request that you immediately repair to Head-Quarters, at New York.[60]

The same day that he wrote the order to Wooster, Washington, wrote a private letter to John Hancock in which he expressed his concern over his brigadier. In the letter he asked; "As General Wooster in all probability will be here in a little time, in compliance with the resolve of Congress and my order transmitted him, I wish to know, what am I to do with him when he comes?"[61] On June 17, Washington corresponded officially to the president of the Congress informing him that General Wooster had arrived, as ordered, and that

General Wooster has repaired to Head-Quarters in obedience to their resolve transmitted him; and shall be extremely glad if they will give me such further directions about him as they may conceive necessary. He is desirous of seeing his family in Connecticut, as I am informed, having been a good while from it. I shall wait their instructions as to his future employment.[62]

Hancock's reply came to Wooster with the enclosed resolution passed on June 21: "General Washington be directed to permit Brigadier General Wooster to return to his family in Connecticut."[63] Wooster's return home, however, would be short-lived.

Wooster was recalled from Canada by the Continental Congress in June 1776.[64] According to historian Mark Anderson, Wooster had performed admirably in Canada despite intense anti–New England animosity brewing in congress.[65] Even John Adams had written about the congressional ill treatment of Wooster in a letter to James Warren.[66] David Wooster returned to Connecticut and continued his military service to the American cause, despite never receiving another command from the Continental Congress. John Adams stated that the failure of the Canadian expedition was entirely the fault of Congress, and that Wooster was not to blame.

In Woosters case there was a manifest Endeavor to lay upon him the blame of their own misconduct in Congress in embarrassing and starving the War in Canada. Wooster was calumniated for Incapacity, Want of Application and even Cowardice, with[out] a Colour of Proof of either. The Charge of Cawardice he soon confut[ed] by a glorious and voluntary Sacrifice of his Life, which compelled his Enemies to confess he was a hero.[67]

While Wooster's military future within the Continental Army hung in the balance, Schuyler commenced a new letter writing campaign to members of the Continental Congress. Schuyler knew that the blame for the failure of the Canadian expedition was ultimately his, as did many of the soldiers and officers who served under him. He was extremely unpopular, especially among the New England troops. To save his credibility, Schuyler once again wrote to the Congress and shifted blame upon Wooster. To him every failure of the Canadian campaign rested on lack of "discipline and subordination." There were ample supplies, Schuyler mentioned, however had Wooster been competent, "I should not have been (as I have to this very day) left in the dark with respect to everything in Canada."[68] Schuyler's feeble defense was unraveling, while Wooster headed for Philadelphia to defend his honor, and the honor of his men in Canada, to Congress itself.

From the time of his placement in command of the troops in Montreal and Quebec on the first of January to April 1776, Wooster wrote no less than fourteen lengthy letters of correspondence to Schuyler. Each of these letters contained a similarly detailed message to the major general in command of the Northern Department; the army in Canada lacked food (flour for bread), meat, shoes, tentage, medicine, and ammunition, not to mention enlistments that expired, and men had threatened to return home. The overall lack of hard currency was transmitted to Schuyler and the Continental Congress repeatedly. Schuyler was hardly "left in the dark" about all things in Canada.

Wooster arrived in New York in June to meet with the commander-in-chief at Headquarters. While there, he requested Washington's permission to "wait on

Congress," and on June 26, 1776, Wooster headed for Philadelphia.[69] In the meantime, upon learning that her husband had been recalled from Canada, Mary Wooster petitioned Governor Trumbull of Connecticut to postpone filling the vacant position of the Naval Office in Connecticut until her husband might appear before him and requested the post on his behalf, if possible. This is the first correspondence of Mary Wooster in the historical record. Hearing that her husband had been recalled from Canada she hoped that the position, which her husband held before the war, might be his once again. She did not realize, however, that her husband was not to be deterred from military duty quite so easily. Even at the age of sixty-six, David Wooster was not ready to retire while the defense of liberty and freedom were required. The letter from Mary Wooster to Governor Trumbull exudes a sense of cordiality, and familiarity, as this was not the first time she had written him:

> Sometime since I wrote to your Honour, soliciting the favour of having the Naval office for the port of New-Haven continued in General Wooster's hands.
> I would now inform your Honour that a letter from the General gives us to understand that he is at present in Philadelphia, and will be in this Colony in a few days. I would therefore ask your Honour to suspend bestowing the above favour to any other person until the General shall be able to wait on your Honour in person, and hive such sureties as the law required for the faithful discharge of the trust, if he should be honoured with it.[70]

Wooster maintained his connection with Connecticut despite being stationed in Canada from October 1775, until June 1776. Even in his absence his leadership was known, as demonstrated by the Connecticut General Assembly, who voted him as justice of the peace for another yearly term during their May session.[71]

The pressure of command on such a large scale, with all its tremendous responsibility, had worn heavily upon Wooster. There is little doubt that he had never experienced anything quite like the challenges presented to him over the past several months. He struggled with the newly created chain of command and chaffed under the authority of commanders and politicians whose personal interest appeared, to him, to outweigh those of the cause and which seemed to negate the very ideals of republicanism and liberty. He arrived in Philadelphia in late June with permission from Washington and requested of the Congress that an investigation be opened into his conduct in Canada. To the president of the Congress, he wrote:

> Sir:
> The unjust severity and unmerited abuse with which my character has been treated in the Colonies by persons who are either secret enemies to the glorious cause in which every virtuous American must heartily join, or whose ambition would by every means (however base) remove all obstacles to their advancement and promotion, added to the harsh treatment I have received from some part of the illustrious body over whom you preside, render it indispensably necessary that I should take some steps towards undeceiving them, satifying the publick, and doing justice to myself and the Army in Canada. If these can be done, it must give satisfaction to every feeling heart. The honour of a soldier being the first thing he should defend, and his honesty the last he should give up, his character must ever be considered as entitled to the protection of the virtuous and the good. I have, therefore, sir, to request that you would move to the honourable Congress that the Committee appointed to examine into the affairs of Canada may be directed to look thoroughly into my conduct while I had the honour of commanding the Continental forces

in that country, or that some other may be appointed for that purpose, that I may be acquitted or condemned upon just grounds and sufficient proof.

> I am, with great respect, sir, your
> most humble servant,
>
> David Wooster[72]

There were several key actions that he had to defend while in Philadelphia. The first involved prisoners that he had detained, with permission of Schuyler, in Montreal and Quebec. These persons were deemed troublesome to the cause of the army. The commissioners from the Congress, upon their arrival in Canada, released these prisoners as a token of goodwill without consultation with Wooster. Immediately upon arriving home the prisoners stirred up anti–American sentiment in the Canada and recruited new men into the king's army. The second involved a merchant in Montreal who claimed that Wooster had stolen his property. Wooster told the committee that the individual was not permitted to travel north of the city to trade goods with the Indians, who were becoming hostile toward the Americans. The man removed himself and his goods under cover of darkness to trade with the Indians. Wooster brought him and his goods back to Quebec, where he ordered them to be cataloged and used by the army if needed, and pledged to pay the individual the amount owed if any were used.[73]

Upon Wooster's request, the Congress opened an investigation into his actions in Canada. From July 1 through July 27, they heard testimony upon the actions of the American Army and the leadership of Wooster in Canada.[74] Twelve men testified regarding the Canadian Campaign. Wooster himself testified for two full days, July 3–4.[75] Eleven days of hearings began on July 1, and the first to testify was Mr. John Blake, a merchant in Montreal. He was followed by Captain Hector McNeil, who testified on July 2. McNeil provided evidence as to the horrid conditions found in Canada upon Wooster's arrival, as well as the lack of morale among the Connecticut and New York Troops. "As soon as Montgomery was killed, the troops being dispirited and dissatisfied, went away in droves." McNeil illuminated the difference between the aged Wooster and the brash, youthful Arnold. "He [McNeil] thinks Wooster's going was lucky, as he kept the men there, which he thinks Arnold could not have done; that the New York troops particularly were dissatisfied with Arnold because he wrote some letters which appeared in the newspapers, reflecting on them." He concluded his testimony on behalf of General Wooster by recounting the tremendous impact smallpox had upon the troops in Canada:

> The small pox was sent out of Quebeck by Carleton, inoculating the poor people at government expense for the purpose of giving it to our army. It had just begun to appear in the army before Montgom's death, after which it spread fast.
>
> When Genl. Wooster arrived which was Apr. 1st, there was something upwards 2,700 men in all of whom 800 were sick. Of these there were 1653 whose time were out the 15th of Apr. "He [McNeil] has never seen anything in Genl. Wooster but the greatest care." Things were carried out more harmoniously under him than would have been under Arnold after the discontent against him.[76]

Following McNeil in the afternoon of July 2 was Doctor Coates who also alluded to the grave impact that disease had upon Wooster's men:

Small pox had made considerable appearance in [the] army before defeat. "Was supposed Carlton sent out people with it." "When Wooster arrived the Yorkers time was to expire the 15th. April the New Englanders also." Most of them Genl. Wooster prevailed to stay. [Coates] Does not think there was any waste of provisions.[77]

Before the commission went any further, Wooster was allowed to testify on his own behalf. The general's testimony involved a two-day long inquiry. The first day involved a lengthy and inclusive examination of all the correspondences from him, Schuyler, the Congress, Washington, and two additional officers. A total of forty-two letters were examined. Of these twenty-one were written by Wooster, while seventeen were written by Schuyler. The commission went through each letter and outlined the contents and weighed the evidence of any wrongdoing. On July 4 the committee heard testimony directly from Wooster. In the notes provided by Thomas Jefferson, who was a member of the investigative committee, he provided an overview of Wooster's actions in Canada. Within Jefferson's notes there contained nothing of a pressing or accusatory nature. In Wooster's testimony, he neither accused nor placed blame for the failure of the events in Canada on anyone.[78]

Official hearings of the committee resumed on July 6 with the testimony of Major Samuel Blackden. He was followed by Wooster's secretary, Major Lockwood. On July 10, Mr. Price testified regarding the situation in Quebec prior to, and immediately following, Montgomery's failed attack. Monsieur Christopher Pelissier, "the owner of iron works at Trois revieres," and John Hamtramck, a Canadian from Quebec, testified on July 11. Francois Guillot dit La Rose, "a captain of Canadian militia under commission from Wooster and Sullivan," Hardoin Merlet, "a Continental major in the Canadian Militia," and William Haywood, "An inhabitant of Montreal," testified on July 18. Haywood commented on the way Wooster prevented merchants from selling goods to the Indians outside of Montreal, which was a tremendous problem prior to the General's orders. It was noted that no one was allowed to sell goods in the "upper country" without a permit. The men who charged Wooster with overstepping his authority had been found guilty of selling without said permit to the Indians whom the Americans were fighting. Several sleighs loaded with goods were seized and bought back by the army.

The investigative committee concluded its hearings with testimony from Mr. Mason on July 19 and Mr. Bonfeild on July 27. The evidence provided was submitted to the Congress who read the report of the committee, debated the findings, and adopted the report. On Tuesday, July 30, 1776, after lengthy discussion regarding the Canadian Campaign, the Congress reported:

That the short inlistments of the Continental Troops in Canada have been one great cause of the miscarriages there, by rendering unstable the number of men engaged in military enterprises, by making them disorderly and disobedient to their officers, and by precipitating the commanding officer into measures which their prudence might have postponed could they have relied on a longer continuance of their troops in service:
That the want of hard money has been one other great source of the miscarriages in Canada, rendering the supplies of necessaries difficult and precarious, the establishment of proper magazines absolutely impracticable, and the pay of Troops of little use to them:

That a still greater and more fatal source of misfortunes has been the prevalence of the small-pox in that Army, a great proportion whereof has therby been usually kept unfit for duty.
    With this Congress concurred.[79]

And, at the very conclusion of Congressional business for that day, Congress passed an official resolution stating, "That General Wooster acted properly in stopping the Goods of Bernard & Wadden, who were carrying the same, without permission, to the Indians in the upper country."[80]

In the meantime, much letter writing occurred from Philadelphia, as the Congress was in the midst of items of great importance. In early July, the colonies became aware that, at the same time Wooster was defending his actions and those of the army in Canada, Congress had unanimously declared the independence of the thirteen united colonies. Their treatment of Wooster, however, proved anything but a united front. His experience, character, and actions had to speak for themselves, for the general had few actual supporters in the Congress. One of the Connecticut delegates to the Continental Congress in 1776, William Williams, wrote to Governor Trumbull about the actions that had taken place regarding Wooster, first on August 7 in which he stated:

Poor Wooster a faithful officer is treated most inhumanly by Mr._____ [Chase] & sundrey men in Congress tho they cant support and thing against him, by any Proof but the most confident assertions of their won. Many of us grieve & lament the Fate of that unhappy Army, but as yet see not how nor what to do. G. Schuyler how good soever he miht be if present &c will be their Ruin to Comand & guide the affairs at a 100 or two miles off.[81]

Four days later Williams again wrote to Trumbull lamenting the state of Wooster and his abuse at the hands of several vocal critics:

Poor Wooster a worthy Officer is neglected boundless Efforts have been used to blast his Character in Congress by one of the Canada Comissioners. He has been represented by him as a most worthless contemptible Felon & the most liberal abuse thrown out against him in Congress, such as I think totally inconsistent with their Honor & Justice to suffer, but so it is. Nor has the author escaped severe Remarks by the Friends of Wooster but the former undauntedly persisted in his Reflections, & has fixed a deep Prejuduce against him in a majority; tho not a single Charge can be supported against him, & He has been honorably acquitted by a Committee, whose Report by address &c, has been yet kept off & recommitted.
I hope in God, they & all will acquit themselves like Men & be strong in the Day of approaching Conflict, & may the Lord of Hosts be on our Side & vindicate our righteous Cause agt our most unjust & more than Savage Foes.

I am Dear Sir your affecte Friend & Brother

W. Williams[82]

An examination of the letters of the delegates to the Continental Congress written during the spring and summer months of 1776 indicates a clear regional divide regarding the general from New England. Samuel Chase was the most outspoken critic of Wooster within Congress. There were Virginians who also penned derogatory comments about Wooster. The most prominent were Richard Henry Lee and Francis Lightfoot Lee. In a letter to Landon Carter on May 21, 1776, Francis Lightfoot Lee referred to Wooster as "an old woman."[83] Despite the southerner's disdain, New

Englanders such as John Adams, William Williams, Roger Sherman, and Elbridge Gerry remained steadfast supporters.[84]

On August 9, the Congress reviewed a list of current officers in consideration of yet another series of officer promotions. Brigadier Generals William Heath, Joseph Spencer, John Sullivan, and Nathaniel Greene were all promoted to major general. Wooster had originally been commission at the same time as these four men, yet, of these original officers still commissioned by the Continental Army, he alone was overlooked for promotion.

Wooster most vocal champion in Congress, John Adams, took pen in hand to note his frustration within the Congress highlighting the bizarre attitude that permeated the chamber regarding Wooster. He commented on August 12, 1776, that "it appeared to me, that the Commodore [Hopkins] was pursued and persecuted by that Anti New England Spirit, which haunted Congress in many other of their proceedings, as well as in this Case and that of General Wooster."[85]

It was not until August 17 that the Congress finally held a vote on the resolution regarding Wooster's conduct, and that of his army in Canada. He was officially exonerated for all wrongdoing:

> The Congress resumed the consideration of the report of the committee to whom was referred General Wooster's letter, requesting an enquiry into his conduct while he had the honour of commanding the continental forces in Canada, which was read, as follows:
> That Brigadier General Wooster produced copies of a number of letters which passed between him and General Schuyler, and of his letters to Congress; from which it appears that he, from time to time, gave seasonable and due notice of the state of the army under his command, and what supplies were, in his opinion, necessary to render the enterprise successful: that a number of officers and other gentlemen from Canada, who were acquainted with his conduct there, and who happened occasionally to be in this city, were examined before the committee; to which letters, and the minutes of the examination of the witnesses herewith exhibited, the committee beg leave to refer Congress for further information, and report, as the opinion of the committee, upon the whole of the evidence that was before them, that nothing censurable or blameworthy appears against Brigadier General Wooster.
> The Report, being again read, was agreed to.[86]

After lengthy testimonies by the investigative committee, the first of its kind held by the Continental Congress, Wooster was acquitted of all charges of wrongdoing. However, there were those who still fumed at what they saw as illiberal justice. John Adams wrote to his wife Abigail that there were men within the Massachusetts delegation to the Congress who argued with him over Wooster's acquittal.[87] Immediately following the resolution and vote to exonerate General Wooster for any wrongdoing, Adams wrote in his diary:

> But not, however, without a great Struggle.—In this Instance again as in many others, when the same anti New England Spirit which pursued Commodore Hopkins, persecuted General Wooster, I had to contend with the whole Host of their Enemies, and with the Utmost Anxiety and most arduous Efforts, was, scarcely able to preserve them from disgrace and Ruin, which Wooster had merited even less than Hopkins. In Woosters case there was a manifest Endeavour to lay upon him the blame of their own misconduct in Congress in embarrassing and starving the War in Canada. Wooster was calumniated for Incapacity, Want of Application and even for Cowardice, with [out] a Colour of Proof of either. The Charge of Cowardice

he soon confut[ed] by a glorious and voluntary Sacrifice of his Life, which compelled his Ene-mies to confess he was a Hero.[88]

By mid–August, with the British threatening to invade New York, which had been a constant concern for over a year, Wooster found himself isolated from mili-tary command and the Continental Congress. He still held the official rank of brig-adier general in the Continental Army, despite being the only one to not receive a promotion. Ten days after the new commissions were approved Wooster wrote a brief missive to the Congress:

Having the pleasure and satisfaction of your approbation of my past conduct in the Army, beg leave to acquaint your Honours, that I am still ready and willing to serve in my proper rank in the Army, and attend your further orders. I am, with due respect, your Honours' most obedi-ent, humble servant.[89]

The Congress received his letter on August 19, noted the receipt of it, and ordered it "To lie on the table."[90] Brigadier General David Wooster never again received orders for military command from the Continental Congress. Three days later, British General Howe landed roughly 32,000 troops off the southern shore of Long Island. From August 27 through November 20, British forces drove northward, captured New York City, and forced Washington and his Continental troops into New Jersey and eventually Pennsylvania. All the while Wooster watched and waited for any word from Congress. None arrived. New York had been a haven of loyalist activity and with the presence of the British army in occupation, the western border of Connecticut was exposed to invasion. Wooster knew where his duty lay. Despite his advanced age he sought to continue to do his duty to the best of his ability.

He traveled home to Connecticut and, not one to sit idle, returned immediately to military service to the very institution of liberty and freedom he knew best, the new state of Connecticut, his friends, family, and business. The accusations levied upon him from men like Philip Schuyler, which had taken such a toll on the sixty-six-year-old soldier, were not finished. Schuyler's pettiness reigned upon members of the Congress. In October, General Schuyler, still in Albany, received word that Wooster had been fully exonerated by the Continental Congress. This only meant one thing, if Wooster was innocent, then he must be the guilty party. His fears and consternations were put to paper. He wrote to General Horatio Gates on October 5, expressing his continued dislike of Wooster as well as his utter disbelief in the congressional resolve:

A letter which I yesterday received from a friend advises me that the Committee appointed to inquire into the causes in Canada, were reported on Monday last. It seems hard that such an inquiry should have been gone into without giving me notice of it, without calling on me to answer for my conduct, or even to explain any matter.
I am informed that Congress has some time since entered into an exculpatory resolve in favour of General Wooster, which has been published in the papers. A total silence with respect to me must therefore indicate to the publick that I am culpable. I shall, however, exculpate myself in a narration, supported by inconvertible proofs, and leave the publick to judge whether I am, or who is in fault. Until then I wish the candid and ingenuous to suspend their judgment.[91]

On October 23, 1776, Schuyler went further to express his disdain for Wooster. This time he addressed the Congress itself. To Schuyler it was all about his reputa-tion, not about his inability to command the Northern Department:

I was greatly at a loss to what cause to impute that very rapid increase of calumny, which I experienced after my return from the Indian treaty. I did not know that I was principally indebted to Congress for this misfortune, until yesterday, when, and never before did I see the resolution of the 17th of August last, which, whilst it exculates General Wooster from any mal-conduct in Canada, is couched in such terms as to leave even to the candid and judicious no alternative but that od supposing that Canada was not properly supplied either by Congress or me. Judge on whom the publick censure would fall, and let every gentleman in Congress for a moment fancy himself in my situation, let him candidly scan that resolve, and then let him conclude what my feeling must be from his own. Is it, sir, consistent with that dignity which should be inseparable from the most respectable body on earth, thus partially and precipitately to enter into a resolution which leaves so much room for the publick to consider me as a faithless servant? Deeply sensible to the injury I have sustained from the hand which ought to have supported me, I shall endeavour yet to be patient, and do my duty in this critical conjuncture with zeal, alacrity and firmness, supported by the consciousness of my integrity, and the expectation of a speedy opportunity of vindicating my character, and of testifying to the world not only the rectitude of my intentions, but the propriety of my conduct.[92]

Addressing the struggle of the army in Canada, as well as the Schuyler-Wooster controversy, historian Jonathan Gregory Rossie noted that "with this latest vituperative attack on Congress, Schuyler finally went too far."[93] Members of the pro–Schuyler faction, like Robert R. Livingston, thought likewise and felt that Schuyler's desire to place the blame for the failed Canadian campaign placed at Wooster's feet was impossible. Other members of Congress who had found themselves supporting Schuyler previously began to distance themselves from him. His ego had become his undoing. All the while Wooster prepared for the defense of western Connecticut, and ironically, setting out to offer his services to the Continental Congress yet again.

The General Assembly of the State of Connecticut, no longer a colony, capitalized on the Congress' error in leaving Wooster in military limbo. In a flurry of orders and resolutions during their October session they reorganized their states' defenses by appointing Wooster major general once more. Apparently, they felt Wooster was not too old to lead in the field. The first resolution reads; "This Assembly do appoint David Wooster, Esq.,' to be Major General of the militia of this State, and his Honor the Governor is hereby desired to commission him accordingly."[94] The Assembly held a grave concern over the presence of British troops in New York. The enemy was rapidly advancing towards the western portion of Connecticut, and was cause for alarm. The following resolution was adopted with great urgency:

That as many of the militia as are fit for service and of other householders etc., able-bodied effective men within the limits of the ninth, tenth, thirteenth and sixteenth regiments within this State, be immediately called forth, well armed and equipped, and embodied under the command of Maj' General Wooster appointed by this State to lead them forth, command and direct them in the necessary operations against our enemy, and to give all possible relief to our army, notifying the General and Commander in Chief of the continental army of his situation and readiness to cooperate with him, taking such directions from him as he may obtain how and in what manner he may most conduce to his assistance and annoy the enemy, and to consult and advise with any other general or commanding officer or officers of our army who may be nearest to him for that purpose.

Resolved by this Assembly, That the third regiment of light horse and the troop of [light*] horse in the tenth regiment of militia be ordered forthwith to march to the western part of this State, to join the forces under the command of Maj' General Wooster, who is hereby directed and impowered to give orders for their march, operations and stations.[95]

The actions of the assembly enlivened and reenergized Wooster. The urgency and necessity of the moment can be felt within the lines of these orders, and Wooster knew exactly what needed to be done. In October he took command, and his leadership never wavered. Despite his age he felt he had service to render to the cause.

He began by reorganizing the four state militia regiments (the 9th, 10th, 13th, and 16th), and placed them in key locations across Connecticut, especially along the western border. The General Assembly had ordered Wooster to send troops to the Connecticut towns of Norwalk, Stratford, and Greenwich, which he immediately did.[96] To further protect the western towns in Connecticut from British or Tory aggression the General Assembly passed a resolution that created a special committee to arrest suspected individuals who were deemed as "inimical to the liberties of this and the other United States of America, who are forming dangerous insurrections, and taking every method in their power to communicate intelligence to comfort, aid, and assist the enemies of these United States, and to distress the inhabitants of said town, and to bring on a general anarchy and confusion among them."[97]

With New York under British occupation, the Assembly was extremely conscious of the precarious position the western towns had been placed in. To strengthen this resolution the following was added; "And it is further Resolved, That his Honour the Governor be desired to direct Major-General Wooster to give the aid and assistance with his troops in his power to said Committee for carrying into execution the aforesaid resolve."[98]

In addition to the threats posed against western Connecticut towns was the threat to shipping in the Long Island sound. New Haven remained a vital shipping port and the Long Wharf continued to attract mercantile business. Major General Wooster remained in contact with the officers of the Continental Army and received word in November from General Charles Lee with instructions to defend the valuable "saw pits" along the coast located southwest of Greenwich and Stamford.[99] Following Lee's letter, Assistant Quartermaster-General Hugh Hughes informed Wooster of the importance of preventing Tories from stealing cattle or forage for the British troops in New York, stating that "whenever there is any booty belonging to Tories that have gone to the enemy, they [Wooster's troops] are to take all."[100] Nothing would be spared to keep all necessary supplies from falling into the hands of the enemy. Although Wooster never received another command from the Continental Congress, he continued to lead as best he could wherever he was needed and remained in contact with the commander-in-chief.

An interesting sidenote to Wooster's achievements occurred in November. The Connecticut sloop *Wooster*, named in his honor, was christened, and received her first sailing orders. The seventy-five-ton ship was equipped with ten cannons and twelve swivel guns. She conducted her first cruise in November 1776, and over the course of the next two years the *Wooster* captured two enemy vessels, the snow *Atlantic*, and the brigantine *Mermaid*. While in the Caribbean in 1779 the *Wooster* was captured by the British. The official inventory of Wooster's estate, made following his death in 1777, listed £ 309..15.. pounds sterling worth of shares in the sloop *Wooster,* an enterprise he fully invested in and supported.[101] The *Wooster* was built in New Haven and commanded by New Haven sailors.[102]

The threatening state of affairs in Connecticut regarding the safety of the western border dominated all activity. Wooster sent an emergency dispatch to Governor Trumbull on November 18. It contained two very important pieces of information. First, his son Thomas, the deliverer of the note, was "at present one of my Aid-de-Camps, and as such entitled to the rank of Major, but as he is desirous of serving in the standing Army, requests that he may be appointed first or second Captain in Colonel Chester's regiment, if there is room, or in some other regiment belonging to the State of Connecticut." The second part of the note alerted the governor that he had only five hundred of the promised two-thousand men in the service, and that the enemy was but a "three hours' march from us."[103] Wooster became increasingly concerned that the militia would not answer the call if a crisis emerged.

The situation became more dire in early December, as word reached Trumbull that British ships-of-the-line were preparing to sail from New York to their winter station at Newport, with orders to ravage the coast along the way. Wooster was on high alert and prepared, to the best of his ability, for the defense of his state. Ever hopeful of receiving some communication from the Congress, he provided necessary information, and informed that them that he still awaited orders for a field command:

> I have not had a line from you since I left Philadelphia, therefore conclude I am entirely forgotten by Congress; but however, I have not forgotten the interest of my distressed country. If the honourable Continental Congress has any further service for me, I shall take it as a favour to be informed of it.
>
> This sir, will be handed you by an express which have forwarded from Governor Trumbull to his Excellency General Washington, General Lee, &c., to acquaint then on the 5th instant a fleet of about eighty transports and eight large ships-of-war, anchored, off New London, and were there on the 6th, being the last accounts from them. They passed this place on the 4th, in the evening. I learn by deserters from Long-Island, who left the fleet, that they have about eight thousand men on board—a bad situation for our eastern people, and not a General Officer in that part of the country; but I hope Providence will work deliverance for us. The express must go on; I can therefore only add, that I am, sir, with the greatest esteem, your Excellency's most obedient, humble servant.[104]

The Congress noted the receipt of Wooster's letter but did not send a reply. Rather than issuing Wooster new orders, as he was still commissioned a brigadier general in the Continental Army, the Congress simply ignored him. Instead, he remained in charge of all the militia units in Connecticut. In this capacity he continued to organize the defense of the state, and guarded deserters sent to him from the various Committees of Safety in New York, who themselves lacked the resources. Despite his protest, the Committee of Safety for the County of Westchester, in White Plains, continued to send deserters to Wooster.[105] There developed a clear distinction in Wooster's mind separating his orders from Trumbull or Washington, and those from the New York Assembly or individual New York communities. On December 23, citizens from Westchester County, New York, expressed their concern that

General Wooster, who is now stationed at the Saw-Pitts, in the eastern part of the County, affords us no assistance; and we have been informed that some of his officers have said that they would not defend the State, and if the enemy should make their appearance, they would retreat to the borders of Connecticut, and there make a stand.[106]

His experience with New Yorkers remained fresh in his mind, as well as the Connecticut men under his command. Following the debacle in Canada, they simply refused to serve under New York officers. After continued abuses at the hands of New York politicians and officers, soldiers in Connecticut washed their hands of the issues and complaints of their neighbors to the west and allowed them to finally fend for themselves, as best they were able.

Over the past year of military service, Wooster had dealt with either the short-term enlistments of his men or, as in the case of troops in Canada, enlistments that had in fact expired. Dealing with state militia on limited short-term enlistments was a never-ending struggle. Encouraging soldiers to reenlist after the disastrous fall campaign in New York was arduous. The Connecticut General Assembly had created a commission whose responsibility it was to find the Connecticut regiments stationed east of the Hudson River to encourage them to reenlist for the following season. The report of the two commissioners, Eliakim Hall and Amos Mead, demonstrated the persuasion, influence, and spirit that Wooster maintained to encourage his men to stay with him in the field.[107] Despite immeasurable setbacks and challenges, as well as his advanced age, Wooster continued to lead his men to the best of his ability.

It is unknown if these Connecticut soldiers stationed at the Saw Pitts with Wooster had received word of Washington's stunning victory at Trenton. However, their enthusiasm, coupled with Washington's success, proved that the cause of liberty remained on the hearts and minds of men in the field. Wooster's leadership proved that. At the close of the December meeting of the Connecticut General Assembly, knowing his quality and character, the members voted the following resolution in the affirmative, that "this Assembly do appoint Maj^r General David Wooster, Esqr to be first Major General over the whole militia of this State."[108] With the confidence of his men and the government of Connecticut behind him, Wooster prepared for what would turn out to be his last military campaign.

8

1777

By the end of 1776 the British Army, under the command of General William Howe and General Charles Cornwallis, occupied New York City. Following the decisive victory at Trenton on December 26, followed by a second victory at Princeton on January 3, 1777, George Washington's army went into winter quarters at Morristown, New Jersey. Despite these American victories, the condition in and around New York City remained the same. The British occupied the city which continued to encourage loyalist activity, and the royal Governor William Tryon took full advantage of the tenuous situation.

For his part, David Wooster returned to the western part of Connecticut to prevent forage from being seized by loyalists and British regulars. He was in command of all the militia forces in Connecticut, both infantry and mounted troops, referred to as light horse. The defense of Connecticut was his primary goal. He also kept a keen eye on New York for an opportunity to attack the enemy.

Examining the map of New York, Morristown is approximately fifty miles west-by-southwest of New York City, while New Rochelle, Wooster's location, was half that distance to the northeast. On January 9, 1777, Wooster wrote a lengthy letter to Governor Jonathan Trumbull, in which he proposed a possible plan of attack to retake New York City. Ever seeking the opportunity to secure the liberty and freedom of his country, Wooster explained to Trumbull:

> That the reason why I formed a design against New York at this present time is from the Certain intelligence that I have of the British Troops being almost all ordered into the Jerseys so that they have not more than fifteen hundred men to defend that city, therefore now is the time, the very time, to give them a fatal stroke, their ships all hauled into the Docks and unrigged so that they cannot be any annoyance to us.[1]

With Howe and Cornwallis preoccupied with Washington in the west, an attack from Wooster upon New York City from the east was a feasible plan. This potentially would remove the British from the occupied city, force them into another engagement in New Jersey, and alleviate the growing military and economic pressure on Connecticut. However, the analysis of history through the lens of time provides an unfair advantage for modern historians. Wooster's plan was never put into action.[2] He simply did not have the troops to implement such an aggressive plan. The presence of British regulars had bolstered loyalist activity; therefore, any attack would be against a two-fold enemy which was much larger than what Wooster could gather.

At the same time, General William Heath had expected to take charge of the

Connecticut troops near New Rochelle to assist the Continental Army in the Peekskill Mountains, north of New York City, along the Hudson River. If this redeployment occurred, it would leave western Connecticut exposed to the ravages and dangers of the New York Tories.

One attempt at taking New York occurred in late January. The garrison at Kingsbridge, a small fortification situated between Manhattan and the Bronx, was lightly defended. The action was unsuccessful, and New York remained a bastion of British activity. An eye-witness account of the action was provided by historian William Gordon and exemplifies the frustration of failed military attempts in 1777.[3]

Throughout February and March, Wooster kept in contact with Washington, still encamped at Morristown. He also corresponded with Heath, who wrote to Wooster on February 7, the contents of which certainly had soured the relationship between the two officers. Heath advised Wooster to work more diligently to remove and secure the forage near New York, and any forage that was not removed was to be burned to deprive it to the enemy. He expressed his agitation against Wooster and his troops who were accused of damaging property of civilians in New York. Heath directed the general to make certain that spoils of war were not removed from New York without the consent of the New York Commissioners.[4]

Heath took pen in hand and wrote another letter to Wooster the following day. In that letter Wooster was ordered to provide a sergeant and twelve soldiers as a guard for James Stevenson, a commissioner of the Continental Army who was in New York. Already hard pressed for men, Wooster complied. However, the subsequent directive caused Wooster a great pause. Heath had passed along an order from Washington that Wooster should continue to collect the forage in the area and then march to the Jerseys and join his army, and that Wooster was to work with the Committee of the state on New York. This was a bitter pill for him to swallow.[5]

By February, the lengthy campaign season was taking its toll on his men. It is difficult to persuade soldiers to remain in the field under a constant heightened state of alarm and readiness, especially with family so nearby, and in the dead of winter. Although Wooster had orders to march his men to the Jerseys to aid Washington, the historic record does not indicate that he joined the commander-in-chief. Instead, he held his position as the only force between British-occupied New York and Connecticut. He repositioned his men from Rye Neck to New Rochelle, closer to New York City. In a letter to Colonel William Duer, Wooster stated that his volunteers were being discharged at the end of the month, however he would send some troops to defend Wright's Mill, a key grain mill in the area. His frustration and growing exhaustion of being in a perpetual state of emergency could be felt through his letters as he expressed the difficulty in sending troops to various stations and protecting forage. There were simply not enough men to do all that was asked of him.[6]

Despite remaining in eastern New York, Wooster continued to correspond with Washington. On February 21, he informed him "that since General Heaths departure to Boston, I have taken Post at this place, with seven hundred men." He went on to say "This Country is much infested with our Tory Enemies, who Use their utmost diligence, both Night & day to convey provisions &c. to the Enemy. I am taking

every precaution in my power to prevent and detect them in their Infamous Prac-
tices." He concluded his report by alerting the commander-in-chief that

> the Troops here under my Command are inlisted only to the 15th of March next; during which
> time I shall do every thing in my power to defend this part of the Country; tho under the great-
> est disadvantages possible; As General Heath after our inglorious expedition towards Kings
> bridge, ordered all the Field Pieces to Peekskill so that I have only small arms to oppose what-
> ever the Enemy may bring against me.[7]

His correspondence throughout the remainder of the spring details the maneuvering of his men throughout Connecticut and Long Island. This was done to prevent plunder by the British troops, and hopefully to enlist new recruits for the main
Continental Army as well as the Connecticut militia which he now commanded.
He discussed with Washington the need for artillery and the urgency of reenlisting
men whose term would end in March.[8] Effectively working with a volunteer militia instead of a regular army was one element of the Revolutionary War that no one
had yet found a solution for. Wooster wrote to Washington from his new encampment at Rye Neck addressing a serious concern. There was a constant problem with
spies leaving New York in the spring of 1777, and Wooster had detained several men
who neither carried official papers nor a flag of truce, and he requested advice from
Washington on how to deal with them. Due to overwhelming number of British regulars at New Rochelle, he had removed his smaller force further to the east. With
a constant reduction of his own force to fill the ranks of the Continental Army,
Wooster saw no possible way to engage the British with such inadequate numbers.[9]
The day following his letter to Washington, March 2, Major General David Wooster
turned sixty-seven years old.

To this Washington sent a scathing letter rebuking Wooster for not harassing
the enemy at New Rochelle and for retreating against a larger force. He stated:

> I was a good deal surprised to find yours of the 2d dated from Rye. Supposing there was a real
> Necessity of your retreating from New Rochelle, you certainly ought to have returned imme-
> diately, upon the Enemy's dropping their design, if they ever had any, of attacking you—All
> Accounts from your Quarters complain loudly of this retreat as a most injudicious Step, as it
> gives fresh spirits to the disaffected and retarded the removal of Forage by the Convention of
> New York, the very end that your Troops were principally intended to answer.[10]

After analyzing the documentation between Washington and Wooster, which
only pertained to eighteen months, from June 1775 to March 1777, it is clear to see
the jaded opinion that Washington had formed concerning New Englanders. The
"Quarters" that "complain loudly" continued to be from New York, and those people, especially the New York politicians, had Washington's ear. Wooster did not. By
the same token, however, it is unclear if Wooster ever desired it.

There remained two letters between Washington and Wooster. Writing from
New Haven, Wooster inquired on March 28 for advice regarding two court marital
cases and forwarded them to Washington for review. He ended the letter by informing his commander that

> I am very sorry to find, the Quota of Men to be raised in This State, for The Continental Army, so
> far from being Completed; and very much fear that thereby, Your Excellency will be prevented
> from taking the Field, with signal Advantage; until The Spring shall be far advanced. Reports

here say, that The Enemy are pressing Artillery, and Baggage Horses from the Inhabitants of Long-Island; form The East End of which, I also expect they will gain much forage, as well from The County of Westchester, where I do not learn, that any Troops have arrived, since the expiration of The Term of Inlistment, and Departure of The Connecticut Troops; who have maintained The Ground, and in a great degree prevented the Ravages of The Enemy, in that Quarter This Winter.[11]

Washington's reply on April 12 simply verified the death sentence for one of the court martial cases and acquitted the second. This was the last letter Wooster received from the commander-in-chief.[12]

By April 1777, Wooster was stationed near his home in New Haven. Nearby in Danbury, the army had stored large amounts of supplies; food, clothing, tentage, and powder. There was great anti-republican sentiment in New York, which led to numerous loyalist plots against those who fought for American independence. The British commanders in New York, along with newly appointed Lieutenant General Tryon, the Tory governor of New York, devised a scheme to invade neighboring Connecticut and destroy the large cache of supplies stored at Danbury. A detachment of British soldiers under the command of Tryon sailed from New York through Long Island Sound. The flotilla of twenty-five ships disembarked near Norwalk, Connecticut, and marched north to Danbury.[13] General Tryon did not care for the citizens of Connecticut. While on the march the troops under his command caused as much destruction of property as well as harm to the civilians as possible, including women, children, and the elderly. The locals sent many of the small children to the surrounding countryside for protection.

His troops landed on April 25 and were led by two Tory guides who directed them towards Danbury. According to accounts, no Tory home or property was destroyed by Tryon's men. In Danbury, where the greatest amount of destruction was committed, patriots who lost their homes noted white crosses on all Tory building and property which marked them to be spared from destruction.[14] Two men fired upon Tryon and his soldiers as they entered Danbury. These defenders were shot and killed, along with an unarmed black man, and all thrown into a nearby house which was then set afire.[15]

While in Danbury, Tryon's men destroyed the entire cache of Connecticut provisions, which included "1,700 barrels of pork, 50 ditto of beef, 7 hogsheads of rum, 11 tierces of claret, 3 quarter casks of wine, between 12 and 1,700 bushels of rye and oats, 17 casks of bread, 36 iron pots, 12 coils of rope, 1,600 tents, some carpenter's tools, 3 loads of hay, [and] 10 wagons."[16] Much of the rum was consumed by his men, leading to drunkenness and increased destruction and devastation. Tryon and his men were not expecting the advancing army of Wooster and therefore saw no need to hasten their return to New York. They burned a great number of homes, farmsteads, barns, churches, and public buildings while they slowly retreated to their ships anchored off the coast.

Generals Wooster and Benedict Arnold were in New Haven when Tryon began his raid into Connecticut. When word reached Wooster of the invasion, he immediately set off with all the militia he could gather. Arnold and General Gold Selleck Silliman of the Connecticut militia also marched with haste towards Danbury. Wooster had informed Washington earlier that his force had dwindled, as enlistment for the Continental Army grew. However, this did not deter Wooster from gathering a formidable force to oppose Tryon. A flurry of letters, orders, and emergency notes sent via express were penned by the major general. From Reading at five o'clock am, Wooster wrote to General James Wadsworth, stationed at Durham, Connecticut, roughly fifty miles east of Danbury, that he had just learned of the enemy's landing earlier on the afternoon of April 25. Their goal appeared to be the stores at Danbury. He urgently requested that Wadsworth march with his men as fast as possible. His post-script was ominous; "A smoke arises this moment over Danbury, which we suppose is from the Stores on fire."[17] After receiving a letter from Wadsworth which included the urgent request from Wooster, Trumbull ordered Wadsworth and Silliman to Wooster's assistance.[18] In the meantime Wooster rushed towards Danbury but arrived after Tryon and his force had already begun their retreat to the coast. Urgency was the driving force, as Wooster penned to Wadsworth "The Importance of a vigorous push at this time is so great that no man will want motives to urge him on instantly."[19] The pursuit was hampered by torrential rains which made the roads all but impassable.

On April 27, Wooster and Arnold arrived on the heels of the retreating enemy. Wooster set in to harass the enemy from the rear, while Arnold and Silliman attempted to hit Tryon's force from their flanks. Wooster's force of roughly 600 men struck the enemy, despite the British having several field guns. Tryon's forces had moved south from Danbury towards the town of Ridgefield. Wooster's men initially surprised the enemy and took several prisoners. Tryon engaged Wooster and began to break the Connecticut line. To rally his troops and encourage them forward, Wooster spurred his horse, waved his sword in encouragement, and was struck in the side by an enemy bullet. The bullet broke his spine and lodged itself in his stomach. An account of the engagement, and of Wooster's martial character, was written by historian G.H. Hollister. Of the battle he wrote:

> On the morning of the 27th, the American troops were astir at a very early hour. General Wooster detached Generals Silliman and Arnold, with about five hundred men, to advance and intercept the enemy in front, while he undertook with the remainder—amounting only to two hundred half-armed militia—to attack them in the rear. About nine o'clock, he came up with them as they were marching upon the Norwalk road, and, taking advantage of the uneven ground, fell upon a whole regiment with such impetuosity as to throw them into confusion, and break their ranks. Before they could be restored to order, he had succeeded in taking forty prisoners; a number equal to one fifth part of his whole force. He continued to hang upon their skirts and harass them for some time, waiting for another favorable opportunity to make an attack. A few miles from Ridgefield, where the hills appeared to offer a chance of breaking their ranks a second time, he again charged furiously upon them. The rear guard, chagrined at the result of the former encounter, now faced about and met him with a discharge of artillery and small arms. His men returned their shot resolutely at first, but as they were unused to battle, they soon began to fall back. Wooster, uniting all the fire of youth with the experience of an old soldier, who had seen hard service in more than one field, sought to inspire them with his own courage. Turning his horse's head and waving his sword, he called out to them in a brisk tone, "Come on, my boys; never mind such random shots." Before he had time to turn his face again toward the enemy, a musket ball, aimed by a tory marksman, penetrated his back, breaking the spinal column, and lodging in the fleshy parts of his body.

He instantly fell from his horse. His faithful friends stripped his sash from his person and bore him upon it from the field.[20]

He was removed from the field in his wine-colored silk waist sash, used as a stretcher, and taken to Danbury. While there his wife arrived. His son Thomas, serving as his aide-de-camp, was with him when he fell mortally wounded. As his men pressed forward, Wooster was carried some distance to the rear. "Dr. Turner, the surgeon in attendance, probed the wound of the venerable Wooster, and informed him that it was mortal. He heard the intelligence with unruffled calmness. A messenger was immediately dispatched to New Haven for Mrs. Wooster, and the wounded man was speedily removed to Danbury."[21]

He lay in agonizing pain and died three days later, May 2, 1777, at the age of sixseven. Word of the battle was first printed in the *Connecticut Journal* on Wednesday, April 30, taking two of the three columns on the front page of the paper. In this initial report stated:

> At 9 o'clock A.M. intelligence was received that the enemy had taken the road leading to Norwalk, of which Gen. Wooster was advised and pursued them, with whom he came up about 11 o'clock, when a smart skirmishing ensued, in which Gen. Wooster, who behaved with great intrepidity, unfortunately received a wound by a musket ball, thro' the groin, which it is feared will prove mortal.[22]

By the time the next edition of the paper was printed the following week, the press had revealed the sober news that "Friday last died at Danbury, of the wound which he received, on the 26th ult. that brave and experienced soldier, the hon. major general David Wooster, of this town."[23] The *Connecticut Journal* prepared a tremendous article in honor of the fallen hero on Wednesday, May 14. Many colonial obituaries can be found throughout the Connecticut newspaper, most are rather short, being only one, perhaps two, paragraphs. David Wooster's was extraordinary in its length of over one full column. After providing an overview of his exemplary life, the paper wrote:

> From the first rise of the present controversy with G. Britain in 1764, tho' his interest, as an half pay officer, might have apologized for him, if he had observed perfect neutrality; yet so fully convinced was he of the ruinous measures of the British court, and so jealous was he for his country's rights, that regardless of his private interest, he took an open and decisive pass, and avowedly espoused the cause of America, and persisted in that line of conduct to the day of his death.
>
> Thus fell a brave and experienced officer, fighting in the cause of his injured country, at a time when his abilities, courage and experience are most wanted? May that providence which hath taken him away in this manner, and at this juncture, raise up and qualify some person, abundantly to fill his place![24]

On May 19, the Continental Congress formed a committee to "consider what honors are due to the memory of the late brigadier Wooster, who died on the 2d of May."[25] The committee reported on June 17, that a monument should be built in his honor with the following inscription:

> In honor of David Wooster, brigadier-general in the army of the United States. In defending the liberties of America, and bravely repelling an inroad of the British forces to Danbury, in Connecticut, he received a mortal wound on the 27th day of April, 1777, and died on the 2d

day of May following, The Congress of the United States, as an acknowledgement of his merit and services, have caused this monument to be erected.[26]

This concluded with the resolution that the state of Connecticut should execute the building of such a monument, and that 500 dollars be allotted for its construction. No such monument was ever erected to honor General Wooster by the Continental Congress. It is worth noting, however, that this resolution to honor Wooster with a monument was passed during the war.

There is some historical discrepancy concerning the Battle of Ridgefield and the death of Wooster. He was mortally wounded on April 27, 1777, and died from the wound on May 2. David Ramsay noted in his *History of the American Revolution* that Wooster was seventy years old, as did historian William Gordan. In fact, Wooster had just turned sixty-seven years old when he died. According to Hollister, while the British were enroute to Danbury they shot cannon balls and canister shot through the oldest church at Reading Ridge. His statement, written in 1855, was corrected by James R. Case in 1927. Case noted that

> the statement (made by Hollister) concerning the firing into the church is a mistake. It is said that the church was not molested at all (except that a soldier with a well-directed ball took off a leg from the gilded weathercock on the spire), and the fact that the pastor, the Rev. James Beach, as well as several of its most prominent members, were most pronounced loyalists, strengthens the assertion.[27]

The most important error pertains to the incorrect narrative that at the Battle of Ridgefield, Thomas Wooster was bayonetted and killed while defending his dying father. This narrative began to circulate due to a letter written by William Carmichael to Charles W.F. Dumas from Paris, June 20, 1777. Carmichael, a native of Maryland, was serving the Congress as a special envoy to France, along with Silas Deane. In the letter to Dumas, Carmichael stated that no news had been forthcoming, other than that which he gained from England. He went on to say, "General Wooster's son was killed defending his father's body, having repeatedly proffered quarter."[28] This was incorrect, and has led to many notable historians repeating the same narrative, thus confuting the true historical record.[29] Thomas Wooster was alongside his father at the Battle of Ridgefield, yet the record also indicates that as a captain of infantry, a position his father had requested from Governor Trumbull, he left the army in 1780. A letter written to General Washington dated September 29, 1780, proves this fact. In that letter Thomas Wooster requested to be readmitted into the army after his resignation from the service which he attested to a disagreement with the commanding officer of the regiment, which apparently others did as well as they too, resigned. Wooster was requesting to:

> serve in your Family as a Volunteer, if it is consistent, with the rules and customs of the Army, and your own inclination; I shou'd expect to continue with the Army, as long as the War lasted, (if my Life was spar'd) and shou'd think myself very happy, to be so near your Excellency, that I might form myself, both by your precepts and example.[30]

Washington replied that to fulfill this request would require him to set a dangerous precedent for the many men who had previously asked the same and been refused. Washington closed his letter to Thomas Wooster by stating, "I entreat you therefore to believe that there is nothing personal in the objection; but on the contrary You may rest assured, the Memory of Your gallant Father, and your own reputation will always entitle you to every mark of consideration and esteem."[31] This series of letters alone corrects the inaccuracies which have permeated the historical record pertaining to Wooster's lineage, which started in June 1777.

Because of the urgent nature of the British invasion under Tryon, Wooster had to be buried in haste, as there was little time for a proper funeral. His wife and son were with him when he died. Before losing consciousness, the general mentioned to his family that "he was dying, but with strong hope and persuasion that his country would gain its independence."[32]

On July 16, 1777, the estate of Major General David Wooster was inventoried and sold. This lengthy inventory sheds great light into the private life of Wooster, his material possessions, what he wore, land that he owned as well as livestock and farming implements. Not only did Wooster own a great deal of furniture, clothing, and land, he also owned shares in the British East India Company.[33] The analysis of the inventory provides an invaluable assessment of a life fully lived.

Upon learning of the death of Wooster, Phillis Wheatley, the female poet who had corresponded with the general in 1773, wrote to Mary Wooster to express her deepest sympathies for her loss. Mary Wooster replied, upon Wheatley's request, to provide her the characteristics of her late husband, which Wheatly then included in a lengthy eulogy poem titled "On the Death of General Wooster."[34] Wheatly wrote once more to Mary Wooster on July 15, 1778, and included in her letter was the eulogy poem:

Madam,

I recd, your favour by Mr. Dennison inclosing a paper containing the Character of the truly worthy General Wooster. It was with the most sensible regret that I heard of his fall in battle, but the pain of so afflicting a dispensation of Providence must be greatly alleviated to you and all his friends in the consideration that he fell a martyr in the Cause of Freedom
You will do me a great favour by returning to me by the first oppy those books that remain unsold and remitting the money for those that are sold—I can easily dispose of them here for 12/ [shillings] each—I am greatly obliged to you for the care you show me, and your condescention in taking so much pains for my Interest—I am extremely sorry not to have been honour'd with a personal acquaintance with you—if the foregoing lines meet with your acceptance and approbation I shall think them highly honour'd. I hope you will pardon the length of my letter, when the reason is apparent—fondness of the subject &—the highest respect for the deceas'd—I sincerely sympathize with you in the great loss you and your family sustain and am sincerely

Your friend & very humble sert
Phillis Wheatley.[35]

The death of David Wooster on May 2, 1777, was clearly devastating to his wife Mary. Unfortunately for her the horrors of war were far from over. Two years after Wooster's death, Tryon once again invaded Connecticut; this time, though, the invasion was directed at New Haven. On July 5, Tryon's men marched into New Haven with the sole purpose of wanton destruction of patriot property. The accounts of the invasion highlighted the purposeful attention given to Wooster's estate. Nathan Beers, Revolutionary War veteran and inhabitant of New Haven, related the destruction to his brother on July 16, 1779; "Old Mrs. Wooster stayed in her house and was most shockingly abused; everything in the house was destroyed or carried off by them, not a bed left or the smallest article in the kitchen."[36] Simeon Baldwin also related the tragedy that befell Mary Wooster. His recollections, made years later, are not quite as historically accurate. However, they are compelling, nonetheless:

> When the British came to New Haven, a detachment marched through town till they came to Gen. Wooster's residence and then grounded their arms and were disbanded for pillage. Madam Wooster remained alone in her house. She came out onto the front Piazza and said to an officer who approached, "Sir, I am your prisoner." "Yes, damn you" was the brutal reply.
>
> Through the day they were robbing the house and store adjoining, breaking and injuring what they could not remove. Once during the day as she was standing in the middle of the room three or four soldiers surrounded her with bayonetts and insisted upon searching her pockets. One stood in front of her and she noticed blood on his bayonet. "Yes," [he] said [to] her, "I have just killed one old rebel over there, he has lived long enough. Mr. English, a very old gentleman who was deaf and sitting in his arm chair, not answering readily they stabbed him."[37]

Mary Wooster not only had possession of her husband's personal papers, but those of her late father, Thomas Clap, the former president of Yale College. After the British troops ransacked her home, they seized the papers of the two men. The president of Yale College at the time of the attack, Ezra Stiles, wrote to Governor Tryon requesting the return of the documents, especially those of Thomas Clap.[38] The personal papers of General Wooster had also been seized by the invading enemy troops. Tryon replied that the officers who led the attack on New Haven had no recollection of the letters in the possession of any of his men and regretted that he could not assist Mr. Stiles in his request.[39] By December, the fate of the missing papers had been confirmed. Stiles wrote once more to Tryon in a state of great agitation and frustration:

Yale College, December 14, 1779.

> Sir,—The latter end of October last, I received your letter of 25th September. It is unnecessary for you to make any further inquiry respecting President Clap's manuscript. Capt. Boswell, of the guard, while here on the fatal 5th of July last, showed some of them in town, which he said he had taken from Gen. Wooster's house, and it is presumed that he well knows the accident which befell the rest. Your troops carried away from Mrs. Wooster's a box and two large trunks of papers. One of them was a trunk of papers which the General took to Canada; the others were his own and the President's. On the night of the conflagration of Fairfield, three whale boats of our people, on their way from Norwalk to the eastward, passed by your fleet, at anchor off Fairfield (then in flames), sailed through a little ocean of floating papers, not far from your shipping. They took up some of them as they passed. I have since separated and reduced them all to three sorts and no more, viz.: Gen. Wooster's own papers; Gen. Carlton's French Commissions and orders to the Canadian Militia; and Mr. Clap's, a few of which last belong to this College, This specimen, Sir, shows us that the rest are unhappily and irrevocably lost, unless, perhaps Capt. Boswell might have selected some before the rest were thrown overboard. If so, your polite attention to my request convinces me that I shall be so fortunate as to recover such as may have been saved.

I am, Sir, your very humble
servant,

Ezra Stiles[40]

With the limited supply of hard currency in the colonial treasury, let alone the treasury of the Continental Congress, Wooster often used his own financial resources to provide for his own men, hoping that if they were victorious the bills would be repaid. With a good sense for business, he had kept meticulous records of his expenditures. Among her husband's personal papers that had been destroyed were the expenditures which documented all the items he had purchased for his troops. Mary Wooster found herself impoverished with little recourse to alleviate her economic situation. Throughout the 1780s, and into the early 1800s she struggled to receive the military pension granted to her late husband, as well as interest owed. On April 20, 1785, William Johnson, a member of the Continental Congress from Connecticut, wrote to Roger Sherman asking for advice on how to help Mary Wooster with her petition for her late husband's military pension and the interest that had accrued on that pension. The financial distress of the states at the close of the Revolution was shocking. It became apparent that the best way to deal with the pension crisis was for the Confederation Congress to return the question to the individual states to pay, while the states, in turn, forwarded the same requests back to the Confederation Congress. Johnson was at a loss on how to assist Mary Wooster. In frustration he wrote:

> I extremely want your opinion and advice relative to the pursuing Mrs. Wooster's petition before Congress. The difficulty is this. Congress have very lately upon the petition of Gen. Thomas' widow of Massachusetts, fully explained the doubt there was, whether he has entitled to brigadier's or Colonel's pay deciding it in the favor of the former. Thus, one of the grounds of Mrs. Wooster's petition is effectually removed. What remains, is only that the State of Connecticut will not pay it, though the requisition of Congress is as full as they can make it, if they should take up the subject again. And is it to be presumed that Congress will take it up themselves, merely because Connecticut will not do what she aught? Nay will the finances of the United States admit of such a measure? Yet more, can they do it when the other States have actually taken upon themselves, and are now in the payment of similar demands, as N. York of Mrs. Montgomery, N. Jersey of Mrs. Barber, &c, &c? Would not this derange everything? Will not the matter now stand solely upon the ground, and appear in the light, of a complaint against the State? If so, can I advocate it? Will not everything of the nature come with a very ill grace from a delegate of the State? Finally, for I dare not presume to ask any more questions, is it not most advisable, since Congress have explained the only doubt there was in the case, and that the session of the General Assembly is so near, for Mrs. Wooster to apply once more to the Assembly before she pursues the matter further here. Your sentiments upon this subject would give great relief to, and extremely oblige, Dear Sir,
>
> > Your most obedient humble servant,
> >
> > Wm. Saml. Johnson[41]

Placed in a desperate situation, and facing economic uncertainty, she petitioned President George Washington in May 1789, to provide employment for her son, Thomas, in the memory of her late husband. It was now twelve years after her husband's death. Her request was not only for financial assistance, but for something more. She feared that her son would leave the United States for a foreign county. Without his help she would face certain poverty. Mary Wooster petitioned the new President of the United States and asked, "your Excellency to become a Father to him, and relieve him in some measure from his troubles, forgive a Mothers feelings whose future happiness Depends on that of her Son."[42] She referenced her late husband's service and sacrifice to the great cause of the Revolution, for which he had lost everything. Now she, too, was on the brink of financial ruin. Her continued petitions for his pension had produced nothing tangible. Her request to Washington was that of a desperate widow.

This request placed Washington in a rather awkward situation. As president of the United States, he could not provide assistance based solely on his political position. Mary Wooster had even gone so far as to ask Washington to be a father figure for her son. Privately, Washington, sympathized, but as a public figure he assured her that he was required to make certain that all government positions under his authority should be filled by those best suited to carry out the office. To her request, President Washington replied, "I have duly received your affecting letter, dated the 8th day of this Month. Sympathysing with you, as I do, in the great misfortunes which have befallen your family in consequence of the war; my feelings, as an individual, would forcibly prompt me to do every thing in my power to repair those misfortunes." Regarding her request that President Washington provide employment for her son, he continued, "But as a public man, acting only with a reference to the public good, I must be allowed to decide upon all points of my duty without consulting my private inclinations & wishes. I must be permitted, with the best lights I can obtain, and upon a general view of characters & circumstances, to nominate such persons alone to offices, as, in my judgment, shall be best qualified to discharge the functions of the departments to which they shall be appointed." It was not proper, as he saw it, to provide a position for anyone who did not warrant the post through their qualifications. He saw that providing such an opportunity would discredit the position that he had been duly elected to. He deeply regrated her situation but was unable to provide the assistance that she requested of him.[43]

Secretary of the Treasury Alexander Hamilton also weighed in on the political debate regarding Wooster's pension. Thirteen years had passed since the death of General Wooster. On March 25, 1790, Hamilton addressed the issue of in a report that was delivered to the Speaker of the House of Representatives which stated:

> That the State of Connecticut having settled the allowance of seven years half pay with the petitioner, in the same manner, as has been customary in like cases, and charged it to the United States, and adjustments at the Treasury having proceeded on a similar principle, the Secretary is of opinion, that a departure from the rule, by granting the interest claimed by the said petition, would operate partially, with regard to many other claims of the same nature, which have been heretofore adjusted, or, if extended to them, would involve the inconvenient precedent of unsettling an established rule.
> All which is humbly submitted
>
> Alexander Hamilton
Secry. of the Treasury[44]

As the years dragged on it became less clear if Mary Wooster would receive the pension due her husband, and if so, would it come from the new United States government, or from the State of Connecticut? She had attempted to remedy her situation with the General Assembly of Connecticut, President Washington, and in 1797, with President John Adams. Her son-in-law, the Rev. John Cosens Ogden, did much to help her procure her husband's military pension. In an attempt to secure the position as customs official in New Haven, and thus provide for his own wife, as well as his mother-in-law, Ogden wrote to President Adams in 1797:

> I am not so totally a stranger of Your Excellency as not to be known as the son in law of that meritorious officer General Wooster, who so valiantly sacrificed his life and fortune together in the late war,—An event which deprived his widow and family of a very valuable property. This has been made doubly poignant to them as the Genl. entered the service, possessed of his military and other lands in Vermont, which have been lost by the independence of that State—of the incomes of the naval office & British half-pay as a captain.—The commutation of his widow was paid at a time when it was greatly depreciated, and the distresses of her affairs from taxation depreciation of public credit—fall of lands in value, and long deprivation of [any] former incomes forced her to part with them, when other sources failed, from public events. She is now totally destitute of any income, and made happy with her daughter at an advanced age.[45]

The struggle continued as Ogden wrote to Thomas Jefferson in 1799, requesting his "readiness to serve so venerable a Lady as Mrs. Wooster, or do honor so distinguished a soldier as General Wooster."[46] Despite the historic record outlining Mary Wooster's plight, no records indicate whether she ever did receive funds from the government of the United States, either through reimbursement of her husband's war-time expenditures, of his military pension. According to the records of Congress in 1793, as a military widow she was granted her husband's pension of seven years half-pay. The resolution read:

> And it will further appear, by the resolve of Congress of the 4th of May, 1785, that is was recommended to the State of Connecticut to pay to the widow of the late Brigadier General Wooster the seven years' half-pay of a brigadier general, the amount whereof they are authorized to charge to the United States.[47]

According to the list of claims from the state of Connecticut, Mary Wooster was owed $5,250 in back pension pay.[48] In the end, both David and Mary Wooster sacrificed everything for the blessings of liberty and independence.

Major General David Wooster had truly sacrificed, and lost, everything. The last line of the Declaration of Independence reads, "We mutually pledge to each other our lives, our fortunes and our sacred honor." It was to these republican ideas that Wooster had pledged his loyalty. In dealing with the trials and tribulations of the Revolution and the successes throughout his entire life, his honor was never impugned. In the end Wooster gave all for the defense of his country and for the Revolution's cause of liberty, freedom, independence, and equality. His leadership never faltered, and his loyalty never wavered.

9

Wooster's Legacy

Although Major General David Wooster's leadership helped to set the stage for American success in the Revolution, with the destruction of his personal papers, little remained to tell his story. Once the veterans who had served with him in the field, business associates with whom he worked, or family members had passed on, the historical record also faded. In the years following the conclusion of the war historians such as Mercy Otis Warren, Benjamin Trumbull, David Ramsay, and William Gordon provided excellent accounts of Wooster's role in the Revolution. The men who survived and remained politically connected, however, such as Philip Schuyler and Benedict Arnold took pen in hand to memorialize their versions of the historic events. Many of these post-war accounts contained negative anecdotes about David Wooster. Arnold's infamy became legend, yet Wooster's was omitted. Schuyler's career in politics was cemented by the Revolution, yet Wooster's eroded. Washington's legacy was cast in marble, yet Wooster's was lost. Only after years of research, and accumulating of copies of letters, documents, and correspondences from across the country, can we begin to analyze the many leadership roles of David Wooster, and in doing so, assess the American Revolution in a new and broader perspective.

Connecticut General Benedict Arnold returned to his home state of Connecticut in 1781, this time as a British officer. After betraying the American cause in 1780, predominantly from extreme frustration over the lack of promotion by the Continental Congress, an experience shared by Wooster. Unlike Wooster, who continued to serve the American cause until his death in battle, Arnold realigned his loyalty and ravaged the coastal town of New London on the southern coast of Connecticut, not out of military necessity, but out of spite. One month later, General Lord Charles Cornwallis surrendered to General George Washington at Yorktown, Virginia, effectively ending military combat in America.

Following the conclusion of the war, the Confederation Congress, unable to pay many of the soldiers with actual hard currency, provided land grants to veterans in the newly established Northwest Territory, lands situated north-west of the Ohio River. In addition, the Congress granted a tract of land known as the Connecticut Western Reserve to those who lost their homes during Arnold's 1780 attack. This land, known as the Firelands, was in northeast Ohio and became the new home for many Connecticut veterans and their families. By the early 1800s, enough civilians had migrated into the Western Reserve that they petitioned to establish counties and designate towns as official county seats. Wayne County, Ohio, was located on the southern edge of the Western Reserve. In 1812, the county had been established and the inhabitants sought to name the county seat. Numerous Connecticut veterans had established themselves in the area and under their influence the country seat was named in honor of the late Major General David Wooster. It is worth noting that this honor was bestowed upon him thirty-two years after his death. There are at least seventeen documented Connecticut Revolutionary War veterans buried in Wayne County, and Wooster, Ohio, became the first town to be named in his honor, thus fortifying his legacy in the western territories.[1]

In 1802, the Senate of the United States passed a bill that mirrored the resolution of the Congress in 1778 that allotted $500 for the construction of the monument to honor the late Brigadier General Wooster. The monument was to be erected in Connecticut.[2] Although the funds were allotted twenty-five years had passed since Wooster's death. A new generation had emerged, and Wooster's monument was once more postponed.

Early histories written in the 1830s through the 1850s highlighted the achievements and character of Wooster. Many of these were written by men who knew him or had secondhand knowledge of him. The fraternal organization of Freemasons in Connecticut, which he founded, pressed for a fitting site for a monument to Wooster. The call went out to brother Masons across the country to raise the necessary funds required to build a fitting monument. Although the Congress provided funds for a monument in 1802, no record of those funds being used for their intended use was ever documented. In 1854, the Connecticut General Assembly ordered that a monument be erected upon the site of the burial of Wooster. The problem arose, however, to ascertain the exact location of Wooster's grave site since the general had been hastily interred following his death in 1777. With the assistance of locals who had helped to dig the grave years earlier, Wooster's remains were correctly located. This discovery is related by historian Benson Lossing:

> When search was made for his grave, it was identified by unmistakable evidences. With the skeleton was found some matted wire (the remains of epaulets), a portion of a plume, and a leaden bullet. The later was a smooth, English bullet, larger than those used by the Americans. These were satisfactory evidence that the right grave had been opened. That bullet undoubtedly gave the death-wound to the patriot.[3]

The body was exhumed and given a full military burial, and the full rites of a Freemason.

Major General Wooster finally received just accolades seventy-seven years after his death. On April 27, 1854, the chief stone was laid in the Danbury Cemetery for the first, and only, monument erected to honor the late general. At the ceremony, led by Freemasons from Connecticut, a collection of items was placed with the remains of Wooster. It was a copper box which contained:

> various gold, silver, and copper coins, public documents, proceedings of Grand Lodge and other high Masonic bodies, the papers, and periodicals of the day, a daguerreotype likeness of Gen. Wooster, the identical bullet with which he was killed, a fragment of his vest, with many other interesting relics.[4]

A lengthy ceremony followed which included songs, poems, and numerous speeches. The M.W. Lodge Grand Master delivered the introductory remarks:

For some good purpose it was left for us, the sons of the heroes of the revolution, to erect this Monument to the sacred memory of Gen. David Wooster who early, yet gloriously, fell a martyr to the cause of Liberty and Independence.

It may with truth be said, he was the father of Freemasonry in Connecticut. General Wooster was a man of keen foresight. Learning, from observation and reflection, the benevolent ends out institution designed to accomplish, he determined to became one of the brotherhood. An honest advocate of the equal and inalienable rights of man, he become satisfied that Masonry had, at all times, and under the severest trials, been the unfaltering supporter of just and free principles; and under all circumstances, he found Masonry, as we now find it, true and steadfast in advancing the moral and intellectual improvements of the masses, and the elevation of man to the condition of equality and happiness.[5]

Connecticut Governor Pond then addressed the gathering:

The living owe it to themselves, as well as to the memory of departed patriots, to raise monumental structures, and especially to the memory of a patriot, who spilt his life's blood in contending for the Independence of his country.

This Monument is the joint product of the General Assembly, the Masonic Fraternity, and the people of Danbury. Although Congress, duly impressed with its importance, made an appropriation for the same object which has convened this vast concourse, yet it has remained for this generation to complete what Congress proposed. The General Assembly made the introductory movement, the Masonic Brotherhood promptly seconded the motion, and the people of Danbury contributed liberally towards the noble enterprise.

There stands the WOOSTER MONUMENT, containing the lesson which all have read in school books. *"My life has been devoted to my country from my youth up, though never before in a cause like this, a cause for which I would most cheerfully risk—nay, lay down my life."*[6]

The ceremonial program contained over twenty congratulatory letters from lodges across the country. The inscriptions which were engraved on the monument were then read:

DAVID WOOSTER
First Maj. Gen. of the Conn. Troops
in the
Army of the Revolution:
Brig. Gen. of the United Colonies:
Born at Stratford, March 2, 1710–11:
Wounded at Ridgefield, April 27, 1777,
while defending the liberties of
America,
and nobly died at Danbury,
May 2d, 1777.
Of his country Wooster said:
"My life has ever been devoted to her service from my youth up, though
never before in a cause like this; a cause for which I would most cheerfully
risk—nay lay down my life!"[7]

The opposite side referenced his role in establishing Freemasonry in Connecticut, and the importance of Hiram Lodge No. 1, whose charter dated to 1750.

The pinnacle of the ceremony was a lengthy oration on the life of General David Wooster delivered by Henry Champion Deming. The extensive speech was well documented and covered the entirety of Wooster's life, although some components had already begun to fade from memory by the 1850s. Deming provided an excellent overview which was the capstone of the grand events of the day.[8]

Photograph of the monument to General Wooster, located in the Danbury Cemetery, Danbury, Connecticut (photograph by the author).

In 1858, famed Italian painter Constantino Brumidi was commissioned to paint several murals throughout the United States Capital Building. In the Senate wing, adorning one archway in the original Senate Military Affairs and Militia Committee Room, now the Senate Appropriations Committee suite, is a fresco painted by Brumidi entitled the "Death of General Wooster, 1777." This painting has recently been

Image of the front of the Wooster Monument in Danbury Cemetery, showing the death of Wooster at the Battle of Ridgefield, April 30, 1777 (photograph by the author).

cleaned and restored to its original brilliance, and depicts Major General Wooster, being carried from the field in his scarlet waist sash turned stretcher, moments after being mortally wounded at the Battle of Ridgefield.[9] For senators who have the occasions to frequent this room, Wooster remains ever present.

By the late 1800s, Wooster's legacy began to fade. The historiography of the Revolution focused on more noteworthy figures such as Washington. Schuyler was memorialized in a two-volume biography written by Benson Losing. In his *Life of*

Additional image from the Wooster Monument in Danbury Cemetery highlighting the Masonic order which Wooster established in Connecticut (photograph by the author).

Philip Schuyler, Lossing highlighted the conflict between Wooster and Schuyler in 1775–76. Understandably it was presented from a pro–Schuyler perspective.

By the Bicentennial in 1976, Wooster had been forgotten. Few authors included him in their work, other than the cursory note that he was made third brigadier general in 1775 and associating him with the failure in Canada in 1776. Biographies of Benedict Arnold began to emerge and these, too, provided an image of the Revolution from his perspective as a youth filled with zeal for the cause who was held back, or ignored, by the aged Wooster who was too slow or overly cautious. Few historians, like Jonathan Rossie, provided an accurate analysis of Wooster's actions in the war, and, despite his years of military experience and leadership, no one mentioned him within the many volumes being written on Colonial America or the history of Connecticut. Most recently historian, Mark Anderson has defended Wooster's military actions in the Canadian campaign of 1776 as instrumental in holding the army together as long as possible.[10]

Unfortunately, there continues to be a repetition of several incorrect accounts of Wooster's life in modern historiography. These have permeated historical writing for generations. In the late 1800s, there appeared a narrative that David Wooster was a drunkard, an officer that was continuously inebriated and incompetent. This assessment of Wooster first appeared in Thomas Jones' *History of New York During the Revolutionary War* (1879). Jones provided a brief one-page biography of Wooster that concluded by incorrectly stating he was "between 70 and 80 years of age at the time of his death."[11] Following, however, he included that "although he had accustomed himself during the greatest part of his life to swallow daily large potations of flip, he was a healthy, hearty, strong, man to the last."[12] Jones included a footnote to this brief passage to explain what "flip" was:

> A mixture of New England rum, pumpkin beer, and brown sugar. In winter it was made warm by putting a red-hot poker into it. Every public-house in Connecticut has in the winter season one of these pokers (known among them by the name of loggerheads) always in the fire, ready upon the travelers or the arriving in of company. It is far from being disagreeable liquor, and is universally drank in Connecticut.[13]

Below this was added a second footnote which subsequent historians have used in perpetuating the myth that Wooster as a drunkard:

> A gentleman who was at Albany in 1775, when Wooster was upon his march to Canada, was asked by the High Sheriff one evening whether he had an inclination to see a curiosity? He asked, what? The Sheriff answered, "I am just come from the jail, and there is General Wooster, my turnkey, and the butcher's boy in the tap-room drinking flip together." Such company one would think even beneath the dignity of a Yankee General.[14]

The second footnote is not referenced in Jones' book. Neither the gentleman nor the sheriff mentioned are named, which makes further research into the notation extremely difficult to verify. In 1947, a collection of journals was compiled by historian Kenneth Roberts that focused on the Canadian expedition led by Benedict Arnold. The accounts are valuable for research; however, Roberts referenced the narrative found in Jones' footnote and included it verbatim as a biographical footnote of his own, adding to it that "he [Wooster] drank large amounts of flip each day."[15] For modern historians, especially those who focus on Benedict Arnold, Roberts' book *March to Quebec: Journals of the Members of Arnold's Expedition* appears to be a common reference, including the notation on Wooster's alleged drinking problem. It is interesting to analyze the development of the allegation of drunkenness, especially considering that public drinking was commonplace in the colonies in the 1700s.

Historian Willard M. Wallace was one of the few biographers of Arnold who cited both Jones and Roberts and provided a broader interpretation of Wooster's account in the war.[16] In *The Fate of a Nation: The American Revolution Through Contemporary Eyes* (1975), historians William P. Cumming and Hugh Rankin noted that Wooster was "a country-looking fellow who considered a day wasted unless he had paid his homage to Bacchus, soon had 'thrown everything into confusion.'"[17] Noted Arnold scholar James Kirby Martin, in his excellent biography *Benedict Arnold, Revolutionary Hero: An American Warrior Reconsidered* (1997), also cited Roberts' work and included the narrative of Wooster's drinking.[18] Christopher Hibbert also referenced Jones' work in *Redcoats and Rebels: The American Revolution Through British Eyes* (2002). In assessing the condition of the army in Canada, Hibbert stated that "he [Arnold] was still in camp before Quebec on 1 April when the bucolic, hard-drinking General Wooster arrived from Montreal with heavy guns to take over the command of the besieging force," and that "having thrown everything into confusion, he [Wooster] was soon himself replaced by General John Thomas."[19] A detailed review of the historic record indicates that Wooster had no heavy guns with which to besiege Quebec, not to mention the inaccuracies of his supposed drunkenness. An overview of Arnold biographies published from the 1950s to today reveal a continuation of the original Jones account and Roberts' interpretation.

And then there began yet another interesting tale; the "periwig" narrative. It is true that Wooster did own a wig, two in fact, as listed in his estate inventory of 1777. In *Angel in the Whirlwind: The Triumph of the American Revolution* (1997), Benson Bobrick was one of the first historians to refer to Wooster as "a rather fussy old man with an enormous periwig."[20] A periwig was a large wig, usually worn in the early 1700s by a man, piled high in the front and which hung down upon the shoulders. This was an outdated style for Colonial America, especially among New England Puritans in the mid–1700s. An analysis of Wooster's 1746 portrait made in London clearly shows him wearing his hair queued. It is highly unlikely that he would have adopted an outdated style in his sixties, if he did not wear his hair in that fashion as a younger man. Even as recently as 2019, historian Rick Atkinson perpetuated that narrative in *The British Are Coming: The War for America, Lexington to Princeton, 1775–1777* (2019), writing of the failure of the Canadian campaign; "Worse yet, General Wooster—an arrogant, despotic Yale graduate in a large periwig—had alienated many Canadians by arresting priests and loyalists, closing Catholic churches, meddling with the fur trade, and telling Montreal citizens, 'I regard the whole of you as enemies and rascals.'"[21]

The origin of the "periwig conspiracy" is found in the journal of British Captain Thomas Ainslie who was stationed in Quebec. Ainslie, the collector of customs in Quebec on the outset of the war, petitioned to serve in the royal army during the American attack against Canadian. As a loyalist he fought to defend the city and his journal provided a unique perspective of events in Canada. On April 2, 1776, Ainslie wrote the following entry:

> Wind SW warm clear weather. Three men were seen near the ruins of Mount Pleasant about 400 yards from Port Louis; one of them wore a large grey periwig, suppos'd to be David Wooster, another was dress'd in scarlet said to be Arnold, the third, said those who had a good glass was Edward Antil—they stood pointing to the walls probably planning an attack, which they never intend to make.[22]

To make an accurate observation at 400 yards would be challenging with the best glass of the eighteenth century. Ainslie's entry does coincide with Wooster's arrival near Quebec. This historic account has been used and exaggerated over the years by numerous historians who have added their own interpretation of the event, with a bit of creativity, as noted in the passages above. This further demonstrates the need to correct the historical record regarding David Wooster.

A perfect example of how Ainslie's journal entry gained prominence within the historical record can be found in Justin H. Smith's *Our Struggle for the Fourteenth Colony: Canada and the American Revolution* (1907). Here Smith expounded upon the journal entry in a rather creative fashion, stating:

> On the second day in April, something new appeared on the Heights, and the glasses were soon levelled that way. It was an enormous grey periwig. On one side of it stood Edward Antill; a figure in scarlet on the other was pronounced Arnold; and the periwig—was General David Wooster.[23]

As humorous as Smith's account might appear, this distortion of the historical record is perpetuated in the modern historiography and is often found among biographies of Benedict Arnold as well as the history of the American Canadian Campaign of 1775–76. In his two-volume work, Smith provided a great deal of information on Wooster, yet none quite as interesting as the passage above.

Aside for these historically inaccurate portrayals of Wooster, the narrative of Wooster's son being killed by his father's side at the Battle of Ridgefield also continued to find its way into modern historiography. Recently Nathaniel Philbrick, who also referenced the works of Jones and Roberts, included in his excellent book *Valiant Ambition: George Washington, Benedict Arnold, and the fate of the American Revolution* (2016) the following passage:

> Before Wooster had a chance to fall back, he received a musket ball in the groin. His son rushed to his aid, and when a regular bore down on the two of them, the younger Wooster refused to ask for quarter and, according to a British officer, "died by the bayonet" at his mortally wounded father's side.[24]

There are two errors in this passage. First, Major General Wooster was not shot in the groin, but rather in the side, the ball piercing his spinal column. That error had been reported in the *Connecticut Journal* on April 30, 1777, but was quickly corrected in his obituary printed on May 14. Second is the reference to his son dying at his side, which, as noted previously, is not supported by further analysis of the historical record. The citation for this account found in the Philbrick passage is "A British Officer's Account of the Danbury Raid" found in the *Naval Documents of the American Revolution* (NDAR) which stated:

Arnold & Wooster opposed us with more Obstinacy than skill—the first narrowly escaped; leaving His Horse dead, & His pistolls dropped a few Yards off; the other was Mortally wounded in the Belly & left to die on the Field by His Son, who behaved remarkably well, refusing Quarter & dyed by the Bayonet.[25]

The original source was a letter from Paul Wentworth to the Earl of Suffolk, May 8, 1777, and is found in *B.F. Steven's Facsimiles of Manuscripts in European Archives Relating to America, 1773–1783* (1898).[26] Wentworth was the "British Officer" referred to in the *Naval Documents of the American Revolution*, cited by Philbrick.

After analyzing hundreds of surviving documents pertaining to David Wooster from the earliest accounts to his death, nowhere in the historical record is there any indication of Wooster being a drunkard. It is evident that there were those who did not like him, both military officers and politicians within the Continental Congress. These accounts have been noted in the previous pages. Historical biographies of men like Philip Schuyler, Benedict Arnold, George Washington, and Samuel Chase, continue to be published. Without an in-depth accumulation of Wooster's personal papers, it is difficult to write his biography relying solely upon his few remaining letters. Suffice it to say it has been a quest to find as many individuals as possible who associated with him, either in business, politics, the military, or in his religious society, and to analyze those additional correspondence to assess their perspective of Wooster. With additional sources now being digitized and made readily available, a treasure trove of primary

The first commissioned bronze statue of Major General David Wooster, created by master sculptor Alan Cottrill, and installed on the front lawn of the Wayne County Public Library, Wooster, Ohio. The project to create this statue was undertaken by Dr. Jason Anderson (photograph by the author).

source documents has enabled a much more comprehensive overview of Wooster than ever before. Now his role, equally placed within the context of a broader republican revolution, can be analyzed for his contribution to colonial Connecticut and his unwavering military leadership.

To catapult this research revival, a project was recently completed to bring Major General David Wooster to light. In the fall of 2018, the "Major General David Wooster Memorial Statue Campaign" was created in Wooster, Ohio. The goal of this project was to commission the first ever bronze statue of David Wooster, and have it erected in downtown Wooster, Ohio, the town dedicated in his honor. After initial investigating as to the best location for the statue, procuring the necessary funding for the cost of such a work of art, and a campaign plan to form the idea into a reality, the project commenced. Throughout 2019, a series of lectures were given to educate the public on the life of General Wooster, and to raise the necessary funding. Mr. Alan Cottrill, a master sculptor in Zanesville, Ohio, was commissioned for the work. He designed a bronze statue of Major General David Wooster as imagined at age sixty-five, in Connecticut uniform, sword drawn, and proudly defiant. By December 2020, just days after Christmas, the seven-foot-tall bronze statue of Wooster was installed on the front lawn of the Wayne County Public Library in downtown Wooster, Ohio. The statue was designed to be at ground level where anyone visiting the library could approach the statue and see the immense detail Mr. Cottrill instilled in the piece of art, as well as take a photograph alongside the general. The statue was officially dedicated on Saturday, July 24, 2021. This event was not a city of Wooster celebration. It was not a Wayne County, Ohio, celebration. It was truly an American Celebration. The Revolutionary War veterans took the first step in honoring Wooster. By connecting to our American heritage, the legacy of Major General David Wooster is being remembered and re-honored.

The purpose of this work is to accurately, and objectively, place David Wooster into the historiography of eighteenth-century Colonial America. Due to primary source material heretofore yet analyzed, Wooster's narrative has been forced into the shadows of history, normally as a sidenote to the failed attempt to take Canada in 1776. This book intertwines Wooster's leadership role within the colony of Connecticut and the events that shaped eighteenth-century New England. This analysis provides a detailed look into the hardships, challenges, and successes of colonial life, as well as the many factors that shaped and propelled the ideals of republicanism and liberty throughout the 1700s.

Prompted by new historical research, there is a renewed interest in the life of David Wooster and the impact that he made upon Connecticut and the founding of the nation. This started with a grass-roots campaign and has included school programs, educational materials for teachers, and public presentations. It is good to see that David Wooster's renewed legacy of undivided loyalty to the cause of republican liberty, freedom, and independence, coupled with his numerous examples of modeled unwavering leadership will continue to influence generations of Americans well into the future.

Appendix I

Historiographic Essay on Eighteenth-Century Colonial Connecticut

To write a comprehensive analysis of how Wooster's leadership shaped Connecticut in the 1700s required a four-pronged assessment of current historiography: eighteenth-century republicanism; colonial economics; political loyalism; and the Revolutionary War.

The first historiographical analysis must focus on eighteenth-century republicanism.[1] The Glorious Revolution of 1689 made a tremendous political impact on New England. The seeds of republicanism had been sown by the time of Wooster's birth in 1710, developing and growing further throughout the 1700s. Republicanism in the eighteenth century encompassed that form of government whose sole power was derived from its enfranchised citizens who, in turn, elected representatives from among them to govern on their behalf—thus the Lockean idea of consent of the governed. These elected officials could be removed from elected office for wrongdoings and, in eighteenth-century political ideology, serve for a limited amount of time before returning to the people from whence they came.

Locke wrote one of the most influential works on political philosophy, his *Two Treatises of Government,* to refute the assertions of Sir Richard Filmer who defended absolute monarchy.[2] In the *Second Treatise of Government,* Locke developed his theory of the role of government and the importance of personal property and its origin. He concluded the *Second Treatise* by describing how a political system, not a social system, could be overthrown and replaced. To Locke, the government's sole purpose was to protect individual property. No man in the state of freedom would give up the right to property to a government that would not protect it. The very idea of giving one's consent was extremely important. Anything less would lead to tyranny or despotism. The writings of John Locke became the foundation for American republicanism and the American Whig political position in the 1770s.

John Locke's writings deeply influenced eighteenth-century Colonial America: Thomas Paine's *Common Sense*, George Mason's *Virginia Declaration of Rights*, and Thomas Jefferson's *Declaration of Independence*, are all applications of Locke's *Second Treatise of Government*. Locke's political theories were so widely read that it is no surprise to see entire sections pulled from his treatise and inserted into the Declaration of Independence. Men like Roger Sherman, George Mason, Thomas Jefferson, and Thomas Paine took the thoughts and writings of John Locke and, through their practical application, started the American Revolution from a political perspective.

The 1960s saw a renewed interest in the founding ideology as well as American republicanism. Historian J.G.A. Pocock's *Political Language & Time: Essays on Political Thought and History* (1960) and J.R. Pole's *Political Representation in England and the Origins of the American Republic* (1966) set the standard for the analysis of American political thought and its eighteenth-century origins. Pocock and Pole examined the influence of enlightened thought upon the British North American colonies. Historian Gordon S. Wood's *The Creation of the American Republic: 1776–1787* (1969) became a landmark piece and defined eighteenth-century American Republicanism. According to Wood:

> Republicanism was the ideology of the Enlightenment. In the eighteenth century, to be enlightened was to be interested in antiquity, and to be interested in antiquity was to be interested in republicanism. Although the classical past could offer meaningful messages for monarchy, there is little doubt that most of what the ancient world had to say to the eighteenth century was latently and often manifestly republican.[3]

The years following the bicentennial of the Revolution produced a change in the historiography of eighteenth-century republicanism which followed other trends in the profession. These new assessments focused on how political thought uniquely impacted different regions of the British North American Colonies, rather than the traditional blanket approach for all thirteen. Pocock again led the way with his *Three British Revolutions: 1641, 1688, 1776* (1980), which examined how the political revolutions of 1641, 1688, and 1776 dramatically changed British politics. His work was followed by Margaret Jacob and James Jacob's *The Origins of Anglo-American Radicalism* (1984). Jacob broadened the field of republicanism by including ways that women and religion helped spread republican ideology. Historian Jack Greene stressed in his *Peripheries and Center: Constitutional Development in the Extended Polities of the British Empire and the United States, 1607–1788* (1986) the immense political and economic uncertainty coupled with the continuation of empirical involvement that followed the French and Indian War in North America. He followed that with an examination of regional history and argued in *Pursuits of Happiness: The Social Development of Early Modern British Colonies and the Formation of American Culture* (1988) that Colonial New England's stance against the institution of black African slavery epitomized the idea of American Republicanism on the eve of the Revolutionary War and set the tone for future political debate.[4]

The 1990s and early 2000s saw another shift in the historiography of eighteenth-century American republicanism. This time the change re-focused the assessment away from Marxist historians who had continued to analyze the American Revolution in terms of the French Revolution. According to such historians, the evils of French capitalist greed and terror therefore must have been rooted in the American colonies. Not true, as noted by the new analysis provided by historians such as Robert Shalhope, Gordon S. Wood, Joyce Appleby, Rebecca Starr, and again J.G.A. Pocock, and Jack Greene.[5] Historians examined the uniqueness of the American Revolution as a political, social, and military rebellion against what many in the British North American colonies saw as an abusive, tyrannical system of oppression.

A system where they were denied the basis rights of an Englishman guaranteed under Magna Carta. Indeed, many referenced that sacred political document in their eighteenth-century documents and pamphlets. To these colonists it was the British parliamentary system that had become corrupt and abusive, and it was their political revolution that in fact defended the rights of Englishmen. This was therefore not at all the same as the French Revolution. Their revolution was something different, as Gordon Wood mentions, that "transformed a monarchical society into a democratic one unlike any that had ever existed."[6]

Because Wooster was a major importer of British goods, economic policies impacted his decision making. Imperial taxation implemented by Parliament had begun to strain economic relations with the American colonies in the 1700s. The impact of this era of taxation upon America has been recently reexamined as a significant steppingstone for the growth of an economically independent colonial system. From the 1940s onward, more analysis has been applied to the historiography of colonial economics. A keystone work on the influence of imperial policy on the British colonies in North American is John Miller's *Origins of the American Revolution* (1943).[7] Miller presented a new approach to the causes of the American Revolution as a combination of economic and political issues and focused upon primary source material to explain the economic impact the taxes of Parliament made upon the American Colonies. Historian Louis Wright's *The Cultural Life of the American Colonies* (1957)[8] further discussed the impact of British economic policy that developed an independent American market-based economy where imported goods were sought after as symbols of social mobility and heighted status.

The economic structure of specific colonies began to be studied on the eve of the bicentennial of the French and Indian War. Historian Robert A. East addressed the intercolonial economic dependency of cities such as Boston upon beef and grain trade from areas such as Connecticut. In *Business Enterprise in the American Revolutionary Era* (1964) East noted that Connecticut was well situated to enhance grain harvesting and shipping of the product to viable markets, the sale and exportation of beef, and the control of their own shipping to the West Indies and European markets.[9] According to East, colonial merchants became financial institutions in themselves for their local communities, often loaning capital.[10] As a leading merchant in New Haven it would be fascinating to locate records indicating Wooster also worked in the financial market for his neighbors. Records do exist, however, to indicate that he was financially able to outfit and provide for his own regiment during the Revolution. In any case, the study of colonial merchants overall within the growing field of colonial economic historiography has particular potential for studying Wooster and his role in the Revolution.

The most fundamental change to the historiography of colonial economics in America came from historian Jack Greene in the 1970s and the concept of Atlantic History.[11] Since then historians have emphasized the importance of economic policy in shaping an independent ideology within the British North American colonies. The historiography has further developed to assess the full nature of the economic structure of the British Empire. No historian has addressed this role of Atlantic History as well as noted historian Bernard Bailyn. His *Atlantic History: Concept and*

Contours, written in 2005, broadened the historic field that Jack Greene had developed to examine the interconnectedness of England and her colonies.[12] To advance an understanding of the economic ties further and to examine the role that Connecticut played in this system, modern historians have combined Atlantic History and regional history to present a more comprehensive image of economic activity in Connecticut, especially within the ship-building industry.[13]

There were great advancements in the historiography of economic activity in Colonial America in the 1980s. Historians began to analyze the impact of shipping within the Atlantic world and how commercial production of goods combined with the shipbuilding industry allowed the colony of Connecticut to become a major center of trade and commerce. This thesis is examined in *The Economy of British America, 1607–1789* (1985) written by historians John J. McCusker and Russell R. Menard. The onset of the Revolutionary War greatly changed the economics of maritime trade. Historian Thomas M. Doerflinger added to the historiography by studying the impact of a civil war—which described the Revolution—upon trade and the economy. To fully understand the eighteenth century and the lead-up to the Revolutionary War, one must understand the vast impact of internal colonial economics in terms of both trade and mercantilism within the British Empire. Doerflinger stated in *A Vigorous Spirit of Enterprise: Merchants and Economic Development in Revolutionary Philadelphia* (1986) that "nothing was more damaging to the economy than the wrenching shift of the interstate transport system from coastal maritime trade to inland carriage."[14] Although he wrote about the trade in Philadelphia, that same assessment applies to Connecticut. Shipping had become the central hub of the Connecticut economy from the 1760s to the outbreak of the Revolution. An additional economic link was the official customs office in the royal colonies. Those who held these positions were charged with tax collecting during the turbulent years leading up to the Revolution. Significantly, Wooster held that position for the port of New Haven.

The economic tax policy of Great Britain and the internal colonial implementation had a massive impact upon the mercantile and shipping industries in Connecticut and drove both economic and political dissent among colonial leaders such as David Wooster. Records of the "David Wooster & Company" mercantile business provide a key to assess the ways that Parliamentary taxes stunted economic activity in both the importation of goods for market sale and domestic production in the Atlantic world. No matter how deep Wooster's loyalty ran, British economic policies that resulted for him in crushed business development and growth were not sustainable.[15]

The analysis of political loyalty, and loyalism in general, is the third area of eighteenth-century historiography. David Wooster was devoted to king and country, yet by 1775 his political loyalty had been refined. While Wooster, and others in similar situations reevaluated the political association with Great Britain in the 1770s, many American colonists remained loyal to king and country. The historiography of loyalists during the American Revolution begins in the Antebellum period. Beginning with *The American Loyalists, or Biographical Sketches of Adherents to the British Crown in The War of the Revolution; Alphabetically Arranged with a Preliminary*

Historical Essay (1847), Lorenzo Sabine's work marked the first major analysis of loyalists in the Revolution.[16]

Historian William Nelson continued the examination of loyalists in his *The American Tory* (1961). The historiography of eighteenth-century British loyalists began to examine the dispute that fueled the internal social and political divisions of Americans. Nelson focused his research to answer the question of defining who the colonial loyalists were, and what did they believe? How did they differ from the more radical element of society? This examination of loyalty in the American Colonies continued into the 1970s.

In *The British-Americans: The Loyalist Exiles in England, 1774–1789* (1972), historian Mary Beth Norton added to the historiography by discussing how American colonists in British North America sought similar political and economic reform. Colonial patriots and British loyalists differed in their reaction to external taxation and how reform would come about. Norton pointed out that from 1765 through the Revolution "Loyalty was the norm: rebellion was not."[17] Still, many struggled against what they perceived as violent fervor and fled to England for their safety. Their exile, however, did not ensure their eventual political or social happiness.

Robert Calhoon's *The Loyalists in Revolutionary America, 1760–1781* (1973), analyzed the loyal political ideology that emerged in the years preceding the Revolution. Calhoon also examined the thousands of loyalists who became refugees due to the radicalization of Revolutionary thought and action. For some historians the radicalization of American society and politics in the 1960s and 1970s provided an excellent comparison with events two hundred years earlier. Noted scholar Bernard Bailyn's *The Ordeal of Thomas Hutchinson: Loyalism and the Destruction of the First British Empire* (1974) provided one such example of comparative history, although Bailyn admitted that his work on the loyalist governor of Massachusetts, Thomas Hutchinson, was not shaped by Bailyn's own experience. To examine the American Revolution was to assume that there were legitimate winners and losers. According to Bailyn:

> The real losers—those whose lives were disrupted, who suffered violence and vilification, who were driven out of the land and forced to resettle elsewhere in middle life and died grieving for the homes they had lost—these were not the English but the Americans who clung to them, who remained loyal to England and to what had been assumed to be the principles of legitimacy and law and order which the British government embodied.[18]

American society on the eve of the bicentennial of the American Revolution reflected the British colonies in America which allowed historians to examine more fully the lives of those who remained loyal to the crown throughout the years of external taxation and political upheaval. This analysis of the Tory mindset was further developed by historian William P. Cumming and Hugh Rankin's *The Fate of a Nation: The American Revolution through Contemporary Eyes* (1975). Cummings and Rankin provided a lengthy tome on both loyalist and patriot perspectives of the war, placing the loyalists on a level plane with the patriots. This perspective had not been previously examined or seen to this extent. Yet, although it contains numerous images, prints, maps, and excellent quotations, *The Fate of a Nation* is poorly referenced, thus making its primary sources nearly impossible to examine or analyze.

The Bicentennial also led to a reevaluation of the impact of loyalists upon Colonial America. Historian John E. Ferling re-interpreted the importance of one such loyalist, Joseph Galloway. Like David Wooster, few of Galloway's personal papers remain. In the book *The Loyalist Mind: Joseph Galloway and the American Revolution* (1977), Ferling analyzed Galloway's importance through his public work as a legislator in the years leading up to the Revolution. Likewise, historian Elizabeth P. McCaughey's *From Loyalist to Founding Father: The Political Odyssey of William Samuel Johnson* (1980), examined the actions and ideology of William Johnson, a Connecticut loyalist who was involved in ventures similar to Wooster's and who remained in contact with numerous loyalists who had fled to England during the war. Johnson remained loyal through much of the Revolution—long past Wooster's death in 1777. Both Galloway and Johnson saw inherent evils in the political revolution spurred on by radicalism in the American colonies; yet, as Ferling and McCaughey pointed out, there were legitimate complaints levied at Parliament and the crown, all of which placed loyalty in question.

As the shift towards regional studies began to emerge in the 1980s and early 2000s, the historiography of the American loyalist focused on individuals in specific colonies and within certain economic fields. Loyalists were included more prominently in the general overview of the war as seen in Robert Middlekauff's *The Glorious Cause: The American Revolution, 1763–1789* (1982). Viewing the war through the eyes of British subjects further advanced the historiography of loyalists, as found in Christopher Hibbert's *Redcoats and Rebels: The American Revolution Through British Eyes* (1990) and H.W. Brand's *Our First Civil War: Patriots and Loyalists in the American Revolution* (2021).[19] Analyzing the historiography of loyalists in the American Revolution thus allows for a more complete assessment of David Wooster within a more balanced view of the context of eighteenth-century Connecticut.

The final historiographical analysis examines the literature of the Revolutionary War. The historiography of eighteenth-century America has developed through a series of distinct analytical cycles. All are anchored to Colonial America and entwined through the American political revolution and the Revolutionary War itself. Importantly, there is a distinction between the "American Revolution" and the "Revolutionary War." The former includes the years following the French and Indian War in North American in 1763 and concludes with the ratification of the Constitution in 1788. This demonstrates a true revolution, political, social, military, and economic. The "Revolutionary War" denotes the armed struggle for independence and autonomy which began in 1775 and concluded with the Treaty of Paris in 1783. Historians first began writing the history of the Revolutionary War using their personal reflections and those of many around them. These first histories often included colonial pre-war analysis in defense of the movement towards political independence and the military struggle of the war itself. In presenting a historical overview, these eighteenth and early nineteenth-century historians provided background into life in Colonial America, the events leading up to and following the French and Indian War, and their culmination in the Revolutionary War.

David Ramsay's *The History of the American Revolution,* published in 1789, is one of the first accounts written of the Revolutionary War. Although born in

Pennsylvania, Ramsay lived in South Carolina during the Revolution. His historical record, however, highlighted the New England perspective of the Revolution and provided a first-hand account of the more obscure actions of the war.[20] Ramsay mentioned David Wooster often and praised him as an honorable soldier and a gentleman.

In 1805, Massachusetts historian Mercy Otis Warren became the first female author to write on the American Revolution with her book *The History of the Rise, Progress, and Termination of the American Revolution, Interspersed with Biographical, Political, and Oral Observations, In Three Volumes,* In the work, Warren mentioned General Wooster at the Battle of Ridgefield, April 27, 1777, as one of two generals present, Silliman being the other, and she noted that Wooster was "an aged and experienced officer, and a very worthy man."[21] She presented Wooster in an admirable light, as there was a great connection between the colony of Massachusetts and Connecticut during the war. Historian J.T. Headley added to the early historiography of the war as well with his two-volume set on *Washington and His Generals,* which was published in 1847.[22] In this overview of the major and brigadier generals of the Revolution, David Wooster received only a cursory biographical overview. Yet as historical accounts of the war were gathered, recorded, and published in the early 1800s, they presented David Wooster in a more positive light.

By the mid-nineteenth century, historians began to change their perspectives on the war. Newer accounts were being written, some by those who experienced the war itself or by those who heard of the tales of the Revolution by family and friends who themselves experienced the conflict. How do historians account for the validity of memory? Historian Daniel B. Rowland has examined the ways that historians utilize memory and the importance of retained memory for an individual, a family, and for a nation.[23] Memory can be faulty. Events of the past can, through the lens of time, become overly dramatic, and those involved appear tremendously heroic. This utilization of memory to recreate past events was applied by many mid-nineteenth-century historians. One excellent example of the application of memory in the historical record is the autobiography of Joseph Plumb Martin, which was written fifty years after the end of the Revolution.[24]

On the centennial of the French and Indian War, popular historian Benson J. Lossing compiled a massive two-volume history of the American Revolution. He combined historical research, historical geography, and historical interviews in his account of the Revolution. His work contained pages of footnotes that included detailed statements and accounts from participants in the Revolutionary War. However, these accounts must be analyzed in the correct perspective, as many were documented over seventy years after the end of the war. Accounts from 1775 were already eighty years old when Lossing's *Pictorial Field-Book of the Revolution* was published in 1859. Regional perspectives dominated the historiography of the 1800s, and Lossing was no exception. Although his *Pictorial Field-Book of the Revolution* provided a detailed overview of the war, as well as information on General Wooster, his New York perspective dominated the two-volume work on *The Life and Times of Philip Schuyler* which was first published in 1860.[25] Tensions between Connecticut and New York were quite high on the eve of the Revolutionary War, and the conflicting interests and personalities of Wooster and Schuyler only added to the heightened situation. The writing style of the mid-nineteenth century exudes a rich tone of regional defense in the many volumes of local history published. Lossing's writing on the life of General Schuyler presented General Wooster in a less-then-flattering manner. This began a transition in the historiography of the Revolution regarding Wooster. Due to the emergency of the Revolution in Connecticut upon Wooster's death, no one compiled his writings, correspondences, or recollections. The dead tell no tales. That is left to the living, and the living were men like Philip Schuyler, Benedict Arnold, and Silas Deane, who found David Wooster an irritant at best. Schuyler, ever the political maneuverer, sought to present his legacy in the best manner, which included denigrating those who disagreed with him, men like David Wooster.

Though historical interest in the Revolution rose in popularity in the 1870s and 1880s with the centennial of the war, it was somewhat diminished during the era of Reconstruction following the devastation of the Civil War. Many of these tomes of Americana focused on key figures and major campaigns. Works such as Henry B. Carrington's *Battles of the American Revolution 1775–1781*, published in 1881, dealt with large-scale history, while omitting many of the key leaders who made such an impact on the early years of the war.[26] There was no mention of David Wooster in Carrington's book.

By the late nineteenth century, the historiography of the American Revolution, and the Revolutionary War itself, began to change. With authors such as Washington Irving immortalizing the Founding Fathers with his four-volume biography on *The Life of George Washington* (1887), stories of the Revolution began to become more myth and fable than actual scholarly history. Biographies of George Washington became very popular, and General Wooster was mentioned briefly in these narratives. As the historiography of the Revolution shifted to focus on Virginians, the role of New Englanders such as Wooster began to fade from popular historical writing.[27] There were a few exceptions. In 1896 historian Lewis Henry Boutell compiled the letters of Connecticut politician Roger Sherman. This included political letters and correspondence of Sherman as well as personal letters written to David Wooster, with whom Sherman was well acquainted.[28] Letters of the early colonial governors of Connecticut were also published at this time. Although these included correspondence with David Wooster, nothing changed in the historiography of Colonial America or the Revolution.

By the late 1940s the historiography of the Revolution had changed, and little was mentioned of General Wooster in print aside from the confrontations with General Schuyler in Quebec. Little was known of his involvement in Connecticut, and less was published of his action in the war. Historian John C. Miller's *Triumph of Freedom: 1775–1783*, published in 1948, is a good example of the obscurity into which Wooster had fallen. Still, Lynn Montross's work *The Reluctant Rebels: The Story of the Continental Congress, 1774–1789* (1950), began to redirect the historiographical record toward the inclusion of General Wooster. Montross is one of the first historians to mention the anti–New England sentiment that pervaded the Continental Congress. As a result of the failed Patriot operation in Canada in 1775–1776, a scapegoat was sought in General David Wooster. Montrose added that Wooster was exonerated from any wrongdoing.[29]

The 1950s and 60s directed new changes in the historiography of Colonial America and the Revolution. This was an era of multi-layered historical analysis, as historian Michael D. Hattem noted in his 2013 article "The Historiography of the American Revolution." According to Hattem, these layers included New Whig, New Left, and Social Historical Ideological Interpretations of the war.[30] These layers can be seen in *Appeal to Arms: A Military History of the American Revolution* (1951) by historian Willard M. Wallace, and the two-volume work *The War of the Revolution* written by Christopher Ward and published in 1952. Ward's analysis began to change the historiography of both the Revolution and the inclusion of David Wooster. Ward not only provided information on Wooster's involvement and leadership in the war, he presented one of the best overviews of the Battle of Ridgefield of 1777 in which Wooster was mortally wounded.[31] New historical assessments of Benedict Arnold such as the 1954 publication of *Traitorous Hero: The Life and Fortunes of Benedict Arnold* by Wallace and *Benedict Arnold: Hero and Traitor*, published in 1965 by Lauren Paine also began to include General Wooster in the historic narrative.[32] Bernard Bailyn's *The Ideological Origins of the American Revolution* (1967) marked an intellectual advancement in the historiography of Colonial America and the Revolution.[33]

The final phase of historiographic development regarding Colonial America and the Revolutionary War emerged from the 1990s through the early 2000s. More primary sources became available, many now digitized, thus dramatically altering the historical record. Colonial newspapers, diaries, journals, letters of correspondence, maps, and notes from colonial legislatures as well as the Continental Congress became readily available to historians who sought to provide a more extensive analysis of the 1700s. Interest waned in military history overall and was replaced with a focus on individual experiences and the common soldier. The ability to study individual men and women through their own writings or contemporary newspaper accounts added to historical understanding. Previously the analysis focused on the major players in history; now the supporting cast was starting to take the limelight.

Continual assessment has been made of regional studies through works such as historian George L. Rockwell's *The History of Ridgefield Connecticut* (1979), and Richard Middleton's *Colonial America: A History, 1585–1776* (1992).[34] New analysis was further applied to additional individuals with whom Wooster had been associated, such as General Richard Montgomery by historian Hal T. Shelton, *General Richard Montgomery and the American Revolution: From Redcoat to Rebel* (1994), including a renewal of interest in Benedict Arnold via James Kirby Martin's *Benedict Arnold Revolutionary Hero: An American Warrior Reconsidered* (1997).[35]

Further developments in the early 2000s prompted the historiography of Colonial America and the Revolution to change once more. Historians began to reexamine the historical record and apply newly available source material to provide new analysis of the 1700s, including studies such as Fred Anderson's *Crucible of War: The Seven Years' War and the Fate of Empire in British North America* (2000), Henry

Steele Commanger and Richard B. Morris's *The Spirit of Seventy-Six: The Story of the American Revolution as told by its Participants* (2002), and Eric Hinderaker and Peter C. Mancall's *At the Edge of Empire: The Backcountry in British North America* (2003). These new historians combined Atlantic history, Continental history, and regional history to freshly assess the importance of inter-colonial disagreements, such as the *Susquehanna Affair* in the Wyoming Valley between Connecticut and Pennsylvania, in which Wooster provided ample argument for support of Connecticut's claim.

Yet, despite a dramatic shift in the historiography of Colonial America and the Revolution as found in many books and articles published, David Wooster has remained elusive to historians. Historians such as Gordon Wood, Bernard Bailyn, Richard Ketchum, David Hackett Fischer, Joseph Ellis, and David McCullough have continued to omit Wooster from the historiography of Colonial America and the Revolutionary War. Popular historian David McCullough's Pulitzer Prize winning *1776* (2005), omitted any detail pertaining to the Canadian Campaign of 1776, or any reference to the general in charge of the Canadian expedition after the death of Montgomery, David Wooster. Despite being recalled from Canada by the Continental Congress, and receiving permission from General Washington, while meeting with him at headquarters in New York, to call upon the congress in Philadelphia, Wooster had completely fallen from the radar of popular Revolutionary history.[36] Some have taken up the anti–Wooster historiography in what I term the "Periwig Conspiracy." These historians, some very recent, perpetuate the pro–Schuyler and Arnold view of Wooster, including William P. Cumming and Hugh Rankin's *The Fate of a Nation; The American Revolution Through Contemporary Eyes* (1975), Benson Bobrick's *Angel in the Whirlwind; The Triumph of the American Revolution* (1997), Christopher Hibbert's *Redcoats and Rebels; The American Revolution Through British Eyes* (2002), and Rick Atkinson's *The British Are Coming; The War for America, Lexington to Princeton, 1775–1777* (2019).[37]

Recent publications show a change in the scholarly approach to Wooster's involvement and leadership in Colonial Connecticut and the Revolutionary War. Historian Mark Anderson has led the field in reengaging Wooster in the Canadian Campaign in 1775–76 in his books *The Battle for the Fourteenth Colony: America's War of Liberation in Canada, 1774–1776* (2013), and *The Invasion of Canada by the Americans, 1775–1776: as Told through Jean-Baptiste Badeaux's Three Rivers Journals and New York Captain William Goforth's Letters* (2016). Other recent works further correcting Wooster's legacy of leadership in the Revolution include Walter R. Borneman's *American Spring: Lexington, Concord, and the Road to Revolution* (2014), Derek W. Beck's *The War Before Independence: Igniting the American Revolution, 1775–1776* (2016), and H.W. Brands' *Our First Civil War: Patriots and Loyalists in the American Revolution* (2021).[38]

Appendix II

"On the Death of General Wooster":
A Poem by Phillis Wheatley, July 1778

From this the Muse rich consolation draws
He nobly perish'd in his Country's cause
His Country's Cause that ever fir'd his mind
Where martial flames, and Christian virtues join'd.
How shall my pen his warlike deeds proclaim
Or paint them fairer on the list of Fame—
Enough, great Chief-now wrapt in shades around,
Thy grateful Country shall thy praise resound—
Tho not with mortals' empty praise elate
That vainest vapour to the immortal State
Inly serene the expiring hero lies.
And thus (while heav'nward roll his swimming eyes):

"Permit, great power, while yet my fleeting breath
And Spirits wander to the verge of Death—
Permit me yet to point fair freedom's charms
For her the Continent shines bright in arms,
By thy high will, celestial prize she came—
For her we combat on the field of fame
Without her presence vice maintains full sway
And social love and virtue wing their way
O still propitious be thy guardian care
And lead Columbia thro' the toils of war.
With thine own hand conduct them and defend
And bring the dreadful contest to an end—
For ever grateful let them live to thee
And keep them ever Virtuous, brave, and free—
But how, presumtuous shall we hope to find
Divine acceptance with th' Almighty mind—
While yet (O deed Ungenerous!) they disgrace
And hold in bondage Afric's blameless race?
Let Virtue reign—And thou accord our prayers
Be victory our's, and generous freedom theirs."

The hero pray'd—the wond'ring spirits fled
And sought the unknown regions of the dead—
Tis thine, fair partner of his life, to find
His virtuous path and follow close behind—

A little moment steals him from thy sight
He waits thy coming to the realms of light
Freed from his labours in the ethereal Skies
Where in succession endless pleasures rise!

Appendix III

Excerpts from the Connecticut Journal
on the Death of Wooster

New Haven, May 14.

Of Friday the 2d instant, May, departed this life at Danbury, the Hon. Major-General WOOSTER. He was born at Stratford, in this State, on the 2d day of March, A.D. 1710–11; was educated at Yale College, where he was graduated in the year 1738. Soon after the Spanish was broke out in 1739, he was employed first as a lieut. and then as the captain of the armed vessel built by this colony for a Guarda-Coasta. After this he engaged in the military service of his country, and was a captain in Col. Burr's regiment. After the reduction of that place, he was sent to France with a part of the prisoners taken there, and from thence went to England, where he received the honor of a captaincy on the establishment, in Sir William Pepperell's regiment. During the peace, which soon followed, he received his half-pay, and was chiefly employed in his private affairs. When the war with France was renewed in 1755, he was soon thought of, as a gentleman qualified for an higher sphere of command, and served his country as colonel, and commandant of a brigade to the end of the war.—From the first rise of the present controversy with G. Britain in 1764, tho' his interest, as an half pay officer, might have apologized for him, if he had observed a perfect neutrality; yet so fully convinced was he of the ruinous measures of the British court, and so jealous was he for his country's rights, that regardless of his private interest, he took an open and decisive part, and avowedly espoused the cause of America, and persisted in that line of conduct to the day of his death. As soon as hostilities were commenced in the Lexington battle, the General Assembly of this colony set about raising an army, and Col. Wooster from his approved abilities, well known courage, and great experience, was appointed to the chief command. The same summer he was appointed a Brigadier-General in the continental service. Honoured with these commissions he first commanded the troops sent to guard New York, where it was expected, that a part of the British army which came over in 1775 would land. In the latter part of that campaign, he, with his troops went into Canada, and assisted much in the reduction of St. John's, Montreal, &c. and after Gen. Montgomery's death, had the chief command in that province.—He returned home in the summer of 1776, and not long after, was appointed first Major General of the militia of the State. He had been out the whole of the last winter, at the head of a body of men raised by the state for our own security, and was but lately returned; when on Saturday the 26th ult. he received the news, that the enemy in a large body had landed at Campo. He immediately set off for Fairfield, leaving orders for the militia to be mustered and sent forward as fast as possible. When he arrived at Fairfield, finding Gen. Silliman had marched in pursuit of the enemy, with the troops then collected, he followed on with all expedition, and at Reading, overtook Gen. Silliman with the small body of militia with him, of which he of course took the command, and proceeded the same evening to the village of Bethel. Here is was determined to divide the troops, and part were sent off under Generals Arnold and Silliman, the rest remained with Gen. Wooster, and them he led by the rout of Danbury, in pursuit of the enemy, whom he overtook on the Sabbath about

N E W - H A V E N, May 7.

Friday laft died at Danbury, of the wound which he received, on the 26th ult. that brave and experienced foldier, the hon. major-general DAVID WOOSTER, of this town.

Top: "Notice of the Death of Major General Wooster." *Connecticut Journal*, May 7, 1777, No. 499. *Bottom:* "Obituary of Major General David Wooster." *Connecticut Journal*, Wednesday, May 14, 1777, No. 500.

THE

C O N N E C T I C U T J O U R N A L:

Containing the frefheft A D V I C E S, Foreign and Domeftic.

W E D N E S D A Y, M A Y 14, 1777.   [N°. 500.

N E W - H A V E N: Printed by T H O M A S and S A M U E L G R E E N, near the College.

4 o'clock, near Ridgefield. Observing a party of the enemy who seemed to be detached from the main body, he determined to attack them, tho' the number of his men were less than two hundred; he accordingly led them on himself with great spirit and resolution, ordering them to follow him. But, being unexperienced militia and the enemy having several field pieces, our men after doing considerable execution, were broken and gave way. The General was rallying them, to renew the attack, when he received the fatal wound. A musket ball from the distance of 50 rods, took him obliquely in the back, broke his back-bone, lodged within him, and never could be found. He was removed from the field, had his wound dressed by Doct. Turner, and was then conveyed back to Danbury, where all possible care was taken of him. The surgeons were from the first sensible of the danger of the case, and informed the General of their apprehensions, which he heard with the greatest composure. The danger soon became more apparent, his whole lower parts became insensible, and a mortification it is thought began very early. However, he liv'd till Friday the 2d of May, and then with great composure and resignation expired. It was designed to bring his remains to New Haven, to be interred there, but this was found impossible, and therefore they were interred at Danbury.

Thus fell a brave and experienced officer, fighting in the cause of his injured country, at a time when his abilities, courage and experience are most wanted! May that providence which hath taken him away in this manner, and at this juncture, raise up and qualify some person, abundantly to fill his place!

Chapter Notes

Preface

1. Resolution to honor the late Brigadier Wooster, in *Journals of the Continental Congress, 1774–1789; Edited from the Original Records in the Library of Congress by Worthington Chauncey Ford, Chief. Division of Manuscripts, Volume VII, 1777* (Washington, D.C.: Government Printing Office, 1907).

2. Governor Trumbull to General Washington, July 13, 1775, in *The Trumbull Papers,* Collections of the Massachusetts Historical Society, Volume X, Fifth Series (Boston: Massachusetts Historical Society, 1888), 1.

3. John Ferling has written such titles as *Whirlwind: The American Revolution and the War That Won It* (2015), *Independence: The Struggle to Set America Free* (2011), *Almost a Miracle: The American Victory in the War of Independence* (2007), *Struggle for a Continent: The Wars of Early America* (1993), *John Adams: A Life* (1992), *The First of Men: A Life of George Washington* (1988), and *A Wilderness of Miseries: War and Warriors in Early America* (1981). Edward Lengel is the former editor and chief of the Washington Papers at the University of Virginia, and author of *The Battles of Connecticut Farms and Springfield, 1780* (2020), *This Glorious Struggle: George Washington's Revolutionary War Letters* (2008), and *General George Washington: A Military Life* (2005). Andrew O'Shaughnessy is the Saunders Director of the Robert H. Smith International Center for Jefferson Studies at Monticello and a professor of history at the University of Virginia and has written such books as *The Men Who Lost America: British Leadership, the American Revolution, and the Fate of the Empire* (2013), and *An Empire Divided: The American Revolution and the British Caribbean* (2000).

4. A comprehensive historiographical essay on the four themes listed, and their impact on Wooster's life, may be found in Appendix I.

Chapter 1

1. Erin Strogoff, "Connecticut's 'The Legend of the Charter Oak,'" *ConnecticutHistory.org,* September 4, 2022, https://connecticuthistory.org/connecticuts-the-legend-of-the-charter-oak/.

2. Samuel Orcutt and Ambrose Beardsley, *The History of the old town of Derby, Connecticut, 1642–1880* (Springfield: Springfield Printing Company, 1880).

3. David Wooster, M.D., F.R.A., *Genealogy of the Woosters in America, Descended from Edward Wooster of Connecticut; Also an Appendix Containing a Sketch Relating to the Author, and a Memoir of Rev. Hezekia Calvin Wooster, and Public Letters of General David Wooster* (San Francisco: M. Weiss, Printer, 1885), Susan Benedict Hill, ed., *History of Danbury, Conn., 1684–1896, from Notes and Manuscript left by James Montgomery Bailey* (New York: Burr Printing House, 1896), and the *Papers of the New Haven Historical Society. Vol. IV* (New Haven: Printed for the Society, 1888).

4. Donald Lines Jacobus, M.A., "Edward Wooster of Derby, Conn., and Some of his Descendants," in *The New England Historical and Genealogical Register, Vol. LXXV, July 1921,* Henry Edwards Scott, ed. (Boston: New England Historic Genealogical Society, 1921), 175.

5. I found this early example of inaccurate historiography fascinating. Researching the life of Major General David Wooster becomes extremely challenging with the many inaccuracies and misinterpretations that have permeated the historiography. His life presents a unique story of colonial leadership. However, even modern historians continued to repeat certain false narratives regarding his lineage, as well as his death. I will refute these throughout the book and provide primary source documentation to support a reinterpretation of the historiography. Like Donald Jacobus I am driven to present an accurate record of the life of David Wooster, free from bias, and continued repeated misinterpretation. Hopefully, as David Wooster, M.D., F.R.A., requested in 1888, this will become the much-needed accurate biography of the late colonial leader.

6. Donald Lines Jacobus, M.A., "Edward Wooster of Derby, Conn., and Some of his Descendants," in *The New England Historical and Genealogical Register, Vol. LXXV, July 1921* (Boston: New England Historic Genealogical Society, 1921), 175–87.

7. There is some debate as to Wooster's birth year. Most sources point to 1710, although there

are a few that indicate 1711 was the year of his birth.

8. Donald Lines Jacobus, M.A., "Edward Wooster of Derby, Conn., and Some of his Descendants," in *The New England Historical and Genealogical Register, Vol. LXXV, July, 1921*, Henry Edwards Scott, ed. (Boston: New England Historic Genealogical Society, 1921), 176.

9. *Ibid.*, 180.

10. Samuel Orcutt and Ambrose Beardsley, *The History of the old town of Derby, Connecticut, 1642–1880* (Springfield: Springfield Printing Company, 1880), 237, 667.

11. *Ibid.*, 667.

12. Donald Lines Jacobus, M.A., "Edward Wooster of Derby, Conn., and Some of his Descendants," in *The New England Historical and Genealogical Register, Vol. LXXV, July, 1921*, Henry Edwards Scott, ed. (Boston: New England Historic Genealogical Society, 1921), 180.

13. Edward E. Atwater, ed., *History of the City of New Haven to the Present Time* (New York: W.W. Munsell & Co., 1887), 113.

14. The colony of Massachusetts chartered the oldest university, Harvard, in 1636. The College of William and Mary in Williamsburg, Virginia, was established in 1693.

15. Edward E. Atwater, ed., *History of the City of New Haven to the Present Time* (New York: W.W. Munsell & Co., 1887), 164–65.

16. In 1718 the Reverend Cotton Mather wrote to Elihu Yale who was living in London and requested his assistance in establishing a fine college in Connecticut. Mather noted that if Yale made donations of material goods and books for the school it very well would be named in his honor and would serve as a more permanent monument to Yale than the pyramids of Egypt. "Yale History Timeline: 1710–1719," *Yale University Library*, 2022, https://guides.library.yale.edu/c.php?g=296074&p=1976320.

17. "Landmarks in Yale History," *Yale University*, 2022, https://www.yale.edu/about-yale/traditions-history.

18. "Resources on Yale History: A Brief History of Yale. By Judith Schiff, Chief Research Archivist, Manuscripts and Archives," *Yale Library*, 2022, https://guides.library.yale.edu/yalehistory.

19. Franklin Bowditch Dexter, M.A., *Biographical Sketches of the Graduates of Yale College with Annals of the College History: October, 1701–May, 1745* (New York: Henry Holt and Company, 1885), 597.

20. *Ibid.*, 598.

21. Peter Colt, Yale class of 1764, served as military secretary for Major General Wooster in 1775, Samuel Lockwood, Yale class of 1766, son of Reverend James Lockwood, class of 1735, served in May 177, as military secretary to Wooster, Mark Leavenworth, Yale class of 1771, son of Reverend Mark Leavenworth, class of 1737, served as Wooster's adjunct general in 1775 and 1776, and Stephen Row Bradley, Yale class of 1775, served as Wooster's

aid-de-camp in 1776 and 1777. Franklin Bowditch Dexter, LITT.D. *Biographical Sketches of the Graduates of Yale College with Annals of the College History: Vol. III. May, 1763–July, 1778* (New York: Henry Holt and Company, 1903), 65, 194, 421, 549.

22. Metaphysics is the study of the nature of reality and is a field of philosophy.

23. Thomas Clap, *The Annals or History of Yale-College, in New-Haven, In the Colony of Connecticut, From The first Founding thereof, in the Year 1700, to the Year 1766: With An Appendix, Containing the Present State of the College, the Method of Instruction and Government, with the Officers, Benefactors, and Graduates* (New Haven: Printed for John Hotchkiss and B. Mecom, 1766), 81–82.

24. *Ibid.*, 89.

25. A "syllogistick form" of debate involved two or more general ideas lead the student to a deeper understanding through debate and discussion.

26. A "declamation memoriter" referred to the student who delivered a lengthy persuasive speech. According to historian Neil W. Bernstein the declamation was a "Standard component of an elite American education." Neil W. Bernstein, *Ethics, Identity, and Community in Later Roman Declamation* (New York: Oxford University Press, 2013).

27. Thomas Clap, *The Annals or History of Yale-College, in New-Haven, In the Colony of Connecticut, From The first Founding thereof, in the Year 1700, to the Year 1766: With An Appendix, Containing the Present State of the College, the Method of Instruction and Government, with the Officers, Benefactors, and Graduates* (New Haven: Printed for John Hotchkiss and B. Mecom, 1766), 82.

28. In 1754 Thomas Clap wrote a twenty-page pamphlet on the role of religion at Yale College, which focused on the ecclesiastical foundations of the many colleges in New England, especially in Connecticut. Clap started the essay by stating, "The original End, and Design of Colleges was to Instruct, Educate, and Train up Persons for the Work of the Ministry." He later stated that "Colleges, are Religious Societies, of a Superior Nature to all others." Thomas Clap, *The Religious Constitutions of Colleges, Especially of Yale-College in New Haven In the Colony of Connecticut* (New-London: T. Green, 1754). The following year he published a second essay which was a reply to a letter he received questioning the purpose of Yale College and the religious nature of the institution. Once more Clap articulated the importance of the religious focus of the college, stating, "That a College or University is an Ecclesiastical Society distinct from and Superior to all other Ecclesiastical Societies; for all other Ecclesiastical Societies are for training up the common People for Religion; whereas Colleges are Societies of Ministers, for training up Persons for the Work of Ministry." Thomas Clap, *The Answer of The Friend in the West, to A Letter From A Gentleman in the East, entitled, The Present State of the Colony of Connecticut*

considered (New Haven: James Parker Printer, 1755), 8. He concludes the letter be reaffirming that "the President indefatigably pursues the religious Interests of the College, according to the ancient Principles of the Country; rightly judging that to be the original and principled worthy End of its Institutions: And tho' in the calm, but steady Pursuit of this, some Gentlemen are disobliged, who have hithertofore appeared friendly to the College; yet if their Friendship can't be secured and continued, but at the Forfeiture of the Religion of the College, he wisely judges it too dear a purchase." Thomas Clap, *The Answer of The Friend in the West, to A Letter From A Gentleman in the East, entitled, The Present State of the Colony of Connecticut considered* (New Haven: James Parker Printer, 1755), 17. This letter was penned ten years after David Wooster married Mary Clap, the daughter of Rev. Thomas Clap. The influence of his father-in-law solidified his own religious conviction.

29. The sermon prepared and derived at the funeral for Thomas Clap exemplifies the importance of religion in the early colonial university setting, as well as the influences of Clap upon Yale College. Rev. Naphtali Daggett, *A Sermon Occasioned by the Death of The Reverend Thomas Calp (President of Yale-College, in New Haven) Who departed this Life, Jan. 7th, 1767; Delivered in the College-Chapel, Jan. 8th, By The Rev'd Naphtali Daggett, Livingstonian Professor of Divinity in Yale-College* (New Haven: B. Mecom, 1767).

30. Edward E. Atwater, ed., *History of the City of New Haven to the Present Time* (New York: W.W. Munsell & Co., 1887), 169–70.

31. Thomas Clap, *The Annals or History of Yale-College, in New-Haven, In the Colony of Connecticut, From The first Founding thereof, in the Year 1700, to the Year 1766: With An Appendix, Containing the Present State of the College, the Method of Instruction and Government, with the Officers, Benefactors, and Graduates.* (New Haven: Printed for John Hotchkiss and B. Mecom, 1766), 83.

Chapter 2

1. The War of Jenkins' Ear (1739–1742) was given this name due to a story of a British merchant captain, Robert Jenkins, who supposedly had his ear cut off by a Spaniard who has attacked his ship on the high seas. He reported this in front of Parliament, in which Parliament, outraged, called for war against Spain. No one ever verified whether Jenkins had lost his ear or not due to the very long wig that he wore.

2. Lawrence Washington, older half-brother to George Washington, fought in the Royal Navy under British Admiral Vernon in the war. The Virginia colonial helped to attack the city of Cartagena in 1741. Washington's Mount Vernon plantation was named by Lawrence in honor of British Admiral Vernon.

3. Franklin Bowditch Dexter, M.A., *Biographical Sketches of the Graduates of Yale College with Annals of the College History: October, 1701–May, 1745* (New York: Henry Holt and Company, 1885), 616–17.

4. Journal of the Lower House, February 1741, Commission of David Wooster as 1st Lieutenant of the sloop *Defense, Colonial Wars, Volume 3.* Connecticut State Archives, Hartford, Microfilm 88.

5. This is one of the earliest known letters of David Wooster. He was in frequent correspondence with all of the colonial governors of the colony of Connecticut. Jonathan Law, *The Law Papers: Correspondence and Documents during Jonathan Law's Governorship of the Colony of Connecticut, 1741–1750, Volume 1, October 1741–July 1745* (Hartford: Connecticut Historical Society, 1907), 47–48.

6. Pay request for the crew of the sloop *Defense,* September 5 to October 20, 1741, *Colonial Wars, Volume 3.* Connecticut State Archives, Hartford, Microfilm 97b, and October 1741 treasury payment for the sloop *Defense, Colonial Wars, Volume 3,* Connecticut State Archives, Hartford, Connecticut, Microfilm 97a.

7. Charles Hoadly, *Public Records of the Colony of Connecticut from October, 1735, to October, 1743, Inclusive. Transcribed and Edited in Accordance with a Resolution of the General Assembly* (Hartford: Press of the Case, Lockwood & Brainard Co., 1874), 530.

8. Jonathan Law, *The Law Papers: Correspondence and Documents during Jonathan Law's Governorship of the Colony of Connecticut, 1741–1750, Volume 1, October 1741–July 1745* (Hartford: Connecticut Historical Society, 1907), 257.

9. The Connecticut sloop *Defense* was in active service during and siege of Louisbourg and in the months following. A letter to Connecticut Governor Jonathan Law from Captain John Prentiss of the *Defense* dated October 28, 1745, and the governor's reply on November 6, 1745, discuss the number of men who have died onboard the sloop and who were too ill to carry on their duties, as the *Defense* was still stationed at Louisbourg. Jonathan Law, *The Law Papers: Correspondence and Documents during Jonathan Law's Governorship of the Colony of Connecticut, 1741–1750, Volume II, August 1745–December 1746* (Hartford: Connecticut Historical Society, 1911), 65, 66, 99. The governor ordered the crew discharged and to "unbend your Sails" and have the ship sent in for repairs. Jonathan Law, *The Law Papers: Correspondence and Documents during Jonathan Law's Governorship of the Colony of Connecticut, 1741–1750, Volume II, August 1745–December 1746* (Hartford: Connecticut Historical Society, 1911), 99, 106. In a letter to Gurdon Saltonstall, who oversaw ship repairs made to the sloop, Governor Law ordered the *Defense* repaired and made ready to sail for Louisbourg on March 3, 1746. Jonathan Law, *The Law Papers: Correspondence and Documents during Jonathan Law's Governorship of the Colony*

of Connecticut, 1741–1750, Volume II, August 1745– December 1746 (Hartford: Connecticut Historical Society, 1911), 186, 187. This caused confusion onboard the ship as to who directed her actions, the governor, or Commodore Warren of the British Navy who was still in Louisbourg. By August 1746 the *Defense* was stationed once more at Louisbourg, but in a letter from Michael Burnham to Governor Jonathan Law, August 19, 1746, the captain stated to the governor that his men were ill prepared with clothing to endure a fall campaign in the north and requested direction as to where necessary supplies were to come. To this Governor Law ordered the sloop home and the men discharged on November 29, 1746. Jonathan Law, *The Law Papers: Correspondence and Documents during Jonathan Law's Governorship of the Colony of Connecticut, 1741–1750, Volume II, August 1745– December 1746* (Hartford: Connecticut Historical Society, 1911), 281, 347. Roger Wolcott provided an exceptional account of the ship's involvement at Louisbourg in a report dated November 15, 1745. Jonathan Law, *The Law Papers: Correspondence and Documents during Jonathan Law's Governorship of the Colony of Connecticut, 1741–1750, Volume II, August 1745–December 1746* (Hartford: Connecticut Historical Society, 1911), 109. Roger Wolcott, *Journal of Roger Wolcott at the Siege of Louisbourg, 1745* (Hartford: Connecticut Historical Society, 1860), 150.

10. In 1747 the sloop *Defense* was made ready to sail by order of Governor Law and granted a letter of marque against any enemy of the colony, or the crown. Jonathan Law, *The Law Papers: Correspondence and Documents during Jonathan Law's Governorship of the Colony of Connecticut, 1741–1750, Volume III, January 1747–October 1750* (Hartford: Connecticut Historical Society: Hartford, 1914), 207, 211, 214. Following a grant from Parliament of £ 800,000 pounds to assist in maintaining the occupation of Louisbourg the *Defense* was repaired and made sea ready and by early March 1747 she was once more at sea. Jonathan Law, *The Law Papers: Correspondence and Documents during Jonathan Law's Governorship of the Colony of Connecticut, 1741–1750, Volume III, January 1747– October 1750* (Hartford: Connecticut Historical Society, 1914), 233. On May 25, 1748, Governor Law wrote to Eliakim Palmer describing the French snow that the *Defense* had captured at sea, which contained 100 hogshead of molasses and 82 hogshead of sugar. Such a prize brought a great deal of money. Jonathan Law, *The Law Papers: Correspondence and Documents during Jonathan Law's Governorship of the Colony of Connecticut, 1741–1750, Volume III, January 1747–October 1750* (Hartford: Connecticut Historical Society, 1914), 239. Eventually, however, on December 6, 1748, the Defense, by order of the Connecticut Assembly, was sold to Mr. Jabez Huntington of Norwich for the price of £ 4,860 pounds "payable to ye Govn & Co in one year wth out Interest." Jonathan Law, *The Law Papers: Correspondence and Documents during Jonathan*

Law's Governorship of the Colony of Connecticut, 1741–1750, Volume III, January 1747–October 1750 (Hartford: Connecticut Historical Society, 1914), 285.

11. Samuel Orcutt and Ambrose Beardsley, *The History of the old town of Derby, Connecticut, 1642–1880* (Springfield: Springfield Printing Company, 1880), 28.

12. Donald Lines Jacobus, M.A., "Edward Wooster of Derby, Conn., and Some of his Descendants," in *The New England Historical and Genealogical Register, Vol. LXXV, July, 1921*, Henry Edwards Scott, ed. (Boston: New England Historic Genealogical Society, 1921), 187.

13. Edward E. Atwater, ed., *History of the City of New Haven to the Present Time* (New York: W.W. Munsell & Co., 1887), 22–25.

14. Richard A. Brayall, *"To the Uttermost of My Power": The Life and Times of Sir William Pepperrell: 1696–1759* (Westminster, MD: Heritage Books, 2008), 65.

15. A 1745 French map of the Louisbourg fortress is drawn from sea level and provides an image that this imposing. "Plan du port et de la ville de Louisbourg, 1745," *Norman B. Leventhal Map & Education Center,* 2022, https://collections.leventhalmap.org/search/commonwealth:z603vm897. Also in 1745 James Gibson created a large map from the perspective of the New England troops and British naval forces. Titled *A Prospect of the City of Lewisbourg Also the Harbours and Garrisons On the Island of Gaspey or Capre Breton in North America. Surrendered to the New England Land Troops On the 17 June 1745 after a Siege of 48 Days Lieut General Pepperril Esqr Commander of the Land Troops And Commodore Petr Warren Esqr Commander of His Majesties Fleet there to Guard the Coast* the map provides an excellent overview of the French fortress, the several batteries, as well as the locations of the New England encampments. Gibson's map was included in the front of his journal account of Louisbourg and served as a fold out. James Gibson, *A Journal of the Late Siege by the Troops from North America, Against the French at Cape Breton, The City of Louisbourg, and the Territories thereunto belonging. Surrendered to the English on the 17th of June 1745, after a Siege of Fort-eight Days. By James Gibson, Gentleman Volunteer at the above Siege. To which is subjoined, Two Letters concerning some farther Advantages and Improvements, that may seem necessary to be made on the taking and keeping of Cape Breton. Humbly offered to public consideration. With a large Pan of the Town and Harbour of Louisbourg* (London: Bible and Sun, St. Paul's Church-Yard, 1747). Both maps provide accurate visualization of the city and the fortification. However the French map appears more imposing than Gibson's. Referencing both while reading and analyzing the various accounts allows for a well-rounded appreciation of the events leading up to the surrender of Louisbourg in 1745, as well as the importance of the city for the security of the New England colonies.

16. George M. Wrong, M.A., *Louisbourg in 1745; The Anonymous Lettre d'un Habitant De Louisbourg (Cape Breton) Containing a narrative by an eye-witness of the siege in 1745, edited with English Translations* (Toronto: Warwick Bros. & Rutter, 1897), 3.

17. *Ibid.*, 13.

18. James Pritchard, *In Search of Empire; The French in the Americas, 1670–1730* (Cambridge: Cambridge University Press, 2004), 368–85.

19. *Ibid.*, 405–06.

20. *Ibid.*, 420.

21. George M. Wrong, M.A., *Louisbourg in 1745; The Anonymous Lettre d'un Habitant De Louisbourg (Cape Breton) Containing a narrative by an eye-witness of the siege in 1745, edited with English Translations* (Toronto: Warwick Bros. & Rutter, 1897), 23–26.

22. *Ibid.*, 15–18.

23. James Pritchard, *In Search of Empire; The French in the Americas, 1670–1730* (Cambridge: Cambridge University Press. 2004), 400.

24. Samuel Adams Drake, *The Taking of Louisbourg 1745* (New York: Lee and Shepard, 1890), 64.

25. James Gibson, *A Journal of the Late Siege by the Troops from North America, Against the French at Cape Breton, The City of Louisbourg, and the Territories thereunto belonging. Surrendered to the English on the 17th of June, 1745, after a Siege of Fort-eight Days. By James Gibson, Gentleman Volunteer at the above Siege. To which is subjoined, Two Letters concerning some farther Advantages and Improvements, that may seem necessary to be made on the taking and keeping of Cape Breton. Humbly offered to public consideration. With a large Pan of the Town and Harbour of Louisbourg* (London: Bible and Sun, St. Paul's Church-Yard, 1747), 10–11.

26. Samuel Niles, *A Brief and Plain Essay on God's Wonder-working Providence for New-England, In the Reduction of Louisburg, and Fortresses thereto belonging on Cape-Breton. With A short hint in the Beginning, on the French Taking & Plundering the People of Canso, which led the several Governments to Unite and Pursue that Expedition. With the Names of the Leading Officers in the Army and the several Regiments to which they belonged* (London: T. Green, 1747), 15–16.

27. Samuel Adams Drake, *The Taking of Louisbourg, 1745* (New York: Lee and Shepard, 1890), 63.

28. Charles Hoadly, *Public Records of the Colony of Connecticut from May, 1744, to November, 1750, Inclusive. Transcribed and Edited in Accordance with a Resolution of the General Assembly* (Hartford: Press of the Case, Lockwood & Brainard Co., 1876), 81.

29. *Ibid.*, 83.

30. *Ibid.*, 85.

31. *Ibid.*, 91.

32. A Press Warrant was formally given by the crown, or the crown's representative, as authority to impress, or seize, men or equipment into the army or navy.

33. David Wooster to Governor Jonathan Law, April 2, 1745. New Haven Museum, New Haven, CT.

34. George M. Wrong, M.A., *Louisbourg in 1745; The Anonymous Lettre d'un Habitant De Louisbourg (Cape Breton) Containing a narrative by an eye-witness of the siege in 1745, edited with English Translations* (Toronto: Warwick Bros. & Rutter, 1897), 41.

35. Roger Wolcott, *Journal of Roger Wolcott at the Siege of Louisbourg, 1745* (Hartford: Connecticut Historical Society, 1860), 151.

36. A print made in 1745 depicts the New England troops disembarking at Louisbourg. *A view of the Landing the New England Forces in ye Expedition against Cape Breton, 1745* engraved by J. Stevens. Text below the image reads:

> A view of the Landing the New England Forces in ye Expedition against Cape Breton, 1745
> When after a siege of 40 days the town and fortress of Louisbourg and the important Territories thereto belonging were recover'd to the British Empire. The brave & active Commodore Warren, since made Knight of the Bath & Vice Admiral of ye White, commanded the British Squadron in this glorious Expedition, The Hon. Will'm Pepperell Esq (since Knighted), went a Volunteer and Commanded the New England Men who bravely offer'd their service and went as private Soldiers in this hazardous but very glorious Enterprize.

37. William Pepperrell, *An Accurate Journal and Account of the Proceedings of the New-England Land-Forces, During the late Expedition Against the French Settlements on Cape Breton, To the Time of the Surrender of Louisbourg* (London: A. and S. Brice, 1746), 8.

38. *Ibid.*, 9.

39. William Shirley, *A Letter from William Shirley, Esq; Governor of Massachusetts's Bay, to his Grace the Duke of Newcastle: with a Journal of the Siege of Louisbourg, and other Operations of the Forces, during the Expedition against the French Settlements on Cape Breton; drawn up at the Desire of the Council and House of Representatives of the Province of Massachusetts's Bay; approved and attested by Sir William Pepperell, and the other Principal Officers who commanded in the said Expedition* (London: E. Owen in Warwick Lane, 1746), 6.

40. *Ibid.*, 7.

41. Samuel Adams Drake was one historian who provided a traveler's perspective of the siege of Louisbourg by describing the terrain, as well as the remines of the fort, in his 1890 account. According to Drake there was little remaining, the fort being destroyed in the 1750s by the British. He presented a bleak image of the area, although his portrayal of the countryside surrounding the fort has seen little change since 1745. Samuel Adams Drake, *The Taking of Louisbourg 1745* (New York: Lee and Shepard, 1890), 15–23. However archaeological work done at Louisbourg since the 1970s have

established foundational features of the fort and buildings and have enabled historical reconstruction of portions of the old fort. Much of the fortress that the New England troops laid siege to in 1745 is visible today. John Fortier and Owen Fitzgerald, *Fortress of Louisbourg.* (Toronto: Oxford University Press, 1979).

42. Robert Carter Goldthwaite, *Record of the Military Service of Captain Joseph Goldthwait, Adjutant of Pepperrel's Regiment (First Mass.) at the Siege of Louisbourg, 1745* (Washington, D.C.: Library of Congress, 1910), 12.

43. William Pepperrell, *An Accurate Journal and Account of the Proceedings of the New-England Land-Forces, During the late Expedition Against the French Settlements on Cape Breton, To the Time of the Surrender of Louisbourg* (London: A. and S. Brice, 1746), 8.

44. Richard A. Brayall, *"To the Uttermost of My Power": The Life and Times of Sir William Pepperrell: 1696–1759* (Westminster, MD: Heritage Books, 2008), 129.

45. The anonymous French account at Louisbourg wrote angrily that the British commanders did not prevent the total looting and destruction of French private property, nor did the French troops defend them. Many of the French prisoners, while in the cartel ships, were looted enroute to France. George M. Wrong, M.A., *Louisbourg in 1745; The Anonymous Lettre d'un Habitant De Louisbourg (Cape Breton) Containing a narrative by an eye-witness of the siege in 1745, edited with English Translations* (Toronto: Warwick Bros. & Rutter, 1897), 62.

46. This story was communicated by Deacon Nathan Beers. It was included in Henry C. Deming's 1854 *Oration at the Dedication of a monument to General Wooster.* The story is difficult to verify. Nathan Beers knew Wooster, and in Beer's own funeral oration a letter was included as a footnote concerning the attack on Lady Wooster's home in 1779. Beers was involved in the Revolution and was in the Canadian campaign in 1775–76 with General Wooster. Samuel W.S. Dutton, *An Address at the Funeral of Deacon Nathan Beers, on the 14th of February, 1849* (New Haven: William H, Stanley, Printer, 1849), 12. The anecdote was included by Deming in his dedication speech in 1854. *Proceedings of the M. W. Grand Lodge of Connecticut, called for the purpose of Laying the Chief Stone of the Monument to Gen. David Wooster, at Danbury, April 27, 1854, with the Oration and Addresses Delivered on the Occasion and Exercises in the Church* (New Haven: Storer & Moorehouse, 1854), 16.

47. Jonathan Law, *The Law Papers: Correspondence and Documents during Jonathan Law's Governorship of the Colony of Connecticut, 1741–1750, Volume II, August 1745–December 1746* (Hartford: Connecticut Historical Society, 1911), 350–52.

48. James Gibson, *A Journal of the Late Siege by the Troops from North America, Against the French at Cape Breton, The City of Louisbourg, and the Territories thereunto belonging. Surrendered to the English on the 17th of June 1745, after a Siege of Fort-eight Days. By James Gibson, Gentleman Volunteer at the above Siege. To which is subjoined, Two Letters concerning some farther Advantages and Improvements, that may seem necessary to be made on the taking and keeping of Cape Breton. Humbly offered to public consideration. With a large Plan of the Town and Harbour of Louisbourg* (London: Bible and Sun, St. Paul's Church-Yard, 1747), 29–33.

49. A detailed analysis of several British newspapers provided a timeline of activity pertaining to Wooster's involvement in the prisoner exchange and subsequent travels to England. None of the newspaper articles specifically mentioned Wooster by name. They did include extensive reports of Sir William Pepperrell and Commodore Warren at Louisbourg and Cape Breton, as well as the arrival of the cartel ships at Rochefort. These were printed from July through November 1745, in *The Derby Mercury* (July 19 and 26, 1745), and *The Newcastle Courant* (September 7, 14, and 21, 1745), and *The London Gazette* (October 15, 22, 26, 29, 1745). *The London Daily Advertiser* printed numerous accounts starting on July 18 that news arrived from Boston that Commodore Warren had captured the Royal Battery at Louisbourg; July 22, news arrived in London of the fall of Louisbourg; July 24, the New England Coffee House in London held a celebration over the capture of Louisbourg; July 29, the first of several repeated articles advertising a fireworks display in London to recreate the capture of Louisbourg; July 30, an account of the arrival of the cartel ships at Rochefort filled with French prisoners; July 3, accounts of the capture of Louisbourg; August 1, accounts of the numerous batteries taken at Louisbourg; August 12, "The King has been pleas'd to grant unto William Pepperrell, Esq; of the Province of New England in North America, the Dignity of a Baronet of the Kingdom of Great Britain"; August 14, two regiment of foot are ordered to Cape Breton for the safeguarding of Louisbourg; August 15, "We are informed that Admiral Warren is created a Baronet of Great Britain, and appointed Governor of Louisbourg"; September 4 and 16, French ships made ready and sailed from Rochefort to the West Indies; and November 4, "We have advice from New England, August 20, that two vessels from Louisbourg, with French Prisoners, are arrived at the Province. They came out with five others, and inform us, that four more were to sail in a few Days for the said Province, with French Inhabitants of Cape Breton." Many of these papers printed news as it arrived, and oftentimes were weeks, if not months, past the actual events which had taken place. All together they provide a clear image of how the success of the reduction of Louisbourg was heralded in London. Together these newspaper articles assist in creating a timeline for Wooster's activities from July through October 1745. Wooster left form Louisbourg on the cartel ships on July 4, arrived at Rochefort, France,

around August 5. He left Rochefort on September 19, and testified to the Admiralty Court on October 8. He returned to Connecticut by mid-January 1746. The trip from Louisbourg to England took approximately twenty days. An express could arrive in fourteen, as noted in the newspapers. Wooster arrived in England at the same time the country celebrated the king's birthday, the anniversary of his coronation, the birth of Prince Henry, and the height of the Jacobite rebellion of Charles Edward, the Young Pretender, who sought to reclaim the British throne for the Stuarts, who had arrived in Scotland and began marching with a formidable force south towards London. These stories filled the London papers in the fall of 1745; and Wooster was privy to it all.

50. For his military achievement for the crown, William Pepperrell was made a baronet by the King and received many additional honors. He traveled to England to procure reimbursement for the cost of the Louisbourg expedition. He was successful. Samuel Adams Drake, *The Taking of Louisbourg 1745* (New York; Lee and Shepard, 1890), 130, and William Pepperrell, *An Accurate Journal and Account of the Proceedings of the New-England Land-Forces, During the late Expedition Against the French Settlements on Cape Breton, To the Time of the Surrender of Louisbourg* (London: A. and S. Brice, 1746), 3–4.

51. Jonathan Law, *The Law Papers: Correspondence and Documents during Jonathan Law's Governorship of the Colony of Connecticut, 1741–1750, Volume II, August 1745–December 1746* (Hartford: Connecticut Historical Society, 1911), 582–84. In the William Pepperrell papers at the Massachusetts Historical Society is a copy of the affidavit that David Wooster signed declaring that he had not received any additional pay from His Majesty between 1769 and 1770, aside for half-pay "as a reduced Captain in Sir William Pepperell's late Regiment of Foot." http://www.masshist. org/database/resource.php?t=William%20 Pepperrell%20Papers%2C%201664-1782&i=/ collection-guides/fulldigital/fa0054/6466_b3_ f20_009.jpg&u=http%3A//www.masshist.org/ collection-guides/digitized/fa0054/b3-f20%239.

52. It is interesting to note that of all the provincial officers who fought both in the siege of Louisbourg or in the French and Indian War, David Wooster was the only one to receive an officer's commission in a royal regiment. For years I have questioned leading historians of both wars, and of Colonial American history, searching for another such instance. No one has ever been able to produce another colonial afforded such an honor, not even the young George Washington who so desperately sought similar recognition.

53. Jonathan Law, *The Law Papers: Correspondence and Documents during Jonathan Law's Governorship of the Colony of Connecticut, 1741–1750, Volume II, August 1745–December 1746* (Hartford: Connecticut Historical Society, 1911), 170–71.

54. The original mezzotint image of David Wooster was made in London in 1748. He is depicted in his British uniform in front of the fortress at Louisbourg. The image was reprinted in London in 1776 during the Revolutionary War. The caption of the 1776 reprint reads "Commander in Chief of the Provincial Army against Quebec"—as Wooster was in command at Montreal and Quebec in 1776 after the death of General Montgomery in December 1775.

55. Samuel Johnson created one of the first eighteenth-century dictionaries. In his original 1755 edition, esquire is defined as "a title of dignity, and next in degree below a knight. Those to whom this title is now of right due, are all the younger sons of noblemen, and their heirs male for ever; the four esquires of the king's body; the eldest sons of all baronets; so also of all knights of the Bath, and knights batchelors, and their heirs male in the right line; those that serve the king in any worshipful calling, as the serjeant chirurgeon, serjeant of the ewry, master cook, &c. such as are created esquires by the king with a collar of S.S. of silver, as the heralds and serjeants at arms. The chief of some ancient families are likewise esquires by prescription; those that bear any superior office in the commonwealth, as high sheriff of any county, who retains the title of esquire during his life, in respect of the great trust he has had of the *posse comitatus.* He who is a justice of the peace has it during the time he is in commission, and no longer, if not otherwise qualified to bear it. Utter barristers, in the acts of parliament for poll-money, were ranked among esquires." Samuel Johnson, A.M., *A Dictionary of the English Language: In Which The Words are deduced from their Originals, and Illustrated in their Different Significations By Examples form the best Writers. Volume I* (London: W. Strahan, 1755).

56. Connecticut State Records, Colonial Wars, Microfilm, Volume 3, 329.

57. *Ibid.*, 366a, 417.

58. Jonathan Law, *The Law Papers: Correspondence and Documents during Jonathan Law's Governorship of the Colony of Connecticut, 1741–1750, Volume II, August 1745–December 1746* (Hartford: Connecticut Historical Society, 1911), 323.

59. Samuel Adams Drake, *The Taking of Louisbourg 1745* (New York: Lee and Shepard, 1890), 128.

Chapter 3

1. According to historian Henry P. Johnson, editor of *The Record of Connecticut Men in the Military and Naval Service During the War of the Revolution: 1775–1783*, the 51st Regiment of Foot was disbanded in 1748, yet Wooster retained his half-pay until the outbreak of the Revolution. Henry P. Johnson, A.M., ed., *The Record of Connecticut Men in the Military and Naval Service During the War of the Revolution: 1775–1783* (Hartford: Lockwood & Brainard, 1889), 37.

2. Captain David Wooster and Mary Clap were

married on March 6, 1745, by the Reverend Mr. Joseph Noyes. Mary was sixteen and David was thirty-five. *Vital Records of New Haven; 1649–1850, Part I* (Hartford: The Connecticut Society of the Order of the Founders and Patriots of America, 1917), 251.

3. The couple had two children die in childhood, Mary being the first. Their second daughter, also named Mary, died at seven months. Donald Lines Jacobus, M.A., "Edward Wooster of Derby, Conn., and Some of his Descendants," in *The New England Historical and Genealogical Register, Vol. LXXV, July, 1921*, Henry Edwards Scott, ed. (Boston: New England Historic Genealogical Society, 1921), 187, and *Vital Records of New Haven; 1649–1850, Part I* (Hartford: The Connecticut Society of the Order of the Founders and Patriots of America, 1917), 309, 439. Their surviving daughter, named Mary as well, was wed to Mr. John Cofen Ogden on October 6, 1774, by the Reverend Jonathan Edwards, Jr., *Vital Records of New Haven; 1649–1850, Part I* (Hartford: The Connecticut Society of the Order of the Founders and Patriots of America, 1917), 340.

4. The first edition of this map was done by Joseph Brown. He constructed a map of New Haven in 1724 and another in 1748. The 1724 map was completed based on his memory of the occupants. "Map of New Haven Drawn by Joseph Brown, 1724, Copied by Prest. Ezra Stiles, 1782," *Yale University Library Digital Collections*, 2022, https://collections.library.yale.edu/catalog/15830185. The 1748 map in the Yale University Digital collections shows the hand-drawn version with additional features. There is a printed version of this hand-drawn map, and from this was made the plan of New Haven owned by the Connecticut Historical Society. These maps omit street names. "Plan of the city of New Haven taken in 1748, drawn by James Wadsworth," *Yale University Library Digital Collections*, 2022, https://collections.library.yale.edu/catalog/2003038. *A Plan of the Town of New Haven With all the Buildings in 1748 Taken by the Hon Gen. Wadsworth of Durham To Which Are Added The Names and Professions of the Inhabitants at that period also the Location of Lots to many of the first Grantees.* January 9, 1806. William Lyon, T. Kensett, engraver. The Connecticut Historical Society. There is a hand-colored Currier engraving of the 1748 Plan of New Haven that does include street names. This map is helpful in making the historical connections in the various narratives of New Haven, while the original hand-drawn maps provide excellent documentation as to the styles of homes and their locations. David R. Brown, *A Plan of the Town of New Haven With all the Buildings in 1748 Taken by the Hon Gen. Wadsworthy of Durham To Which Are Added The Names and Professions of the Inhabitants at that period also the Location of Lots to many of the first Grantees.* Barry Lawrence Ruderman Map Collection, November 11, 2022, https://exhibits.stanford.edu/ruderman/catalog/vt541rb3690. An additional

map of New Haven was made and copied by President Ezra Stiles in 1775 during the Revolution and shows a clear development of the city in the seventy-seven years since the Wadsworth map was made. "A plan of New Haven and harbour by President Stiles of Yale College, Sept. 27th, 1775." *Yale University Library Digital Collections*, 2022, https://collections.library.yale.edu/catalog/15827429.

5. Public Records of the Colony of Connecticut, Vol. 9, 493.

6. *Ibid.*, 342.

7. *Ibid.*, 580.

8. It was also mentioned in *History of the City of New Haven to the Present Time* that, in 1887, "near the foot of Hamilton Street was a small ravine, over which was built a stone bridge. This ravine had been used before the Revolutionary War by General Wooster to convey his cargoes taken from vessels in the harbor, across the fields in scows, to his storehouse near the corner of Wooster and Chestnut streets." Edward. E. Atwater, *History of the City of New Haven to the Present Time* (New York: W.M. Munsell & Co., 1887), 300, 302.

9. The names of the four major harbors in Connecticut, as well as the roads noted, can be found on the 1776 Bowles's Map of the Seat of War. Carington Bowles, *Bowles's Map of the Seat of War in New England. Comprehending the Provinces of Massachusetts Bay, and New Hampshire; with the Colonies of Connecticut and Rhode Island; Divided into their Townships; from the best Authorities* (London: Carington Bowles, 1776).

10. A rope walk was a long building in which hemp rope would be run the length and twisted into larger ropes for ships. Multiple strands of rope would be twisted and entwined together to create suitable rope for the rigging of a variety of ships. As noted on the 1812 Doolittle *Plan of New Haven*, the town had two rope walks. One was to the south near the Oyster Point Quarter, off Water Street. The other was to the northwest off Olive Street.

11. By the 1830s the Long Wharf had extended three thousand nine hundred and forty-three feet into the harbor. Edward R. Lambert, *History of the Colony of New Haven Before and After the Union with Connecticut* (New Haven: Hitchock & Stafford, 1838), 80.

12. Charles J. Hoadly, *The Public Records of the Colony of Connecticut, From May, 1751, to February, 1757, Inclusive* (Hartford: Press of the Case, Lockwood & Brainard Co., 1877), 295–96.

13. J.W. Barber, *History and Antiquities of New Haven, Conn., From the Earliest Settlement to the Present Time, Collected and Compiled from the most Authentic Sources* (New Haven: J.W. Barber, 1831), 21.

14. *Ibid.*, 62.

15. "Letter now remaining in the Post-Office at New-Haven," *The Connecticut Gazette*, June 14, 1755, No. 10.

16. Edward E. Atwaer, *History of the City of New Haven to the Present Time* (New York: W.M. Munsell & Co., 1887), 31.

17. 1751 County Merchant's Petition, in *The Wolcott Papers; Correspondence and Documents During Roger Wolcott's Governorship of the Colony of Connecticut, 1750–1754, with some of earlier dates* (Hartford: Connecticut Historical Society, 1916), 60–62.

18. Charles H. Levermore, Ph.D., *The Republic of New Haven; A History of Municipal Evolution* (Baltimore: Johns Hopkins University Press, 1886), 202.

19. Edward R. Lambert, History *of the Colony of New Haven Before and After the Union with Connecticut* (New Haven: Hitchock & Stafford, 1838), 4.

20. Bernard Bailyn, *The Ideological Origins of the American Revolution* (Cambridge: The Belknap Press of Harvard University Press, 2017).

21. It is unclear if John Locke joined the fraternity when he arrived in London. Masonic histories quote John Locke often. There are various historical accounts that do state John Locke become a "brother" in Freemasonry, however the primary sources do not support this claim. It should be noted that they do not prove otherwise, though. The letter quoted was written to the Earl of Pembroke, and Locke did take time to read over and express his opinion about Freemasonry. According to Locke's biographer H. R. Fox Bourne the letter was written in a sarcastic lone and was no to be taken seriously. This analysis, however, was not shared by Freemasons throughout the nineteenth century. H.R. Fox Bourne, *The Life of John Locke in Two Volumes, Volume II* (New York: Harper & Brothers, 1876), 307–08, Claude E. Jones, "John Locke and Masonry, a Document," *Neuphiliogische Mitteilunge* 67, no. 1 (1966), 72–81.

22. Dorothy Ann Lipson, *Freemasonry in Federalist Connecticut, 1789–1835* (Princeton: Princeton University Press, 1977), 31.

23. Steven C. Bullock, *Revolutionary Brotherhood; Freemasonry and the transformation of the American Social Order, 1730–1840* (Chapel Hill: University of North Carolina Press, 1996), 2–4.

24. Upon his return Wooster petitioned the St. John Lodge in Boston for a charter to organize the first Freemasonry Lodge in Connecticut. To do this, Wooster needed to have been admitted into the society of Freemasons. Although there is no record of his admission, England was flourishing with various lodges at the time, and Wooster would have been exposed to them while overseas.

25. Dorothy Ann Lipson, *Freemasonry in Federalist Connecticut, 1789–1835* (Princeton: Princeton University Press, 1977), 51.

26. Steven C. Bullock, *Revolutionary Brotherhood; Freemasonry and the Transformation of the American Social Order, 1730–1840* (Chapel Hill: University of North Carolina Press, 1996), 11–12.

27. On April 26, 1854, the cornerstone was laid for the memorial to General Wooster in Danbury, Connecticut. The ceremony was led by the Freemasons of Union Lodge in Connecticut. At the beginning of the ceremony the Most Worshipful Grand Master David Clark, in his opening address, stated that "masonry has done … more than all other associations for the establishment of the just and equal rights of man." He further noted that it has "resisted wrong and oppression in every form. It has defied and overcome alike the demands of despotism." The praises of Freemasonry, founded in Connecticut by David Wooster, were clearly made. Charity, hospitality, equality, freedom, and the refuting of tyranny are interwoven throughout this address. *Proceedings of the M. W. Grand Lodge of Connecticut, Called for the Purpose of Laying the Chief Stone of the Monument to Gen. David Wooster, at Danbury, April 27, 1854, with the Oration and Addresses Delivered on the Occasions, and Exercises in the Church* (New Haven: Storer & Morehouse, 1854), 11–12.

28. To calculate years according to the Freemason calendar requires the origin of humanity at 4000 B.C., then adding the actual year which, in the account noted was 1750, thus the Masonic calendar year would be 5750. According to historian E.G. Storer; "One thing can be said of Hiram Lodge, No. 1, which cannot be said of any other Lodge in the State—that in no instance, since the formation of the Grand Lodge [in 1789], has she failed of being represented and making returns at the Grand Communications of that body. Another thing is also true,—that in no instance has her own regular communications been omitted." E.G. Storer, *The Records of Freemasonry in the State of Connecticut, with a brief account of its origin in New England, and the entire Proceedings of the Grand Lodge, from its First Organization, A.L. 5789* (New Haven: E.G. Storer, 1859), 50.

Chapter 4

1. Frank D. Andrews, *Connecticut Soldiers in the French and Indian War; Bills, Receipts, and Documents, Printed from the original manuscripts* (Vineland, NJ: Private Printer, 1925), 1.

2. The Connecticut General Assembly called for the enlistment of 1,000 men to serve under General William Johnson and Phineas Lyman, *Rolls of the Connecticut Men in the French and Indian War, 1755–1762, Volume 1, 1775–1757* (Hartford: Connecticut Historical Society, 1905), 4.

3. Phineas Lyman became a prominent lawyer in Connecticut and Massachusetts prior to the French and Indian War. Upon the outbreak of the war Lyman was placed in command of the Connecticut forces raised by order of the General Assembly. His command focused on the area north of Albany, New York, near Crown Point. Commanding under British General James Abercrombie in 1758 at Fort Carilion (Ticonderoga), in which the force was repulsed by the French, and General Jeffery Amherst in 1759, during which Fort Ticonderoga was successfully taken. Lyman gained excellent military experience, as well as insight into the growing change in attitude between the

British regulars and those "provincials" in the colonies. Lyman was sent to England to seek financial gains in the form of land grants in the west following the war. He was unsuccessful and remained in England until 1772 when his son was sent for him. He did eventually gain a grant of twenty acres of land in Mississippi. Franklin Bowditch Dexter, M.A., *Biographical Sketches of the Graduates of Yale College with Annals of the College History, October, 1701–May, 1745* (New York: Henry Holt and Company, 1885), 603–06.

4. Franklin Bowditch Dexter, M.A., *Biographical Sketches of the Graduates of Yale College with Annals of the College History, October, 1701- May, 1745* (New York: Henry Holt and Company, 1885), 605.

5. "To the Governors of the several Colonies who raised the Troops on the present Expedition from Major-General Johnson, Camp at Lake George. Sept. 9, 1755," *The Maryland Gazette*, NO. 544, Thursday, October 9, 1755.

6. Samuel Blodget, *A Prospective-Plan of the Battle near Lake George, on the Eighth Day of September, 1755. With an Explanation thereof; Containing A full, tho' short, History of that important Affair* (Boston: Richard Draper Pinter, 1755).

7. Charles J. Hoadly, *The Public Records of the Colony of Connecticut, From May, 1757, to March, 1762, Inclusive.* (Hartford: Press of the Case, Lockwood & Brainard Company, 1880), 422.

8. *Ibid.*, 423.

9. An analysis of the inventory list of David Wooster's effects compiled in July 1777 list several military maps, but no reference to any specific military manuals. However, an inventory of Connecticut officer Colonel Ephraim Williams, who was killed at the Battle of Lake George in September 1755, list his personal effects which included the following books: four volumes of *Cato's Letters*, two volumes of *Y'd Independent Whigg* (indicative of eighteenth-century republicanism), *A New Roman History of Quest'n and Answer*, and Bland's *Military Discipline*. William's College owns the original inventory list. *Inventory of Ephraim Williams, Jr.'s Effects from September 15, 1755, Number 44: 1755.*

10. An analysis of several of the most popular military manuals of that Wooster would have seen, and quite possibly may have owned at one time, include Humphry Bland, *A Treatise of Military Discipline; in Which is Laid down and Explained The Duty of the Officer and Soldier, Thro' the Several Branches of the Service* (London: Daniel Midwinter, 1743), Geo. Townshend, *A Plan of Discipline, Composed for the USE of the MILITIA of the County of Norfolk* (London: J Shuckburgh, 1759), *The Manual Exercise as Ordered by His Majesty, in the Year 1764. Together with Plans and Explanations of the Method generally Practiced at Reviews and Field-Days* (Philadelphia: J. Humphreys, R. Bell, and R. Aitken, 1776), Bennett Cuthbertson, *A System for the Complete Interior Management and Economy of a Battalion of Infantry* (London, 1759), George Grant, *The New Highland Military Discipline of a short Manual Exercise Explained with the Words of Command; in which is laid down the Duty of the Officer and Soldier through the several Branches of that Concise Service* (London: George Bickham, 1757), *New Manual Exercise As Performed by His Majesty's Dragoons, Foot-Guards, Foot, Artillery, Marines, And by the MILITIA, To which is added Two Copper Plates, and the New Forms of Encampments for Dragoons and Foot* (London: J. Millian, 1759), *The Manual Exercise as Ordered by His MAJESTY in 1764, Together with Plans and Explanations of the Methods generally Practic'd at Reviews and Field-Days, Etc.* (New York: H. Gaine, 1764), *A System of Camp Discipline, Military Honours, Garrison-Duty, And other Regulations for the Land Forces* (London, 1757).

11. Sandra L. Powers, "Studying the Art of War: Military Books Known to American Officers and Their French Counterparts During the Second Half of the Eighteenth Century," *The Journal of Military History* 70, no. 3. (July 2006), 789–91.

12. Virginia Steel Wood, "George Washington's Military Manuals," Library of Congress.

13. Thomas Mante, *The History of the Late War in North-America and the Islands of the West-Indies, Including the Campaigns of MDCCLXIII and MDCCLXIV Against His Majesty's Indian Enemies* (London: W. Strahan and T. Cadell in the Strand, 1772), 32–33. Charles J. Hoadly, *The Public Records of the Colony of Connecticut, From May, 1757, to March, 1762, Inclusive* (Hartford: Press of the Case, Lockwood & Brainard Company, 1880), 470.

14. "Deserted from Col. David Wooster's Regiment." *Connecticut Gazette*, May 29, 1756, no. 60.

15. Victualizing Rolls for Colonel Wooster's Regiment, May 12, 1756. Microfilm. *Colonial Wars, Volume 1*, 339.

16. The maps created in the 1700s of the British Colonies in North America provide excellent tools to place troop movements and military actions throughout the French and Indian War. Even though the majority of maps used in Connecticut were from British cartographers, many of the French outposts and towns retained their French names, and several, such as the Popple and Mitchel maps, took French descriptions of geographic features and included them onto their own maps verbatim. In 1772 Thomas Mante published an account of the French and Indian War which included plate maps of the many battles of the war, especially those in New York in which Connecticut troops were engaged. Printed only nine years following the Treaty of Paris of 1763, Mante's book in invaluable in following the actions and movements of troops from Albany to Forth Edward, Fort William Henry, and Crown Point. These smaller engraved maps also include wagon trails from one fort to another, as well as "roads" north of Albany. Henry Popple, *A Map of the British Empire in America with the French and Spanish Settlements adjacent thereto. by Henry Popple. C. Lempriere inv. & del. B Baron Sculp. To the Queen's*

Most Excellent Majesty This Map is most humbly Inscribed by Your Majesty's most Dutiful, most Obedient, and most Humble Servant Henry Popple (London Engrav'd by Willm. Henry Toms & R.W. Seale, 1733), Thomas Jefferys, Engraver, and Samuel Blodget, *A prospective view of the battle fought near Lake George, on the 8th of Sepr. bewteen 2000 English with 250 Mohawks under the Command of Genl. Johnson; & 2500 French & Indians under the command of Genl. Dieskau in which the English were victorious captivating the French Genl. with a Number of his Men killing 700 & putting the rest to flight. Samuel Blodget delin; T. Jeffreys sculp.* (New York, 1756), Thomas Johnston, *Plan of Hudson's River from Albany to Fort Edward* (Boston, 1756), Tho's Jefferys, Engraver, *A PLAN of the TOWN and FORT of CARILLON at TICONDEROGA; with the ATTACK made by the BRITISH ARMY Commanded by Genl. Abercombrie, 8 July 1758* (London: Tho's Jefferys near Charing Cross, 1758), and Thomas Mantes, *The History of the Late War in North-America and the Islands of the West-Indies, Including the Campaigns of MDCCLXIII and MDCCLXIV Against His Majesty's Indian Enemies* (London: W. Strahan and T. Cadell in the Strand, 1772).

17. Edward E. Atwater, ed., *History of the City of New Haven to the Present Time* (New York: W.W. Munsell & Co., 1887), 440.

18. Charles J. Hoadly, *The Public Records of the Colony of Connecticut, From May, 1757, to March, 1762, Inclusive* (Hartford: Press of the Case, Lockwood & Brainard Company, 1880), 1.

19. *Ibid.*, 56.

20. *Rolls of the Connecticut Men in the French and Indian War, 1755–1762, Volume 1, 1755–1757* (Hartford: Connecticut Historical Society, 1905), 166.

21. Wooster's business partner, Aaron Day, was also one of the members of this committee. This is the last notation that Wooster and Day collaborated during the war. Zera Jones Powers, ed., *Ancient Town Records, Volume III; New Haven Town Records, 1684–1769* (New Haven: New Haven Colony Historical Society, 1962), 332.

22. Officer's Petition to the Connecticut General Assembly for equal pay, May, 1758, Colonial Wars, 241, Microfilm.

23. Rev. Samuel Niles, A.M., *A Summary Historical Narrative of The Wars in New England With the French and Indians in the Several Parts of the Country* (Boston: John Wilson & Sons, 1861), 464–65.

24. An excellent map depicting the location of the Connecticut regiments at the 1758 attack upon Fort Carillon may be seen in Thomas Mante's *The History of the Late War in North-America and the Islands of the West-Indies, Including the Campaigns of MDCCLXIII and MDCCLXIV Against His Majesty's Indian Enemies* (London: W. Strahan and T. Cadell in the Strand, 1772), 144–45.

25. Charles J. Hoadly, *The Public Records of the Colony of Connecticut, From May, 1757, to March,*

1762, Inclusive (Hartford: Press of the Case, Lockwood & Brainard Company, 1880), 240.

26. *Ibid.*, 323–25.

27. *Ibid.*, 2.

28. *Ibid.*, 4.

29. *Ibid.*, 5.

30. *Ibid.*, 6.

31. *Ibid.*, 14.

32. *Ibid.*, 16.

33. *Ibid.*, 18.

34. *Ibid.*, 19.

35. *Ibid.*, 23.

36. *Ibid.*, 3.

37. To see historic maps of Fort Edward, Lake George, Fort Ticonderoga and Crown Point, see Appendix C. Thomas Mante, *The History of the Late War in North America and the Islands of the West-Indies, Including the Campaigns of MDCCLXIII and MDCCLXIV Against His Majesty's Indian Enemies* (London: W. Strahan and T. Cadell in the Strand, 1772).

38. Charles J. Hoadly, *The Public Records of the Colony of Connecticut, From May, 1757, to March, 1762, Inclusive* (Hartford: Press of the Case, Lockwood & Brainard Company, 1880), 365.

39. Approximate travel mileage by foot and boat: New Haven to New York City—80 miles, New York to Albany—150 miles, Albany to Fort Edward—50 miles, Fort Edward to Lake George—15 miles, Lake George to Fort Ticonderoga—50 miles, Fort Ticonderoga to Crown Point—10 miles.

40. Colonel David Wooster's Orderly Book, Fort Edward, Lake George, Ticonderoga and Crown Point, from 19th June to the 10th October, 1759, The National Archives, Washington D.C., Microfilm.

41. A review of a complete inventory of David Wooster's effects taken upon his death in 1777 reveals that he owned twenty-one different maps, some which were of the New England and New York areas where he served during the French and Indian War, including *Bowles's map of the seat of war in New England. Comprehending the provinces of Massachusetts Bay, and New Hampshire; with the colonies of Connecticut and Rhode Island; divided into their townships; from the best authorities, 1776.* See Appendix D.

42. A sutler was a merchant who was issued a license from the army to sell good to the soldiers that were not rationed or issued to them. Sutlers often sold items, such as strong liquor, that was forbidden from army use. At the end of the Orderly Book, Wooster noted a list of items that the army commanders reviewed for sale to the soldiers, including the price each item was to cost the soldiers. "Colonel David Wooster's Orderly Book: Fort Edward, Lake George, Ticonderoga and Crown Point from 19th June to 10th October, 1759." National Archives, Washington, D.C.

43. Colonel David Wooster's Orderly Book, Fort Edward, Lake George, Ticonderoga and Crown Point, from 19th June to 10th October, 1759, The

National Archives, Washington D.C., Microfilm 366.

44. Bennett Cuthbertson, *A System for the Complete Interior Management and Economy of a Battalion of Infantry* (London, 1759), 85.

45. Colonel David Wooster's Orderly Book, Fort Edward, Lake George, Ticonderoga and Crown Point, from 19th June to 10th October, 1759, The National Archives, Washington D.C., Microfilm 54.

46. This advertisement shed light on personal material possessions of a soldier in the field during the French and Indian War. Wooster may have retrieved these personal items, as an inventory of his personal effects, done on May 20h, 1777, after his death, show *one camp beadstead and sacking, and one camp beadstead bolster and pillows.* Colonel David Wooster's Orderly Book, Fort Edward, Lake George, Ticonderoga and Crown Point from 19th June to 10th October, 1759, National Archives, Washington, D.C., Microfilm.

47. *The Fitch Papers; Correspondence and Documents During Thomas Fitch's Governorship of the Colony of Connecticut, 1754–1766. Volume II, January 1759–May 1766* (Hartford: Connecticut Historical Society, 1920), 29–30.

48. *Ibid.*, 30–32.

49. The letter addressed to General Amherst was dated November 10, 1759, and his reply was sent on December 16, 1759. Amherst was essential in the capture of Montreal in 1760, following the Battle of Quebec. King George II died on October 25, 1760. It is probable that the petition was never sent to the king for consideration, or that the king died before his consent was given or denied.

50. 3rd Regiment of Connecticut Troops Hospital Return, August 18–September 23, 1760, at Oswegatchie, Colonial War, Connecticut State Archives. Microfilm, 101–02.

51. Charles J. Hoadly, *The Public Records of the Colony of Connecticut, From May, 1757, to March, 1762, Inclusive* (Hartford: Press of the Case, Lockwood & Brainard Company, 1880), 542.

52. J.W. Barber, *History and Antiquities of New Haven (CONN.) From its Earliest Settlement to the Present Time, Collected and Compiled From the Most Authentic Sources* (New Haven: J.W. Barber, 1831), 63.

53. *The Fitch Papers; Correspondence and Documents During Thomas Fitch's Governorship of the Colony of Connecticut, 1754–1766. Volume II, January 1759–May 1766* (Hartford: Connecticut Historical Society, 1920), 92.

54. David Wooster to the General Assembly requesting equal pay and rations, October 13, 1761, Colonial Wars, Microfilm, 186.

55. *Rolls of the Connecticut Men in the French and Indian War, 1755–1762, Volume 2, 1758–1762* (Hartford: Connecticut Historical Society, 1905), ix.

56. David Wooster to Cadwallader Colden, December 29, 1763, New York Historical Society.

57. A survey map of the land between Fort Ticonderoga north to Lake Champlain displays four distinct tracts of land surveyed to the east of Lake Champlain. One of those four surveyed tracts contains the name Capt. Wooster. His surveyed plot is exactly as listed in his letter to Cadwallader Colden in 1763 and is roughly 3,000 acres of land directly across the lake from Crown Point. Notation on the map further indicates that Wooster himself was directed to survey the land, which he apparently did. The survey map contains the signature of Governor Colden. *A Map of the bay from Tunderoga to Crown Point*, New York Historical Society Museum and Library.

58. Charles J. Hoadly, *The Public Records of the Colony of Connecticut, From May, 1757, to March, 1762, Inclusive* (Hartford: Press of the Case, Lockwood & Brainard Company, 1880), 3.

Chapter 5

1. Wooster broadened his community involvement and civic leadership on December 12, 1763, and again for an additional year in December 1764, by accepting the appointment as surveyor of the highways in and around New Haven. This position utilized his surveying skills learned at Yale and required him to maintain quality transportation within the community. In an era of few roads the surveyor of highways was an important position. Earlier in the summer he had also been engaged by New Haven to apprehend several rioters who had disturbed the peace on the night of July 30. His bill for travel expenses was recorded and noted as paid by the New Haven treasury. "Travel cost apprehending Ralph Isaacs, August 29, 1763," Connecticut Historical Society.

2. Yuichi Hiono, "Sustaining British Naval Power Through New England Masts During the Seven Years War," *Taylor & Francis Online*, January 28, 2020.

3. Charles H. Levermore, PhD, *The Republic of New Haven: A History of Municipal Evolution* (Baltimore: Johns Hopkins University Press, 1886), 203–04.

4. *Ibid.*, 204.

5. "The Sugar Act: 1764," The Avalon Project, Yale Law School, 2008, https://avalon.law.yale.edu/18th_century/sugar_act_1764.asp.

6. "The Sugar Act: 1764," The Avalon Project, Yale Law School, 2008, https://avalon.law.yale.edu/18th_century/sugar_act_1764.asp.

7. Edward E. Atwater, *History of the City of New Haven to the Present Time* (New York: W.W. Munsell & Co., 1887), 33.

8. "An act to encourage the importation of pig and bar iron from his Majesty's colonies in America; and to prevent the erection of any mill or other engine for slitting of rolling of iron; or any plateing forge to work with a tilt hammer; or any furnace for making steel, in any of the said colonies." *A Collection of all the Statutes Now in Force Relating to the Revenue and Officers of the Customs in Great*

Britain and the Plantations, Volume II. (London: Charles Eyre and Willian Strahan, 1780), 976–79.

9. Colonel Isaac Barré referred to those in America who opposed the passage as the Sons of Liberty. Opposition leaders in Boston took the phrase as the name of their organization in 1766.

10. Edward E. Atwater, *History of the City of New Haven to the Present Time* (New York: W.W. Munsell & Co. 1887), 33.

11. Timothy Pitkin married Temperance Clap, sister to Mary Clap who married David Wooster. Pitkin and Wooster were brothers-in-law. Timothy Pitkin's father, William Pitkin, served as governor of Connecticut from 1766 to 1769.

12. "The Stamp Act, March 22, 1765." *The Avalon Project, Yale Law School,* 2008. https://avalon.law.yale.edu/18th_century/stamp_act_1765.asp.

13. "The Quartering Act, May 15, 1765." *The Avalon Project, Yale Law School,* 2008, https://avalon.law.yale.edu/18th_century/quartering_act_165.asp.

14. J.W. Barber, *History and Antiquities of New Haven (CONN.) From its Earliest Settlement to the Present Times* (New Haven: J.W. Barber, 1831), 67.

15. *Ibid.,* 71.

16. Jared Ingersoll's older brother, Jonathan, was a friend of David Wooster. Jonathan Ingersoll became a minster in Ridgefield and served during the French and Indian War as the chaplain for Colonel Wooster's regiment in both 1758 and 1759. In a letter to his brother Jared the night he left for the front, dated June 9, 1758, he stated: "I remarked in particular, your observing something of the heaviness of my countenance at parting with you at New Haven—upon which I would observe that this bidding farewell is a difficult thing, and tends greatly to move the passions." "I have this day received a line form Colonel Wooster, by which I am informed that I must be at Norwalk tomorrow in order to embark for Albany. I am ready and rejoice at the news. He also informs me that you are appointed agent, and have accepted at which I greatly rejoice, and hope your courage will hold out, and desire that you will be made a blessing to your country and government in this important undertaking." George Rockwell, *The History of Ridgefield Connecticut* (New York: Harbor Hill, 1979), 85–86.

17. "The Declaratory Act, March 18, 1766," *Avalon Project, Yale Law Library,* 2008, https://avalon.law.yale.edu/18th_century/declaratory_act_1766.asp.

18. Several histories of New Haven contain the article found in the *Connecticut Gazette* that reported the repeal of the Stamp Act. Two prominent volumes are J.W. Barber, *History and Antiquities of New Haven (CONN.) From its Earliest Settlement to the Present Times* (New Haven: J.W. Barber, 1831), 73, and Edward E. Atwater, *History of the City of New Haven to the Present Time* (New York: W.W. Munsell & Co., 1887), 38.

19. Charles H. Levermore, PhD, *The Republic of New Haven: A History of Municipal Evolution* (Baltimore: Johns Hopkins University Press, 1886), 207.

20. Bills for repairs to the White Haven Society Meeting House, 1766, Papers of the New Haven Museum and Historical Society.

21. Receipt of payment for land sale to James Fitch, April 11, 1766, Connecticut Historical Society.

22. G.H. Hollister, *The History of Connecticut, From the First Settlement of the Colony to the Adoption of the Present Constitution. Volume II* (New Haven: Durie and Peck, 1855), 306, and David Wooster, M.D., F.R.A., *Genealogy of the Woosters in America, Descended from Edward Wooster of Connecticut; Also an Appendix Containing a Sketch Relating to the Author, and a Memoir of Rev. Hezekia Calvin Wooster, and Public Letters of General David Wooster* (San Francisco: M. Weiss, Printer, 1885), 28.

23. Charles H. Levermore, PhD, *The Republic of New Haven: A History of Municipal Evolution* (Baltimore: Johns Hopkins University Press, 1886), 207.

24. J.W. Barber, *History and Antiquities of New Haven (CONN.) From its Earliest Settlement to the Present Times* (New Haven: J.W. Barber, 1831), 72.

25. *Ibid.*

26. Sutlers were merchants, bakers, or brewers who were licensed to travel with the army and sell their goods to the troops. At times these goods were purchased with hard currency that the soldiers had. They were also allowed credit which could be to the soldier's disadvantage if hard specie was unavailable.

27. Charles J. Hoadly, *The Public Records of the Colony of Connecticut, from May, 1762, to October, 1767, Inclusive* (Hartford: Press of the Case, Lockwood & Brainard Co., 1881), 618.

28. "The Townshend Act, November 20, 1767," *Avalon Project, Yale Law Library,* 2008, https://avalon.law.yale.edu/18th_century/townsend_act_1767.asp.

29. This original letter was transcribed by me and adds a great deal of insight to Wooster's thoughts towards loyalty and dedication, as well as his position within the colony of Connecticut as the Governor a sked his input in the proposal and offered him the position of Naval Customs Official for New Haven. David Wooster to Governor William Pitkin, New Haven, 26th March 1768, Connecticut Historical Society.

30. Zera Jones Powers, ed., *Ancient Town Records, Volume III, New Haven Town Records 1684–1769* (New Haven: New Haven Colony Historical Society, 1962), 803.

31. *An Act for laying and collecting a Duty on Goods and Merchandize brought in for Sale by Persons not Inhabitants of this Colony.*

Be it enacted by the Governor's Council and Representatives, in General Court assembled, and by the authority of the same. That there shall be paid a duty of five pounds for every hundred pounds worth of goods, wares and merchandize (except lumber) brought into this Colony, either by water or land carriage, by all and. every person and persons, who are not inhabitants within the same. The value of which goods, wares and merchandize, at the place or port from whence they shall be brought, shall be esteemed and allowed to be the value thereof, and the said duties shall be paid accordingly at the rate aforesaid for a greater or lesser quantity. And, that the said duties hereby laid may be effectually collected and paid,

Be it further enacted by the authority aforesaid. That the collectors chosen to collect the country rate shall for the current year in their several respective towns collect and receive all such duties as shall become due and payable by virtue of this act.

That all and every person or persons not being inhabitants of this Colony, who shall bring in by water or land carriage any goods, wares or peace; at which time the importer or owner of such goods shall give a bond with a good surety to the Treasurer of this Colony for the payment of the duties laid by this act, to be paid in three months at furthest from that time. And in case any part of said goods unsold shall be exported or carried out of this Colony within said three months, the importer or owner, on making proof thereof by his own oath or other credible witness, shall be allowed out of his said bond at the rate of five *per cent*, for such goods so carried or transported out as aforesaid.

That if any person or persons shall neglect or refuse to conform to this act by not giving a manifest or attesting thereto when required, or in not paying said duties or giving security according to the directions in this act contained, all such goods, wares and merchandize, by him or them so imported or brought into this Colony, shall be forfeited, one half to the Colony Treasurer for the use of the government, and the other half to him or them who shall inform thereof and prosecute the same to effect.

That the said goods, wares or merchandize, or arty part thereof, may be accordingly seized by such collector or. by warrant from any one Assistant or justice of the peace and on information made to any court, assistant or justice of the peace proper to try the same. And when the same cannot be seized as aforesaid, the said court. Assistant or justice of the peace may proceed to hear and determine the cause, and give judgment therein either for the forfeiture of such goods, wares and merchandize as shall be seized, and order the same to be sold for the purposes aforesaid; or in case there be no seizure, then judgment shall be given for the forfeiture of the value thereof against such person or persons who imported the same contrary to the intent and meaning of this act, and award execution there on accordingly. In the tryal whereof the burthen of proof respecting the conformity to this act shall lie on the importer or claimer.

That where securities or bonds are taken for such duties as aforesaid and the money not paid by the time it becomes due, the collector to whom such bond or security was delivered is hereby authorized and fully impowered and directed, to put the same in suit ; and he is hereby authorized to appear and prosecute the same to all intents and purposes, for the recovery thereof ; and to recover all forfeitures which shall be- come due to the Treasurer of this Colony by virtue of this act, within the respective towns for which they are appointed, and shall annually account to said Treasurer therefor, or on neglect thereof the Treasurer shall give information thereof to the King's Attorney in the county where such collector dwells, who shall thereupon sue such negligent collector to account.

And be it further enacted by the authority aforesaid, That each town in this Colony shall hereafter annually appoint a collector for the purpose aforesaid, and every town shall be responsible for the ability and fidelity of their respective collectors in discharge of this trust. And the said collectors shall be sworn to the faithful discharge of their duty herein, and shall have a reward of ten per cent, for their service, on all monies by them collected and paid into the Colonial treasury as aforesaid [Charles J. Hoadly, *The Public Records of the Colony of Connecticut, from May, 1768, to October, 1772, Inclusive* (Hartford: Press of the Case, Lockwood & Brainard Co., 1885), 72–73].

32. Charles H. Levermore, PhD, *The Republic of New Haven; A History of Municipal Evolution* (Baltimore: Johns Hopkins University Press, 1886), 208.

33. Sir William Pepperrell died in 1759, yet the 51st Regiment of Foot remained intact. An affidavit sheet from 1770 made out for David Wooster claimed:

"DAVID WOOSTER, maketh Oath, that he had not between the 29 of Decr 1769 and the 24th of June 1770 any other Place or Employment of Profit, Civil or Military, under His Majesty, besides His Allowance of Half-Pay, as a reduced Captain in Sir William Pepperill's late Regiment of Foot. [signed] David Wooster. Sworn before Me this 4th Day of July in the Year of Our Lord, 1770. [signed] Danl Lyman Jus. Of the Peace for New Haven County. I do Attest and Declare, that I verily believe the above Affidavit to be Genuine and Authintick ["Affidavit of David Wooster, July 4, 1770." William Pepperrell Papers, 1669–1772 financial sheets, Massachusetts Historical Society].

34. Charles J. Hoadly, *The Public Records of the Colony of Connecticut, from May, 1768, to October, 1772, Inclusive* (Hartford: Press of the Case, Lockwood & Brainard Co., 1885), 419.

35. "Justice of the Peace," Connecticut Secretary of State Justice of Peace Manual, July 2022, https://uwc.211ct.org/justice-of-the-peace/.

36. Charles J. Hoadly, *The Public Records of the Colony of Connecticut, from May, 1768, to October, 1772, Inclusive* (Hartford: Press of the Case, Lockwood & Brainard Co., 1885), 526.

37. *Ibid.*, 378.

38. The cost for a "whole share" was nine Spanish Dollars. Julian R. Boyd, ed., *The Susquehanna Company Papers, Volume I: 1750–1755* (New York: Cornell University Press, 1962), 13, 179–80.

39. *Ibid.*, lxx–lxxxvii.

40. There is a dispute over the legality of the land sale and the manner in which the signature of the Indian chiefs of the Six Nations were acquired by the representatives of the Susquehanna Company. Julian R. Boyd, ed., *The Susquehanna Company Papers, Volume I: 1750–1755* (New York: Cornell University Press, 1962), 190.

41. Charles J. Hoadly, *The Public Records of the Colony of Connecticut, from May, 1768, to May, 1772, Inclusive* (Hartford: Press of the Case, Lockwood & Brainard Co., 1885), 427.

42. *Ibid.*, 427.

43. *Ibid.*, 218–19.

44. *Report of the Commissioners Appointed by the General Assembly of this Colony, To Treat With the Proprietaries of Pennsylvania Respecting the Boundaries of this Colony And That Province* (Norwich: Green & Spooner, 1774), and Charles J. Hoadly, *The Public Records of the Colony of Connecticut, from October, 1772, to April, 1775, Inclusive* (Hartford: Press of the Case, Lockwood & Brainard Co., 1888), 161.

45. David Wooster's letter to the General Assembly concerning the Susquehanna Company and Connecticut charters, March 1774, Yale Archive Collection.

46. "Tickets for sale for Lottery Scheme to build the Long Wharf," *The Connecticut Journal, and New Haven Post Boy* January 1, 1773, *The Connecticut Journal, and New Haven Post Boy*, January 3, 1773, *The Connecticut Journal, and New Haven Post Boy*, January 15, 1773, *The Connecticut Journal, and New Haven Post Boy*, January 22, 1773, *The Connecticut Journal, and New Haven Post Boy*, February 12, 1773, and *The Connecticut Journal, and New Haven Post Boy*, February 19, 1773.

47. *Just Imported from London, in the ship Albany, via New York, By David Wooster and Co.*, Yale Archive Collection. This listing also ran as an advertisement in *The Connecticut Journal, and New Haven Post Boy* from January 1 through January 22, 1773.

48. "Extract from a letter concerning Liberty and the Freedom of the Press," *The Connecticut Gazette*, February 7, 1756, "A Song to the Tune of Heart of Oak," *The Connecticut Journal and New Haven Post Boy*, July 22, 1768, and "Advertisement from the Sons of Liberty" *Connecticut Journal*, February 19, 1773.

49. *Ibid.*, 115.

50. *Ibid.*, 191.

51. This is the only noted book in Wooster's inventory that can be correctly traced. There are two volumes of Watt's Sermons, volume one is five hundred and four pages in length and volume two is five hundred and twenty. Both contain pulpit sermons, hymn, and psalms, and both volumes are hardbound. It is unclear which of the two volumes Wooster owned, as only one volume was mentioned in his inventory. I. Watts, D.D., *Sermons on Various Subject, Divine and Moral: With a Sacred Hymn Suited to each Subject, In Two Volumes* (London: Printed at the Bible in Pater-noster Rom, 1734).

52. Accounts for the White Haven Society for building repairs and services rendered, 1772, Connecticut Historical Society.

53. Phillis Wheatley to Colonel David Wooster, October 18, 1773, Massachusetts Historical Society:

> Sir, Having an opportunity by a servant of Mr. Badcock's who lives near you, I am glad to hear you and your Family are well, I take the Freedom to transmit to you, a short sketch of my voyage and return from London where I went for the recovery of my health as advis'd by my Physician, I was reciev'd in England with such kindness Complaisance, and so many marks of esteem and real Friendship, as astonishes me on the reflection, for I was no more than 6 weeks there.—Was introduced to Lord Dartmouth and had near half an hour's conversation with his Lordship, with whom was Alderman Kirkman,—Then to Lord Lincoln, who visited me at my own Lodgings with the Famous Dr. Solander, who accompany'd Mr. Banks in his late expedition round the World.
>
> Then to Lady Cavendish, and Lady Carteret Webb,—Mrs. Palmer a Poetess, an accomplishd Lady.—Dr. Thos. Gibbons, Rhetoric Professor, To Israel Mauduit Esqr. Benjamin Franklin Esqr. F.R.S. Grenville Sharp Esqr. who attended me to the Tower Show'd the Lions, Panthers, Tigers, &c. the Horse Armoury, small Armoury, the Crowns, Sceptres, Diadems, the Font for christening the Royal Family. Saw Westminster Abbey, British Museum Coxe's Museum, Saddler's wells, Greenwich Hospital, Park and Chapel, The royal Observatory at Greenwich, &c. &c. too many things & Places to trouble you with in a Letter.—The Earl of Dartmouth made me a Compliment of 5 Guineas, and desir'd me to get the whole of Mr. Pope's Works, as the best he could recommend to my perusal, this I did, also got Hudibrass, Don Quixot, & Gay's Fables—was presented with a Folio Edition of Milton's Paradise Lost, printed on a Silver Type, so call'd from its elegance (I suppose) By Mr. Brook Watson Mercht. whose Coat of Arms is prefix'd.—Since my return to America my Master, has at the desire of my friends in England given me my freedom. The Instrument is drawn, so as to secure me and my property from the hands of the Executrs. administrators, &c. of my master, & secure whatsoever should be given me as my Own, a Copy is sent to Isra. Mauduit Esqr. F.R.S.

I expect my Books which are publishd in London in Capt. Hall, who will be here I believe in 8 or 10 days. I beg the favour that you would honour the enclos'd Proposals, & use your interest with Gentlemen & Ladies of your acquaintance to subscribe also, for the more subscribers there are, the more it will be for my advantage as I am to have half the sale of the Books, This I am the more solicitous for, as I am now upon my own footing and whatever I get by this is entirely mine, & it is the Chief I have to depend upon. I must also request you would desire the Printers in New Haven, not to reprint that Book, as it will be a great hurt to me, preventing any further Benefit that I might recieve from the Sale of my Copies from England. The price is 2/6.d Bound or 2/ Sterling Sewed.

Should be so ungenerous as to reprint them the Genuine Copy may be known, for its sign'd in my own handwriting. My dutiful respects attend your Lady and Children and I am ever respectfully your oblig'd Hume sert.

Phillis Wheatley, Boston October 18th. 1773.

I found my mistress very sick on my return. But she is some what better, we wish we could depend on it. She gives her Compliments to you & your Lady

54. Here Lamb provides a confused chronology. Wooster encouraged his son to stay in England to avoid the rising tensions in the British North American Colonies, however Thomas returned before the Revolution began. Roger Lamb, *An Original and Authentic Journal of Occurrences During the Late American War, From its Commencement to the Year 1783* (Dublin: Wilkenson & Courtney, 1809), 218–19.

55. £ 814 pounds sterling in 1773 is roughly equal to £ 159,000 pounds sterling in 2023—which is estimated to be equal to $189,000 American.

56. Indenture for land sales in New York to John Gilbert, April 22, 1773, New Haven Museums and Historical Society, and, Indenture for land sales in New York to John Gilbert, April 23, 1773, New Haven Museum and Historical Society.

57. "Tribe of Zebulon" referred to those in antiquity who gained their money from commerce and trade through their ports and access to the sea—just as New Haven did in the 1700s. David Wooster to John Lawrance, May 10, 1773, Connecticut Historical Society.

58. Charles J. Hoadly, *The Public Records of the Colony of Connecticut, from October, 1772, to April, 1775, Inclusive* (Hartford: Press of the Case, Lockwood & Brainard Co., 1888), 387.

59. *Heads of Inquiry Relative to the Present STATE and CONDITION of His Majesty's Colony of CONNECTICUT, Signed by His Majesty's Secretary of State, in his Letter of the 5th of July, 1773: With the Answers THERETO* (New-London: T. Green, 1775), 494–99, and Charles Hoadly, *The Public Records of the Colony of Connecticut, from October, 1772, to April, 1775, Inclusive* (Hartford: Press of the Case, Lockwood & Brainard Co., 1888), 344..

Below is a transcription of the seven questions posed to Wooster and his replies. (Note: his response to questions 1, 5, 7, 9, 10, and 11 are the only that were recorded or remain.)

From Colonel David Wooster.
New Haven 16 May, 1774.
Sir: I have your Honor's letter before me of the 18th of February last, and for answer:
Question 1: *What is the Situation of the Colony under your Government, the Nature of the Country, Soil and Climate, the Latitudes and Longitudes of the most considerable Places in it? Have those Latitudes and Longitudes been settled by good Observations, or only by common Computations, and from whence are the Longitudes comuted?*
1. The latitude of New Haven is 41° 18' north, and long. 73° 30' west from London, taken by good observations.
Question 5: *What are the principal Harbours, how situated, of what extent, and what is the depth of Water, and nature of Anchorage each?*
5. New Haven has the principal harbor in the western part of the Colony, situated north and south, half a mile wide at the entrance, and from the entrance to the town four miles, having two fathoms and an half water at low water, and three fathoms and four feet at common tides, and very good anchorage.
Question 7: *What is the Trade of the Province? The number os Shipping belonging thereto, their Tonnage, and number of Seafaring Men, with their respective Increase of Diminution within ten Years past?*
7. The trade from this part of the Colony is entirely to the West India Islands, and the exports are horses, oxen, pork, beef, tallow, and lumber, and the imports West India produce. The shipping belonging to this port are one hundred and eight vessels, consisting of brigantines, sloops and schooners, amounting to seven thousand one hundred and seventy tons, carpenter's measure. The number of seafaring men are seven hundred and fifty-six. As for their increase or diminution I must refer your Honor to the last return, ten years ago.
Question 8: *What Quantity and Sorts of British Manufacturers do the Inhabitants annually take from hence? What Goods and Commodities are exported from thence to Great Britain, and what is the annual Amount at Average?*
8. British manufactures and India goods, imported annually from Great Britain into the port of New Haven, on an average amount to about £4000 sterling; for which remittances are made in pot and pearl ashes and bills of exchange. European and India goods taken from Boston and New York annually amount to about £40,000 sterling, for which remittances are made in pork, beef, wheat, rye, indian corn, flax-seed, pot and pearl ashes.
Question 9: *What Trade has the Province under your Government with any foreign Plantation,*

or any Part of Europe besides Great Britain? How is that Trade carried on? What Commodities do the People under your Government send to, or receive from foreign Plantations; and whit is the annual Amount at an Average?
9. We trade with no foreign plantation, except the French islands in the West Indies, nor to any parts of Europe but Great Britain. We carry to the French plantations horses, oxen and lumber, and receive in return sugar and molasses, to the amount of about £3000 sterling annually, on an average.
Question 10: *What Methods are there used to prevent illegal Trade? And are the same effectual?*
10. The methods to prevent illegal trade are, the custom-house officers go on board all vessels as soon as they come into port, and after due search being made their report to the King's collector the cargo on board, which proves very effectual.
Question 11: *What is the Natural Produce of the Country, staple Commodities and Manufacturers; and what Value thereof in Sterling Money may you annually export?*
11. The natural produce of the country is wheat, rye, indian corn and flax; the staple commodities are pork, beef, wheat, rye, indian corn, flaxseed, pot and pearl ashes. Our manufactures are coarse linens and woollens for the poorer sort of people and servants, also iron-mongery, but we export none

60. Charles H. Levermore, PhD, *The Republic of New Haven: A History of Municipal Evolution* (Baltimore: Johns Hopkins University Press, 1886), 210.
61. Charles Hoadly, *The Public Records of the Colony of Connecticut, from October, 1772, to April, 1775, Inclusive* (Hartford: Press of the Case, Lockwood & Brainard Co., 1888), 349.
62. Charles H. Levermore, PhD, *The Republic of New Haven: A History of Municipal Evolution* (Baltimore: Johns Hopkins University Press, 1886), 210.
63. David Brooks, A.M., *The Religion of the Revolution: A Discourse, Delivered at Derby, Conn., 1774* (Rochester: Curtis & Butts, 1854), 6.
64. *Ibid.*, 8.
65. *Ibid.*, 9.
66. *Ibid.*
67. *Ibid.*, 10.

Chapter 6

1. Charles J. Hoadly, *The Public Records of the Colony of Connecticut, from October, 1772, to April, 1775, Inclusive* (Hartford: Press of the Case, Lockwood & Brainard Co.,1887), 422–23.
2. Henry P. Johnson, A.M., ed., *The Record of Connecticut Men in the Military and Naval Service During the War of the Revolution: 1775–1783* (Hartford: Lockwood & Brainard, 1889), 37.
3. Edward W. Richardson, *Standards and Colors*

of the American Revolution (Philadelphia: University of Pennsylvania Press, 1982), 73–81.
4. G.H. Hollister, *The History of Connecticut, From the First Settlement of the Colony to the Adoption of the Present Constitution. Volume II* (New Haven: Durrie and Peck, 1855), 163.
5. *Ibid.*
6. The first published account of Arnold's aggressive action was found in William Gordon's work. The first publications of these four volumes were in London in 1788 and was geared more for a European audience. The following year he published a three-volume set in New York which is considered the American version. William Gordon, D.D., *The History of the Rise, Progress, and Establishment, of the Independence of the United States of America: Including An Account of the Late War; and of the Thirteen Colonies, from their origin to that period. Volume I* (New York: Hodge, Allen, and Campbell, 1789), 340.
7. J.W. Barber, *History and Antiquities of New Haven (CONN), From its Earliest Settlements to the Present Time* (New Haven: J. W. Barber, 1831), 73.
8. G.H. Hollister, *The History of Connecticut, From the First Settlement of the Colony to the Adoption of the Present Constitution. Volume II* (New Haven: Durrie and Peck, 1855), 165.
9. Charles J. Hoadly, *The Public Records of the Colony of Connecticut, from June 7, 1772, to October 2, 1776, Inclusive* (Hartford: Press of the Case, Lockwood & Brainard Co.,1890), 9, 39.
10. G.H. Hollister, *The History of Connecticut, From the First Settlement of the Colony to the Adoption of the Present Constitution. Volume II* (New Haven: Durrie and Peck, 1855), 306–07.
11. An Humble address and exhortation to the provincial general, officers, and soldiers in Connecticut, June 1775 (New Haven: Thomas and Samuel Green, 1775).
12. Charles J. Hoadly, *The Public Records of the Colony of Connecticut, from June 7, 1772, to October 2, 1776, Inclusive* (Hartford: Press of the Case, Lockwood & Brainard Co.,1890), 89–90.
13. Letters from June 1775 include, Orders from the New York Assembly, June 14, 1775, in *American Archives*, Peter Force, Fourth Series, Volume 2 (Washington, D.C.: M. St. Clair Clark and Peter Force, 1839), Isaac Sears to Wooster, June 14, 1775, in *American Archives*, Peter Force, Fourth Series, Volume 2 (Washington, D.C.: M. St. Clair Clark and Peter Force, 1839), Orders from the New York Assembly, June 15, 1775, in *American Archives*, Peter Force, Fourth Series, Volume 2 (Washington, D.C.: M. St. Clair Clark and Peter Force, 1839), Orders from the New York Assembly, June 15, 1775, in *American Archives*, Peter Force, Fourth Series, Volume 2 (Washington, D.C.: M. St. Clair Clark and Peter Force, 1839), Wooster to Governor Trumbull, June 15, 1775, in *American Archives*, Peter Force, Fourth Series, Volume 2 (Washington, D.C.: M. St. Clair Clark and Peter Force, 1839), Wooster to the New York Congress, June 15, 1775, in *American Archives*, Peter Force,

Fourth Series, Volume 2 (Washington, D.C.: M. St. Clair Clark and Peter Force, 1839), Resolution of the Continental Congress, June 16, 1775, in *American Archives,* Peter Force, Fourth Series, Volume 2 (Washington, D.C.: M. St. Clair Clark and Peter Force, 1839), Wooster to Governor Trumbull, June 16, 1775, in *American Archives,* Peter Force, Fourth Series, Volume 2 (Washington, D.C.: M. St. Clair Clark and Peter Force, 1839), New York General Assembly to General Wooster, June 17, 1775, in *American Archives,* Peter Force, Fourth Series, Volume 2 (Washington, D.C.: M. St. Clair Clark and Peter Force, 1839), General Wooster to the New York Assembly, June 17, 1775, in *American Archives,* Peter Force, Fourth Series, Volume 2 (Washington, D.C.: M. St. Clair Clark and Peter Force, 1839), Wooster to Governor Trumbull, June 18, 1775, in *American Archives,* Peter Force, Fourth Series, Volume 2 (Washington, D.C.: M. St. Clair Clark and Peter Force, 1839), Wooster to the New York Assembly, June 18, 1775, in *American Archives,* Peter Force, Fourth Series, Volume 2 (Washington, D.C.: M. St. Clair Clark and Peter Force, 1839), Governor Trumbull to the New York Congress, June 19, 1775, in *American Archives,* Peter Force, Fourth Series, Volume 2 (Washington, D.C.: M. St. Clair Clark and Peter Force, 1839), New York Assembly to Governor Trumbull, June 20, 1775, in *American Archives,* Peter Force, Fourth Series, Volume 2 (Washington, D.C.: M. St. Clair Clark and Peter Force, 1839), New York Assembly to General Wooster, June 20, 1775, in *American Archives,* Peter Force, Fourth Series, Volume 2 (Washington, D.C.: M. St. Clair Clark and Peter Force, 1839).

14. General Wooster to Governor Trumbull, June 15, 1775, in *American Archives,* Peter Force, Fourth Series, Volume 2 (Washington, D.C.: M. St. Clair Clark and Peter Force, 1839), 1001–02.

15. General Wooster to Governor Trumbull, June 16, 1775, in *American Archives,* Peter Force, Fourth Series, Volume 2 (Washington, D.C.: M. St. Clair Clark and Peter Force, 1839), 1010.

16. General Wooster to Governor Trumbull, June 15, 1775, in *American Archives,* Peter Force, Fourth Series, Volume 2 (Washington, D.C.: M. St. Clair Clark and Peter Force, 1839), 1001.

17. An extensive review of letters written to Wooster and by Wooster from June 14–25 include the following: New York Assembly to General Wooster, June 14, 1775, in *American Archives,* Peter Force, Fourth Series, Volume 2 (Washington, D.C.: M. St. Clair Clark and Peter Force, 1839), 1299, Isaac Sear to General Wooster, June 14, 1775, in *American Archives,* Peter Force, Fourth Series, Volume 2 (Washington, D.C.: M. St. Clair Clark and Peter Force, 1839), 1002, New York Congress to General Wooster, June 15, 1775, in *American Archives,* Peter Force, Fourth Series, Volume 2 (Washington, D.C.: M. St. Clair Clark and Peter Force, 1839), 1299, Provincial Congress of New York, June 15, 1775, in *American Archives,* Peter Force, Fourth Series, Volume 2 (Washington,

D.C.: M. St. Clair Clark and Peter Force, 1839), 1000, Provincial Congress of New York to General Wooster, June 15, 1775, in *American Archives,* Peter Force, Fourth Series, Volume 2 (Washington, D.C.: M. St. Clair Clark and Peter Force, 1839), 1301, General Wooster to Governor Trumbull, June 15, 1775, in *American Archives,* Peter Force, Fourth Series, Volume 2 (Washington, D.C.: M. St. Clair Clark and Peter Force, 1839), 1001–02, General Wooster to New York Congress, June 15, 1775, in *American Archives,* Peter Force, Fourth Series, Volume 2 (Washington, D.C.: M. St. Clair Clark and Peter Force, 1839), 1001, Resolution of the Continental Congress, June 16, 1775, in *American Archives,* Peter Force, Fourth Series, Volume 2 (Washington, D.C.: M. St. Clair Clark and Peter Force, 1839), 734, General Wooster to Governor Trumbull, June 16, 1775, in *American Archives,* Peter Force, Fourth Series, Volume 2 (Washington, D.C.: M. St. Clair Clark and Peter Force, 1839), 1010, New York Congress to General Wooster, June 17, 1775, in *American Archives,* Peter Force, Fourth Series, Volume 2 (Washington, D.C.: M. St. Clair Clark and Peter Force, 1839), 1020–21, General Wooster to the New York Congress, June 17, 1775, in *American Archives,* Peter Force, Fourth Series, Volume 2 (Washington, D.C.: M. St. Clair Clark and Peter Force, 1839), 1306, General Wooster to Governor Trumbull, June 18, 1775, in *American Archives,* Peter Force, Fourth Series, Volume 2 (Washington, D.C.: M. St. Clair Clark and Peter Force, 1839), 1020, General Wooster to New York Congress, June 18, 1775, in *American Archives,* Peter Force, Fourth Series, Volume 2 (Washington, D.C.: M. St. Clair Clark and Peter Force, 1839), 1306, 1025–26, New York Congress to Governor Trumbull, June 20, 1775, in *American Archives,* Peter Force, Fourth Series, Volume 2 (Washington, D.C.: M. St. Clair Clark and Peter Force, 1839), 1306, New York Provincial Congress to General Wooster, June 20, 1775, in *American Archives,* Peter Force, Fourth Series, Volume 2 (Washington, D.C.: M. St. Clair Clark and Peter Force, 1839), 1306–07, and Thaddeus Burr to General Wooster, June 25, 1775, in *American Archives,* Peter Force, Fourth Series, Volume 2 (Washington, D.C.: M. St. Clair Clark and Peter Force, 1839), 1089.

18. New York Assembly to General Wooster, June 20, 1775, in *American Archives,* Peter Force, Fourth Series, Volume 2 (Washington, D.C.: M. St. Clair Clark and Peter Force, 1839), 1306–07.

19. Roger Lamb, *An Original and Authentic Journal of Occurrences During the Late American War, From its Commencement to the Year 1783* (Dublin: Wilkenson & Courtney, 1809), 217.

20. *Ibid.,* 218.

21. Seth Pomeroy did not accept his appointment and John Thomas took his place. Had Pomeroy accepted he would have been the oldest general in the army. With his withdrawal Wooster became the oldest, as Pomeroy was four years older than he. Wooster was sixty-five when the war began in 1775.

22. *Rolls and Lists of Connecticut Men in the Revolution, 1775–1783* (Hartford: Connecticut Historical Society, 1901), 9, 37.

23. *Rolls and Lists of Connecticut Men in the Revolution, 1775–1783* (Hartford: Connecticut Historical Society, 1901), 39–44.

24. Franklin Bowditch Dexter, *Biographical Sketches of the Graduates of Yale College with Annals of the College History, Vol. III, May, 1763–July, 1778* (New York: Henry Holt and Company, 1903), 65–67, 193–94, 300–01, 421–22, 549–52.

25. The Connecticut Delegates to the Governor of Connecticut (Jonathan Trumbull), Philadelphia, June 16, 1775, in *Letters of Members of the Continental Congress, Volume 1, August 29, 1774, to July 4, 1776*, Edmund C. Burnett, ed. (Washington, D. C.: Carnegie Institution of Washington, 1921).143–44.

26. Resolutions of the Connecticut General Assembly, July 5, 1775, in *American Archives,* ed. Peter Force, Fourth Series, Volume 2 (Washington, D.C.: M. St. Clair Clark and Peter Force, 1839), 1584–86.

27. From John Adams to James Warren, 23 July 1775, in *The Adams Papers, Papers of John Adams, vol. 3, May 1775–January 1776*, ed. Robert J. Taylor (Cambridge: Harvard University Press, 1979), 86–89.

28. Letter from Roger Sherman to David Wooster, June 23, 1775, in *The Life of Roger Sherman,* Lewis Henry Boutell (Chicago: A.C. McClurg and Company,1896), 86–87.

Dear Sir

The Congress having determined it necessary to keep up an army for the defence of America at the charge of the united colonies, have appointed the following general officers. George Washington Esq., Commander-in-Chief, Major Generals Ward, Lee, Schuyler, and Putnam, Brigadier Generals Pomeroy, Montgomery, yourself, Heath, Spencer, Thomas, Major Sullivan of New Hampshire, and one Green of Rhode Island. I am sensible that according to your former rank you were entitled to the place of Major General; and as one was to be appointed in Connecticut I heartily recommended you to the Congress. I informed them of the arrangement made by our Assembly, which I thought would be satisfactory, to have them continue in the same order: but as General Putnam's fame was spread abroad and especially his successful enterprise at Noodle's Island, the account of which had just arrived, it gave him a preference in the opinion of the Delegates in general so that his appointment was unanimous among the colonies. Bit from your known abilities and firm attachment to the American cause we were very desirous of your continuance in the army, and hope you will accept the appointment made by the Congress. I think the pay of a Brigadier is about one hundred and twenty-five dollars per month. I suppose a commission is sent to you by

General Washington. We received intelligence yesterday of an engagement at Charlestown, but have not had the particulars. All the Connecticut troops are now taken into the Continental army. I hope proper care will be taken to secure the Colony against any sudden invasion, which must be at their own expense. I have nothing further that I am at liberty to acquaint you with of the doings of Congress but what have been made public. I would not have anything published in the papers that I write, lest something may inadvertently escape one which ought not to be published. I should be glad if you write to me every convenient opportunity and inform me of such occurrences and other matters as you may think proper and useful for me to be acquainted with. I am with great esteem,Your humble servant, Roger Sherman

P.S. The General officers were elected in the Congress, not by nomination but by ballot.

29. Thaddeus Burr to General Wooster, June 25, 1775, in *American Archives,* Peter Force, Fourth Series, Volume 2 (Washington, D.C.: M. St. Clair Clark and Peter Force, 1839), 1089.

30. General Washington to the Continental Congress, June 25, 1775, in *The Papers of George Washington* (Charlottesville: University of Virginia Press, 2007).

31. Jonathan Gregory Rossie, *The Politics of Command in the American Revolution* (Syracuse: Syracuse University Press, 1975), 28.

32. Justus Bellamy's Revolutionary War pension record is an excellent source for personal accounts of the war, especially those actions which involved General Wooster. His full pension application, over twenty hand-written pages, can be found online on Fold3. It is also fully transcribed by historian John C. Dann. His book is an invaluable tool, as are the accounts provided by Bellamy. Pension records can be challenging, especially if taken down many years after the war. However, they remain an excellent source of primary material. John C. Dann, ed., *The Revolution Remembered: Eyewitness Accounts of the War for Independence* (Chicago: University of Chicago Press, 1980), 381.

33. Letter from David Wooster to Roger Sherman, July 7, 1775, in *The Life of Roger Sherman,* Lewis Henry Boutell (Chicago: A.C. McClurg and Company, 1896), 88–89.

34. Edmund C. Burnett, ed., *Letters of Members of the Continental Congress, Volume 1, August 29, 1774, to July 4, 1776* (Washington, D.C.: Carnegie Institution of Washington, 1921), and Worthington Chauncey Ford, ed., *Journals of the Continental Congress, 1774–1789, Volume II. 1775, May 10–September 20* (Washington, D.C.: Government Printing Office, 1905).

35. Letter from Silas Deane to Elizabeth Deane, July 15, 1775, in *The Deane Papers, Volume I, 1774–1777* (New York: New York Historical Society, 1887).

36. John Adams to James Warren, July 23, 1775,

in *The Adams Papers, Volume 3, May 1775–January 1776*, Robert J. Taylor, ed. (Cambridge: Harvard University Press, 1979), 86–89.

37. Jonathan Trumbull to John Adams, November 14, 1775, in *The Adams Papers, Volume 3, May 1775–January 1776*, Robert J. Taylor, ed. (Cambridge: Harvard University Press, 1979), 298–301.

And now for Connecticut Politics, which you desire and Account of. We are Sir a People of a very independent Spirit, and think ourselves as good as any Body, or on the whole a little better—wiser at least, and more intelligent Politicisan. Do you wish to know Sir, what ousted Col. Dyer and Mr. Deane? The Spirit of shewing our own Power, and reminding our Delegates of their mortality, influenced us to change some of the men. Indeed so far, I cannot blame it. But the reason of dropping out those two Men was principally this, that the Congress, last spring being led away by a vain opinion of their own importance and forgetting their inferiority to the venerable Assembly of this Colony, did wickedly and willingly of their own forethought and malice prepense, wholly pass by, disregard and overthrow the Arrangement of General Officers for the said Colony, and the said two Delegates were aiding, abetting, advising and Comforting them therein; against the Appointment and Commissions of this Colony.

38. Jonathan Trumbull to John Adams, November 14, 1775, in *The Adams Papers, Volume 3, May 1775–January 1776,* Robert J. Taylor, ed. (Cambridge: Harvard University Press, 1979), 298–301.

39. Frank Moore, *Diary of the American Revolution from Newspapers and Original Documents, Volume I* (New York: Charles Scribner, 1860), 105.

40. *Ibid.*, 106.

41. *Ibid.*, 107–08. The eighteen toast are as follows

1, The king—better counsellors to him. 2, The hon. Continental Congress. 3, General Washington, and the army under his command. 4, The several provincial congresses and committees in the confederated colonies. 5, A speedy union on constitutional principles between Great Britain and America. 6, Conquest and laurels to all those heroes who draw their swords in support of freedom. 7, Confusion and disappointment to the friends of despotism and the enemies of America. 8, May the disgrace of the rebels against the constitution be as conspicuous as that of the rebels against the house of Hanover. 9, All those worthies in both Houses of Parliament, who stood forth advocates of America and the rights of mankind. 10, The Lord Mayor, and worthy citizens of London. 11, The glorious memory of King William. 12, The immortal memory of Hampden, Sydney, and every patriot who fell in defence of liberty.

13, May the enemies of America be turned into saltpetre, and go off in hot blasts. 14, May Great Britain see her error before America ceases in affection. 15, May America ever be the

dread and scourge of tyrants. 16, The daughters of America in the arms of their brave defenders only. 17, Death and jackboots, before dishonor and wooden shoes. 18, The glorious nineteenth of April, when the brave Americans convinced General Gage and the friends of tyranny, that they dare fight and conquer also.

42. G.H. Hollister, *The History of Connecticut, From the First Settlement of the Colony to the Adoption of the Present Constitution. Volume II* (New Haven: Durrie and Peck, 1855), 178–79.

43. Wooster to the New York Congress, July 7, 1775, in *American Archives,* Peter Force, Fourth Series, Volume 2 (Washington, D.C.: M. St. Clair Clark and Peter Force, 1839), 1604.

44. New York Congress to General Wooster, June 14, 1775, in *American Archives,* Peter Force, Fourth Series, Volume 2 (Washington, D.C.: M. St. Clair Clark and Peter Force, 1839), 1299.

45. Henry P. Johnson, A.M., ed., *The Record of Connecticut Men in the Military and Naval Service During the War of the Revolution: 1775–1783* (Hartford: Lockwood & Brainard, 1889), 36.

46. General Wooster to New York Congress, July 11, 1775, in *American Archives,* Peter Force, Fourth Series, Volume 2 (Washington, D.C.: M. St. Clair Clark and Peter Force, 1839), 1645.

47. New York Committee of Safety to General Wooster, July 13, 1775, in *American Archives,* Peter Force, Fourth Series, Volume 2 (Washington, D.C.: M. St. Clair Clark and Peter Force, 1839), 1785–86, 1778–79.

48. General Wooster the New York Committee of Safety, July 15, 1775, in *American Archives,* Peter Force, Fourth Series, Volume 2 (Washington, D.C.: M. St. Clair Clark and Peter Force, 1839), 1665.

49. General Schuyler to the Continental Congress, July 17, 1775, in *American Archives,* Peter Force, Fourth Series, Volume 2 (Washington, D.C.: M. St. Clair Clark and Peter Force, 1839).

50. General Wooster to John Hancock, July 22, 1775, in *American Archives,* Peter Force, Fourth Series, Volume 2 (Washington, D.C.: M. St. Clair Clark and Peter Force, 1839), 1711.

51. General Schuyler to the Continental Congress, July 17, 1775, in *American Archives,* Peter Force, Fourth Series, Volume 2 (Washington, D.C.: M. St. Clair Clark and Peter Force, 1839).

52. Colonel Joseph Reed to General Wooster, July 26, 1775, in *American Archives,* Peter Force, Fourth Series, Volume 2 (Washington, D.C.: M. St. Clair Clark and Peter Force, 1839), 1731.

53. Letters during the military actions of July 1775 include: General Schuyler to Washington, July 1, 1775, in *American Archives,* Peter Force, Fourth Series, Volume 2 (Washington, D.C.: M. St. Clair Clark and Peter Force, 1839), 1525–26, Connecticut Assembly to Governor Trumbull, July 5, 1775, in *American Archives,* Peter Force, Fourth Series, Volume 2 (Washington, D.C.: M. St. Clair Clark and Peter Force, 1839), 1585–86, Wooster to New York Congress, July 7, 1775, in *American Archives,*

Peter Force, Fourth Series, Volume 2 (Washington, D.C.: M. St. Clair Clark and Peter Force, 1839), 1604, Committee of Safety in New York to General Wooster, July 11, 1775, in *American Archives,* Peter Force, Fourth Series, Volume 2 (Washington, D.C.: M. St. Clair Clark and Peter Force, 1839), 1778–89, General Wooster to New York Congress, July 11, 1775, in *American Archives,* Peter Force, Fourth Series, Volume 2 (Washington, D.C.: M. St. Clair Clark and Peter Force, 1839), 1645, Committee of Safety in New York to General Wooster, July 13, 1775, in *American Archives,* Peter Force, Fourth Series, Volume 2 (Washington, D.C.: M. St. Clair Clark and Peter Force, 1839), 1785–86, General Wooster to the New York Committee of Safety, July 15, 1775, in *American Archives,* Peter Force, Fourth Series, Volume 2 (Washington, D.C.: M. St. Clair Clark and Peter Force, 1839), New York Committee of Safety to General Wooster, July 15, 1775, in *American Archives,* Peter Force, Fourth Series, Volume 2 (Washington, D.C.: M. St. Clair Clark and Peter Force, 1839), 1789–90, Resolution of the Continental Congress ordering Wooster to send troops of Schuyler, July 17, 1775, in *American Archives,* Peter Force, Fourth Series, Volume 2 (Washington, D.C.: M. St. Clair Clark and Peter Force, 1839), 1884, General Wooster to the Continental Congress, July 22, 1775, in *American Archives,* Peter Force, Fourth Series, Volume 2 (Washington, D.C.: M. St. Clair Clark and Peter Force, 1839), 1711, and Colonel Joseph Reed to General Wooster, July 26, 1775, in *American Archives,* Peter Force, Fourth Series, Volume 2 (Washington, D.C.: M. St. Clair Clark and Peter Force, 1839), 1731.

54. General Wooster to Governor Trumbull, Oyster Pond, August 9, 1775, in *American Archives,* Peter Force, Fourth Series, Volume 2 (Washington, D.C.: M. St. Clair Clark and Peter Force, 1839), 73.

55. General Wooster to Governor Trumbull, August 14, 1775, in *American Archives,* Peter Force, Fourth Series, Volume 2 (Washington, D.C.: M. St. Clair Clark and Peter Force, 1839), 134.

56. G.H. Hollister, *The History of Connecticut, From the First Settlement of the Colony to the Adoption of the Present Constitution. Volume II* (New Haven: Durrie and Peck, 1855), 241.

57. General Wooster to Governor Trumbull, August 24, 1775, in *American Archives,* Peter Force, Fourth Series, Volume 2 (Washington, D.C.: M. St. Clair Clark and Peter Force, 1839), 262.

58. General Wooster to the New York Congress, August 27, 1775, in *American Archives,* Peter Force, Fourth Series, Volume 2 (Washington, D.C.: M. St. Clair Clark and Peter Force, 1839), 562.

59. General Schuyler to Governor Trumbull, August 31, 1775, in *American Archives,* Peter Force, Fourth Series, Volume 3 (Washington, D.C.: M. St. Clair Clark and Peter Force, 1843), 469.

60. General Washington to General Wooster, September 2, 1775, in *American Archives,* Peter Force, Fourth Series, Volume 3 (Washington, D.C.: M. St. Clair Clark and Peter Force, 1843), 632.

61. General Washington to General Wooster,

September 2, 1775, in *American Archives,* Peter Force, Fourth Series, Volume 3 (Washington, D.C.: M. St. Clair Clark and Peter Force, 1843), 632, Committee of Safety to General Wooster, September 13, 1775, in *American Archives,* Peter Force, Fourth Series, Volume 3 (Washington, D.C.: M. St. Clair Clark and Peter Force, 1843), 734, General Wooster to Benjamin Trumbull, September 14, 1775, in *American Archives,* Peter Force, Fourth Series, Volume 3 (Washington, D.C.: M. St. Clair Clark and Peter Force, 1843), General Wooster to the New York Council, September 15, 1775, in *American Archives,* Peter Force, Fourth Series, Volume 3 (Washington, D.C.: M. St. Clair Clark and Peter Force, 1843), 734, and New York Committee of Safety to General Wooster, September 16, 1775, in *American Archives,* Peter Force, Fourth Series, Volume 3 (Washington, D.C.: M. St. Clair Clark and Peter Force, 1843), 734–36.

62. General Wooster to the New York Committee of Safety, September 17, 1775, in *American Archives,* Peter Force, Fourth Series, Volume 3 (Washington, D.C.: M. St. Clair Clark and Peter Force, 1843), 734–36.

63. John Hancock to General Wooster, September 20, 1775, in *American Archives,* Peter Force, Fourth Series, Volume 3 (Washington, D.C.: M. St. Clair Clark and Peter Force, 1843). 749.

64. General Wooster to the President of Congress, September 23, 1775, in *American Archives,* Peter Force, Fourth Series, Volume 3 (Washington, D.C.: M. St. Clair Clark and Peter Force, 1843), 778.

65. General Washington to General Schuyler, October 6, 1775, in *American Archives,* Peter Force, Fourth Series, Volume 3 (Washington, D.C.: M. St. Clair Clark and Peter Force, 1843), 976.

66. General Schuyler to General Washington, October 14, 1775, in *American Archives,* Peter Force, Fourth Series, Volume 3 (Washington, D.C.: M. St. Clair Clark and Peter Force, 1843), 1065.

67. *Journals of the American Congress: From 1774 to 1778, Volume I: From September 5, 174, to December 31, 1776, inclusive* (Washington: Way and Gibson, 1823), 150.

68. Gunning Bedford to the Continental Congress, August 30, 1775, in *American Archives,* Peter Force, Fourth Series, Volume 3 (Washington, D.C.: M. St. Clair Clark and Peter Force, 1843), 460.

69. Gunning Bedford to Philip Schuyler, October 15, 1775, Philip Schuyler papers, Manuscripts and Archive Division, The New York Public Library.

70. *Ibid.*

71. General Schuyler to the President of the Congress, John Hancock, October 18, 1775, in *American Archives,* Peter Force, Fourth Series, Volume 3 (Washington, D.C.: M. St. Clair Clark and Peter Force, 1843), 1065.

72. General Wooster to General Schuyler, October 19, 1775, in *American Archives,* Peter Force, Fourth Series, Volume 3 (Washington, D.C.: M. St. Clair Clark and Peter Force, 1843), 1108.

73. General Schuyler to the President of the

Congress, October 18, 1775, in *American Archives,* Peter Force, Fourth Series, Volume 3 (Washington, D.C.: M. St. Clair Clark and Peter Force, 1843), 1093–95.

74. General Schuyler to the President of the Congress, October 18, 1775, in *American Archives,* Peter Force, Fourth Series, Volume 3 (Washington, D.C.: M. St. Clair Clark and Peter Force, 1843), 1093–95.

75. General Schuyler to General Wooster, October 19, 1775, in *American Archives,* Peter Force, Fourth Series, Volume 3 (Washington, D.C.: M. St. Clair Clark and Peter Force, 1843), 1007.

76. General Wooster to General Schuyler, October 19, 1775, in *American Archives,* Peter Force, Fourth Series, Volume 3 (Washington, D.C.: M. St. Clair Clark and Peter Force, 1843), 1108.

77. President of Congress to General Wooster, October 19, 1775, in *American Archives,* Peter Force, Fourth Series, Volume 3 (Washington, D.C.: M. St. Clair Clark and Peter Force, 1843), 1107

78. *Ibid.,* 36.

79. General Schuyler to General Wooster, October 23, 1775, in *American Archives,* Peter Force, Fourth Series, Volume 3 (Washington, D.C.: M. St. Clair Clark and Peter Force, 1843).

80. General Schuyler to General Washington, October 26, 1775, in *American Archives,* Peter Force, Fourth Series, Volume 3 (Washington, D.C.: M. St. Clair Clark and Peter Force, 1843), 1195.

81. General Schuyler to Governor Trumbull, October 27, 1775, in *American Archives,* Peter Force, Fourth Series, Volume 3 (Washington, D.C.: M. St. Clair Clark and Peter Force, 1843), 1207.

82. John C. Dann, ed., *The Revolution Remembered: Eyewitness Accounts of the War for Independence* (Chicago: University of Chicago Press, 1980), 382.

83. Benjamin Trumbull was born on December 19, 1735, and died on February 2, 1840. He was a graduate of Yale College and became a minister. He served in the Revolution under Wooster. Following the war Trumbull published numerous histories of both the Revolution as well as New Haven and Connecticut. His journal during the siege of St. John and the New York campaign of 1776 provide insight into the real experiences of soldiers in the field in all conditions.

84. Benjamin Trumbull, *A concise Journal of Minutes of the principal Movements Towards St. John's of the siege and Surrender of the Fort There in 1775* (Hartford: Connecticut Historical Society, 1899), 150.

85. John C. Dann, ed., *The Revolution Remembered: Eyewitness Accounts of the War for Independence* (Chicago: University of Chicago Press, 1980), 382.

86. General Schuyler to the President of the Congress, October 18, 1775, in *American Archives,* Peter Force, Fourth Series, Volume 3 (Washington, D.C.: M. St. Clair Clark and Peter Force, 1843), 1093–95.

87. *Ibid.,* 160.

88. *Ibid.,* 162.

89. John C. Dann, ed., *The Revolution Remembered: Eyewitness Accounts of the War for Independence* (Chicago: University of Chicago Press, 1980), 385.

90. *Ibid.,* 171–72.

91. "Extract of a Letter from a Gentleman at St. John's," *The Connecticut Journal,* Wednesday, November 22, 1775, No. 423.

92. Silas Deane, *The Deane Papers, Volume I, 1774–1777* (New York: New York Historical Society, 1886), 83–85.

93. Continental Congress to General Wooster, November 30, 1775, in *American Archives,* Peter Force, Fourth Series, Volume 3 (Washington, D.C.: M. St. Clair Clark and Peter Force, 1843), 1718–19.

Sir;

That a conscious pleasure arise from patriotism, your experience must have already evinced to you. Your brethren in America, on whose behalf that patriotism has been exerted, will not withhold that accession of pleasure which you ought to receive form their just and grateful applauses. I am directed by the Congress to transmit to you the thanks of the United Colonies for the very important assistance which you have contributed in reducing St. John's, and spreading the banners of freedom over the greatest part of Canada. I am, &c.,

John Hancock, President

94. Jonathan Gregory Rossie, *The Politics of Command in the American Revolution* (Syracuse: Syracuse University Press, 1975), 32–33.

95. Extract of a letter from an Officer in the Northern Army, December 2, 1775, in *American Archives,* Peter Force, Fourth Series, Volume 3 (Washington, D.C.: M. St. Clair Clark and Peter Force, 1843), 156–57.

96. General Wooster to General Schuyler, December 18, 1775, in *American Archives,* Peter Force, Fourth Series, Volume 3 (Washington, D.C.: M. St. Clair Clark and Peter Force, 1843), 310.

97. General Montgomery to General Schuyler, December 5, 1775, in *American Archives,* Peter Force, Fourth Series, Volume 3 (Washington, D.C.: M. St. Clair Clark and Peter Force, 1843), 188–89, General Montgomery to General Wooster, December 16, 1775, in *American Archives,* Peter Force, Fourth Series, Volume 3 (Washington, D.C.: M. St. Clair Clark and Peter Force, 1843), 288–89, General Montgomery to General Schuyler, December 26, 1775, in *American Archives,* Peter Force, Fourth Series, Volume 3 (Washington, D.C.: M. St. Clair Clark and Peter Force, 1843), 464–65.

98. Colonel Arnold to General Wooster, December 31, 1775, in *American Archives,* Peter Force, Fourth Series, Volume 3 (Washington, D.C.: M. St. Clair Clark and Peter Force, 1843), 481, and Colonel Donald Campbell to General Wooster, December 31, 1775, in *American Archives,* Peter Force, Fourth Series, Volume 3 (Washington, D.C.: M. St. Clair Clark and Peter Force, 1843), 480.

Chapter 7

1. Henry P. Johnson, A.M., ed., *The Record of Connecticut Men in the Military and Naval Service During the War of the Revolution: 1775–1783* (Hartford: Lockwood & Brainard, 1889), 39.

2. Colonel David Campbell to General Wooster, January 2, 1776, in *American Archives,* Peter Force, Fourth Series, Volume 4 (Washington, D.C.: M. St. Clair Clark and Peter Force, 1843), 670.

3. One interesting item that Benedict Arnold requested from General Wooster, aside from arms and ammunition was "three to four hundred pair of snowshoes, [and] a few barrels of sugar for the Hospital." Benedict Arnold to General Wooster, January 4, 1776, in *American Archives,* Peter Force, Fourth Series, Volume 3 (Washington, D.C.: M. St. Clair Clark and Peter Force, 1843), 668.

4. General Wooster to General Schuyler, January 5, 1776, in *American Archives,* Peter Force, Fourth Series, Volume 4 (Washington, D.C.: M. St. Clair Clark and Peter Force, 1843), 668.

5. General Wooster to General Schuyler, January 5, 1776, in *American Archives,* Peter Force, Fourth Series, Volume 4 (Washington, D.C.: M. St. Clair Clark and Peter Force, 1843), 668.

6. General Wooster to General Schuyler, January 5, 1776, in *American Archives,* Peter Force, Fourth Series, Volume 4 (Washington, D.C.: M. St. Clair Clark and Peter Force, 1843), 668.

7. General Wooster to Colonel Warner, January 5, 1776, in *American Archives,* Peter Force, Fourth Series, Volume 4 (Washington, D.C.: M. St. Clair Clark and Peter Force, 1843), 852–55.

8. General Orders, November 5, 1775, *The Papers of George Washington*, Revolutionary War Series, vol. 2, *16 September 1775–31 December 1775,* ed. Philander D. Chase (Charlottesville: University Press of Virginia, 1987), 300–01.

9. General Wooster to General Schuyler, January 5, 1776, in *American Archives,* Peter Force, Fourth Series, Volume 4 (Washington, D.C.: M. St. Clair Clark and Peter Force, 1843), 668.

10. General Washington to General Schuyler, January 14, 1776, in *American Archives,* Peter Force, Fourth Series, Volume 4 (Washington, D.C.: M. St. Clair Clark and Peter Force, 1843), 696–97.

11. John C. Dann, ed., *The Revolution Remembered: Eyewitness Accounts of the War for Independence* (Chicago: University of Chicago Press, 1980), 382.

12. General Wooster to General Washington, January 21, 1775, in *American Archives,* Peter Force, Fourth Series, Volume 4 (Washington, D.C.: M. St. Clair Clark and Peter Force, 1843), 796–97.

13. General Wooster to General Schuyler, January 14, 1776, in *American Archives,* Peter Force, Fourth Series, Volume 4 (Washington, D.C.: M. St. Clair Clark and Peter Force, 1843), 1002.

14. General Wooster to General Schuyler, January 19, 1776, in *American Archives,* Peter Force, Fourth Series, Volume 4 (Washington, D.C.: M. St. Clair Clark and Peter Force, 1843), 855.

15. General Wooster to General Schuyler, January 29, 1775, in *American Archives,* Peter Force, Fourth Series, Volume 4 (Washington, D.C.: M. St. Clair Clark and Peter Force, 1843), 1006–07.

16. General Schuyler to General Wooster, January 25, 1775, in *American Archives,* Peter Force, Fourth Series, Volume 4 (Washington, D.C.: M. St. Clair Clark and Peter Force, 1843), 1003–04.

17. General Schuyler to General Washington, January 25, 1775, in *American Archives,* Peter Force, Fourth Series, Volume 4 (Washington, D.C.: M. St. Clair Clark and Peter Force, 1843), 1003–04. Subacity refers to having a rancorous tone, especially in writing.

18. General Washington to General Schuyler, January 27, 1776, in *American Archives,* Peter Force, Fourth Series, Volume 4 (Washington, D.C.: M. St. Clair Clark and Peter Force, 1843), 872.

19. General Wooster to Governor Jonathan Trumbull, January 27, 1775, Connecticut Historical Society collection.

20. General Wooster to General Schuyler, January 14, 1775, in *American Archives,* Peter Force, Fourth Series, Volume 4 (Washington, D.C.: M. St. Clair Clark and Peter Force, 1843), 869–70.

21. Wooster replied to John Hancock that "to a man who engages in this glorious struggle form the pure principle of love for his country, if he meets with the applause of his countrymen for any service, it must certainly give him very sensible pleasures. My brethren, in America, were not only entitled to any little services I may have rendered them, but ever will be to my most strenuous efforts to serve them, and I shall always think myself exceeding happy, and most amply rewarded, if they prove successful." General Wooster to the President of Congress, January 27, 1776, in *American Archives,* Peter Force, Fourth Series, Volume 4 (Washington, D.C.: M. St. Clair Clark and Peter Force, 1843), 869.

22. A Copy of General Wooster's Orders, Head Quarters, Montreal, Jan. 27, 1776, Connecticut Historical Society.

23. General Wooster to General Schuyler, January 27, 1776, in *American Archives,* Peter Force, Fourth Series, Volume 4 (Washington, D.C.: M. St. Clair Clark and Peter Force, 1843), 1002.

24. General Washington to General Wooster, January 27, 1776, in *American Archives,* Peter Force, Fourth Series, Volume 4 (Washington, D.C.: M. St. Clair Clark and Peter Force, 1843), 873.

25. General Schuyler to the President of Congress, January 29, 1775, in *American Archives,* Peter Force, Fourth Series, Volume 4 (Washington, D.C.: M. St. Clair Clark and Peter Force, 1843), 880–81.

26. General Schuyler to the President of the Congress, February 1, 1775, in *American Archives,* Peter Force, Fourth Series, Volume 4 (Washington, D.C.: M. St. Clair Clark and Peter Force, 1843), 906–08.

27. General Schuyler to the President of the Congress, February 6, 1775, in *American Archives,*

Peter Force, Fourth Series, Volume 4 (Washington, D.C.: M. St. Clair Clark and Peter Force, 1843), 939.

28. General Wooster to the President of the Continental Congress, February 11, 1776, in *American Archives,* Peter Force, Fourth Series, Volume 4 (Washington, D.C.: M. St. Clair Clark and Peter Force, 1843).1001.

29. *Ibid.*, 1001.

30. General Wooster to the President of the Continental Congress, February 11, 1776, in *American Archives,* Peter Force, Fourth Series, Volume 4 (Washington, D.C.: M. St. Clair Clark and Peter Force, 1843), 1001.

31. General Wooster to General Schuyler, February 11, 1775, in *American Archives,* Peter Force, Fourth Series, Volume 4 (Washington, D.C.: M. St. Clair Clark and Peter Force, 1843), 1217.

32. General Wooster to Roger Sherman, Montreal, February 11, 1776, in *The Life of Rogers Sherman,* Lewis Henry Boutell (Chicago: A. C. McClurg and Company, 1896), 343–45.

33. General Schuyler to the President of the Congress, February 20, 1776, in *American Archives,* Peter Force, Fourth Series, Volume 4 (Washington, D.C.: M. St. Clair Clark and Peter Force, 1843), 1499.

34. General Wooster to General Schuyler, February 13, 1776, in *American Archives,* Peter Force, Fourth Series, Volume 4 (Washington, D.C.: M. St. Clair Clark and Peter Force, 1843), 1218.

35. General Wooster to the President of Congress, February 21, 1776, in *American Archives,* Peter Force, Fourth Series, Volume 4 (Washington, D.C.: M. St. Clair Clark and Peter Force, 1843), 1470.

36. General Wooster to the President of Congress, February 21, 1776, in *American Archives,* Peter Force, Fourth Series, Volume 4 (Washington, D.C.: M. St. Clair Clark and Peter Force, 1843), 1470.

37. The Committee of Secret Correspondence: a Report to Congress, on or before 14 February 1776, in *The Papers of Benjamin Franklin, vol. 22, March 23, 1775, through October 27, 1776,* ed. William B. Wilcox (New Haven: Yale University Press, 1982), 350–53

38. Edward R. Lambert, *History of the Colony of New Haven, Before and After the Union with Connecticut* (New Haven: Hitchcock & Stafford, 1838), 135.

39. J.W. Barber, *History and Antiquities of New Haven (CONN.) From its Earliest Settlement to the Present Time* (New Haven: J.W. Barber, 1831), 88.

40. General Schuyler to the President of Congress, March 5, 1776, in *American Archives,* Peter Force, Fourth Series, Volume 4 (Washington, D.C.: M. St. Clair Clark and Peter Force, 1848), 91.

41. General Schuyler to Governor Trumbull, March 9, 1776, in *American Archives,* Peter Force, Fourth Series, Volume 4 (Washington, D.C.: M. St. Clair Clark and Peter Force, 1848), 147.

42. General Wooster to General Schuyler, March 16, 1776, in *American Archives,* Peter Force,

Fourth Series, Volume 4 (Washington, D.C.: M. St. Clair Clark and Peter Force, 1848), 416–17.

43. "NEW- YORK, April 25, Extract of a letter from a Gentleman at Albany to his friend in New-York," *The Connecticut Journal,* Wednesday, May 1, 1776, No. 446.

44. In 1898 historian Kate Mason Rowland published a book a regional history on Charles Carroll of Carrollton and included in the first volume a series of letters and historical analysis of the commission sent by Congress in 1776 to Canada. In the book Rowland states that "the journal of Charles Carroll of Carrollton, which gives in outline the details of the expedition, has been preserved; while the correspondence of the Commissioners with Congress, and with the generals operating in Canada, Thomas, Schuyler, Arnold, Thompson, and Wooster, picture the deplorable condition of the American troops, and convey a vivid impression of the annoyances and perplexities which confronted the Commissioners, and of the patience and tact required to surmount them. Arnold, who since the fall of General Montgomery in the assault on Quebec in December, had been keeping his ground with a small, undisciplined, and ill-fed force, was superseded early in April by his ranking officer General Wooster, who, weak and incompetent, had remained in masterly inactivity at Montreal all the winter. And now he assumed to conduct the difficult siege of Quebec while Arnold took his place at Montreal where there was no enemy to contend with." This presented a totally one-sided perspective of the argument, lacked any analysis of the previous condition in the Northern Department, and continued the eighteen-century ill treatment of New Englanders, especially General Wooster. Shown only from the point of view of the commissioners from Maryland, no objective interpretation was provided within the letters of the commissioners. Kate Mason Rowland, *The Life of Charles Carroll of Carrollton, 1737–1832, with his Correspondence and Public Papers. Volume I* (New York: G.P. Putnam's Sons, 1898), 147, 166, 169.

45. Charles Carroll of Carrollton and John Carroll were Catholic. John Carroll became the first Archbishop of Baltimore in 1789. These two men had an obvious pro–Catholic view upon arriving in Canada in 1776 and were sympathetic to the plight against Catholics in Montreal and Quebec. General Wooster detained several Roman Catholics as they continued to cause trouble for the Continental Army in the area. Despite the Catholic position, the Bishop of Quebec continued to deny any French priest the right to say Mass or absolve sins of any American Catholic. In fact, he went further to threaten excommunication to any priest who joined the American cause.

46. Commissioners in Canada to the President of Congress, May 27, 1776, in *American Archives,* Peter Force, Fourth Series, Volume 6 (Washington, D.C.: M. St. Clair Clark and Peter Force, 1848), 589.

47. *Ibid.*

48. *Ibid.*

49. It is interesting to note that at the same time General Washington was writing to General Schuyler requesting that he, Schuyler, send him as many arms as he could possibly spare, as Washington, still headquartered at Cambridge, did not have enough weapons for his own men laying siege to Boston. General Washington to General Schuyler, February 25, 1776, in *American Archives,* Peter Force, Fourth Series, Volume 4 (Washington, D.C.: M. St. Clair Clark and Peter Force, 1848), 1493.

50. Mark R. Anderson, *The Battle for the Fourteenth Colony: America's War of Liberation in Canada, 1774–1776* (Hanover: University Press of New England, 2013), 287–88.

51. General Schuyler to the President of Congress, March 6, 1776, in *American Archives,* Peter Force, Fourth Series, Volume 5 (Washington, D.C.: M. St. Clair Clark and Peter Force, 1843), 91.

52. John Adams to John Thomas, 7 March 1775, in *The Adams Papers, Papers of John Adams, vol. 4, February–August 1776* (Cambridge: Harvard University Press, 1979), 43–44, and *Journals of the American Congress: From 1774 to 1778, Volume I, From September 5, 1774, to December 31, 1776, inclusive* (Washington: Way and Gibson, 1823), 279.

53. Historical accounts of the intentional spread of smallpox among the American troops can be found in the following accounts: Lothrop Withington, ed., *Caleb Haskell's Diary. May 5, 1775–May 30, 1776: A Revolutionary Soldier's Record Before Boston and the Arnold's Quebec Expedition* (Newburyport: William H. Huse & Company, 1881), 14–15, and Fred C. Wurtlee, ed., *Blockade of Quebec in 1775–1776 by the American Revolutionists* (Quebec: Daily Telegraph Job Publishing House, 1906), also Paul R. Reynolds, *Guy Carleton, A Biography* (New York: William Morrow and Company, 1980), 80, 89, 93. For an overview of smallpox in the war; Harold B Gill, Jr., "Colonial Germ Warfare," *Colonial Williamsburg Journal,* Spring 2004.

54. Historian Mark Anderson provides an excellent source on the American Army in Canada in 1775–1776. He has researched the role that General Wooster played in his defense of Canada and has been of great help in this dissertation research. His works are well written and scholarly in their approach to both Wooster and the winter of 1775–76. Mark R. Anderson, *The Battle for the Fourteenth Colony: America's War of Liberation in Canada, 1774–1776* (Hanover: University Press of New England, 2013), 287–88, 318–20, 323–24, 332–38.

55. General Arnold to General Washington, May 8, 1776, in in *American Archives,* Peter Force, Fourth Series, Volume 6 (Washington, D.C.: M. St. Clair Clark and Peter Force, 1843), 389.

56. Theodore Sedgwick to General Wooster, May 27, 1776, in *American Archives,* Peter Force, Fourth Series, Volume 6 (Washington, D.C.: M. St. Clair Clark and Peter Force, 1843), 589.

57. L.H. Butterfield, ed., *The Adams Papers, Diary and Autobiography of John Adams, Vol. 3, Diary, 1782–1804; Part One to October 1776* (Cambridge: Harvard University Press, 1961), 381–82.

58. Julian P. Boyd, ed., *The Papers of Thomas Jefferson, Volume I, 1760–1776* (Princeton: Princeton University Press, 1950), 292–93.

59. President of Congress to General Washington, June 7, 1776, in *American Archives,* Peter Force, Fourth Series, Volume 6 (Washington, D.C.: M. St. Clair Clark and Peter Force, 1843), 740.

60. General Washington to General Wooster, June 9, 1776, in *American Archives,* Peter Force, Fourth Series, Volume 6 (Washington, D.C.: M. St. Clair Clark and Peter Force, 1843), 770.

61. Philander D. Chase, ed., *The Papers of George Washington, Revolutionary War Series, Vol. 4, 1 April 1776–15 June 1776* (Charlottesville: University Press of Virginia, 1991), 470–73.

62. General Washington to the President of Congress, June 17, 1776, in *American Archives,* Peter Force, Fourth Series, Volume 6 (Washington, D.C.: M. St. Clair Clark and Peter Force, 1843), 937.

63. Philander D. Chase, ed., *The Papers of George Washington, Revolutionary War Series, Vol. 5, 16 June 1776–12 August 1776* (Charlottesville: University Press of Virginia, 1993), 68–70.

64. General Washington to General Wooster, June 9, 1776, in *American Archives,* ed. Peter Force, Fourth Series, Volume 6 (Washington, D.C.: M. St. Clair Clark and Peter Force, 1846), 770.

65. Mark Anderson, "David Wooster Kept the Men at Quebec: Giving Credit to a Much-Maligned General," *Journal of the American Revolution,* May 13, 2020, https://allthingsliberty.com/2021/05/david-wooster-kept-the-men-at-quebec-giving-credit-to-a-much-maligned-general.

66. John Adams to James Warren, May 18, 1776, in *Papers of John Adams,* ed. Robert J. Taylor, Volume 4, February–August 1776 (Cambridge: The Belknap Press of Harvard University Press, 1979), 192–93.

67. L.H. Butterfield, ed. *The Adams Papers: Diary and Autobiography of John Adams, Volume 3, Diary 1782–1804, Autobiography Through 1776* (Cambridge: The Belknap Press of Harvard University Press, 1961), 408–09.

68. General Schuyler to the President of Congress, June 1, 1776, in *American Archives,* Peter Force, Fourth Series, Volume 6 (Washington, D.C.: M. St. Clair Clark and Peter Force, 1843), 679.

69. General Washington to the President of Congress, June 20, 1776, in *American Archives,* Peter Force, Fourth Series, Volume 6 (Washington, D.C.: M. St. Clair Clark and Peter Force, 1843), 922.

70. Mary Wooster to Governor Trumbull, June 17, 1776, in *American Archives,* Peter Force, Fourth Series, Volume 6 (Washington, D.C.: M. St. Clair Clark and Peter Force, 1843), 945.

71. Charles J. Hoadley, *The Public Records of the Colony of Connecticut, From May, 1775, to June, 1776, inclusive, with the Journal of the Council of Safety from June 7, 1775, to October 2, 1776 and an Appendix Containing Some Council Proceedings, 1663–1710, Volume XV* (Hartford: Press of the Case, Lockwood & Brainard Co., 1890), 277.

72. General Wooster to the President of

Congress, June 26, 1776, in *American Archives,* Peter Force, Fourth Series, Volume 6 (Washington, D.C.: M. St. Clair Clark and Peter Force, 1843), 1081.

73. General Wooster to the Committee of Congress, July 5, 1776, in *American Archives,* Peter Force, Fifth Series, Volume 1 (Washington, D.C.: M. St. Clair Clark and Peter Force, 1843), 12, and a second letter on the same date, General Wooster to the Committee of Congress, July 5, 1776, in *American Archives,* Peter Force, Fifth Series, Volume 1 (Washington, D.C.: M. St. Clair Clark and Peter Force, 1843), 13.

74. There is tremendous irony in the fact that while General Wooster was in Philadelphia defending his actions against false pretenses and charges, in a sense against a type of political tyranny, the Continental Congress was itself debating the exact same notion regarding American Independence. Republicanism triumphed for both causes.

75. Notes of Witnesses' Testimony concerning the Canadian Campaign, July 1–27, 1776, in *The Papers of Thomas Jefferson, Volume I, 1760–1776,* Julian P. Boyd, ed. (Princeton: Princeton University Press, 1950), 433–54.

76. *Ibid.*

77. *Ibid.*

78. *Ibid.*

79. Reports of the Continental Congress, Tuesday, July, 30, 1776, in *American Archives,* Peter Force, Fifth Series, Volume 1 (Washington, D.C.: M. St. Clair Clark and Peter Force, 1843), 1611–12.

80. *Ibid.,* 1593–94.

81. William Williams to Jonathan Trumbull, August 7, 1776, in *Letter of Delegates to Congress, 1774–1789; May 16–August 15, 1776,* Paul H. Smith, ed. (Washington: Library of Congress, 1979), 637.

82. William Williams to Jonathan Trumbull, August 11, 1776, in *Letter of Delegates to Congress, 1774–1789; May 16–August 15, 1776,* Paul H. Smith, ed. (Washington: Library of Congress, 1979), 650–51.

83. Richard Henry Lee to Charles Lee, May 18, 1776, in *Letter of Delegates to Congress, 1774–1789; May 16–August 15, 1776,* Paul H. Smith, ed. (Washington: Library of Congress, 1979), 36–37, and Francis Lightfoot Lee to Landon Carter, May 21, 1776, in *Letter of Delegates to Congress, 1774–1789; May 16–August 15, 1776,* Paul H. Smith, ed. (Washington: Library of Congress, 1979), 57–58.

84. Elbridge Gerry to John Adams and Samuel Adams, July 21, 1776, in *Letter of Delegates to Congress, 1774–1789; May 16–August 15, 1776,* Paul H. Smith, ed. (Washington: Library of Congress, 1979), 506–08, and John Adams to Daniel Hitchcock, August 3, 1776, in *Letter of Delegates to Congress, 1774–1789; May 16–August 15, 1776,* Paul H Smith, ed. (Washington: Library of Congress, 1979), 613–15.

85. Monday August 12, 1776, in *The Adams Papers, Diary and Autobiography of John Adams, Volume 3, Diary, 1782–1804; Autobiography, Part One to October 1776,* L.H. Butterfield, ed.

(Cambridge: Harvard University Press, 1961), 405–06.

86. Proceedings of the Continental Congress, August 17, 1776, in in *American Archives,* Peter Force, Fifth Series, Volume 1 (Washington, D.C.: M. St. Clair Clark and Peter Force, 1843).

87. John Adams to Abigail Adams, 18 August 1776, in *The Adams Papers,* Adams Family Correspondence, Volume 2, June 1776–March 1778, L.H. Butterfield, ed. (Cambridge: Harvard University Press, 1963), 99–100.

88. Saturday, August 17, 1776, in *The Adams Papers, Diary and Autobiography of John Adams, Volume 3, Diary, 1782–1804; Autobiography, Part One to October 1776,* L.H. Butterfield, ed. (Cambridge: Harvard University Press, 1961), 408–09.

89. General Wooster to the Continental Congress, August 19, 1776, in *American Archives,* Peter Force, Fifth Series, Volume 1 (Washington, D.C.: M. St. Clair Clark and Peter Force, 1843), 1060.

90. *Journals of the American Congress: From 1774 to 1788, In Four Volumes, Volume I: From September 5, 1774, to December 31, 1776, inclusive* (Washington, D.C.: Way and Gibson, 1823), 447

91. General Schuyler to General Gates, October 5, 1776, in *American Archives,* Peter Force, Fifth Series, Volume 3 (Washington, D.C.: M. St. Clair Clark and Peter Force, 1843), 909

92. General Schuyler to the President of Congress, October 23, 1776, in *American Archives,* Peter Force, Fifth Series, Volume 3 (Washington, D.C.: M. St. Clair Clark and Peter Force, 1843), 1205–06.

93. Jonathan Gregory Rossie, *The Politics of Command in the American Revolution* (Syracuse: Syracuse University Press, 1975), 131–33.

94. Charles J Hoadley, *The Public Records of the State of Connecticut, from October, 1776, to February, 1778, Inclusive* (Hartford: Case Lockwood & Brainard, 1894), 16.

95. *Ibid.,* 16–17.

96. *Ibid.,* 42.

97. *Ibid.,* 16–17

98. *Ibid.,* 27–28.

99. The "saw pits" are located in present day Port Chester, New York. General Lee to General Wooster, November 13, 1776, in in *American Archives,* Peter Force, Fifth Series, Volume 3 (Washington, D.C.: M. St. Clair Clark and Peter Force, 1843), 711.

100. Commissary Hughes to General Wooster, November 16, 1776, in in *American Archives,* Peter Force, Fifth Series, Volume 3 (Washington, D.C.: M. St. Clair Clark and Peter Force, 1843), 711.

101. Inventory of General Wooster, 1777, Connecticut Historical Society.

102. Louis F. Middlebrook, *History of Maritime Connecticut During the American Revolution, 1775–1783, Volume 2* (Salem: The Essex Institute, 1925), 244–45, 267.

103. General Wooster to Governor Trumbull, November 18, 1776, in in *American Archives,* Peter Force, Fifth Series, Volume 3 (Washington, D.C.: M. St. Clair Clark and Peter Force, 1843), 755.

104. General Wooster to the President of Congress, December 8, 1776, in *American Archives,* Peter Force, Fifth Series, Volume 2 (Washington, D.C.: M. St. Clair Clark and Peter Force, 1843), 1607.

105. Joseph Youngs to General Wooster, December 10, 1776, in *American Archives,* Peter Force, Fifth Series, Volume 3 (Washington, D.C.: M. St. Clair Clark and Peter Force, 1843), 1251, Governor Trumbull to James Bowdoin, December 11, 1776, in *American Archives,* Peter Force, Fifth Series, Volume 3 (Washington, D.C.: M. St. Clair Clark and Peter Force, 1843), 1175, and Joseph Youngs to General Wooster, December 16, 1776, in *American Archives,* Peter Force, Fifth Series, Volume 3 (Washington, D.C.: M. St. Clair Clark and Peter Force, 1843), 1251.

106. Petition of Inhabitants of Westchester County, New York, December 23, 1776, in *American Archives,* Peter Force, Fifth Series, Volume 3 (Washington, D.C.: M. St. Clair Clark and Peter Force, 1843), 1379.

107. Charles J. Hoadley, *The Public Records of the State of Connecticut, from October, 1776, to February, 1778, Inclusive* (Hartford: Case Lockwood & Brainard, 1894), 126–27.

That in pursuance of your Honors' directions, on the 23rd of instant December we set out and with all possible diligence pursued our journey towards the army; and on our way we call'd on all the officers of the 4 battalions and in the name of the Gen' Assembly commanded them to hasten the raising the men and as soon as possible to march, according to the order of his Honor the Governor to their stations; and in the evening of the 24th instant, on the road between Fairfield and Norwalk, we met the Honble Maj' Gen' Spencer, to whom we communicated the subject matter of our commission, upon which Gen' Spencer informed us that we were too late to make application to the troops who had been station'd at Peekskill and North-castle, for that he had given orders to Gen' Wadsworth to dismiss the whole of his brigade the next morning and that there was no possibility of making any proposals to any of the troops of this State except those under the command of Gen' Wooster at the Sawpits. Pursuant to which intelligence we prosecuted our journey directly to Gen' Wooster at the Sawpits and there shewed him the resolution of your Honors and conversed with him upon the subject matter thereof; and on motion the general sent for all the field officers of his corps to attend immediately at headquarters. The general informed us that he had fully wrote his Honor by express that morning, therein acquainting him that he had used the utmost of his influence to and had engaged them to stay untill Monday the 30th instant. The field officers immediately came to the generals quarters, to whom we communicated our orders, who all shewed the greatest readiness to assist us by exerting their influence in their

several regiments to induce them to comply with your Honors' request, and agreeable to orders by the general issued for that purpose to the several regiments there under his command they were paraded, and the general with the field officers attended, when we acquainted them with your Honors' resolution and the same being read to them we then address'd them with all the arguments we were master of, to stimulate them into a compliance, in which we were ably assisted by the Revd Mr. Waterman and also in a sensible and soldier-like manner by the general himself, when, to try their minds, the general proposed to them to shew their complyance by raising their firelocks, in which the great part appeared to consent, except the regiment of horse and but few of them consented to tarry—their reasons for noncompliance we afterwards learned from Maj' Starr and his officers were that they had rec'd no pay for the summer or this campaign, that they were under the necessity of purchasing all the oats for their horses with their own money, that their money was expended, that for want of a sutler, or a commissary, to attend them they had been much imposed upon. The officers of the other regiments told us that the complaints among their men were similar as to the pay and want of a commissary. We farther take leave to mention to your Honors that antecedent to our arrival at the Sawpits, Gen' Wooster had ordered 10 companies of the 9th Reg' of militia immediately to march in for the support and defence of the lines there untill other troops should arrive, which was immediately complyed with by Col. Mead and the necessary orders issued by him for that purpose. All which is submitted by your Honors obed' humble servts

Midletown, 28th day of Decbr 1776.

Eliakim Hall, Amos Mead.

108. *Ibid.,* 134.

Chapter 8

1. General Wooster to Governor Trumbull, January 9, 1777, Connecticut Historical Society.

2. It is interesting to consider what might have happened if General Washington and General Wooster had collaborated on a joint attack on New York city in the spring of 1777, Washington from the west and Wooster from the east?

3. William George, D.D., *The History of the Rise, Progress, and Establishment of the Independence of the United States of America: Including an Account of the Late War and of the Thirteen Colonies, from their origins to that period. Volume II* (New York: John Woods, 1781), 107–08.

Toward the end of January a plan was fixed for taking Fort Independence, near Kingsbridge, and by so doing, to obtain a passage into New-York island. About 1,000 militia of the Massachusetts, Connecticut, and New-York states, in four divisions, under Generals Heath, Wooster, Parsons and Lincoln, were destined for the service. Gen. Heath was commander in chief. They marched, the division under Heath from White-Plains—under Wooster and Parsons from New-Rochelle—and under Lincoln from toward Tarrytown, All met on the heights about and near Kingsbridge. The fort had but a trilling garrison, which could have made no effectual resistance, had a vigorous push been instantly made; and the men were in spirits for the attempt. In this way only could it be carried, was defence attempted, as the Americans had no other artillery than three field-pieces. With these they fired a number of shots at eighty or a hundred Hessians, and a few light-horse, who collected on the other side of Harlem river; the Hessians were thrown into a momentary confusion, but soon formed again. Gen. Heath demanded a surrender of the fort, and threatened in case of non-compliance. The threat was disregarded. The troops were employed chiefly in picking-up Tories and in foraging and taking stores that had been in the possession of the enemy, till move artilery should arrive from Peek'skill which a council of war had agreed to send for. About nine days from the first appearance of the Americans before the fort, the artillery came to hand, and consisted of one brass 24 pounder, and two howitzers, The twenty-four pounder was fired twice, when the carriage broke; and a few shells were thrown without any execution. A great number of teams were then employed in carrying off forage, &c. The enemy who had been reinforced during these delays, sallied out, but were repulsed: soon after the Americans retired, upon a report that some ships were gone up the North-River. Gen Heath's conduct was censured by men of sense and judgment, who were with him on the expedition. It was fraught with so much caution, that the array was disappointed, and in some degree disgraced.

4. General Wooster to General Washington, February 15, 1777, Connecticut Historical Society, General Wooster to General Washington, February 21, 1777, in *The Papers of George Washington Digital Edition*, Theodore J. Crackel, ed. (Charlottesville: University of Virginia Press, 2007), General Wooster to General Washington, March 2, 1777, in *The Papers of George Washington Digital Edition*, Theodore J. Crackel, ed. (Charlottesville: University of Virginia Press, 2007), General Washington to General Wooster, March 11, 1777, in *The Papers of George Washington Digital Edition*, Theodore J. Crackel, ed. (Charlottesville: University of Virginia Press, 2007), General Wooster to General Washington, March 28, 1777, in *The Papers of George Washington Digital Edition*, Theodore J. Crackel, ed. (Charlottesville: University of Virginia Press, 2007), General Washington to General Wooster, April 12, 1777, in *The Papers of George Washington Digital Edition*, Theodore J. Crackel, ed. (Charlottesville: University of Virginia Press, 2007), and General Heath to General Wooster, February 8, 1777, New York Historical Society.

5. General Heath to General Wooster, February 8, 1777, New York Historical Society.

6. General Wooster to Colonel Duer, February 15, 1777, Connecticut Historical Society.

7. Brigadier General David Wooster to General Washington, February 21, 1777, in *The Papers of George Washington Digital Edition*, Theodore J. Crackel, ed. (Charlottesville: University of Virginia Press, 2007).

8. *Ibid.*

9. General Wooster the General Washington, March 1, 1777, The George Washington Presidential Library. Mount Vernon, Virginia.

10. General Washington to General Wooster, March 11, 1777, in *The Papers of George Washington Digital Edition*, Theodore J. Crackel, ed. (Charlottesville: University of Virginia Press, 2008).

11. Brigadier General Wooster to General Washington, March 28, 1777, in *The Papers of George Washington Digital Edition*, Theodore J. Crackel, ed. (Charlottesville: University of Virginia Press, 2007).

12. General Washington to Brigadier General Wooster, April 12, 1777, in *The Papers of George Washington Digital Edition*, Theodore J. Crackel, ed. (Charlottesville: University of Virginia Press, 2008).

13. William George, D.D., *The History of the Rise, Progress, and Establishment of the Independence of the United States of America: Including and Account of the Late War and of the Thirteen Colonies, from their origins to that period. Volume II* (New York: John Woods, 1781), 195–96.

14. G.H. Hollister, *The History of Connecticut, From the First Settlement of the Colony to the Adoption of the Present Constitution. Volume II* (New Haven: Durrie and Peck, 1855), 300–02.

15. William George, D.D., *The History of the Rise, Progress, and Establishment of the Independence of the United States of America: Including and Account of the Late War and of the Thirteen Colonies, from their origins to that period. Volume II* (New York: John Woods, 1781), 195.

16. "NEW-HAVEN, May 7," *The Connecticut Journal*, May 7, 1777.

17. General Wooster to General Wadsworth, April 26, 1777, Connecticut Historical Society.

18. Governor Jonathan Trumbull to General Wadsworth, April 26, 1777, Connecticut Historical Society.

19. General Wooster to General Wadsworth, April 26, 1777, Connecticut Historical Society.

20. G.H. Hollister, *The History of Connecticut, From the First Settlement of the Colony to the Adoption of the Present Constitution. Volume II* (New Haven: Durrie and Peck, 1855), 303.

21. *Ibid.*, 305.

22. "NEW-HAVEN, April 30," *The Connecticut Journal*, April 30, 1777.

23. "NEW-HAVEN, May 7," *The Connecticut Journal*, May 7, 1777.

24. For a full transcription of the obituary to Major-General Wooster, see Appendix III. "NEW-HAVEN, May 14," *The Connecticut Journal*, May 14, 1777.

25. *Journal of the Continental Congress: From 1774 to 1788, in Four Volumes. Volume II: From January 1, 1777, to July 31, 1778, Inclusive* (Washington, D.C.: Way and Gideon, 1823), 133.

26. *Ibid.*, 168.

27. James R. Case, *An account of Tryon's Raid on Danbury in April, 1777, and The Battle of Ridgefield and The Career of Gen. David Wooster, From written authorities on the subject with much original matter hitherto unpublished* (Danbury: Danbury Printing Company, 1927), 19.

28. William Carmichael to Charles W.F. Dumas, June 20, 1777, in *The Deane Papers, Volume II, 1777–1778*, Collections of the New-York Historical Society for the year 1887 (New York: Printed for the Society, 1888), 73–76.

29. In *Benedict Arnold, Revolutionary Hero: An American Warrior Reconsidered* (New York: New York University Press,1997), noted historian James Kirby Martin wrote that after General Wooster had fallen mortally wounded the enemy "charged forward, and when Wooster's son refused to ask for quarter, a soldier ran him through with a bayonet, killing him instantly" (319). More recently this has been repeated in *Valiant Ambition: George Washington, Benedict Arnold, and the Fate of the American Revolution* (New York: Penguin, 2016). Here historian Nathaniel Philbrick mentioned that after General Wooster was wounded, "his son rushed to his aid, and when a regular bore down on the two of them, the younger Wooster refused to ask for quarter and, according to a British officer, 'died by the bayonet' at his mortally wounded father's side" (95).

30. To George Washington from Thomas Wooster, 29 September, 1780, in *The Papers of George Washington, Revolutionary War Series, Volume 28, 28 August–27 October 1780*, William M. Ferraro and Jeffrey L. Zvengrowski, ed. (Charlottesville: University of Virginia Press, 2020), 443–45.

31. George Washington to Thomas Wooster, 23 October, 1780, in *The Papers of George Washington, Revolutionary War Series, Volume 28, 28 August–27 October 1780*, William M. Ferraro and Jeffrey L. Zvengrowski, ed. (Charlottesville: University of Virginia Press, 2020), 443–45.

32. James B. Longacres and James Herring, *The National Portrait Gallery of Distinguished Americans, Volume II* (Philadelphia: Henry Perkins, 1835), 156.

33. Inventory of the estate of General Wooster, Connecticut Historical Society.

34. To read "On the Death of General Wooster" by Phillis Wheatly, see Appendix.

35. Phillis Wheatley to Lady Mary Wooster, July 15, 1778, Massachusetts Historical Society.

36. Edward E. Atwater, *History of the City of New Haven to the Present Time* (New York: W.M. Munsell & Co., 1887), 54.

37. Account of General Wooster's Death, Simeon Baldwin papers, Connecticut Historical Society.

38. Edward E. Atwater, *History of the City of New Haven to the Present Time* (New York: W.M. Munsell & Co., 1887), 56.

New Haven, July 14, 1779. Sir,—The troops of the separate expedition under your Excellency's command, when they left New Haven on the 6th inst., carried away with them, among other things, the papers MSS. [manuscripts] of the Rev. President Clap, the late head of this seat of learning. They were in the hands of his daughter, Mrs. Wooster, lady of the late General Wooster, and lodged in the General's house. Among them, besides some compositions, were letters and papers of consequence respecting the college, which can be of no service to the present possessor. This waits upon you, Sir, to request this box of MSS., which can have no respect to the present times, as Mr. Clap died in 1767. A war against science has been reprobated for ages by the wisest and most powerful generals. The irreparable loss sustained by the republic of letters by the destruction of the Alexandrian Library and other ancient monuments of literature, have generously prompted the victorious commanders of modern ages to exempt these monuments from ravages and desolations inseparable from the highest rigor of war. I beg leave upon this occasion to address myself only to the principles of politeness and honor, humbly asking the return of those MSS., which to others will be useless—to us valuable. I am. Sir, Your Excellency's most obedient and very humble servant.

Ezra Stiles, President

39. *Ibid.*, 56.

New York, 25th September, 1779. Sir,—Disposed by principle, as well as inclination, to prevent the violence of war from injuring the right of the republic of learning, I very much approve of your solicitude for the preservation of Mr. Clap's MSS. Had they been found here, they should most certainly have been restored, as you desire; but, after dilligent inquiry, I can learn nothing concerning them. The officer of the party at the house where the box is supposed to have been deposited, has been examined, and does not remember to have seen it, nor apprehends that any such papers fell into the hands of the soldiery. I would therefore indulge a hope that better care has been taken of the collection than you were led to imagine at the date of your letter. This however will not abate my attention and inquiry; nor shall I, if I succeed, omit the gratification of your wishes.

I am. Sir, your very obedient servant,

Wm. Tryon

40. *Ibid.*, 56.

41. William Samuel Johnson to Roger Sherman, April 20, 1785, in *The Life of Roger Sherman*, Lewis Henry Boutell, ed. (Chicago: A.C. McClurg and Company, 1896), 345–46.

42. Mary Wooster to President Washington, May 8, 1789, in *The Papers of George Washington, Presidential Series, vol. 2, 1 April 1789–15 June 1789*, Dorothy Twohig, ed. (Charlottesville: University Press of Virginia, 1987), 234–35.

New Haven May 8, 1789. Sir, Permit me to address your Excellency on a subject which perhaps may be thought improper for a Woman, but I rely on my particular unfortunate situation and the candor of your Excellency for my justification. My Son having been excedingly unfortunate during the course of the last War by the loss of his pay, receiving his debts in Continental Money, by being plunder'd to a very considerable amount by the British and Various other ways, but more particularly by the untimely death of his Father which left him in a very disagreable situation at the close of the war, and from which he has never been able to recover, altho he has made every exertion in his power, and at present is entirely out of business with a large Family to support; he has been preposeing for some time past to go and settle in a foreign Country, but his friends have advis'd him to Stay in this Country if he can with propriety, for this end I know he has petition'd your Excellency for a Post under the new Constitution but I am afraid that with his fortune he has lost his friends, as is too frequently the case, and must entreat of your Excellency to become a Father to him, and relieve him in some measure from his troubles, forgive a Mothers feelings whose future happiness Depends on that of her Son.—I have lost my Husband, I have only one Son to depend on, and if he cannot get into Some place or business here whereby he can support his family, is determind to remove into a foreign Country and leave me in a worse than Widow'd State I must therfore entreat your Excellency to consider his and my Situation, and by relieving us in Some way, receive from us with gratitude the Blessings of the Widow and Orphan. I am with respect & Esteem Your Excellencys most Obedt and Very Humble Servt

Mary Wooster

43. President Washington to Mary Wooster, May 21, 1789, in *The Papers of George Washington, Presidential Series, vol. 2, 1 April 1789–15 June 1789*, Dorothy Twohig, ed. (Charlottesville: University Press of Virginia, 1987), 361–62.

44. Report on the Petition of Mary Wooster, 12 April, 1792, in *The Papers of Alexander Hamilton, vol. 11, February 1792–June 1792*, Harold C. Syrett, ed. (New York: Columbia University Press, 1966), 271.

45. "To John Adams from John Cosens Ogden, 9 March 1797," *Founders Online*, National Archives, https://founders.archives.gov/documents/Adams/99–02–02–1887.

46. To Thomas Jefferson form John C. Ogden, 7 February, 1799, in *The Papers of Thomas Jefferson, vol. 31, 1 February 1799–31 May 1800*, Barbara B. Oberg, ed. (Princeton: Princeton University Press, 2004), 16–18.

47. *American State Papers. Documents, Legislative and Executive, of the Congress of the United States, from the First Session to the Second Session of the Seventeenth Congress, Inclusive: Commencing March 4, 1789, and Ending March 3, 1823* (Washington, D.C.: Gales and Seaton, 1834), 71.

48. *Ibid.*, 72.

Chapter 9

1. Marvin R. Oswald, *In Memoriam, A compilation of the locations of the grave sites of Veterans buried in Wayne County, Ohio*, 1996.

2. "In the Senate of the United States, April 29, 1802. A bill to carry into effect a resolution of Congress to erect a monument to the memory of the late general David Wooster," Library of Congress.

3. Benson J. Lossing, *The Pictorial Field-Book of the Revolution, Volume II* (New York: Harper & Brother, 1859), 408.

4. *Proceedings of the M. W. Grand Lodge of Connecticut, Called for the Purpose of Laying the Chief Stone of the Monument to Gen. David Wooster, at Danbury, April 27, 1854, with the Oration and Addresses Delivered on the Occasion, and Exercises in the Church* (New Haven: Storer & Morehouse, 1854), 9.

5. *Ibid.*, 10–11.

6. *Ibid.*, 12–14.

7. *Ibid.*, 28.

8. Henry Champion Deming, *An Oration Upon the Life and Services of General David Wooster. Delivered at Danbury, April 27th, 1854, When a Monument was Erected to His Memory* (Hartford: Case, Tiffany and Company, 1854), 1–60.

9. Amy Elizabeth Burton, *To Make Beautiful the Capitol: Rediscovering the Art of Constantino Brumidi* (Washington, D.C.: U.S. Government Printing Office, 2014), 74.

10. Mark Anderson, "David Wooster Kept the Men at Quebec: Giving Credit to a Much-Maligned General," *Journal of the American Revolution*, May 13, 2020, https://allthingsliberty.com/2021/05/david-wooster-kept-the-men-at-quebec-giving-credit-to-a-much-maligned-general.

11. Thomas Jones, *History of New York During the Revolutionary War, and of the Leading Events in the Other Colonies at that Period* (New York: Trow's Printing and Bookbinding, 1879), 180.

12. *Ibid.*

13. *Ibid.*

14. *Ibid.*

15. Kenneth Roberts, *March to Quebec: Journals of the Members of Arnold's Expedition* (New York: Doubleday & Company, 1947), 103–04.

16. Willard Wallace, *Traitorous Hero: The Life and Fortunes of Benedict Arnold* (New York: Harper Brothers, 1954).

17. William P. Cumming and Hugh Rankin, *The Fate of a Nation: The American Revolution Through Contemporary Eyes* (New York: Phaidon Press, 1975), 74.

18. James Kirby Martin, *Benedict Arnold, Revolutionary Hero: An American Warrior Reconsidered* (New York: New York University Press, 1997), 180, 478.

19. Christopher Hibbert, *Redcoats and Rebels: The American Revolution Through British Eyes* (New York: W.W. Norton, 2002), 93.

20. Benson Bobrick also referenced both Jones and Roberts in his book. He did not refer to Wooster as a drunkard in his own work. Benson Bobrick, *Angel on the Whirlwind: The Triumph of the American Revolution* (New York: Penguin, 1997), 175.

21. Rick Atkinson, *The British Are Coming: The War for America, Lexington to Princeton, 1775–1777* (New York: Henry Holt and Company, 2019), 277.

22. Sheldon S. Cohen, ed., *Canada Preserved: The Journal of Captain Thomas Ainslie* (New York: New York University Press, 1968), 71–72.

23. Justin H. Smith, *Our Struggle for the Fourteenth Colony: Canada and the American Revolution, Volume II* (New York: Knickerbocker Press, 1907), 255.

24. Nathaniel Philbrick, *Valiant Ambition: George Washington, Benedict Arnold, and the fate of the American Revolution* (New York: Penguin, 2016), 95.

25. William James Morgan, ed., *Naval Documents of the American Revolution, Volume 8* (Washington: Naval History Division, Department of the Navy, 1980), 455–57.

26. Benjamin Franklin Steven, *B.F. Steven's Facsimiles of Manuscripts in European Archives Relating to America, 1773–1783, with Descriptions, Editorial Notes, Collections, References, and Translations, Volume II, Nos. 131 to 234* (London, 1898) Document 155.

Appendix I

1. A comprehensive examination of the historiography on 18th-century republicanism can be obtained by analyzing the following: Bernard Bailyn, *The Ideological Origins of the American Revolution* (Cambridge: The Belknap Press of Harvard University Press, 1967), Caroline Robbins, *The Eighteenth-Century Commonwealthman* (Indianapolis: Liberty Fund, 1959), Michael G. Hall and Lawrence H. Leder. *The Glorious Revolution in America: Documents on the Colonial Crisis of 1689* (Chapel Hill: University of North Carolina Press, 1964), R.R. Palmer, *The Age of the Democratic Revolution: A Political History of Europe and America, 1760–1800* (Princeton: Princeton University Press, 2014), Robert Middlekauff, *The Glorious Cause: The American Revolution, 1763–1789* (New York: Oxford University Press, 1982), Gordon Wood, *The Radicalism of the American Revolution* (New York: A.A. Knopf, 1992), J.R. Pole, *Political Representation in England and the Origin of the American Republic* (London: The Macmillan Company, 1966), and Jack Greene, *Peripheries and Center: Constitutional Development in the Extended Polities of the British Empire and the United States, 1607–1788* (Athens: University of Georgia Press, 1986).

2. John Locke, *Two Treatises of Government and A Letter Concerning Toleration* (New Haven: Yale University Press, 2003).

3. Gordon S. Wood. *The Creation of the American Republic: 1776–1787* (Chapel Hill: University of North Carolina Press, 1969), viii.

4. Jack P. Greene, *Pursuits of Happiness: The Social Development of Early Modern British Colonies and the Formation of American Culture* (Chapel Hill: University of North Carolina Press, 1988).

5. Robert Shalhope, *The Roots of Democracy: American Thought and Culture, 1760–1800* (Boston: Twayne, 1990), Gordon Wood, *The Radicalism of the American Revolution: How a Revolution Transformed a Monarchical Society into a Democratic One Unlike Any That Had Ever Existed* (New York: Alfred A. Knopf, 1992), and *The American Revolution: A History* (New York: Random House, 2002), Joyce Appleby, *Liberalism and Republicanism in the Historical Imagination* (Cambridge: Harvard University Press, 1992), Rebecca Starr, ed., *Articulating America: Fashioning a National Political Culture in Early America, Essays in Honor of J.R. Pole* (New York: Rowman & Littlefield, 2000), J.G.A. Pocock, ed., et. al., *The Varieties of British Political Thought, 1500–1800* (Cambridge: Cambridge University Press, 1993), and Jack P. Greene, *The Constitutional Origins of the American Revolution* (Cambridge: Cambridge University Press, 2011).

6. Gordon Wood, *The Radicalism of the American Revolution: How a Revolution Transformed a Monarchical Society into a Democratic One Unlike Any That Had Ever Existed* (New York: Alfred A. Knopf, 1992).

7. John C. Miller, *Origins of the American Revolution* (Boston: Little, Brown, 1943).

8. Louis B. Wright, *The Cultural Life of the American Colonies* (New York: Harper and Row, 1957).

9. Robert East, *Business Enterprise in the American Revolutionary Era* (Gloucester: P. Smith, 1964), 16–17.

10. *Ibid.,* 22.

11. Historian Jack Green taught the concept of Atlantic history at Johns Hopkins University for twenty years. Jack P. Greene and Philip D. Morgan, ed., *Atlantic History: A Critical Appraisal* (Oxford: Oxford University Press, 2009).

12. Bernard Bailyn, *Atlantic History: Concept*

and Contours (Cambridge: Harvard University Press, 2005).

13. Yuichi Hiono, "Sustaining British Naval Power Through New England Masts During the Seven Years War," *Taylor & Francis Online*, January 28, 2020, 18–29.

14. Thomas M. Doerflinger, *A Vigorous Spirit of Enterprise: Merchants and Economic Development in Revolutionary Philadelphia* (Chapel Hill: University of North Carolina Press, 1986), 204–05.

15. For a comprehensive historiographical study of colonial economics see Robert A. East, *Business Enterprise in the American Revolutionary Era* (Gloucester: P. Smith, 1964), John J. McCusker and Russell R. Menard, *The Economy of British America, 1607–1789* (Chapel Hill: University of North Carolina Press, 1985), John J. McCusker and Russell R. Menard, *The Economy of British America, 1607–1789* (Chapel Hill: University of North Carolina Press, 1985), Thomas M. Doerflinger, *A Vigorous Spirit of Enterprise: Merchants and Economic Development in Revolutionary Philadelphia* (Chapel Hill: University of North Carolina Press, 1986), and Ronald Hoffman, et al., *The Economy of Early America: The Revolutionary Period, 1763–1790* (Charlottesville: University Press of Virginia, 1988).

16. Lorenzo Sabine, *The American Loyalists, or Biographical Sketches of Adherents to the British Crown in The War of the Revolution; Alphabetically Arranged with a Preliminary Historical Essay* (Boston: Charles C. Little and James Brown, 1847), *Biographical Sketches of Loyalists of the American Revolution with an Historical Essay, Volume I* (Boston: Little, Brown, 1864), and *Biographical Sketches of Loyalists of the American Revolution with an Historical Essay, Volume II* (Boston: Little, Brown, 1864).

17. Mary Beth Norton, *The British-Americans: The Loyalist Exiles in England, 1774–1789* (Boston: Little, Brown, 1972), 8.

18. Bernard Bailyn, *The Ordeal of Thomas Hutchinson: Loyalism and the Destruction of the First British Empire* (Cambridge: Belknap Press of Harvard University Press, 1974), xi.

19. Mary Beth Norton, *The British-Americans: The Loyalist Exiles in England, 1774–1789* (Boston: Little, Brown, 1972), Robert M. Calhoon, *The Loyalists in Revolutionary America, 1760–1781* (New York: Harcourt Brace Jovanovich, 1973), Bernard Bailyn, *The Ordeal of Thomas Hutchinson: Loyalism and the Destruction of the First British Empire* (Cambridge: Belknap Press of Harvard University Press, 1974), William P. Cumming and Hugh Rankin, *The Fate of a Nation: The American Revolution through Contemporary Eyes* (London: Phaidon Press, 1975), John E. Ferling, *The Loyalist Mind: Joseph Galloway and the American Revolution* (University Park: Pennsylvania State University Press, 1977), Elizabeth P. McCaughey, *From Loyalist to Founding Father: The Political Odyssey of William Samuel Johnson* (New York: Cambridge University Press, 1980), Robert Middlekauff, *The Glorious Cause: The American Revolution, 1763–1789* (New York: Oxford University Press, 1982), Christopher Hibbert, *Redcoats and Rebels: The American Revolution Through British Eyes* (New York: Avon Books, 1990), William Nelson, *The American Tory* (Boston: Northeastern University Press, 1992), and H.W. Brands, *Our First Civil War: Patriots and Loyalists in the American Revolution* (New York: Doubleday, 2021).

20. David Ramsay, *The History of the American Revolution, Volume I and II* (Indianapolis: Liberty Press, 1990).

21. Mercy Otis Warren, *The History of the Rise, Progress, and Termination of the American Revolution, Interspersed with Biographical, Political, and oral Observations, In Three Volumes* (Boston: Manning and Loring Printers, 1805).

22. J.T. Headley, *Washington and His Generals, Volume I and II* (New York: Baker and Scribner, 1847).

23. Daniel B. Rowland. *God, Tsar & People: The Political Culture of Early Modern Russia* (Ithaca: Northern Illinois University Press, 2020).

24. Joseph P. Marin, *Narrative of Some of the Adventures, Dangers and Sufferings of a Revolutionary Soldier* (Hallowell, ME: Glazier, Masters & Co.,1830).

25. Benson J. Lossing, *A Pictorial Field Book of the Revolution*. New York; Harper Brothers, 1859, and *The Life and Times of Philip Schuyler, Volume I and II* (New York: Sheldon and Company, 1860).

26. Henry B. Carrington, *Battles of the American Revolution including Battle Maps and Charts of the American Revolution* (New York: Promontory Press, 1881).

27. Washington Irving, *The Life of George Washington in Four Volumes* (New York: John B. Alden Publisher, 1887).

28. Lewis Henry Boutell, *The Life of Roger Sherman* (Chicago: A.C. McClurg and Company, 1896).

29. Post World War II historiography include John C. Miller, *Triumph of Freedom: 1775–1783* (Boston: Little, Brown, 1948), Lynn Montross, *The Reluctant Rebels: The Story of the Continental Congress, 1774–1789* (New York: Barnes and Nobles, 1950), Willard M. Wallace, *Appeal to Arms: A Military History of the American Revolution* (New York: Harper Brothers, 1951).

30. Historian Michael Hattem has outlined the historiography of the American Revolution in the following manner: 1780–1820: Revolutionary Interpretations and Loyalist Interpretation, 1820–1880: Whig Interpretation, 1900–1940: Progressive Interpretation, 1960–1980: New-Whig, Ideological Interpretation, New Left, Social History, and 1980-Present: Neo-Progress and Founders Chic Interpretation. Michael D. Hattem, "The Historiography of the American Revolution." *Journal of the American Revolution*, August 27, 2013, https://allthingsliberty.com/2013/08/historiography-of-american-revolution/, and "The Historiography of the American Revolution: A Timeline," August 2017,

https://cdn.knightlab.com/libs/timeline3/latest/embed/index.html?source=19P0MD9TrV5Tx-62DC3fImj_uNLA5lAsnV6TmRu2fWdL4&font=PT&lang=en&initial_zoom=1&height=800.

31. Willard M. Wallace, *Appeal to Arms: A Military History of the American Revolution* (New York: Harper Brothers, 1951), Christopher Ward, *The War of the Revolution* (New York: Macmillan, 1952).

32. Historians who impacted this new era of Colonial American and Revolutionary War historiography include Willard M. Wallace, *Traitorous Hero: The Life and Fortunes of Benedict Arnold* (New York: Harper and Brothers, 1954), Lauren Paine, *Benedict Arnold: Hero and Traitor* (London: Robert Hale, 1965), Charles Royster, *A Revolutionary People at War: The Continental Army & American Character, 1775–1783* (Chapel Hill: University of North Carolina Press, 1979), Robert Middlekauff, *The Glorious Cause: The American Revolution, 1763–1789* (New York: Oxford University Press, 1982), Louis Birnbaum, *Red Dawn at Lexington: "If They Mean to Have a War, Let It Begin Here!"* (Boston: Houghton Mifflin, 1986), and Christopher Hibbert, *Redcoats and Rebels: The American Revolution Through British Eyes* (New York: Avon Books, 1990).

33. Bernard Bailyn, *The Ideological Origins of the American Revolution.* (Cambridge: The Belknap Press of Harvard University Press, 1967).

34. George L. Rockwell, *The History of Ridgefield Connecticut* (New York: Harbor Hill, 1979), and Richard Middleton, *Colonial America: A History, 1585–1776* (Oxford: Blackwell, 1992).

35. Hal T. Shelton, *General Richard Montgomery and the American Revolution: From Redcoat to Rebel* (New York: New York University Press, 1994), and James Kirby Martin, *Benedict Arnold Revolutionary Hero: An American Warrior Reconsidered* (New York: New York University Press, 1997).

36. David McCullough, *1776* (New York: Simon & Schuster, 2005).

37. William P. Cumming and Hugh Rankin, *The Fate of a Nation; The American Revolution Through Contemporary Eyes* (New York: Phaidon Press, 1975), 74, "Wooster, a country-looking fellow who considered a day waisted unless he had paid his homage to Bacchus, soon had 'thrown everything into confusion,'" Bobrick Benson, *Angel in the Whirlwind; The Triumph of the American Revolution* (New York: Penguin, 1997), 17,

"A rather fussy old man with an enormous periwig," Christopher Hibbert, *Redcoats and Rebels; The American Revolution Through British Eyes* (New York: W.W. Norton, 2002), "Wooster was an incompetent drunkard," Rick Atkinson, *The British Are Coming; The War for America, Lexington to Princeton, 1775–1777* (New York: Henry Holt and Company, 2019), 277, "Worse yet, General Wooster—an arrogant, despotic Yale graduate in a large periwig—had alienated many Canadians by arresting priests and loyalists, closing Catholic churches, meddling with the fur trade, and telling Montreal citizens, 'I regard the whole of you as enemies and rascals.'"

38. Mark R. Anderson, *The Battle for the Fourteenth Colony: America's War of Liberation in Canada, 1774–1776* (Hanover: University Press of New England, 2013), and *The Invasion of Canada by the Americans, 1775–1776: as Told through Jean-Baptists Badeaux's Three Rivers Journals and New York Captain William Goforth's Letters* (Albany: State University of New York Press, 2016), Walter R. Borneman, *American Spring: Lexington, Concord, and the Road to Revolution* (New York: Little, Brown, 2014), Derek W. Beck, *The War Before Independence: Igniting the American Revolution, 1775–1776* (Naperville, IL: Sourcebook, 2016), and H.W. Brands, *Our First Civil War: Patriots and Loyalists in the American Revolution* (New York: Doubleday, 2021).

Bibliography

Primary Unpublished Sources

Account of General Wooster's Death, Document Found Among Simeon Baldwin Papers. Connecticut Historical Society, Hartford, CT.

Administration of the estate of the late Major Gen. David Wooster granted to Mary Wooster, widow, and Thomas, son of the deceased. May 15, 1777. New Haven Probate Court. Probate Records, Vol. 12, page 188.

Benedict Arnold to General Wooster, December 31, 1775. Connecticut Historical Society, Hartford, CT.

The Connecticut Gazette, 1755–1759 (New Haven, CT). Microfilm. Library of Congress, Washington, D.C.

The Connecticut Journal, May 21, 1773–August 26, 1778 (New Haven, CT). Microfilm. Library of Congress, Washington, D.C.

The Connecticut Journal, Oct. 23, 1767–May 14, 1773 (New Haven, CT). Microfilm. Library of Congress, Washington, D.C.

David Wooster Accounts for the White Haven Society, November 5, 1773. Connecticut Historical Society, Hartford, CT.

David Wooster Accounts of Bonds Payable, May 4, 1774. Connecticut Historical Society, Hartford, CT.

David Wooster Bill of Return, August 29, 1765. Connecticut Historical Society, Hartford, CT.

David Wooster Land Sale Certificate, April 11, 1766. Connecticut Historical Society, Hartford, CT.

David Wooster to Governor William Pitkin, March 26, 1768. Connecticut Historical Society, Hartford, CT.

David Wooster to Jonathan Law, April 2, 1745. Connecticut Historical Society, Hartford, CT.

David Wooster to the Sheriff of New Haven County, October 27, 1774. Connecticut Historical Society, Hartford, CT.

David Wooster to Treasurer John Lawrence, May 10, 1773. Connecticut Historical Society, Hartford, CT.

David Wooster's Land Sale Indenture, April 22, 1773. Connecticut Historical Society, Hartford, CT.

David Wooster's Land Sale Indenture, April 23, 1773. Connecticut Historical Society, Hartford, CT.

Eliphalet Dyer to David Wooster, June 17, 1775. Connecticut Historical Society, Hartford, CT.

General Heath to General Wooster, February 7, 1777. Connecticut Historical Society, Hartford, CT.

General Wooster to Benjamin Trumbull, September 14, 1775. Connecticut Historical Society, Hartford, CT.

General Wooster to Colonel Dyer, February 15, 1777. Connecticut Historical Society, Hartford, CT.

General Wooster to General Washington, March 1, 1777. The George Washington Presidential Library, Mount Vernon, VA.

General Wooster to Governor Trumbull, August 22, 1775. Connecticut Historical Society, Hartford, CT.

General Wooster to Jonathan Trumbull, January 27, 1775. Connecticut Historical Society, Hartford, CT.

General Wooster to Jonathan Trumbull, January 9, 1777. Connecticut Historical Society, Hartford, CT.

Jonathan Spencer to General Wooster, December 2, 1776. Connecticut Historical Society, Hartford, CT.

Just Imported from London, in the ship Albany, via New-York, by David Wooster and Co., and to be sold by wholesale ... at their store in New-Haven. July 2018. Broadside print. Yale University Library Collection, New Haven, CT.

Last Will and Testament of Abraham Wooster. Connecticut Probate Court Fairfield District. Probate Records, Vol. 9–10, 1741–1755.

Major General Wooster's Inventory, July 16, 1777. Connecticut Historical Society, Hartford, CT.

A Map of the bay from Tunderoga to Crown Point. New York Historical Society Museum and Library.

Minutes of the Commission for Lord High Admiral, 8 Oct. 1745; Capts. John Tufton Maison and David Wooster report to the Board the details of their detention at Rochfort after going there with prisoners from Louisbourg. Public Records Office. Manuscript Report Series #140, Volume 2. London: Admiralty: 3. Ottawa, National Historic Site Service. 1965. Volume 52.

"Pay request for the crew of the sloop Defense, September 5, to October 20, 1741." *Colonial Wars,*

Volume 3. Connecticut State Archives, Hartford, CT. Microfilm 97b, and "October 1741 treasury payment for the sloop Defense," *Colonial Wars Volume 3,* Connecticut State Archives, Hartford, CT, Microfilm 97a.

Phillis Wheatley to Lady Mary Wooster, July 15, 1778. Massachusetts Historical Society, Boston, MA.

Sale of the Estate of Major Gen. David Wooster, July 16, 1777. New Haven Probate Court. Probate Records, Vol. 12.

A view of the Landing the New England Forces in ye Expedition against Cape Breton, 1745. Engraved by J. Stevens.

Wooster, David. *Orderly book of David Wooster, 1759.* Library of Congress. Microfilm.

Primary Published Sources

"Account of the Proceedings of the American Colonists, since the Passing of the Boston Port-Bill, The Gentlemen's Magazine, page 231–32, May, 1776." *Internet Archives Vol 46, Issue 5,* https://archive.org/details/sim_gentlemans-magazine_1776-05_46_5/mode/2up?q=woofter.

Adams, John. *The Adams Papers, Volume 4, February–August 1776.* Cambridge: Harvard University Press, 1979.

American State Papers. Documents, Legislative and Executive, of the Congress of the United States from the First Session to the Second Session of the Seventeenth Congress, Inclusive: Commencing March 4, 1789, and Ending March 3, 1823. Washington, D.C.: Gales and Seaton, 1834.

Andrews, Frank D. *Connecticut Soldiers in the French and Indian War; Bills, Receipts, and Documents, Printed from the original manuscripts.* Vineland, NJ: Private Printer, 1925.

Atwater, Edward. E. *History of the City of New Haven to the Present Time.* New York: W.M. Munsell & Co., 1887.

Bird, Rev'd Samuel V.D.M. *The Importance of the divine Presence with our Host. A Sermon, Delivered In New-Haven, April 27th, 1759. To Col. David Wooster, and His Company; At the Request of the Colonel.* New-Haven: James Parker, and Company, 1759.

Blodget, Samuel. *A Prospective-Plan of the Battle near Lake George, on the Eighth Day of September, 1755. With an Explanation thereof; Containing A full, tho' short, History of that important Affair.* Boston: Richard Draper Pinter, 1755.

Boutell, Lewis Henry. *The Life of Roger Sherman.* Chicago: A.C. McClurg and Company, 1896.

Bowles, Carington. *Bowles's Map of the Seat of War in New England. Comprehending the Provinces of Massachusetts Bay, and New Hampshire; with the Colonies of Connecticut and Rhode Island; Divided into their Townships; from the best Authorities.* London: Carington Bowles, 1776.

Boyd, Julian P., ed. *The Papers of Thomas Jefferson, Volume I, 1760–1776.* Princeton: Princeton University Press, 1950.

Brown, David R. *A Plan of the Town of New Haven With all the Buildings in 1748 Taken by the Hon Gen. Wadsworth of Durham To Which Are Added The Names and Professions of the Inhabitants at that period also the Location of Lots to many of the first Grantees.* Barry Lawrence Ruderman Map Collection, November 11, 2022, https://exhibits.stanford.edu/ruderman/catalog/vt541rb3690.

Burnett, Edmund C., ed., *Letters of Members of the Continental Congress, Volume 1, August 29, 1774, to July 4, 1776.* Washington, D.C.: Carnegie Institution of Washington, 1921.

Butterfield, L.H., ed. *The Adams Papers, Adams Family Correspondence, Volume 2, June 1776–March 1778.* Cambridge: Harvard University Press, 1963.

_____. *The Adams Papers: Diary and Autobiography of John Adams, Volume 1–4.* Cambridge: The Belknap Press of the Harvard University Press, 1961.

_____. *The Adams Papers: Diary and Autobiography of John Adams, Volume 3, Diary, 1782–1804; Part One to October 1776.* Cambridge: Harvard University Press, 1961.

Case, James R. *An account of Tryon's Raid on Danbury in April, 1777, and the Battle of Ridgefield and The Career of Gen. David Wooster, From written authority on the subject with much original matter hitherto unpublished.* Danbury: Danbury Printing Company, 1927.

Charter of the Colony of Connecticut, 1662. The Case, Lockwood & Brainard Company, 1900.

Chase, Philander D., ed. *The Papers of George Washington, Revolutionary War Series, Vol. 1, 16 June 1775–15 September 1775.* Charlottesville: University Press of Virginia, 1985.

_____. *The Papers of George Washington, Revolutionary War Series, Vol. 3, 1 January 1776–31 March 1776.* Charlottesville: University Press of Virginia, 1988.

_____. *The Papers of George Washington, Revolutionary War Series, Vol. 4, 1 April 1776–15 June 1776.* Charlottesville: University Press of Virginia, 1991.

_____. *The Papers of George Washington, Revolutionary War Series, Vol. 5, 16 June 1776–12 August 1776.* Charlottesville: University Press of Virginia, 1993.

_____. *The Papers of George Washington, Revolutionary War Series, Vol. 9, 28 March 1777–10 June 1777.* Charlottesville: University Press of Virginia, 1999.

Clap, Thomas. *The Annals or History of Yale-College, in New-Haven, In the Colony of Connecticut, From The first Founding thereof, in the Year 1700, to the Year 1766: With An Appendix, Containing the Present State of the College, the Method of Instruction and Government, with the Officers, Benefactors, and Graduates.*

New Haven: Printed for John Hotchkiss and B. Mecom, 1766.

_____. *The Answer of The Friend in the West, to A Letter From A Gentleman in the East, entitled, The Present State of the Colony of Connecticut considered.* New Haven: James Parker Printer, 1755.

_____. *The Religious Constitutions of Colleges, Especially of Yale-College in New Haven In the Colony of Connecticut.* New-London: T. Green, 1754.

Clark, William Bell. *Naval Documents of the American Revolution, Volume 2.* Washington, D.C.: U.S. Government Printing Office, 1966.

Coffin, Charles. *The Life and Services of Major General John Thomas.* New York: Egbert, Hovey & King, 1844.

Cohen, Sheldon S., ed., *Canada Preserved: The Journal of Captain Thomas Ainslie.* New York: New York University Press, 1968.

A Collection of all the Statutes Now in Force Relating to the Revenue and Officers of the Customs in Great Britain and the Plantations, Volume II. London: Charles Eyre and Willian Strahan, 1780.

Collections of the Connecticut Historical Society, Containing The Lexington Alarm List, Continental Regiments, 1775–1776, Connecticut Line, 1777–1783, State Troops, 1775–1777, Militia Regiments, 1778–1782, Naval Records, and Pensions, Volume VIII. Hartford: Connecticut Historical Society, 1901.

Crackel, Theodore J. *The Papers of George Washington Digital Edition.* Charlottesville: University of Virginia Press, 2007.

Cutherbertson, Bennett. *A System for the Complete Interior Management and Economy of a Battalion of Infantry.* London, 1759.

Daggett, Rev. Naphtali. *A Sermon Occasioned by the Death of The Reverend Thomas Calp (President of Yale-College, in New Haven) Who departed this Life, Jan. 7th, 1767; Delivered in the College-Chapel, Jan. 8th, By The Rev'd Naphtali Daggett, Livingstonian Professor of Divinity in Yale-College.* New Haven: B. Mecom, 1767.

David Wooster Affidavit in the 51st Regt. July 4, 1770. Papers of William Pepperell, http://www.masshist.org/collection-guides/digitized/fa0054/b3-f20#9.

Deane, Silas. *The Deane Papers, Volume II, 1777–1778.* New York: The New York Historical Society, 1888.

_____. "Letters of Silas Deane." *The Pennsylvania Magazine of History and Biography* 11, no. 2 (1887): 199–206.

De Forest, Louis Effingham, ed. *Louisbourg Journals, 1745.* New York: The Society of Colonial Wars in the States of New York, Through Its Committee on Historical Documents, 1932.

Deming, Henry Champion. *An Oration Upon the Life and Services of General David Wooster. Delivered at Danbury, April 27th, 1854, When a Monument was Erected to His Memory.* Hartford: Case, Tiffany and Company, 1854.

Dutton, Samuel W.S. *An Address at the Funeral of Deacon Nathan Beers, on the 14th of February, 1849.* New Haven: William H, Stanley, Printer, 1849.

Edwards, Jonathan, and John Willison. *Sinners In the Hands of an Angry God. A Sermon preached at Enfield, July 8th, 1741. With a preface by John Willison.* Edinburg: Lumisden and Robertson; Edinburgh, 1745.

Egle, William Henry, M.D. *Documents Relating to the Connecticut Settlement in the Wyoming Valley.* Harrisburg: E.K. Meyers, State Printer, 1893.

Ferraro, William M., and Jeffrey L. Zvengrowski. *The Papers of George Washington, Revolutionary War Series, Volume 28, 28 August–27 October 1780.* Charlottesville: University of Virginia Press, 2020.

The Fitch Papers; Correspondence and Documents During Thomas Fitch's Governorship of the Colony of Connecticut, 1754–1766, Volume 1, May 1754–December 1758. Hartford: Connecticut Historical Society, 1918.

_____. *Volume 1I, January 1759–May 1766.* Hartford: Connecticut Historical Society, 1920.

Force, Peter. *American Archives: Consisting of a Collection of Authentick Records, State Papers, Debates, and Letters and other Notices of Publick Affairs, the Whole Forming a Documentary History of the Origin and Progress of the North American Colonies; of the causes and Accomplishments of the American Revolution; and of the Constitution of Government for the United States, the Final Ratification Thereof, Fourth Series: Volume 2.* Washington, D.C.: M. St. Clair Clark and Peter Force, 1839.

_____. *American Archives: Consisting of a Collection of Authentick Records, State Papers, Debates, and Letters and other Notices of Publick Affairs, the Whole Forming a Documentary History of the Origin and Progress of the North American Colonies; of the causes and Accomplishments of the American Revolution; and of the Constitution of Government for the United States, the Final Ratification Thereof, Fourth Series: Volume 3.* Washington, D.C.: M. St. Clair Clark and Peter Force, 1840.

_____. *American Archives: Consisting of a Collection of Authentick Records, State Papers, Debates, and Letters and other Notices of Publick Affairs, the Whole Forming a Documentary History of the Origin and Progress of the North American Colonies; of the causes and Accomplishments of the American Revolution; and of the Constitution of Government for the United States, the Final Ratification Thereof, Fourth Series: Volume 4.* Washington, D.C.: M. St. Clair Clark and Peter Force, 1843.

_____. *American Archives: Consisting of a Collection of Authentick Records, State Papers, Debates, and Letters and other Notices of Publick*

Affairs, the Whole Forming a Documentary History of the Origin and Progress of the North American Colonies; of the causes and Accomplishments of the American Revolution; and of the Constitution of Government for the United States, the Final Ratification Thereof, Fourth Series: Volume 5. Washington, D.C.: M. St. Clair Clark and Peter Force, 1844.

_____. *American Archives: Consisting of a Collection of Authentick Records, State Papers, Debates, and Letters and other Notices of Publick Affairs, the Whole Forming a Documentary History of the Origin and Progress of the North American Colonies; of the causes and Accomplishments of the American Revolution; and of the Constitution of Government for the United States, the Final Ratification Thereof, Fourth Series: Volume 6.* Washington, D.C.: M. St. Clair Clark and Peter Force, 1846.

_____. *American Archives: Consisting of a Collection of Authentick Records, State Papers, Debates, and Letters and other Notices of Publick Affairs, the Whole Forming a Documentary History of the Origin and Progress of the North American Colonies; of the causes and Accomplishments of the American Revolution; and of the Constitution of Government for the United States, the Final Ratification Thereof, Fifth Series: Volume 1.* Washington, D.C.: M. St. Clair Clark and Peter Force, 1848.

_____. *American Archives: Consisting of a Collection of Authentick Records, State Papers, Debates, and Letters and other Notices of Publick Affairs, the Whole Forming a Documentary History of the Origin and Progress of the North American Colonies; of the causes and Accomplishments of the American Revolution; and of the Constitution of Government for the United States, the Final Ratification Thereof, Fifth Series: Volume 2.* Washington, D.C.: M. St. Clair Clark and Peter Force, 1851.

_____. *American Archives: Consisting of a Collection of Authentick Records, State Papers, Debates, and Letters and other Notices of Publick Affairs, the Whole Forming a Documentary History of the Origin and Progress of the North American Colonies; of the causes and Accomplishments of the American Revolution; and of the Constitution of Government for the United States, the Final Ratification Thereof, Fifth Series: Volume 3.* Washington, D.C.: M. St. Clair Clark and Peter Force, 1853.

Ford, Worthington Chauncey, ed., *Journals of the Continental Congress, 1774–1789, Volume II. 1775, May 10–September 20.* Washington, D.C.: Government Printing Office, 1905.

General Orders of 1757; Issued by The Earl of Loudoun and Phineas Lyman in the Campaign Against the French. New York: Gilliss Press, 1899.

George, William, D.D. *The History of the Rise, Progress, and Establishment of the Independence of the United States of America: Including an Account of the Late War and of the Thirteen Colonies, from their origins to that period. Volume II.* New York: John Woods, 1781.

Gibson, Capt. James. *A Journal of the Late Siege by the Troops from North America Against the French at Cape Breton, the city of Louisburg, and the Territories Thereunto Belonging.* London: Bible and Sun,1745.

Grizzard, Frank E., Jr., ed. *The Papers of George Washington, Revolutionary War Series,* vol. 8, *6 January 1777–27 March 1777.* Charlottesville: University Press of Virginia, 1998.

Hanley, Thomas O'Brien. *The John Carroll Papers, Volume 1, 1755–1791.* Notre Dame: University of Notre Dame, 1976.

Hoadly, Charles J. *The Public Record of the Colony of Connecticut, From May, 1726, to May, 1735, inclusive. (Volume VII).* Hartford: Press of the Case, Lockwood & Brainard Co., 1873.

_____. *The Public Records of the Colony of Connecticut, From May, 1717, to October, 1725. (Volume VI).* Hartford: Press of the Case, Lockwood & Brainard Co., 1872.

_____. *The Public Records of the Colony of Connecticut, From May, 1744, to November, 1750, inclusive. (Volume IX).* Hartford: Press of the Case, Lockwood & Brainard Co., 1876.

_____. *The Public Records of the Colony of Connecticut, From May, 1751, to February, 1757, inclusive. (Volume X).* Hartford: Press of the Case, Lockwood & Brainard Co., 1877.

_____. *The Public Records of the Colony of Connecticut, From May, 1757, to March, 1762, inclusive. (Volume XI).* Hartford: Press of the Case, Lockwood & Brainard Co., 1880.

_____. *The Public Records of the Colony of Connecticut, From May, 1768, to May, 1772, inclusive. (Volume XIII).* Hartford: Press of the Case, Lockwood & Brainard Co., 1885.

_____. *The Public Records of the Colony of Connecticut, From May, 1775, to June, 1776, inclusive, with the Journal of the Council of Safety from June 7, 1775, to October 2, 1776 and an Appendix Containing Some Council Proceedings, 1663–1710 (Volume XV).* Hartford: Press of the Case, Lockwood & Brainard Co., 1890.

_____. *The Public Records of the Colony of Connecticut, from October 1772, to April, 1775, inclusive. (Volume XIV).* Hartford: Press of the Case, Lockwood & Brainard Co., 1887.

_____. *The Public Records of the Colony of Connecticut, From October, 1706, to October, 1716, with the Council Journal from October, 1710, to February, 1717. (Volume V).* Hartford: Press of the Case, Lockwood & Brainard Co., 1870.

_____. *The Public Records of the Colony of Connecticut, From October, 1735, to October, 1743, inclusive (Volume VIII).* Hartford: Press of the Case, Lockwood & Brainard Co., 1874.

_____. *The Public Records of the Colony of Connecticut. From May, 1762, to October, 1767, inclusive. (Volume XII).* Hartford: Press of the Case, Lockwood & Brainard Co., 1881.

_____. *The Public Records of the State of Connecticut, from October, 1776, to February, 1778, Inclusive.* Hartford: Case Lockwood & Brainard, 1894.

Hollister, G.H. *The History of Connecticut, From the First Settlement of the Colony to the Adoption of the Present Constitution. Volume II.* New Haven: Durie and Peck, 1855.

An humble address and exhortation to the Provincial general officers, and soldiers in Connecticut, June l. 1775. Library of Congress, https://www.loc.gov/item/rbpe.00303400/.

"In the Senate of the United States, April 29, 1802. A bill to carry into effect a resolution of Congress to erect a monument to the memory of the late general David Wooster." Library of Congress.

Jefferys, Thomas, Engraver, and Samuel Blodget. *A prospective view of the battle fought near Lake George, on the 8th of Sepr. bewteen 2000 English with 250 Mohawks under the Command of Genl. Johnson; & 2500 French & Indians under the command of Genl. Dieskau in which the English were victorious captivating the French Genl. with a Number of his Men killing 700 & putting the rest to flight. Samuel Blodget delin; T. Jeffreys sculp.* New York, 1756.

Jefferys, Tho's, Engraver. *A PLAN of the TOWN and FORT of CARILLON at TICONDEROGA; with the ATTACK made by the BRITISH ARMY Commanded by Genl. Abercrombie, 8 July 1758.* London: Tho's Jefferys near Charing Cross, 1758.

Johnson, Henry P., ed. *The Record of Connecticut Men in the military and Naval Service During the War of the Revolution: 1775–1783.* Hartford: Lockwood & Brainard, 1889.

Johnson, Samuel, A.M. *A Dictionary of the English Language: In Which The Words are deduced from their Originals, and Illustrated in their Different Significations By Examples form the best Writers. Volume I.* London: W. Strahan, 1755.

Johnston, Thomas. *Plan of Hudson's River from Albany to Fort Edward.* Boston, 1756.

"Journal of the Lower House, February 1741, Commission of David Wooster as 1st Lieutenant of the sloop Defense." *Colonial Wars Volume 3.* Connecticut State Archives, Hartford, CT. Microfilm.

Journals of the American Congress: From 1774–1788: Four Volumes, Volume I, From September 5, 1774, to December 31, 1776, inclusive. Washington, D.C.: Way and Gideon, 1823.

Journals of the American Congress: From 1774–1788: Four Volumes, Volume II, From January 1, 1777, to July 31, 1778, inclusive. Washington, D.C.: Way and Gideon, 1823.

Journals of the Continental Congress, 1774–1775; Edited from the original records in the Library of Congress by Worthington Chauncey Ford, Chief, Division of Manuscripts, Volume II, 1775, May 10–September 20. Washington, D.C.: Government Printing Office, 1905.

Lamb, Roger. *An Original and Authentic Journal of Occurrences During the Late American War, From its Commencement to the Year 1783.* Dublin: Wilkenson & Courtney, 1809.

Law, Jonathan. *The Law Papers: Correspondence and Documents during Jonathan Law's Governorship of the Colony of Connecticut, 1741–1750, Volume I, October 1741–July 1745.* Hartford: Connecticut Historical Society, 1907.

_____. *The Law Papers: Correspondence and Documents during Jonathan Law's Governorship of the Colony of Connecticut, 1741–1750, Volume II, August 1745–December 1746.* Hartford: Connecticut Historical Society, 1911.

_____. *The Law Papers: Correspondence and Documents during Jonathan Law's Governorship of the Colony of Connecticut, 1741–1750, Volume III, January 1747–October 1750.* Hartford: Connecticut Historical Society, 1914.

Letters and Papers of John Singleton Copley and Henry Pelham, 1739–1776. Boston: Massachusetts Historical Society, 1914.

Lists and returns of Connecticut Men in the Revolution; 1775–1783. Hartford: Connecticut Historical Society, 1909.

Lowrie, Walter, and Walter S. Franklin. *American State Papers. Documents, Legislative and Executive, of the Congress of the United States, From the First Session of the First to the Second Session of the Seventeenth Congress, Inclusive: Commencing March 4, 1789, and Ending March 3, 1823.* Washington, D.C.: B. Gales and Seaton, 1834.

Mante, Thomas. *The History of the Late War in North-America and the Islands of the West-Indies, Including the Campaigns of MDCCLXIII and MDCCLXIV Against His Majesty's Indian Enemies.* London: W. Strahan and T. Cadell in the Strand, 1772.

"Map of New Haven Drawn by Joseph Brown, 1724, Copied by Prest. Ezra Stiles, 1782." *Yale University Library Digital Collections,* 2022, https://collections.library.yale.edu/catalog/15830185.

Marin, Joseph P. *Narrative of Some of the Adventures, Dangers and Sufferings of a Revolutionary Soldier.* Hallowell, ME: Glazier, Masters & Co., 1830.

Moore, Frank. *Diary of the American Revolution From Newspapers and Original Documents, Volume I.* New York: Charles Scribner's, 1860.

_____. *Diary of the American Revolution From Newspapers and Original Documents, Volume II.* New York: Charles Scribner's, 1860.

Morgan, William James. *Naval Documents of the American Revolution, Volume 8.* Naval History Division, Department of the Navy, 1980.

Niles, Samuel. *A Brief and Plain Essay on God's Wonder-working Providence for New-England, In the Reduction of Louisburg, and Fortresses thereto belonging on Cape-Breton. With A Short Hint in the Beginning, on the French Taking & Plundering the People of Canso, which led the several Governments to Unite and Pursue that Expedition. With the Names of the Leading*

Officers in the Army and the several Regiments to which they belonged. London: T. Green, 1747.

_____. *New England's Victory at Louisburg in 1745.* East Greenwich: Society of Colonial Wars in the State of Rhode Island and Providence Plantation, 1986.

_____. *A Summary Historical Narrative of The Wars in New England With the French and Indians in the Several Parts of the Country.* Boston: John Wilson & Sons, 1861.

Oberg, Barbara B. *The Papers of Thomas Jefferson, vol 31, 1 February 1799–31 May 1800.* Princeton: Princeton University Press, 2004.

Paine, Thomas. *A Dialogue Between the Ghost of General Montgomery Just arrived from the Elysian Fields; and an American Delegate, in a Wood Near Philadelphia.* Philadelphia: R. Bell, 1776.

Paper of the New Haven Colony Historical Society, Vol. III. New Haven: New Haven Colony Historical Society, 1882.

Pepperell, William. *An Accurate Journal and Account of the proceedings of the New England Land-Forces, During the late Expedition Against the French Settlements on Cape Breton, To the Time of the Surrender of Louisbourg.* London: Northgate Press, 1746.

"Plan du Port et de la ville de Louisbourg: Isle royale; Veüe de la ville de Loüisbourg; Veüe de la batterie royale, 1745." *Edward E. Ayer Digital Collection (Newberry Library),* July 19, 2021, https://collections.carli.illinois.edu/digital/collection/nby_eeayer/id/3550.

"A plan of New Haven and harbour by President Stiles of Yale College, Sept. 27th, 1775." *Yale University Library Digital Collections,* 2022, https://collections.library.yale.edu/catalog/15827429.

Plan of the City of New Haven. http://emuseum.chs.org/emuseum/objects/17601/plan-of-new-haven.

"Plan of the city of New Haven taken in 1748, drawn by James Wadsworth." *Yale University Library Digital Collections,* 2022, https://collections.library.yale.edu/catalog/2003038.

Plan of the Town of New Haven With all the Buildings in 1748. http://emuseum.chs.org/emuseum/objects/15952/plan-of-the-town-of-new-haven-with-all-the-buildings-in-1748.

A Plan of the Town of New Haven With all the Buildings in 1748 Taken by the Hon Gen. Wadsworth of Durham To Which Are Added The Names and Professions of the Inhabitants at that period also the Location of Lots to many of the first Grantees. The Connecticut Historical Society. January 9, 1806. William Lyon, engraver.

Popple, Henry. *A Map of the British Empire in America with the French and Spanish Settlements adjacent thereto. by Henry Popple. C. Lempriere inv. & del. B Baron Sculp. To the Queen's Most Excellent Majesty This Map is most humbly Inscribed by Your Majesty's most Dutiful, most Obedient, and most Humble Servant Henry Popple.* London: Engrav'd by Willm. Henry Toms & R.W. Seale, 1733.

Powers, Zera Jones, ed. *Ancient Town Records, Volume III; New Haven Town Records, 1684–1769.* New Haven: New Haven Colony Historical Society, 1962.

Prince, Thomas. *Extraordinary events the doings of God and marvellous in pious eyes: illustrated in a sermon at the South Church in Boston, N.E., on the general thanksgiving, Thursday, July 18, 1745: occasion[e]d by taking the city of Louisbourg on the isle of Cape-Breton, by New-England soldiers, assisted by a British squadron,* 3rd ed. London: Reprinted and sold by J. Lewis, 1746. *Sabin Americana: History of the Americas, 1500–1926.* June 19, 2022.

Proceedings of the M.W. Grand Lodge of Connecticut, Called for the Purpose of Laying the Chief Stone of the Monument to Gen. David Wooster, at Danbury, April 27, 1854, with the Oration and Addresses Delivered on the Occasion, and Exercises in the Church. New Haven: Storer & Morehouse, 1854.

Proceedings of the M.W. Grand Lodge of Connecticut, Called for the Purpose of Laying the Chief Stone of the Monument to Gen. David Wooster at Danbury, April 27, 1854, with the Oration and Address Delivered on the Occasion and Exercises in the Church. New Haven: Storer & Morehouse, 1854.

Ramsay, David M.D. *The History of the American Revolution, Volume I.* Indianapolis: Liberty Fund, 1990.

_____. *The History of the American Revolution, Volume II.* Indianapolis: Liberty Fund, 1990.

Record of Service of Connecticut Men in the War of the Revolution, the War of 1812, & the Mexican War. Hartford, 1889.

Rolls of Connecticut Men in the French and Indian War 1755–1762, Vol. I. Hartford: Connecticut Historical Society, 1905.

_____. *Vol. II.* Hartford: Connecticut Historical Society, 1905.

Rowland, Kate Mason. *The Life of Charles Carroll of Carrollton, 1737–1832, with his Correspondence and Public Papers. Volume I.* New York: G.P. Putnam's Sons, 1898.

Shields, John ed. *The Collected Works of Phillis Wheatley.* Oxford: Oxford University Press, 1988.

Shirley, William. *A Letter from William Shirley, Esq, Governor of Massachuset's Bay, to His Grace the Duke of Newcastle: with a journal of the Siege of Louisbourg, and other operations of the forces, during the expedition against the French settlements on Cape Breton drawn up at the Desire of the Council and House of Representatives of the Province of Massachuset's Bay; approved and attested by Sir William Pepperrell, and the other Principal Officers who commanded in the said Expedition.* London: E. Owen in Warwick Lane, 1746.

Smith, Paul H., ed. *Letters of Delegates to Congress,*

1774–1789; May 16–August 15, 1776. Washington, D.C.: Library of Congress, 1979.

Steven, Benjamin Franklin. *B.F. Steven's Facsimiles of Manuscripts in European Archives Relating to America, 1773–1783, with Descriptions, Editorial Notes, Collections, References, and Translations, Volume II, Nos. 131 to 234*. London, 1898.

Syrett, Harold C., ed., *The Papers of Alexander Hamilton, vol. 11, February 1792–June 1792*. New York; Columbia University Press, 1966.

_____. *The Papers of Alexander Hamilton, vol. 25, July 1800–April 1802*. New York: Columbia University Press, 1977.

Taylor, Robert J., ed. *The Adams Papers: Papers of John Adams, vol 3, May 1775–January 1776*. Cambridge: Harvard University Press, 1979.

_____. *The Adams Papers: Papers of John Adams, vol 4, February–August 1776*. Cambridge: Harvard University Press, 1979.

"To the Governors of the several Colonies who raised the Troops on the present Expedition from Major-General Johnson, Camp at Lake George. Sept. 9, 1755." *The Maryland Gazette*, Numb. 544, Thursday, October 9, 1755.

Trumbull, Jonathan. *The Trumbull Papers, Vol II*. Boston: Massachusetts Historical Society, 1888.

Twohig, Dorothy, ed. *The Papers of George Washington, Presidential Series, vol. 2, 1 April 1789–15 June 1789*. Charlottesville: University Press of Virginia, 1987.

Vital Records of New Haven; 1649–1850, Part I. Hartford: The Connecticut Society of the Order of the Founders and Patriots of America, 1917.

Warren, Mercy Otis. *The History of the Rise, Progress, and Termination of the American Revolution, Interspersed with Biographical, Political, and oral Observations, In Three Volumes*. Boston: Manning and Loring Printers, 1805.

Watts, I., D.D., *Sermons on Various Subject, Divine and Moral: With a Sacred Hymn Suited to each Subject, In Two Volumes*. London: Printed at the Bible in Pater-noster Rom, 1734.

Wheatley, Phillis. *Memoir and Poems of Phillis Wheatley, a Native African and a Slave*. Boston: Geo. W. Light, 1834.

Wilcox, William B., ed. *The Papers of Benjamin Franklin, vol. 22, March 23, 1775, through October 27, 1776*. New Haven: Yale University Press, 1982.

"William Heath to David Wooster, discussing general military matters, 1777." *American History* August 7, 2021, http://www.americanhistory.amdigital.co.uk.ezproxy.liberty.edu/Documents/Details/GLC01139.

William Williams to Jonathan Trumbull, August 10, 1776. *American Memory, Letters of Delegates to Congress* Vol. 4, May 16, 1776–August 15, 1776.

Withington, Lothrop, ed. *Caleb Haskell's Diary. May 5, 1775–May 30, 1776: A Revolutionary Soldier's Record Before Boston and the Arnold's Quebec Expedition*. Newburyport: William H. Huse & Company, 1881.

Wolcott, Roger. *Journal of Roger Wolcott at the Siege of Louisbourg, 1745*. Hartford: Connecticut Historical Society, 1860.

The Wolcott Papers; Correspondence and Documents During Roger Wolcott's Governorship of the Colony of Connecticut, 1750–1754, with some of earlier dates. Hartford: Connecticut Historical Society, 1916.

Wrong, George M., M.A. *Louisbourg in 1745; The Anonymous Lettre d'un Habitant De Louisbourg (Cape Breton) Containing a narrative by an eye-witness of the siege in 1745, edited with English Translations*. Toronto: Warwick Bros. & Rutter, 1897.

Wurtlee, Fred C. ed., *Blockade of Quebec in 175–1776 by the American Revolutionists*. Quebec: Daily Telegraph Job Publishing House, 1906.

Secondary Books

Anderson, Fred. *Crucible of War: The Seven Years' War and the Fate of Empire in British North America, 1754–1766*. New Yok: Vintage, 2000.

Anderson, Mark R. *The Battle for the Fourteenth Colony; America's War of Liberation in Canada, 1774–1776*. Hanover: University Press of New England, 2013.

_____. *The Invasion of Canada by the Americans, 1775–1776*. Albany: State University of New York Press, 2016.

Appleby, Joyce. *Liberalism and Republicanism in the Historical Imagination*. Cambridge: Harvard University Press, 1992.

Atkinson, Rick. *The British Are Coming: The War for America, Lexington to Princeton, 1775–1777*. New York: Henry Holt and Company, 2019.

Atwater, Edward E., ed., *History of the City of New Haven to the Present Time*. New York: W.W. Munsell & Co., 1887.

Bailyn, Bernard. *Atlantic History: Concept and Contours*. Cambridge: Harvard University Press, 2005.

_____. *The Ideological Origins of the American Revolution*. Cambridge: The Belknap Press of Harvard University Press, 1967.

_____. *The Ordeal of Thomas Hutchinson: Loyalism and the Destruction of the First British Empire*. Cambridge: Belknap Press of Harvard University Press, 1974.

Barber, J.W. *History and Antiquities of New Haven, Conn., From the Earliest Settlement to the Present Time, Collected and Compiled from the most Authentic Sources*. New Haven: J.W. Barber, 1831.

Barrett, Brian S. *Wooster's Invisible Enemies*. Monee, Illinois, 2018.

Beck, Derek W. *The War Before Independence: Igniting the American Revolution, 1775–1776*. Naperville, IL: Sourcebook, 2016.

Bernstein, Neil W. *Ethics, Identity, and Community in Later Roman Declamation*. New York: Oxford University Press, 2013.

Birnbaum, Louis. *Red Dawn at Lexington*. Boston: Houghton Mifflin, 1986.

Bobrick, Benson. *Angel in the Whirlwind: The Triumph of the American Revolution*. New York; Penguin Books, 1997.

Borneman, Walter R. *American Spring: Lexington, Concord, and the Road to Revolution*. New York: Little, Brown, 2014.

Bourne, H.R. Fox. *The Life of John Locke in Two Volumes, Volume II*. New York: Harper & Brothers, 1876.

Boutell, Lewis Henry. *The Life of Roger Sherman*. Chicago: A.C. McClurg and Company, 1896.

Brands, H.W. *Our First Civil War: Patriots and Loyalists in the American Revolution*. New York: Doubleday, 2021.

Brayall, Richard A. *"To the Uttermost of My Power": The Life and Times of Sir William Pepperrell, 1696–1759*. Westminster, MD: Heritage Books, 2008.

Bullock, Steven C. *Revolutionary Brotherhood: Freemasonry and the Transformation of the American Social Order, 1730–1840*. Chapel Hill: University of North Carolina Press, 1996.

Burton, Amy Elizabeth. *To Make Beautiful the Capitol: Rediscovering the Art of Constantino Brumidi*. Washington, D.C.: U.S. Government Printing Office, 2014.

Calhoon, Robert M. *The Loyalists in Revolutionary America, 1760–1781*. New York: Harcourt Brace Jovanovich, 1973.

Carrington, Henry B. *Battles of the American Revolution including Battle Maps and Charts of the American Revolution*. New York: Promontory Press, 1881.

Carter, Robert Goldthwaite. *Record of the Military Service of Captain Joseph Goldthwait, Adjutant of Pepperrel's Regiment (First Mass.) at the Siege of Louisbourg, 1745*. Washington, D.C.: Library of Congress, 1845.

Commanger, Henry Steel, and Richard B. Morris. *The Spirit of Seventy-Six: The Story of the American Revolution as Told by Its Participants*. New York: Castle Books, 1967.

Cumming, William P., and Hugh Rankin. *The Fate of a Nation: The American Revolution Through Contemporary Eyes*. New York: Phaidon Press. 1975.

Dawson, Henry B. *Westchester-County, New York, During The American Revolution*. New York: Morrisania, 1886.

Dexter, Franklin Bowditch. *Biographical Sketches of the Graduates of Yale College with Annals of the College History: October, 1701–May, 1745*. New York: Henry Holt and Company, 1885.

_____. *Biographical Sketches of the Graduates of Yale College with Annals of the College History: Vol. III. May, 1763–July, 1778*. New York: Henry Holt and Company, 1903.

Doerflinger, Thomas M. *A Vigorous Spirit of Enterprise: Merchants and Economic Development in Revolutionary Philadelphia*. Chapel Hill: University of North Carolina Press, 1986.

Drake, Samuel Adams. *The Taking of Louisbourg 1745*. New York: Lee and Shepard, 1890.

East, Robert A. *Business Enterprise in the American Revolutionary Era*. Gloucester: P. Smith, 1964.

Ferling, John. *Almost a Miracle: The American Victory in the War of Independence*. Oxford: Oxford University Press, 2007.

_____. *The Loyalist Mind: Joseph Galloway and the American Revolution*. University Park: Pennsylvania State University Press, 1977.

Flick, Alexander Clarence. *Loyalism in New York During the American Revolution*. New York: Columbia University. 1901.

Greene, Jack P. *The American Revolution: Its Character and Limits*. New York: New York University Press, 1987.

_____. *The Blackwell Encyclopedia of the American Revolution*. Cambridge: Blackwell Reference, 1991.

_____. *The Constitutional Origins of the American Revolution*. Cambridge: Cambridge University Press, 2011.

_____. *Peripheries and Center: Constitutional Development in the Extended Polities of the British Empire and the United States, 1607–1788*. Athens: University of Georgia Press, 1986.

_____. *Pursuits of Happiness: The Social Development of Early Modern British Colonies and the Formation of American Culture*. Chapel Hill: University of North Carolina Press, 1988.

Greene, Jack P., and Phillip D. Morgan, ed. *Atlantic History: A Critical Appraisal*. Oxford: Oxford University Press, 2009

Griffin, Martin I.J. *Catholics and the American Revolution*. Ridley Park: Griffin, 1907.

Hall, Michael G., and Lawrence H. Leder. *The Glorious Revolution in America: Documents on the Colonial Crisis of 1689*. Chapel Hill: University of North Carolina Press, 1964.

Headley, J.T. *Washington and His Generals, Volume I*. New York: Baker and Scribner's, 1847.

_____. *Washington and His Generals, Volume II*. New York: Baker and Scribner's, 1847.

Hibbert, Christopher. *Redcoats and Rebels: The American Revolution Through British Eyes*. New York: Avon Books, 1990.

Hill, Susan Benedict. *History of Danbury, Conn.: 1684–1896*. New York: Burr Printing House, 1896.

"History of Freemasonry." *Massachusetts Freemasons*, November 15, 2022, https://massfreemasonry.org/what-is-freemasonry/history-of-freemasonry/.

Hoffman, Ronald, et al. *The Economy of Early America: The Revolutionary Period, 1763–1790*. Charlottesville: University Press of Virginia, 1988.

Irving, Washington. *The Life of George Washington in Four Volumes*. New York: John B. Alden Publisher, 1887.

Jacob, Margaret, and James Jacob. *The Origins of Anglo-American Radicalism*. Boston: George Allen & Unwin, 1984.

Jacob, Margaret C. *The Origins of Anglo-American Radicalism.* London: Allen & Unwin, 1984.

Jacobus, Donald Lines, M.A. "Edward Wooster of Derby, Conn., and Some of His Descendants." In *The New England Historical and Genealogical Register, Vol. LXXV, July, 1921.* Henry Edwards Scott, ed. Boston: New England Historic Genealogical Society, 1921.

Kidd, Thomas S. "'A Shower of Divine Blessing': Jonathan Edwards and A Faithful Narrative." In *The Great Awakening: The Roots of Evangelical Christianity in Colonial America,* 13–23. New Haven: Yale University Press, 2007.

Lambert, Edward R. *History of the Colony of New Haven Before and After the Union with Connecticut.* New Haven: Hitchock & Stafford, 1838.

"Landmarks in Yale History." *Yale University,* 2022, https://www.yale.edu/about-yale/traditions-history.

Laurence, David. "Jonathan Edwards, John Locke, and the Canon of Experience." *Early American Literature* 15, no. 2 (Fall 1980): 107.

Levermore, Charles H., PhD. *The Republic of New Haven: A History of Municipal Evolution.* Baltimore: Johns Hopkins University Press, 1886.

Lipson, Dorothy Ann. *Freemasonry in Federalist Connecticut, 1789–1835.* Princeton: Princeton University Press, 1977.

"Lodge History." *Hiram Lodge No, 1,* November 15, 2022, https://www.hiramlodgeno1.org/lodge-history.

Longacres, James B., and James Herring. *The National Portrait Gallery of Distinguished Americans, Volume II.* Philadelphia: Henry Perkins, 1835.

Lossing, Benson. *The Life and Times of Philip Schuyler, Volume I.* New York: Sheldon and Company, 1872.

_____. *The Life and Times of Philip Schuyler, Volume II.* New York: Sheldon and Company, 1872.

_____. *The Pictorial Field-Book of The Revolution; or, Illustrations, by pen and pencil, of the history, biography, scenery, relics, and traditions of the War for Independence, Volume 1.* New York: Harper & Brothers, 1851.

_____. *The Pictorial Field-Book of The Revolution; or, Illustrations, by pen and pencil, of the history, biography, scenery, relics, and traditions of the War for Independence, Volume 2.* New York: Harper & Brothers, 1851.

Martin, James, Kirby. *Benedict Arnold, Revolutionary Hero: An American Warrior Reconsidered.* New York: New York University Press. 1997.

McCaughey, Elizabeth P. *From Loyalist to Founding Father: The Political Odyssey of William Samuel Johnson.* New York: Cambridge University Press, 1980.

McCusker, John J., and Russell R. Menard. *The Economy of British America, 1607–1789.* Chapel Hill: University of North Carolina Press, 1985.

Middlebrook, Louis F. *History of Maritime Connecticut During the American Revolution, 1775–1783, Volume 2.* Salem: The Essex Institute, 1925.

Middlekauff, Robert. *The Glorious Cause: The American Revolution, 1763–1789.* New York: Oxford University Press, 1982.

Middleton, Richard. *Colonial America: A History, 1585–1776.* Oxford: Blackwell, 1992.

Miller, John C. *Origins of the American Revolution.* Boston: Little, Brown, 1943.

_____. *Triumph of Freedom: 1775–1783.* Boston: Little, Brown, 1948.

Montross, Lynn. *The Reluctant Rebels; The Story of the Continental Congress, 1774–1789.* New York: Barnes and Noble, 1950.

Nelson, William H. *The American Tory.* Boston: Northeastern University Press, 1992.

Norton, Mary Beth. *The British-Americans: The Loyalist Exiles in England, 1774–1789.* Boston: Little, Brown, 1972.

Orcutt, Samuel, and Ambrose Beardsley. *The History of the old town of Darby, Connecticut, 1642–1880.* Springfield: Springfield Printing Company, 1880.

_____. *A History of the Old Town of Stratford and the City of Bridgeport Connecticut, Part II.* Fairfield: Fairfield County Historical Society, 1886.

_____. *A History of the Old Town of Stratford and the City of Bridgeport Connecticut., Part I.* Fairfield: Fairfield County Historical Society, 1886.

Oswald, Marvin R. *In Memoriam, A compilation of the locations of the grave sites of Veterans buried in Wayne County, Ohio.* 1996.

Otis, James. *The Boys of 1745 at the Capture of Louisbourg.* Boston: Estes and Lauriat, 1895.

Paine, Lauren. *Benedict Arnold: Hero and Traitor.* London: Robert Hale, 1965.

Palmer, R.R. *The Age of the Democratic Revolution: A Political History of Europe and America, 1760–1800.* Princeton: Princeton University Press, 2014.

Parkinson, Robert G. *The Common Cause: Creating Race and Nation in the American Revolution.* Chapel Hill: University of North Carolina Press, 2016.

Philbrick, Nathaniel. *Valiant Ambition: George Washington, Benedict Arnold, and the Fate of the American Revolution.* New York: Penguin, 2016.

Pocock, John Grenille Agard. *Politics, Language, and Time: Essays on Political Thought and History.* Chicago: University of Chicago Press, 1989.

_____. *Three British Revolutions, 1641, 1688, 1776.* Princeton: Princeton University Press, 1980.

_____. *The Varieties of British Political Thought, 1500–1800.* Cambridge: Cambridge University Press, 1993.

Pole, Jack R. *Articulating America: Fashioning a National Political Culture in Early America: Essays in Honor of J.R. Pole.* Lanham: Rowman & Littlefield, 2000.

_____. *Political Representation in England and the Origin of the American Republic.* London: Macmillan, 1966.

Pritchard, James. *In Search of Empire; The French*

in the Americas, 1670–1730. Cambridge: Cambridge University Press, 2004.

"Resources on Yale History: A Brief History of Yale. By Judith Schiff, Chief Research Archivist, Manuscripts and Archives." *Yale Library,* 2022, https://guides.library.yale.edu/yalehistory.

Reynolds, Paul R. *Guy Carleton, A Biography.* New York: William Morrow and Company, 1980.

Richardson, Edward W. *Standards and Colors of the American Revolution.* Philadelphia: University of Pennsylvania Press, 1982.

Robbins, Caroline. *The Eighteenth-Century Commonwealthman.* Indianapolis: Liberty Fund, 1959.

Rockwell, George L. *The History of Ridgefield Connecticut.* New York: Harbor Hill Books, 1979.

Rossie, Jonathan Gregory. *The Politics of Command in the American Revolution.* Syracuse: Syracuse University Press, 1975.

Rowland, Daniel B. *God, Tsar & People: The Political Culture of Early Modern Russia.* Ithica: Northern Illinois University Press, 2020.

Sabine, Lorenzo. *The American Loyalists, or Biographical Sketches of Adherents to the British Crown in The War of the Revolution; Alphabetically Arranged with a Preliminary Historical Essay.* Boston: Charles C. Little and James Brown, 1847.

_____. *Biographical Sketches of Loyalists of the American Revolution with an Historical Essay, Volume I.* Boston: Little, Brown, 1864.

_____. *Biographical Sketches of Loyalists of the American Revolution with an Historical Essay, Volume II.* Boston: Little, Brown, 1864.

Shalhope, Robert E. *The Roots of Democracy: American Thought and Culture, 1760–1800.* Boston: Twayne, 1990.

Shapiro, Ian, ed. *Two Treatises of Government and a Letter Concerning Toleration.* New Haven: Yale University Press, 2003.

Shelton, Hal T. *General Richard Montgomery and the American Revolution; From Redcoat to Rebel.* New York: New York University Press, 1994.

Smith, Justin H. *Our Struggle for the Fourteenth Colony: Canada and the American Revolution, Volume I.* New York: Knickerbocker Press, 1907.

_____. *Our Struggle for the Fourteenth Colony: Canada and the American Revolution, Volume II.* New York: Knickerbocker Press, 1907.

Starr, Rebecca, ed. *Articulating America: Fashioning a National Political Culture in Early America, Essays in Honor of J.R. Pole.* New York: Rowman & Littlefield, 2000.

Storer, E.G. *The Records of Freemasonry in the State of Connecticut, Compiled From the Journals of the Proceedings of the Grand Lodge, From 1845 to 1854.* New Haven: E.G. Storer, 1861.

_____. *The Records of Freemasonry in the State of Connecticut, with a brief account of its origin in New England, and the entire Proceedings of the Grand Lodge, from its First Organization, A.L. 5789.* New Haven: E.G. Storer, 1859

Todd, Charles Burr. *A General History of the Burr Family, with a Genealogical Record from 1193 to 1891.* New York: Knickerbocker Press, 1891.

Trumbull, Benjamin D.D. *A Complete History of Connecticut, Civil and Ecclesiastical, From the Emigration of its First Planters, From England, in the Year 1630, to the Year 1764: and to the Close of the Indian Wars. Vol. II.* New Haven: Maltby, Goldsmith and Co., 1818.

Wallace, Willard M. *Appeal to Arms: A Military History of the American Revolution.* New York: Harper and Brothers, 1951.

_____. *Traitorous Hero: The Life and Fortunes of Benedict Arnold.* New York: Harper and Brothers, 1954.

Ward, Christopher. *The War of the Revolution.* New York: Macmillan, 1952.

White, Lorraine Cook, ed. *The Barbour Collection of Connecticut Town Vital Records. Vol. 1–5.* Baltimore: Genealogical Publishing Co., 1994–2002.

Wood, Gordon. *The American Revolution: A History.* New York: Random House, 2002.

_____. *The Creation of the American Republic: 1776–1787.* Chapel Hill: University of North Carolina Press, 1969.

_____. *The Radicalism of the American Revolution: How a Revolution Transformed a Monarchical Society into a Democratic One Unlike Any That Had Ever Existed.* New York: Alfred A. Knopf, 1992.

Wooster, David, M.D., F.R.A. *Genealogy of the Woosters in America, Descended from Edward Wooster of Connecticut; Also an Appendix Containing a Sketch Relating to the Author, and a Memoir of Rev. Hezekia Calvin Wooster, and Public Letters of General David Wooster.* San Francisco: M. Weiss, Printer, 1885.

"Wooster Connecticut Sloop." *American War for Independence at Sea, the American Privateers,* April 2020, https://awiatsea.com/Privateers/W/Wooster%20Connecticut%20Sloop%20%5bMcCleave%20Staples%20Peck%20Brintnall%5d.pdf.

Wright, Louis B. *The Cultural Life of the American Colonies.* New York: Harper and Row, 1957.

Wrong, George McKinnon. *Louisbourg in 1745; The Anonymous Lettre D'un Habitant De Louisbourg (Cape Breton) Containing a Narrative by an Eyewitness of the Siege in 1745.* Toronto: University of Toronto Press, 1897.

Wurtele, Fred C., ed. *Blockade of Quebec in 1775–1776 by the American Revolutionists.* Quebec: The Daily Telegraph Job Printing House, 1909. https://archive.org/stream/blockadeof quebec02wr#page/8/mode/2up/search/general+Wooster.

Secondary Articles

Ali Isani, Mukhtar. "Phillis Wheatley in London: An Unpublished Letter to David Wooster." *American Literature* 51, no. 2 (May 1979): 255–260.

Anderson, Mark. "David Wooster Kept the Men at

Quebec: Giving Credit to a Much-Maligned General." *Journal of the American Revolution,* May 13, 2020, https://allthingsliberty.com/2021/05/david-wooster-kept-the-men-at-quebec-giving-credit-to-a-much-maligned-general.

Bosse, David, Joshua Lane, Amanda Lange, and Philip Zea. "Furnishing the Frontier: The Material World of the Connecticut River Valley, 1680–1720." *Historical Journal of Massachusetts* 41, no. 1 (Winter 2013).

Debrincat, Dominic. "The Spanish Ship Affair: Wreck, Salvage, and Contested Legal Authority in Colonial Connecticut." *Early American Studies, An Interdisciplinary Journal* 19, no. 4 (2021): 699–734.

Ellison, Amy Noel. "Montgomery's Misfortune: The American Defeat at Quebec and the March towards Independence, 1775–1776." *Early American Studies* 15, no. 3 (Summer 2017): 591–616.

Gerber, Scott D. "Law and Religion in Colonial Connecticut." *The American Journal of Legal History* 55, no. 2 (2015): 149–93.

Gill, Harold B., Jr., "Colonial Germ Warfare" *Colonial Williamsburg Journal,* Spring 2004.

Gilmore, Jodie. "The Fire That Backfired." *The New American* 20, no. 9 (May 3, 2004): 36.

Goldstein, Kalman. "Silas Deane: Preparation for Rascality." *The Historian* 43, no. 1 (November 1, 1980): 75.

Hales, John. "The Landscape of Tragedy: Crèvecoeur's 'Susquehanna.'" *Early American Literature* 20, no. 1 (1985): 39–63.

Hattem, Michael D. "The Historiography of the American Revolution: A Timeline." August 2017, https://cdn.knightlab.com/libs/timeline3/latest/embed/index.html?source=19P0MD9TrV5Tx-62DC3fImj_uNLA5lAsnV6TmRu2fWdL4&font=PT&lang=en&initial_zoom=1&height=800.

———. "The Historiography of the American Revolution." *Journal of the American Revolution,* August 27, 2013, https://allthingsliberty.com/2013/08/historiography-of-american-revolution/.

Hiono, Yuichi. "Sustaining British Naval Power Through New England Masts During the Seven Years War." *Taylor & Francis Online,* January 28, 2020, 18–29.

"History of Freemasonry." *Massachusetts Freemasons,* November 15, 2022, https://massfreemasonry.org/what-is-freemasonry/history-of-freemasonry/.

Jones, Claude E. "John Locke and Masonry, a Document." *Neuphiliogische Mitteilunge* 67, no. 1 (1966).

Kidd, Thomas S. "'A Shower of Divine Blessing': Jonathan Edwards and A Faithful Narrative." In *The Great Awakening: The Roots of Evangelical Christianity in Colonial America,* 13–23. New Haven: Yale University Press, 2007.

Lacey, Barbara E. "Gender, Piety, and Secularization in Connecticut Religion, 1720–1775." *Journal of Social History* 24, no. 4 (1991): 799–821.

Laurence, David. "Jonathan Edwards, John Locke, and the Canon of Experience." *Early American Literature* 15, no. 2 (Fall 1980): 107.

Mayer, Holly A. "Canada, Congress, and the Continental Army: Strategic Accommodations, 1774–1776." *Journal of Military History* 78, no. 2 (April 2014): 503–35.

Nash, Gary B. "The Quest for the Susquehanna Valley: New York, Pennsylvania, and the Seventeenth-Century Fur Trade." *New York History* 48, no. 1 (1967): 3.

Ousterhout, Anne M. "Frontier Vengeance: Connecticut Yankees vs. Pennamites in the Wyoming Valley." *Pennsylvania History: A Journal of Mid-Atlantic Studies* 62, no. 3 (1995): 330–63.

Powers, Sandra L. "Studying the Art of War: Military Books Known to American Officers and Their French Counterparts During the Second Half of the Eighteenth Century." *The Journal of Military History* 70, no. 3 (July 2006): 789–91.

Roche, John F. "Quebec Under Siege, 1775–1776: The 'Memorandums' of Jacob Danford." The Canadian *Historical Review* 50, no. 1 (March 1969): 68–85.

"Some Memoirs of Major General David Wooster (with an Elegant Engraving.)." *Hibernian Magazine, Or, Compendium of Entertaining Knowledge, Jan.1771-Apr.1785* (1776): 362.

Strogoff, Erin. "Connecticut's 'The Legend of the Charter Oak.'" *ConnecticutHistory.org,* September 4, 2022. https://connecticuthistory.org/connecticuts-the-legend-of-the-charter-oak/.

Winiarski, Douglas L. "Jonathan Edwards, Enthusiast? Radical Revivalism and the Great Awakening in the Connecticut Valley." *Church History* 74, no. 4 (2005): 683–739.

Wood, Virginia Steel. "George Washington's Military Manuals." Library of Congress.

"Yale History Timeline: 1710-1719." *Yale University Library,* 2022, https://guides.library.yale.edu/c.php?g=296074&p=1976320.

Index

Numbers in **_bold italics_** indicate pages with illustrations.